THE
WORD

THE
WORD

The History of
THE BIBLE
and How it
Came to Us

ROD GRAGG
Author of FORGED IN FAITH

 WND Books

THE WORD

Unless otherwise noted, all Scripture quotations in this work are taken from the New American Standard Bible ® (NASB), Copyright © 1960, 1962, 1963, 1968, 1971, 1972, 1973, 1975, 1977, 1995 by The Lockman Foundation Used by permission. www.Lockman.org Scripture quotations marked KJV are taken from the Holy Bible, King James Version (public domain). Scripture quotations marked NKJV are taken from the New King James Version (NKJV) Scripture taken from the New King James Version®. Copyright © 1982 by Thomas Nelson. Used by permission. All rights reserved.

Also cited:

The New Life Version (NLV). Copyright © 1969 by Christian Literature International. Young's Literal Translation (YLT) (public domain).

Published by WND Books, Washington, D.C. WND Books is a registered trademark of WorldNetDaily.com, Inc. ("WND")

Book designed by Mark Karis

WND Books are available at special discounts for bulk purchases. WND Books also publishes books in electronic formats. For more information call (541) 474-1776, email orders@wndbooks.com, or visit www.wndbooks.com.

Hardcover ISBN: 978-1-944229-81-8
eBook ISBN: 978-1-944229-82-5

Library of Congress Cataloging-in-Publication Data

Printed in the United States of America
18 19 20 21 22 XXX 9 8 7 6 5 4 3 2

To the Reverend John R. "Randy" Riddle—
my friend and mentor in the Lord

Contents

Introduction

THE KING TORE HIS CLOTHES

For the word of God is living and active.
—HEBREWS 4:12

HE WAS EIGHT YEARS OLD WHEN HE BECAME KING. His name was Josiah, and in 640 BC his father was assassinated in the royal palace by some of his staff, making Josiah the boy king of Judah. He inherited a disaster. More than three hundred years earlier, Israel's "Golden Age" had ended with the death of King Solomon, and his heirs had split the kingdom as they competed for the throne. The northern kingdom was called Israel; the southern kingdom was named Judah, and both had suffered from godless leadership. Perhaps the wickedest ruler was Josiah's grandfather, King Manasseh.[1]

Manasseh had ruled for fifty-five years, and his godless reign had done grave damage to Judah's spiritual foundation. He had embraced the Baal worship of the nation's Canaanite predecessors, reestablished child sacrifice, erected idols in prominent places throughout the country, engaged in witchcraft, consulted mediums, slaughtered countless innocent citizens—and in a shocking act of rebellion, had even placed an idol of the Canaanite fertility goddess, Asherah, in Jerusalem's temple.

Near the end of his life, he had repented and attempted to undo the harm he had done, but his son and heir, Amon—Josiah's father—had thoroughly reinstated Manasseh's godless acts. Worse, either Manasseh or Amon—or both—had apparently directed a campaign to purge the nation of the Word of God.[2]

So, the boy king Josiah inherited a nation left in spiritual darkness and decay. In the absence of God's Word, the people of Judah had been left with only the shadow of tradition to follow—a vague guide distorted by disobedience and ignorance. Josiah was different. Rejecting the godless examples of his father and grandfather, he yearned to do "right in the sight of the LORD" Even so, for the first eighteen years of his reign, as documented in the Old Testament books of 2 Kings and 2 Chronicles, Josiah was left to rule over a grim and disturbed kingdom. Even the great temple in Jerusalem—once the beloved site of worship for a God-centered people—had fallen into neglect and decay.[3]

Then, when Josiah was twenty-six, an extraordinary event occurred that transformed king and country. Josiah had ordered a restoration of the temple, and as work crews were making repairs—perhaps tearing out old walls—they discovered a copy of the book of the law, preserved in a secret place. The scrolls apparently had been hidden decades earlier. Who hid them? No one knows. Presumably, a priest or a temple attendant had saved them from destruction during Manasseh's or Amon's purge.[4]

The recovered Scriptures may have been the book of Deuteronomy, or more likely, the Pentateuch—the first five books of the Old Testament—or perhaps the Pentateuch and some of the Bible's historical and poetic books. From the workmen, the discovery was carried up the chain of command, through the ranks of the priesthood—until at last the scrolls were in the hands of King Josiah's principal advisor, Shaphan the scribe. Undoubtedly realizing the providential nature of the discovery and its enormous importance, Shaphan took the Scriptures to the king. "Hilkiah the priest has given me a book," he announced simply. "And—the Bible reports—Shaphan read it in the presence of the king."[5]

It was a dramatic moment. For the first time in his life, the youthful king of Judah fully heard what God expected of His people. *Hear, O Israel! The LORD is our God, the LORD is one!* How the Word must have pierced his heart. *You shall love the LORD your God with all your heart and with all your soul and with all your might.* How did they even know how to love God without knowing His Word? *These words, which I am commanding you today, shall be on your heart.* Without the Word, how could they ever introduce their children to the Lord and continue the truth He had revealed in ages past? *You shall teach them diligently to your sons and shall talk of them when you sit in your house and when you walk by the way and when you lie down and when you rise up.*[6]

And what of all the idolatry that held the people of Judah in the grip of sin? The vile worship rites—the sacrificing of children in ovens of flame, the obscene worship rituals, the bizarre demands of the priests of Baal, the idol shrines erected on hillsides throughout the nation, the conjuring of occult mediums, the dark practices of witchcraft, the sex idol brazenly erected in the temple—all must have risen before Josiah as a mighty, rebellious affront to the living God of the Bible. *You shall have no other gods before Me. You shall not make for yourself an idol, or any likeness of what is in heaven above or on the earth beneath or in the water under the earth. You shall not worship them or serve them.*[7]

How far the nation had fallen! What blessings God's people had denied themselves—and what opportunities to share God's truth they had forsaken. *Now it shall be, if you diligently obey the LORD your God, being careful to do all His commandments . . . , the LORD your God will set you high above all the nations of the earth. All these blessings will come upon you and overtake you if you obey the LORD your God* as King Josiah heard the Word of God, he tore his clothes—the traditional Israelite reaction to grief or blasphemy. He was grieved that the Scriptures had been lost—surely an act of blasphemy—and that the people were living in such spiritual darkness that even the king had never been able to read God's law. So he took action: He ordered the nation's spiritual leaders and heads of households to assemble in Jerusalem.[8] On the appointed day, they came—"all the men of Judah and all the inhabitants of

Jerusalem, and all the priests and all the prophets." They assembled in a giant audience before the temple of the Lord, and King Josiah read aloud to them every word of the newly discovered Scriptures. How many hours—days—did this extraordinary exercise continue? Was it accomplished in one assembly? Or were the people dismissed overnight and recalled at daybreak until it was done? Did this grand mass of people stand there, transfixed, as their king read them the Word of life? Or did they too rip their clothing and cry out in despair and repentance, sending wails of remorse echoing over the walls of Jerusalem?[9]

When Josiah finally concluded—when the last sentence was read—he exercised godly leadership. In the silence that followed the public reading of the Scriptures, the king publicly committed himself to follow the Word of God as a man and as a king—"to walk after the LORD, and to keep His commandments and His testimonies and His statutes with all his heart and all his soul." The people of Judah had now heard God's truth. Now they knew how much God loved them and what He expected of them. And the Word made an impact, just as God promises: "My word . . . will not return to Me empty, without accomplishing what I desire." As promised to every surrendered heart, God's Word transformed a people and a nation that day. A revival came to those who were spiritually parched, and "all the people entered into the covenant."[10]

Repentant and determined, Josiah directed a campaign to regain lost ground—to purge the nation of the idolatry that had led Judah to such godless, evil days. First, he ordered every idol, every graven image, hauled from the Lord's temple—the sensual-looking figurines of Asherah, the prized utensils that were central to the worship of Baal, and other astrological objects of devotion. Everything was burned to ashes in the nearby garbage dump of Kidron; then the ashes were dumped far from Jerusalem, on defiled ground at Bethel, or scattered on the old graves of idol worshippers, rendering both graves and ashes unclean and unfit for veneration. The young king ordered the temple stripped of the prostitutes' booths that had been erected there in a sprawl of debauchery, and his forces destroyed the horrible center of child sacrifice that lay south of Jerusalem in the valley of Gehenna—"the place of burning"—where countless infants had been flung into the flames in an attempt to appease the "god" Molech. He also obliterated the idolatrous worship sites that had become landmarks on the Mount of Olives. Out too went the mediums and the spiritists "and all the abominations that were seen in the land of Judah."[11]

Throughout the nation, King Josiah spread his reforms, directing a crusade that tore down idolatrous temples, wrecked hillside worship centers, toppled towering pillars, and rid the nation of the idol-worshipping priests who reigned at the heart of darkness. Then, at the end of his successful purge, he restored the Passover in conformity to the directions of Scripture—focusing on the unblemished lamb that pointed in a scarlet line of redemption to the cross to come. And "before him," states 2 Kings 23, "there was no king like him who turned to the LORD with all his heart and with all his soul and with all his might . . . nor did any like him arise after him."[12]

The truth of Scripture transformed both Josiah and the nation. The young king heard the infallible Word of God, and was convicted of its truth. He repented of his sins and surrendered his heart to the Lord—the God of the Bible—and then he made a commitment to obey the Word. He removed the objects of sin and temptation from his life and his nation, replaced them with obedience to the law of God, and sought to witness to others—to set an example of a surrendered heart. Repentance, surrender, commitment, removal, replacement, obedience and a faithful witness—they were life-changing, nation-changing actions that came from the never-failing Word of God.[13]

Throughout the ages, countless attempts have been made to destroy or suppress the Bible—but none have succeeded. "The grass withers, the flower fades, but the word of our God stands forever." And because it *is* the inspired, inerrant, infallible, and authoritative Word of God, the Bible continues to hold the potential to change lives—and nations—even today.[14]

1

INSPIRED BY GOD

All Scripture is inspired by God.
—2 TIMOTHY 3:16

WHILE WAITING TO DIE, both men were thinking of the Bible. In 1536, English clergyman William Tyndale sat in the bone-chilling cold of a castle cell, waiting to be burned alive for translating the Bible into English. A letter he wrote in those miserable surroundings has survived through the centuries. In it, he asked prison authorities for warmer clothing and some lighting for his cell—but he mainly wanted the Bible. "But most of all," he wrote, "I beg . . . to have the Hebrew Bible, Hebrew grammar and Hebrew Dictionary, that I may pass the time in that study." Fifteen centuries earlier, the apostle Paul had made a similar request from prison before he was beheaded by Roman authorities. "When you come," Paul wrote his protégé Timothy, "bring the cloak which I left at Troas with Carpus, and the books, especially the parchments." At the end of their earthly days—more than a millennium apart—both Paul and Tyndale were focused on the Bible—which both professed to be the Word of God.[1]

At the dawn of the twentieth century, an Orthodox Jewish scribe in Jerusalem uses traditional methods to copy the Hebrew Bible onto parchment. Ancient parchment accepted ink well, and was durable enough for the writing to be washed away and the parchment used again if necessary. Source: Library of Congress.

Throughout eons of human history, men and women have sought to live according to the Bible, and countless numbers have given their lives for it. Why? Why has the Bible been so revered? How did it come to us? And why have billions of believers through the ages considered it to be inspired by God? "Suppose a nation in some distant region should take the Bible for their only lawbook . . . What a Paradise would this region be," wrote American founding father John Adams. "The Bible is stamped with a specialty of origin, and an immeasurable distance separates it from all competitors," observed William Gladstone, Great Britain's famed nineteenth-century prime minister. "All the miseries and evils which men suffer from vice, crime, ambition, injustice, oppression, slavery, and war, proceed from their despising or neglecting the precepts contained in the Bible," asserted Noah Webster, author of America's first dictionary. "[It is] by the wisdom of God that he has framed the scriptures," concluded the renowned British physicist Isaac Newton. American author and educator Helen Keller, famed for her accomplishments despite being blind and deaf, observed, "The Bible is a book to live with, to think from, and to die by." Of God and the Bible, twentieth-century Christian philosopher and theologian Francis Schaeffer declared, "He is not silent. The . . . infinite-person God, the full Trinitarian God, has not been silent. He has told us who he is." Revered, rejected, obeyed, and ignored, the Bible has made an impact on the history of man unlike any other work, from antiquity through postmodern culture.[2]

Nineteenth century Middle-Eastern Bedouins carry bundled stalks of papyrus, which could be crafted into rope and baskets—as well as writing material. In ancient Egypt, papyrus production was a well-kept trade secret. Source: Library of Congress.

The term *Bible* is believed to have originated with the use of a reed plant called *biblos* that grew along the Nile River in ancient Egypt. The plant's scientific name is *Cyperus papyrus*. The Egyptians used it to manufacture various products, such as rope, baskets, and boats—but its main use was in the production of writing material through a process that the Egyptians protected as a trade secret for generations. Ancient Alexandria was the center of papyrus production, and the final product was used primarily by the wealthy and the government because production was complicated and expensive. The stalks of the plant were harvested, and the inner pitch was removed, cut into lengthy strips, then soaked in water and pounded until pliable. The strips were trimmed, laid in a crisscross pattern between cotton sheets, then pressed until all moisture was absorbed by the cotton. After a final pressing, the papyrus was dyed and then polished with smooth stones. The final product was a thick, well-crafted sheet of pale-colored, paperlike material that eventually became known simply as *papyrus*.[3]

Reed pens were used for writing on papyrus, and the ancient Egyptians produced a variety of colored inks—although the most common colors used on papyrus appear to have been black and red. Usually, writing was placed on a single side of papyrus. Rarely were both sides used—two-sided writing was a practice reserved for critical communication. In the New Testament book of Revelation, for example, the apostle John reported seeing "Him who sat on the throne" holding in His right hand "a book written inside and on the back" —an apparent reference to the importance of God's revelation, which was deserving of a two-sided papyrus scroll. Some papyrus scrolls were thirty-five yards in length, and had to be grasped in both hands by the reader, and the scroll was unrolled while being read. In Latin, a form of the verb *volvere*—"to roll"—is *volumen*, which means "an object rolled up" or a "roll-book." Papyrus was used to record both Old and New Testament manuscripts. The Old Testament prophet Isaiah predicted that at God's final judgment on the earth and its inhabitants, "all the host of heaven shall be dissolved, and the heavens shall be rolled together as a scroll." Likewise, the apocalyptic prophecy in the book of Revelation described the same event with an analogy to a scroll: "and the heaven departed as a scroll when it is rolled together." Some extensive papyrus works required multiple scrolls. The Greeks called such multivolume works *logos,* which translates as "word." They were also called *tomos*, from which the English word "tome" is derived.[4]

A written scroll became known as a biblion . . . which likely gave birth to the familiar name of the book—the Bible.

The Hebrew term for the papyrus plant is *gome*, which is found in Exodus 2:3, where the infant Moses is hidden in a basket made of *gome* (sometimes rendered "wicker" or "bulrushes" in English). The Hebrew term is translated *papuros* in Greek and *papyrus* in Latin. From the Latin translation comes the German *Papier,* the French *papier*, and the English word *paper.* Multiple sheets of papyrus and rolls of it were known as *chartes* in Greek and later as *charta* in Latin—from which the English words *chart* and *charter* derived. Papyrus scrolls were rolled around a pole or a stick known as a "navel." A written scroll became known as a *biblion*—"book" in English—a word that holds a linguistic connection to the *biblos*, or papyrus plant, and which likely gave birth to the familiar name of *the* book—the Bible. Greek-speaking Christians referred to the books of the Old and New Testaments collectively as *ta biblia*—"the books"—and eventually Latin-speaking believers called the Scriptures *biblia*—which over time became the English word *Bible.*[5]

Ancient samples of papyrus discovered in Egypt have been dated as early as 4,000 BC, proving the product to have been remarkably durable. Even more durable was cuneiform—a soft clay tablet inscribed with writing, then baked to a hard consistency. It was rock-hard and was the inexpensive choice of the common people of the ancient Mideast. Archaeological excavations have unearthed vast numbers of cuneiform tablets from the modern sites of the ancient Babylonian and Assyrian empires, in Egypt, ancient Persia, and elsewhere in the

Mideast. Although durable and inexpensive, cuneiform was too weighty for practical transporting, and the small size of the baked clay tablets limited the scope of their messages.[6]

In the nineteenth century, archaeologists recovered this Egyptian papyrus fragment from a burial site near Thebes. In Egypt, reed pens were used to write on papyrus. The most common colors of ink: black or red. Source: New York Public Library.

Parchment was another form of writing material from antiquity, and it too was used to record Scripture. Both Paul and William Tyndale referred to it. It was even more expensive to produce than papyrus. It was reserved not only for documents considered of great importance, but for those that required frequent and continuous use—such as the Scriptures. Both the Old and New Testaments were copied on parchment. The word *parchment—pergamentum* in Latin—comes from the name of Pergamum, an ancient city in what is now modern Turkey. Today named Bergama, it was called Gebal in the Old Testament. Although parchment was sometimes used in ancient Egypt, it was popularized in Pergamum as a substitute for papyrus in the second century BC. It was manufactured by scraping and stretching animal skins—usually goat or sheep—into a thin, paperlike sheet. Some parchment was made from calfskin—called *vellum* in Latin—and the Greek word used for "parchment" in the Bible is *membrana,* from which the English word *membrane* originated. Parchment took ink well and was durable enough for the writing to be washed away and the parchment used repeatedly if necessary. Eventually, because it was easier to manufacture and more practical, parchment would largely replace papyrus. Other writing material used in the ancient Mideast included leather, wood, stone, and even rolled copper, but the primary materials for recording the Bible in antiquity were papyrus and parchment.[7]

What was written on those ancient writing materials came to be known as "Scripture," revered by historic Christianity as the ultimate revealed truth—inspired by God in the original autographs and faithfully transmitted through reliable texts to the present day. Almost five thousand partial or complete biblical manuscripts exist from the days of antiquity. Christian apologists hold that the remarkable abundance of ancient manuscripts and the close proximity of the oldest manuscripts to the era in which they were recorded make a compelling case for the authenticity and authority of the Bible. The oldest surviving New Testament manuscripts, they believe, date to within a single long lifetime or to within a few generations (70 to 170 years) of the era in which they were recorded. More than a century of modern-style, organized archaeological activity has confirmed and explained countless biblical references to events, figures, and cultural expressions, which are also reinforced by extrabiblical works by historians of antiquity, such as Pliny the Younger, Suetonius, Lucian, Tacitus, and Flavius Josephus.[8]

A sixth-century B.C. cuneiform cylinder records information about repairs to the temple of the Moon-god Sin in the ancient Sumerian city of Ur. When baked rock-hard, cuneiform was durable, but its small size limited the scope of its message and use. Source: Marie-Lan Nguyen/Wikimedia Commons.

Such is the basic external evidence of biblical inspiration. The internal evidence is obvious and extensive: the Bible declares itself to be inspired by God. In the Old Testament, for instance, Psalm 119 refers to Scripture as God's Word a total of twenty-four times, and that claim is made repeatedly in the New Testament. "All Scripture is inspired by God and profitable for teaching, for reproof, for correction, for training in righteousness," states 2 Timothy 3:16-17, "so that the man of God may be adequate, equipped for every good work." More than forty diverse writers recorded the Bible over the course of more than fifteen hundred years—perhaps longer. Some were kings, scribes, priests, poets, and scholars; one was a physician, and another was a tax collector. However, many were professionally ill prepared to record anything—they were commercial fishermen with no formal education—and yet they did. Christians believe, and the Bible teaches, that they and the other writers of Scripture were inspired by the Holy Spirit. Over time, sixty-six books were compiled—thirty-nine in the Old Testament, twenty-seven in the New Testament—written in three languages:

Hebrew, Aramaic, and Greek. Considering the enormous span of time over which the Bible was written, the diversity of its human writers, the vast scope of history it covered, and the various languages that were used in it—the unity of the Bible is extraordinary. Throughout the ages and through all sixty-six books, the Bible follows one central, progressive, consistent theme: God's offer of salvation through Jesus Christ.[9]

Historically, Christian Bible scholars have viewed the unity of the Bible as proof of the inspiration of Scripture by the Holy Spirit. Renowned twentieth-century American Bible scholar Norman Geisler spoke for countless Christian scholars through the ages when he observed, "Both the authenticity and the historicity of the New Testament documents are firmly established . . . The authentic nature and vast amount of the manuscript evidence is overwhelming." Theologian Charles D. Ryrie, longtime professor of systematic theology at Dallas Theological Seminary, agreed: "Indeed, the Bible claims inerrancy for itself. Neither do we deny that there are problems in the text that we presently have. But problems are quite different from errors. Indeed, in the face of the claims that the Bible apparently makes for itself about inspiration and inerrancy, it would seem more reasonable when confronted with problems to place one's faith in the Scriptures, which have been proved to be true again and again." Thus, Christianity has historically based its doctrine on the Bible, which believers through the ages have accepted as God's revealed truth.[10]

Almost two thousand years before the crucifixion of Jesus Christ, God revealed His plan of salvation to the patriarch Abraham: someday the Creator of the universe would wrap Himself in flesh and enter this world as Messiah to redeem humankind. "Abraham rejoiced to see my day," Jesus would explain in John 8:56, "and he saw it and was glad." To implement His sovereign plan, God called Abraham from the ancient city of Ur, according to the book of Genesis. Ur was the center of Mesopotamia's powerful Sumerian empire—which may have been the biblical "land of Shinar" and in Abraham's day it had been inhabited for almost two thousand years. According to archaeological evidence, it was located adjacent to the Euphrates River, about two hundred miles southeast of modern Baghdad, Iraq. Large and prosperous, Ur was near its peak of power and influence, and was known for its sprawling commercial and residential centers, elaborate architecture, and a royal cemetery where servants willingly drank poison to escort their dead rulers to the afterlife. Rising above the city skyline was a towering Babel-like ziggurat honoring the Mesopotamian moon god, who was known as "Nanna," or "Sin."[11]

Excavated in modern Iraq in the 1930s, the ruins of a ziggurat on the site of ancient Ur stand as a reminder of the city's power and influence in Abraham's day. Archaeological excavations at the site of Ur and Nippur would recover more than thirty thousand cuneiform texts dating to 2500 B.C. Source: Library of Congress.

Ur was sophisticated, technologically advanced, and idolatrous. Abraham was set apart from the prevailing culture by both calling and conviction. He was one of the "remnant"—those who believed in God and His revealed truth—and he obeyed His call. Abraham "believed in the Lord," reports Genesis 15:6, "and He reckoned it to him as righteousness." Lying to the west by a trek of more than fifteen hundred miles from Ur was the region to which Abraham was called: Canaan—an area between the Mediterranean and the Jordan River that lay on the approximate site of modern Israel. "Go forth from your country, and from your relatives and from your father's house, to the land which I will show you; and I will make you a great nation," God promised Abraham. "And in you all the families of the earth shall be blessed." The land would become Israel. The nation would become the Hebrew people—the descendants of Abraham—and those who professed faith in the God of Abraham would eventually become known as the Jews. And the world's blessing, as God promised to Abraham, would be God's offer of eternal life through Y'shua Messiah—Jesus Christ. In Canaan, the future Israel, God would establish the Jewish people as the community from which He would bring forth the Messiah. As His chosen people—first known as Hebrews, then Israelites and then Jews—they were also divinely selected to receive, record, preserve, and transmit His Word: the Bible.[12]

Abraham appears to have left Ur sometime between 2000 and 1900 BC. Did he bring with him the Genesis accounts of Creation, the Fall, the Flood, the dispersion of humanity, and the chronology of the believing remnant? If so, was it a memorized, venerated oral history, providentially and reverently transferred through the ages? Or was it written in some form? Archaeological excavations at the site of Ur and the nearby Sumerian worship center of Nippur have recovered more than thirty thousand cuneiform texts dating to 2500 BC. The extensive evidence of early Sumerian writing—which includes accounts of creation and a biblical-style flood—suggests that even the common people of Ur may have been literate by Abraham's day. By some accounts, literacy began even earlier: Flavius Josephus, the renowned Jewish historian of the first century AD, believed that the art of writing developed at the beginning of human history—soon after Adam's epoch.[13]

A camel caravan photographed near Jerusalem in the early twentieth century evokes Abraham's exodus from Ur to a faraway land that would one day be known as Israel. When he left Ur, did Abraham bring with him the biblical account of the Fall, the Flood and the salvation of God's believing remnant? Source: Library of Congress.

Pictograph writing was practiced in a variety of early ancient cultures, and archaeology indicates that an organized system of writing was practiced in Sumer at least by 3000 BC. By Abraham's time, the Sumerians had more than a thousand years of experience in the art, and their writing system had spread throughout the Mideast. Did the art of writing develop accidentally? Or was it an act of providence—a gift of God for the primary purpose of sharing His divine revelation? "Believers in the providence of God," observed F. F. Bruce, a prominent, twentieth-century English Bible scholar, "may well conclude that it was by that providence that, when the Bible first began to be written, there lay ready to hand . . . a form of writing, recently invented, the understanding of which was not restricted to specially trained readers but lay within the capacity of Everyman."[14]

The Hebrew-Phoenician alphabet was the ancestor of ancient Greek, which in turn influenced the development of Latin and, eventually, English.

Of the three languages originally used to record the Bible—Hebrew, Aramaic, and Greek—Hebrew was used earliest. Most of the Hebrew Bible—the Old Testament—was written in Hebrew, which is related to what became known as the Phoenician alphabet, so named because it was first used by the ancient, seafaring Phoenicians on the Mediterranean's eastern shore. The Hebrew and Phoenician alphabets were closely related—"two branches of a common stem," observed one scholar—and belong to the Northwest Semitic division of the Semitic group of languages. The Hebrew-Phoenician alphabet was the ancestor of ancient Greek, which in turn influenced the development of Latin and eventually English. The English alphabet is directly descended from the Hebrew-Phoenician alphabet, which, according to some authorities, is the mother of the world's alphabets. The term "Semitic" is derived from the name of Noah's oldest son, Shem, and the Semitic languages also include Classical and modern Arabic. Ancient Hebrew, called "the language of Canaan" or, literally, the "lip of Canaan" in the Old Testament, was written from right to left, and consisted of a twenty-two-symbol alphabet of consonants only. No signs for vowels existed, although eventually a complicated system emerged that designated vowels by placing strokes and dots above, within, or below some consonants. The characteristic square look of the Hebrew letters may have developed during the Babylonian captivity under the influence of the script style used by the Babylonians.[15]

Biblical Hebrew is also known for its direct style and a vivid imagery drawn from everyday life. In the book of Jeremiah, for instance, those in rebellion to God are literally described in Hebrew as walking "backward and not forward." A superlative song is described as the "song of songs," and God's wrath is literally described in one passage as angry "reddened nostrils." Hebrew also employs rich metaphors: rebellious Israel is described as "a wild heifer" and "a crooked bow." Such vivid imagery was undoubtedly useful in the memorization of Scripture. Despite the challenges created by a lack of vowels, Hebrew is said to be relatively easy to translate because of its memorable imagery and simple, direct style. "In its brevity and directness," observed nineteenth-century Hebrew scholar J. A. Paterson, "Hebrew corresponds with the simplicity and naturalness of the unsophisticated life in which it gradually evolved." Such distinctions proved to be advantageous in preserving and sharing Scripture.[16]

Abraham and the community he brought into Canaan may have been influenced by the local language—although it is possible that the reverse is true. Was it Abraham's band of newcomers who linguistically influenced the Canaanites? When Jacob and his family joined Joseph in Egypt in about 1700 BC, did they carry the Hebrew language with them? Eventually, the Hebrew language would become a principal cultural distinction of the Jewish people, along with their unique, monotheistic God-centered faith. According to the Bible, the Hebrew people clearly maintained their religious and cultural identity in Egypt, even as they were enslaved. And according to the book of Exodus, when the Hebrew people emerged from Egypt after more than four hundred years in the land of the pharaohs, they did so as a nation—with their religious and cultural identity intact. Did that also include the Hebrew language?[17]

Following their conquest and occupation of Canaan—the "promised land"—under Joshua's leadership, the Hebrew people became known as the Israelites, and at least by the fourteenth century BC, Hebrew was established as their language. "Hebrew has a long history," notes Hebrew language scholar Angel Sáenz-Badillos. "It has persisted as a written language for more than 3,000 years. As a spoken language, it has had to survive in many different situations, following the complicated historical course of the Jewish people." Eventually, however, Hebrew was supplanted by Aramaic as the common language of the Israelites. The official language of the ancient Assyrian, Babylonian, and Persian empires, Aramaic was spread throughout the Mideast by conquest and commerce. Following the reign of King Solomon, Israel was torn by civil war and divided into two nations, with Judah to the south and Israel to the north. Between 738 and 722 BC, the northern kingdom was conquered by the Assyrian empire, and almost all its people were marched away to Assyria and captivity. Two centuries later, over the course of two invasions between 601 and 586 BC, the people of the southern kingdom of Judah were defeated by invading Babylonian forces, who razed Jerusalem, destroyed the temple, and forced Judah's people into exile in Babylon. There, they and their children and grandchildren gradually acquired the use of Aramaic to a degree that rivaled Hebrew use. The Babylonian Talmud and the Jerusalem Talmud, important collections of Jewish law and tradition, were recorded largely in Aramaic, and so were parts of other ancient texts, such as the Midrash, an ancient commentary on the Hebrew Bible.[18]

Although the gradual shift from Hebrew to Aramaic many have threatened the exiled Israelites' cultural identity, it also may have sparked the historic Jewish practice of recording *targums*—relevant commentaries or paraphrases of Scripture that would later provide valuable insight into period Jewish thought and culture. To enable the people to retain knowledge of the Scriptures as use of the Hebrew language declined, *targums* were recorded in Aramaic. The people of the Northern Kingdom never returned from Assyria, but after the Persian ruler Cyrus the Great conquered Babylon in 539 BC, the exiles from Judah were allowed to return to their homeland to rebuild the temple and Jerusalem—and they apparently brought Aramaic to Israel with them. Remarkably, they emerged from exile with a strong national and cultural identity and for the first time bearing the name of Jews—adopted apparently at the time of Esther—but with Aramaic, not Hebrew, as their primary language. The decline of Hebrew as the common language of the Jewish people—along with intermarriage to their pagan conquerors—so enraged the Jewish leader Nehemiah that at one point he personally whipped some offenders and yanked out their hair. After the Jews returned from Babylon, according to the biblical account, Nehemiah and Ezra the priest called them to a giant assembly in Jerusalem, and had the Scriptures read aloud to them in Hebrew—with a public translation in Aramaic. Despite such efforts to preserve and restore the Hebrew language, the use of Aramaic increased in Israel, and by the time of Christ, it was widely used by the Jewish people.[19]

Residents pack the narrow streets of Zaoud-el-Mara, the Jewish neighborhood of Alexandria, Egypt in the late nineteenth century. It was here in Alexandria that Jewish scholars first translated the Old Testament into Greek in the third century, B.C. Source: Library of Congress.

The first use of the Aramaic language in the Old Testament occurs in Genesis, when Jacob made a treaty with his father-in-law, Laban, and the two marked the agreement with a pile of stones. Jacob called the monument *Galeed,* which means "heap of witness" in Hebrew, and Laban called it by the same—but used the Aramaic words *Jegar-sahadutha.* The book of Daniel is believed to have used Aramaic to report the events in Nebuchadnezzar's court in Babylon. In the book of Ezra, several sections were originally written in Aramaic, including official Persian communications, and one verse of the book of Jeremiah was rendered in Aramaic. Although Hebrew would remain the language of the Jewish Scriptures, it would eventually be supplanted by Aramaic as the popular language of Israel. However, Aramaic would also eventually be replaced as the common language of Israel—by Greek. "While Aramaic was the language of the nursery and the home," concluded the Scottish Old Testament scholar William Ewing, "in the street and the market-place the language that was used was Greek." The influence of Greek culture, which was spread in the fourth century BC by the conquests of Alexander the Great, made Greek the common language of the Mediterranean basin and the Mideast (with Latin becoming the official language upon the rise of the Roman Empire).[20]

By the beginning of the third century BC, there was genuine concern in the international Jewish community that knowledge of Hebrew was becoming lost, and with it the ability to read or understand the Word in its original language. Demand for a translation of the Hebrew Scriptures in Greek resulted in production of the Septuagint—the first translation of the Old Testament in Greek. It was translated and assembled over more than a century by scholarly members of the Jewish community in Alexandria, Egypt. The Septuagint is often referred to by the letters LXX—Roman numerals for the number seventy—based on the tradition that seventy or seventy-two Jewish scholars independently translated it in a miraculous manner. It was the Bible used by the first followers of Christ, and became a Christian missionary tool as the Old Testament reference for spreading the gospel in the apostolic age. Eventually, the Septuagint became the authoritative Greek-language source for numerous English translations of the Old Testament. And the fate of the Hebrew language? By the time of Christ, the Scriptures were more often read in Greek than in Hebrew even among the Jews of Palestine, and within a few more centuries, Hebrew fell into disuse except as a biblical language. Over time, under the influence of Greek, Latin, Arabic, and other languages, Hebrew was reduced to little more than a traditional element of Jewish culture and the language of scholarly Bible study. It appeared that the language might even be doomed to become another "dead" language from antiquity. Then, in 1948—two-thousand years after Greek and Aramaic supplanted Hebrew in ancient Israel—the modern nation of Israel was established, and its predominant official language, revived and protected, became Hebrew.[21]

2

THE OLD TESTAMENT

Then the LORD *said . . . "Write down these words . . ."*
—EXODUS 34:27

IT BEGAN WITH A LOST GOAT. In 1947, three young Arab Bedouin goat-herders were searching for strays from their herd among the rugged cliffs near Wadi Qumran, which was located about a mile northwest of the Dead Sea in what is now modern Israel. They approached the entrance to a remote cave, reportedly tossed a rock into the darkness, and heard the clatter of breaking pottery. Later, one of them—Muhammad adh-Dhib—returned to the cave and edged inside, hoping to find hidden treasure. Instead, he discovered a cache of large, cylindrical earthenware jars, which contained "some smelly parchments." The parchments proved to be treasure of another sort: Muhammad and his companions had discovered what became known as the Dead Sea Scrolls, which have been called "the greatest manuscript discovery of modern times."[1]

From the cave, the boys removed seven scrolls, which made their way to a Bethlehem antiques dealer, and from there to a professor from Hebrew University and an official of the Syrian Orthodox Church in Jerusalem. For a while, no one seemed to realize the significance of the discovery—on a trip to New York City, the church official even tried to sell his scrolls through an ad in the *Wall Street Journal,* which read, "Biblical Manuscripts dating back to at least 200 BC are for sale. This would be an ideal gift to an educational or religious institution by an individual or group."[2]

The yawning mouth of an isolated cave opens to a vista of the Dead Sea in modern Israel. In 1947, a Bedouin goat-herder dared to go inside Qumran Cave 1, and discovered a biblical treasure—the Dead Sea Scrolls. Source: Library of Congress.

Soon afterwards, the importance of the scrolls was recognized by the international scholarly community, religious leaders, and the news media. Soon archaeological expeditions were at work in the Qumran caves—along with more than a few Bedouin entrepreneurs. More discoveries were made in other caves—more by the Bedouins than the archaeologists—and an extraordinary horde of manuscripts was uncovered by 1956, with more caves discovered in 2017. The manuscripts may have belonged to a nearby settlement of the Essenes or another sect, and were hidden in the caves to save them from the invading Roman army during the Jewish war of AD 66–70. Or, they may have been a library. Some speculated that they may have been the library from the second temple in Jerusalem—moved for safekeeping from pillaging Roman troops. The arid conditions of the Dead Sea region perhaps allowed the scrolls to remain exceptionally well-preserved. Eventually, twelve caves yielded almost a thousand manuscripts, including tens of thousands of ancient parchment fragments, numerous examples of secular and apocryphal works, and portions of every Old Testament book except Esther. The Old Testament books date from what is known as the Second Temple period—from five hundred years before Christ to AD 70, when Roman troops destroyed the temple. Although scroll fragments are found in museums around the world, almost all of the Dead Sea Scrolls collection is now owned by the State of Israel, and is preserved and displayed in a wing of the Israel Museum in Jerusalem called the Shrine of the Book.[3]

Since their discovery, the Dead Sea Scrolls have been the focus of continuous study and debate. "Few documents have been more intensively studied, and, indeed, more recklessly interpreted," observed Edward M. Blaiklock, a twentieth-century classic and biblical scholar. Critics of Christianity rushed to find ammunition to attack the Bible and the faith. The Dead Sea Scrolls posed "a challenge to the Church far greater than was ever presented by Darwin's theory of evolution," proclaimed one critic. However, after more than a half century of investigation—scholarly and otherwise—the Dead Sea Scrolls have instead reinforced the authenticity of the Scriptures. The Old Testament scrolls underscored the credibility of modern English translations based on the Septuagint, the Masoretic texts and other ancient sources. Various minor textual questions were resolved from comparison with the Dead Sea Scroll texts, and understanding of the Old Testament text and the New Testament era were both sharpened. The official commentary from an exhibit on the Dead Sea Scrolls in the U.S. Library of Congress in the twenty-first century aptly summarized their value:

> The Dead Sea Scrolls, which date back to the events described in the New Testament, have added to our understanding of the Jewish background of Christianity. The fact that they survived for twenty centuries, that they were found accidentally by Bedouin shepherds, that they are the largest and oldest body of manuscripts relating to the Bible and to the time of Jesus of Nazareth make them a truly remarkable archaeological find.[4]

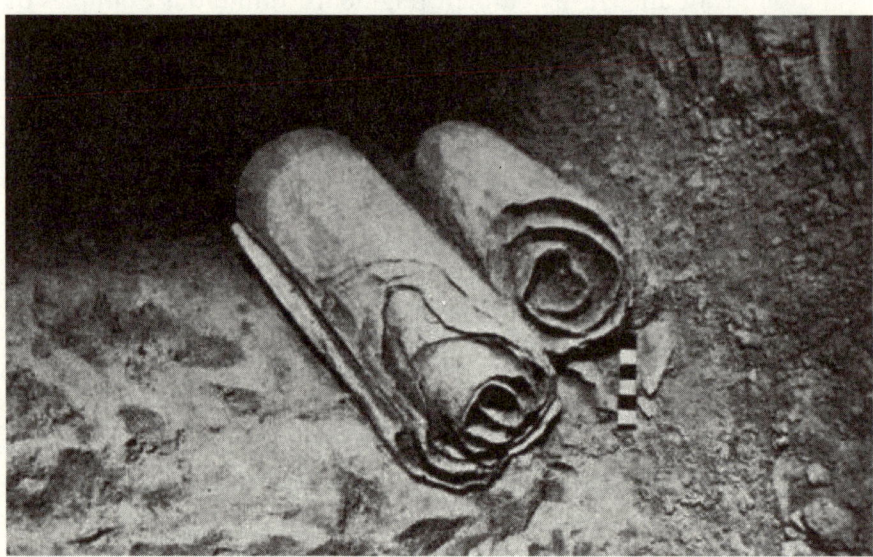

Awaiting scientific examination and preservation, two of the Dead Sea Scrolls lie unrolled on the floor of one of the Qumran caves. The first scrolls found their way into the antiquities market, and were offered for sale in a newspaper classified ad. Source: Wikimedia Commons.

A smattering of the texts from the Dead Sea Scrolls are written in Greek. A few are written in Aramaic. Most, however, are written in Hebrew—and thus the Dead Sea Scrolls provide significant evidence that the Jewish people used Hebrew at least as a religious and scholarly language in the centuries preceding and at the time of Christ in what is known as the Second Temple period. "Since the discovery of the scrolls from the Qumram caves in the late 1940s to the early-to-mid 1950s, the process of sorting, identifying and editing the fragmentary manuscripts has occupied the attention of scholars," concluded Dead Sea Scrolls authority Sidnie White Crawford.

> Now . . . more and more attention has been drawn to the contents of the texts [and we] can say several things about this collection. First, the majority of the texts are written in Hebrew, thus pointing to Hebrew as a living language (at least in literature) in the Second Temple Period. Second, a large percentage of the texts found in the caves (about 25 percent) are copies of books later considered to be part of the canon of the Hebrew Bible.[5]

Other significant archaeological discoveries have underscored the contribution of the Jewish people and the Hebrew language to the recording and preservation of the Bible. In the autumn of 1908, British archaeologist Robert Armstrong Stewart Macalister was excavating Israel's ancient city of Gezer, where biblical accounts attest that Joshua and the Israelites defeated the king of Gezer. The ruins of Gezer, which would become an Israeli national park, are located in the modern Judean hill country midway between Jerusalem and Tel Aviv, and Gezer is one of Israel's principal archaeological sites. Macalister was a pioneer archaeologist at Gezer, and he uncovered extraordinary discoveries—including a fortification from Israel's Late Bronze Age, the Canaanite city wall, and what is believed to be the home of the governor of Gezer. His most significant discovery at Gezer, however, was not a formidable ruin, but a small, four-inch cuneiform tablet, inscribed on one side, with traces of writing on the other. It was a handwritten calendar of the agricultural seasons, with instructions for appropriate farming activities—and it might even have been a student's homework assignment. At first glance, the tablet's message seemed trivial. Upon careful study, however, the inscriptions on the tiny calendar were discovered to be written in Paleo-Hebrew, a predecessor to classic Hebrew. When placed in its proper archaeological context and dated, the Gezer calendar—as it came to be known—was generally considered to have been written during the reign of Israel's King Solomon about 1,000 BC. Although the Hebrew language is believed to be much older, many archaeologists accept the Gezer calendar as the earliest definitive physical evidence of Hebrew writing, which, based on the calendar, may have been widespread in ancient Israel.[6]

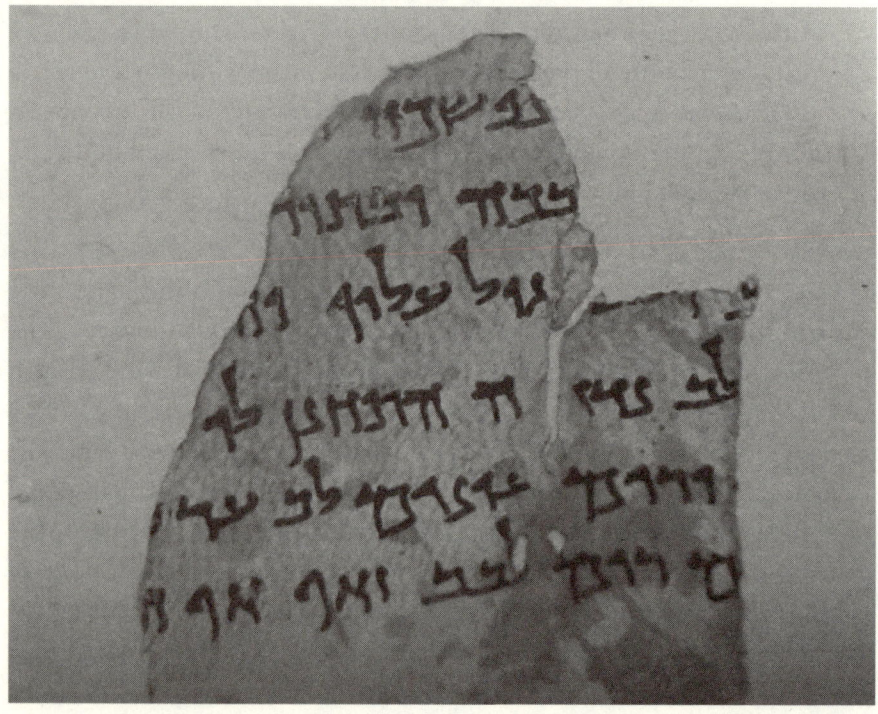

Delicate Hebrew script adorns a fragment of parchment from the Dead Sea Scrolls. By 1956, an extraordinary cache of scrolls and fragments had been recovered from the Qumran caves, and more caves were discovered in 2017. Source: Oriental Institute Museum / Wikimedia Commons.

Other archaeological discoveries that reveal the use of the Hebrew language during antiquity include following:

- THE KETEF HINNOM PLAQUES—two miniature silver plaques uncovered in Jerusalem's Old City in 1979, inscribed with scripture from the Old Testament books of Numbers, Psalms, and Daniel, dating to the sixth or seventh century BC;

- THE MOABITE STONE—an ancient stone slab discovered east of the Dead Sea in 1868, dating to about 830 BC and inscribed with the extinct Moabite language, which was related to Hebrew;

- THE SAMARITAN OSTRACA—sixty-five receipts in Hebrew script, inscribed on pottery shards and excavated at the site of a Samaritan palace dating to the era of Jeroboam II, about 750 BC;

- THE LACHISH LETTERS—twenty-one pottery fragments discovered at the site of the ancient Israelite city of Lachish in 1935, inscribed with Hebrew military correspondence related to Nebuchadnezzar's invasion of Israel, and dating to Jeremiah's day in the eighth century BC;

- THE SILOAM INSCRIPTION—cursive Hebrew script carved into the wall of Hezekiah's tunnel in Jerusalem, discovered in 1880, and dating to 701 BC.[7]

To fulfill His promise, the Bible teaches, God used Abraham to establish a wonderfully unique people.

God's promise to Abraham was specific and far-reaching: "In you . . . shall all the families of the earth be blessed." To fulfill His promise, the Bible teaches, God used Abraham to establish a wonderfully unique people. As noted previously, they were first known as Hebrews, then—after conquering Canaan—as Israelites, and eventually, as the Jews. *From* them, God would bring forth His Son—Y'shua Messiah: Jesus—and *through* them, He would preserve and transmit His written revelation: the Word of God. Thus, the people of the promise became the people of the Book. And through the centuries, they copied and protected the Scriptures with the uniquely Jewish attitude of awe and legalistic attention that marked them as God's chosen people—chosen in part to be the keepers of His Word. It was with such extraordinary care and commitment that the Scriptures were preserved through peacetime, wartime, eras of obedience, seasons of sin, invasions, dispersions, and repeated enemy occupations. Under the inspiration of the Holy Spirit, it was Hebrew/Israelite/Jewish writers who recorded the Bible—both the Old Testament and the New Testament. "The treasuries of the Jewish people are not filled with precious objects," observed Dr. Hava Katz, chief of the Bureau of Israel Archaeology, "but with written words that have contributed to the cultural and spiritual development of mankind." But why is that first division called the Old *Testament?* The use of the term "Old" in relation to the newer, New Testament is obvious, but where did the name "Testament" originate?[8]

The English word "testament" is derived from the Latin *Testamentum,* which was used in early Latin Bibles for the titles of both testaments. The Old Testament was known in Latin as the *Vetus Testamentum* (and the New Testament was called the *Novus Testamentum*). The word *Testamentum* was a Latin translation of the Greek word *diatheke,* which could refer to a declaration such as a "last will and testament." However, it could also mean "covenant"—a lawful alliance granted by an authority—which is the sense of the term when it refers to the Bible. A "testament" in the biblical sense refers to a covenant established by God as an act of grace upon His people. As documented in the Old Testament, God established a covenant of law through Moses—often called the Mosaic Covenant—between Himself and His chosen people, the Israelites. As revealed by the New Testament, the Mosaic covenant led to conviction of sin and a unique, final atonement under a new covenant of grace—provided to believers by the death and resurrection of Jesus, the "Christ" (the Greek translation of "Messiah").[9]

An archeologist's assistant puts a pickaxe to work at Gezer, an early nineteenth century archaeological site northwest of Jerusalem. At this site, British archaeologist R.A.S. McAlister would uncovered the Gezer Calendar—a small cuneiform tablet written in a predecessor to the Hebrew language. Source: Library of Congress.

All the books of the Old Testament are generally believed to have been completed by the time of Ezra, the Old Testament scribe and priest, by about 445 BC. Within Judaism, the Old Testament, or Hebrew Bible, is known as the *Tanakh*, which is not really a word but instead is an acronym: TNK. It is derived from the first letters of the three main divisions of the Hebrew Bible—the *Torah* (the Law), *Nevi'im* (the Prophets), and *Ketuvin* (the Writings). For Jews, it *is* the Bible, but for Christians, it is only the first part, and the Bible's revelation is made complete in the New Testament. By about 250 BC, when translation of the Septuagint is believed to have begun, Jewish rabbinical leaders believed the Old Testament canon was complete, meaning that all thirty-nine books were inspired by the Holy Spirit and deemed authoritative as the Word of God. A definition of biblical inspiration was recorded in the first century AD by the apostle Peter, who was also Jewish. "But know this first of all," he wrote, "that no prophecy of Scripture is a matter of one's own interpretation, for no prophecy was ever made by an act of human will, but men moved by the Holy Spirit spoke from God." Collectively, the books of the Old Testament chronicle an extraordinary story:

- God's creation of humanity, the Fall, the Flood, the call of Abraham, and the development of his line through Isaac, Jacob and the Hebrews, Israelites and Jewish people;

- the history of God's relationship with His chosen people, including their sojourn into Egypt, their enslavement there and their exodus, the establishment of the Ten Commandments and Mosaic covenant at Mount Sinai, the wilderness wandering of the Hebrew people, and their conquest of Canaan under Joshua;

- development of a system of worship through the tabernacle and temple;

- Israel's experience under judges and a united monarchy, and the division of the nation into the southern and northern kingdoms of Judah and Israel;

- the Israelites' repeated rebellion against God, and His prophetic warnings to them;

- the conquering of Israel and Judah, and the captivity and exile of their people under the Assyrians and Babylonians;

- the return of the people of Judah from exile as Jews, and their efforts under Ezra and Nehemiah to restore Israel and rebuild the temple;

- Hebrew psalms, prayers, hymns, proverbs, and poetry;

- a continuous flow of prophecy about the advent of Messiah and God's plan of salvation, and the promise of a new covenant.[10]

An ancient tree on the Mount of Olives frames Jerusalem in this early twentieth century photograph. Archaeological excavations around the city in the nineteenth and twentieth centuries revealed examples of the Hebrew language from antiquity. Source: Library of Congress.

The Old Testament is actually a library—a collection of books believed to be inspired by God over the course of more than fourteen hundred years, and recorded by a diverse body of human writers in different lands. It consists of a remarkable variety of literature styles—history, law, biography, poetry, personal memoirs—with an astonishing unity of theme: God made us, loves us despite our inherent rebellious attitude toward Him, entered this world as Jesus Christ, and offers humanity a plan for eternal salvation through Christ's atoning death. God's revelation of Himself and His plan as recorded in the Old Testament is progressive and cumulative. Principal biblical doctrines, such as the triune nature of God, are progressively revealed through the Old Testament until God's complete revelation cumulates in the New Testament with Jesus Christ. For example, the doctrine of the Trinity—one God expressing Himself in three persons—is exposed in Genesis 1:26 through the use of the plural pronoun, expressed in later Old Testament references, and clearly revealed in New Testament in passages such as Luke 3:21–22 (an expression of the Trinity at the baptism of Christ) and Matthew 28:19 (where Jesus issued the Great Commission in the name of the triune God). The New Testament is built on the Old Testament, and it also fulfills the revealed truth of the Old Testament—such as messianic prophecy—and thus it completes God's revelation.[11]

All of them are believed to be the human agents—writers—who were inspired by the same author: the Holy Spirit.

Christians generally divide the Old Testament into four sections: the Pentateuch, or Law (Genesis to Deuteronomy); History (Joshua to Esther); Poetry and Wisdom (Job to the Song of Solomon); and the Major and Minor Prophets (Isaiah to Malachi). (The same books are organized into the three main divisions in the Hebrew Bible—the Law, the Prophets and the Writings.) Moses is identified as the primary writer of the first five books of the Old Testament, the Pentateuch—a name derived from the Greek word for the number five. Other authors include Joshua, Samuel, Jeremiah, Ezra, Nehemiah, David, Solomon, Isaiah, Ezekiel, Daniel, the other prophets whose books bear their names, and some writers who are anonymous. All of them are believed to be the human agents—writers—who were inspired by the same author: the Holy Spirit. The Hebrew Bible consists of twenty-two or twenty-four books, compared to the thirty-nine books of today's Protestant Old Testament. All thirty-nine books are contained in the Hebrew arrangement, but they are organized differently—perhaps according to the twenty-two letters of the Hebrew alphabet. For example, the twelve minor prophets are grouped as a single book in the Hebrew Bible instead of arranging them as twelve separate books. The organization of the thirty-nine books in today's Protestant Old Testament is based on how the Jewish translators arranged the books in the Greek Septuagint:

GENESIS	1 KINGS	ECCLESIASTES	OBADIAH
EXODUS	2 KINGS	SONG OF SOLOMON	JONAH
LEVITICUS	1 CHRONICLES	ISAIAH	MICAH
NUMBERS	2 CHRONICLES	JEREMIAH	NAHUM
DEUTERONOMY	EZRA	LAMENTATIONS	HABAKKUK
JOSHUA	NEHEMIAH	EZEKIEL	ZEPHANIAH
JUDGES	ESTHER	DANIEL	HAGGAI
RUTH	JOB	HOSEA	ZECHARIAH
1 SAMUEL	PSALMS	JOEL	MALACHI
2 SAMUEL	PROVERBS	AMOS	

Canonization of the thirty-nine Old Testament books occurred over a long period of time, and was unofficially verified in the first century AD. Then, as had occurred during the Babylonian captivity, the Jewish people were driven to the Word of God by the threat of destruction. In AD 70, a Roman army commanded by Titus Vespasianus Augustus, a future Roman emperor, conquered Jerusalem and destroyed the second temple, which obliterated the physical center of the Jewish faith. After the loss of the temple, a Jewish intellectual center with an important focus on the Hebrew Bible developed in the city of Jamnia, or Yavne, which was located about thirty miles northwest of Jerusalem. There over the next generation, a team of Jewish rabbis led by a respected rabbinical scholar named Yoḥanan ben Zakkai studied and debated which books of the Hebrew Bible were considered canonical. They most likely did not compose an official council and took no official action: but their scholarly conclusions reinforced the canonization of the Old Testament. According to Jewish tradition, ben Zakkai and the other Jewish scholars at Yavne recognized that the thirty-nine books of the Hebrew Bible—the Old Testament—were self-authenticated and had been so for centuries, and thus were indeed the inspired Word of God. "This point is crucial," observed Old Testament expert Paul D. Wegner. "The books did not receive their authority because they were placed in the canon; rather, they were recognized by the nation of Israel as having divine authority and were therefore included in the canon." Thus, by AD 90, the Old Testament's thirty-nine books had been long recognized as canonical.[13]

Jews and Christians alike believe the Old Testament text was providentially preserved and transmitted. "Take a scroll and write on it all the words I have spoken to you," God commanded the prophet Jeremiah in the sixth century BC. By 500 BC, and perhaps even long before, a remarkable group of biblical scholars and guardians known as Sopherim, or "scribes," had arisen to preserve and transmit Scripture as a methodical, disciplined craft. Over the centuries, they were succeeded by others, such as the Tannaim and the Amoraim, all of whom followed meticulous methods of copying and preserving the Word of God. Eventually, beginning about AD 500, there arose a dedicated, disciplined body of Jewish scholars and scribes who followed the example of the scribes and the rabbis of Yavne and became renowned for their devotion to faithfully preserving Scripture and accurately transmitting it. They became known as the Masoretes—from the Hebrew *masorah* or "tradition"—and they worked diligently and skillfully to produce accurate texts of the Hebrew Bible from aged manuscripts. Their work eventually became known as the Masoretic text. Hebrew Bibles from the era of the Masoretes onward generally followed the Masoretic text, and all English translations of the Old Testament have been influenced by it. When a finalized system of verses was added to the Hebrew Bible about AD 900, it was largely the work of the family of ben Asher, especially tenth-century Masorete Aaron ben Moses ben Asher, whose method of adding vowels to the Hebrew text became the standard for the Hebrew Bible/Old Testament. The Masoretes' scholarly, disciplined zeal for the accurate transmission of Scripture reflected the uniquely Jewish tradition that had revered, protected, and transmitted God's Word through the ages.[14]

To preserve the ancient texts that they deemed to have been revealed by God, every translator followed painstaking, exacting rules. Before copying a text of Scripture, he had to bathe himself and dress in formal scribal attire. If the copyist used parchment instead of papyrus, the only parchment allowed to bear the Word of God was that made from the skin of "clean" or *kosher* animals; likewise, even its threads were required to be made from the hides of clean animals. Nothing could be rendered from memory—not a single letter, nor a single jot (the smallest letter in the Hebrew alphabet) nor a single tittle (a tiny, decorative accent mark). Each column of words had to have at least forty-eight lines and no more than sixty. Every word had to be pronounced aloud before it was written, the spaces between letters were carefully measured, and crafting of each letter had to meet regulated specifications. Lined paper, prepared to rigid standards, was used to ensure neatness and clarity of the text, and only black ink made from a special recipe could be used. And while writing the name of God, the scribe could not allow himself to pause to answer or look up at anyone—even if addressed by the king.[15]

An editor, or editors, examined each page within thirty days of its completion. Every letter of every word was counted and compared to the source. Only three corrections could be made on a page. If more than three errors were found on a single page, no more corrections were made; instead, the roll was destroyed. And when writing a reference to God, the scribe was required to stop and reverently, carefully clean the point of his pen before proceeding. Thus, God's chosen people—according to Scripture—were used to produce and preserve the Word of God. But they did not do it alone. "All Scripture is inspired by God," according to 2 Timothy 3:16, "and profitable for teaching, for reproof, for correction, for training in righteousness, so that the man of God may be adequate, equipped for every good work."[16]

Photographed at the end of the nineteenth century, a Samaritan high priest in the city of Nablus—site of the biblical Samaria—opens an ancient scroll containing the Pentateuch—the first five books of the Bible. Source: Library of Congress.

In the Jewish community before the time of Christ, a book was accepted as inspired because it contained compelling evidence of divine authority through the standards of canonicity depicted in the Old Testament, such as these:

- Was the book written by a prophet of God or someone recognized as having divine authority, as depicted in Jeremiah 26:2? (False prophecy was a capital crime during the age of the Old Testament.) Was the writer confirmed by acts of God, as reported in Exodus 4:1–9 and 1 Kings 18?

- Did the book claim to be inspired by God, or demonstrate evidence that it was divinely inspired, as stated in Isaiah 1:10-20?

- Did the message depict God consistently with earlier revelations— as required by Deuteronomy 13:1–3?

- Did the book convincingly demonstrate the authority of God as depicted in Exodus 24:7?

- Was the book accepted by the people of God to whom it was addressed, as in Joshua 24:22–27?[17]

While such canonization sometimes occurred over extended time, divine authority was sometimes accepted immediately. Immediate acceptance, for example, was demonstrated by the people's response— "All that the LORD has spoken we will do"—when Moses publicly read the Book of the Covenant in Exodus, when King Josiah spurred a national revival by reading lost Scriptures, or when Ezra proclaimed the Book of the Law to the people. The Pentateuch—the Bible's first five books—was deemed canonical during Moses' lifetime, and was preserved alongside the ark of the covenant in the Holy of Holies. Evidence suggests that all the books of the Old Testament canon were recognized by the Old Testament scribe Ezra in the fifth century B.C. New Testament verification of the Old Testament canon, attest generations of Bible scholars, was established when Jesus used the expression "from . . . Abel to . . . Zechariah" in Luke 11:51—which verified the Old Testament books accepted by Jews and Protestants.[18]

Other books were circulated among the Jewish people in antiquity, but they were not accepted into the Jewish canon—the books of the Hebrew Bible or Old Testament that were revered by the Jews as inspired by God. The word *canon*, or *kanon* in Greek, refers to a standard or body of laws, and originated from the Hebrew *qaneh*—a reed that was apparently used for measuring. Most notable among the books that the Jews rejected as non-canonical was the Apocrypha, which means "hidden" in Greek. Depending on how they are organized, they consist of fourteen to fifteen books that were mostly written in the last two centuries before Christ—1 and 2 Esdras, Tobit, Judith, additions to Esther, the Wisdom of Solomon, Ecclesiasticus, Baruch, the Letter of Jeremiah, the Prayer of Azariah (also called the Song of the Three Young Men), Susanna, Bel and the Dragon, the Prayer of Manasseh, and 1 and 2 Maccabees. Most were translated into Greek along with the Septuagint, but the Jews viewed them as "outside books" that failed to meet canonical standards for inspiration, yet were valuable as history, literature, and cultural expression. While some of the early church fathers accepted part or all of the Apocrypha; others, including Jerome—"the greatest Bible scholar of the ancient Western Church"—did not. Critics noted that none of the books were ever referred to in the New Testament by the apostles or Jesus, who did endorse the scope of canonical books when He spoke of "the Law of Moses, the Prophets and the Psalms" in Luke 24:44. Unlike the Old Testament canonical books, the books of the Apocrypha were always shadowed by uncertainty within much of Christendom. They gained acceptance in the medieval church—only to fall into question again in the revival of Hebrew-language scholarship that followed the Dark Ages.[19]

In 1534, the Reformer Martin Luther included the Apocrypha in his German-language Bible, but he pointedly set those books apart from the Old Testament and wrote in a foreword that they should not be equated with Scripture—a position also taken by the English Westminster Confession of Faith in 1646. In reaction to Luther's German Bible, the

Roman Catholic Church declared most of the Apocrypha's books to be canonical at the 1546 Council of Trent. Many Protestant translations of the Bible treated the books as did Luther's Bible—grouping them separately—although the 1640 edition of the Geneva Bible omitted them, and so did the first English Bible printed in the United States. As required by the Vatican, Catholic Bibles since the sixteenth century have treated them as Scripture, and Catholic scholars sometimes refer to them as the *deuterocanonical books*. The Greek Orthodox churches followed the Roman Catholic Church in accepting most of them, and the Russian Orthodox Church accepts some. Like the Jews, Protestant denominations generally came to reject all of the Apocrypha except as non-canonical literature.[20]

And how faithfully have the canonized Old Testament Scriptures been transmitted to the modern era? The answer is extraordinary. The texts of the Dead Sea Scrolls, the Septuagint, and other ancient manuscripts demonstrate a remarkable, faithful textual transmission from antiquity to a dependable modern translation of the Old Testament. "The historicity of the Old Testament should be taken seriously," concludes Old Testament scholar and author Kenneth A. Kitchens. "As for the Old Testament text itself, the Dead Sea Scrolls provide good evidence of a carefully transmitted core-text tradition through almost a thousand years down to the Masoretic scribes. Thus, the basic text of Old Testament Scripture can be established as essentially soundly transmitted, and the evidence shows that the form and content of the Old Testament fits with known literary and cultural realities of the Ancient Near East." The scribes' veneration for the Word of God led them to follow a tradition of burying and destroying biblical manuscripts when they were worn, tattered, and delicate. Therefore, compared to the New Testament, fewer Old Testament manuscripts exist—perhaps fifteen hundred complete or fragmentary manuscripts. Most date no later than about AD 850, but some are much older.[21]

Aside from the oldest, the Dead Sea Scrolls, other major Old Testament manuscripts include the following:

- THE NASH PAPYRUS—a papyrus fragment from c. 150 BC containing the Hebrew text of Ten Commandments from Exodus and the Shema from Deuteronomy ("Hear, O Israel, the Lord our God is one");

- THE JOHN RYLANDS PAPYRI—a large collection of papyrus fragments in Great Britain's John Rylands Library that date to about 125 BC, and include what is believed to be the oldest surviving fragment of the Greek-language Septuagint;

- THE CHESTER BEATTY PAPYRI—dating to about AD 200, these papyri fragments from Egypt include portions of eight Old Testament books from the Greek Septuagint, which were acquired by American antiquities collector Chester Beatty and were eventually housed in Ireland's Chester Beatty Museum;

- CODEX VATICANUS—acquired by the Vatican library in 1448, and dating to about AD 325, it contains most of both Testaments in Greek on more than seven hundred folios of superbly crafted vellum;

- CODEX SINAITICUS—dating from about AD 350, the antelope skin vellum manuscript was reportedly discovered in 1844 in a monastery at Mount Sinai in Egypt, and consists of hundreds of pages of the Greek Septuagint and the New Testament, most of which is held by the British Library in London;

- CODEX ALEXANDRINUS—also held by the British Library, is believed to have possibly originated with the early church in Alexandria, Egypt, dates to about AD 425, consists of 773 parchment leaves, and is missing only a small portion of the Old Testament text;

- CODEX EPHRAEMI RESCRIPTUS—dating to about AD 450 and now preserved in the National Library of France in Paris, it includes a small portion of the Septuagint on vellum;

- ALEPPO CODEX—believed to have been written in Tiberius, Israel, about AD 1000, and now housed in Israel's Shrine of the Book, it was zealously protected by Jewish guardians in the Syrian city of Aleppo for more than five hundred years, and is often described as "the oldest most complete" manuscript version of the Old Testament, although several entire books are missing;

- CODEX LENINGRAD—preserved in National Library of Russia, it is said to have been produced in Egypt by Masoretic master Moses ben Asher soon after the *Aleppo Codex* was written, and because it is more complete, it too is also frequently described as "the oldest surviving complete copy" of the Old Testament;

- SAMARITAN PENTATEUCH—dating to Israel's Samaritan community c. AD 1150, it contains the first five books of the Old Testament, with a distinctly Samaritan perspective, and is most valuable for its preservation of an ancient form of Hebrew.[22]

The compatibility of the ancient and historic texts is remarkable and reinforces the historic Judeo-Christian position that God inspired the original manuscripts and preserved His revealed truth through the ages—despite the ravages of time, continuous attacks, and the fallibility of man. According to numerous Bible scholars, the survival of the Scriptures intact and faithfully transmitted over the ages is nothing less than astonishing. So too, many believe, is the extraordinary survival of the Jewish people, who were uniquely equipped and preserved to protect and transmit the Word of God. "No book from antiquity comes to the modern world with greater evidence for its authenticity than does the Bible," asserted theologian Norman Geisler. "One can but conclude that the Bible as a whole claims to be the Word of God, and the evidence confirms that claim."[23]

3

THE NEW TESTAMENT

*"But the Helper, the Holy Spirit, whom the Father will send in My name, He will
teach you all things and bring to your remembrance all that I said to you."*
—JOHN 14:26

THEY DID NOT EXPECT AN EMPTY TOMB. Roman and Jewish authorities
obviously believed the ministry of Jesus would end with his death. They
had not reckoned with the Resurrection, and His empty tomb left them
confounded. Roman troops from legions posted in Syria were quartered
in Jerusalem, and the Roman procurator Pontius Pilate had ordered a
guard detail posted at the tomb in response to an official request from
the Jewish high priest's office. Jesus had said publicly that He would
rise from the dead—as foretold by Old Testament prophecy—and the
authorities had intended to safeguard the tomb so Jesus' followers would
not remove His body and provoke rumors. "And they went and made
the grave secure," reports the gospel of Matthew, "and along with the
guard they set a seal on the stone." The seal was serious: it probably
consisted of a cord stretched from side to side across the entrance to
the tomb, held in place by wax, on which was impressed the seal of the
imperial Roman Empire. To break it was to confront the full power and
authority of the Roman government.[1]

As depicted in a nineteenth century Russian icon, the apostle Matthew records the Gospel. According to Scripture, Jesus had promised his apostles that "the Holy Spirit…will teach you all things and bring to your remembrance all that I said to you." Source: Wikimedia Commons

It was broken anyway. "And behold, a severe earthquake had occurred," reports Matthew, "for an angel of the Lord descended from heaven and came and rolled away the stone and sat upon it. And his appearance was like lightning, and his clothing as white as snow. The guards shook for fear of him and became like dead men." The reports of the empty tomb and the risen Messiah confounded Jewish authorities, who should have known and respected the Old Testament prophecies. However, they had not believed Jesus when He predicted His resurrection, and they still denied it after it occurred. They bribed the guards, telling them to report that Jesus' body had indeed been stolen by His followers. And the Romans? They too were confounded. Even the Roman historian Tacitus seemed mystified: He noted that devotion to Jesus Christ as Lord and Savior—which he called a "pernicious superstition"—though it appeared to have been "checked for a short time" by the crucifixion, for some reason "broke out afresh" afterward.[2]

It "broke out afresh" with world-changing power. The apostles were also surprised by the empty tomb—even though Jesus had told them plainly to expect it—but they were not confounded by it. According to the New Testament accounts, Jesus appeared to them in a series of postresurrection encounters over a forty-day period. He appeared to individuals. He appeared to groups. At one point He appeared to an assembly of hundreds. And then, in the presence of a multitude of witnesses, He was "lifted up while they were looking on, and a cloud received Him out of their sight." Into what "cloud" did He disappear? Was it the *Shekinah* glory—the wholly unique luminous cloud of God's radiance that had led the Hebrews from Egypt, and had at times filled the Holy of Holies in the tabernacle and the temple? As eyewitnesses to the incredible events following the Resurrection, the apostles were dramatically transformed. From a group of frightened, timid men hiding behind closed doors, they became men who "turned the world upside down"—carrying the gospel of Jesus Christ from Israel to points as far distant as modern India and modern Spain.[3]

"Go therefore and make disciples of all the nations," Jesus told them in the Great Commission, "baptizing them in the name of the Father and the Son and the Holy Spirit, teaching them to observe all that I commanded you, and lo, I am with you always, even to the end of the age" Transformed, empowered and obedient, they preached, they taught—and some of them wrote. And apparently, all but one died doing it. James, the son of Zebedee and the brother of John, was first to die—executed by King Herod Agrippa in AD 44. Others were martyred over the following decades, according to tradition. Thomas reputedly took the gospel to what is now India, where he was eventually speared to death. Philip may have been crucified in Greece. Bartholomew (or Nathanael) is said to have been flayed alive in Turkey. After a long ministry of preaching to his fellow Jews, Matthew reportedly died in what is now Iran—stoned, beheaded, or burned alive. Simon the Zealot is thought to have been crucified after preaching from the Black Sea to what is now Britain. James, the son of Alphaeus, may have been sawn in pieces. Jude, who may have taken the gospel to the border of modern Russia and Turkey, was reportedly shot to death by arrows. Peter was executed in Rome—reportedly crucified upside down—and Andrew, who preached from Asia Minor to Greece, is said to have been crucified on an X-shaped cross. Matthias, who was selected by the apostles to replace Judas Iscariot, was reportedly stoned and then beheaded in Turkey. Paul, an apostle by a post-Resurrection call, was also beheaded, executed on the road to Rome after conducting extraordinary missionary activity in the Mediterranean world. Of the original apostles, only John is believed to have died a natural death in old age, and besides imprisonment, he reportedly suffered attempts to poison him and boil him in oil.[4]

They were willing to die, according to Scripture, because they had seen the risen Christ, were convinced of the gospel, and were committed to sharing the revealed truth that became the New Testament. "For we did not follow cleverly devised tales," wrote the apostle Peter, "when we made known to you the power and coming of our Lord Jesus Christ, but we were eyewitnesses of His majesty." And according to the New Testament, they were directed by the Holy Spirit, who also inspired the Scripture they wrote. That was Christ's promise to them: "But the Helper, the Holy Spirit, whom the Father will send in My name, He will teach you all things and bring to your remembrance all that I said to you . . . and you shall be My witnesses both in Jerusalem, and in all Judea and Samaria, and even to the remotest part of the earth." When they preached, when they taught, and when they wrote the accounts and letters that compose the New Testament, they claimed the authority of Jesus Christ and the inspiration of the Holy Spirit. "But know this first of all," wrote Peter a year or two before his death, "that no prophecy of Scripture is a matter of one's own interpretation, for no prophecy was ever made by an act of human will, but men moved by the Holy Spirit spoke from God."[5]

Relief sculpture on the Arch of Titus, erected in Rome in A.D. 81, depicts treasures looted from the Temple when Jerusalem was sacked by Roman troops under Titus Vespasianus Augustus in A.D. 70. By then, countless early Christians were spreading the Gospel throughout the Roman world. Source: Steerpike/Wikimedia Commons.

It was no accident that the first Christians were Jews. That had been God's promise—He would first extend the salvation offer to the Jews, then to the Gentiles. The remnant would be expanded to non-Jews, as predicted centuries earlier by the prophet Amos, but like Jesus (Y'shua

Messiah), the apostles and most of Christ's earliest followers were Jewish. They possessed the same reverence for God's Word that was common to generations of Jews before them, and they had equally high standards for Scripture. They believed that God had promised the advent of Messiah, and that He had come as Jesus Christ—making atonement for sin as prophesied in the Old Testament. They also believed that the accounts and letters that would become the New Testament were Scripture—as equally inspired and authoritative as the Old Testament. "God, after He spoke long ago to the fathers in the prophets in many portions, and in many ways," penned the writer of the New Testament book of Hebrews, "in these last days has spoken to us in His Son, whom He appointed heir of all things, through whom also He made the world." Initially, the apostles preached and taught—first in the synagogues and later in churches—as the Old Testament was publicly read and applied to the coming of Christ. Then they wrote, recording the Gospels, the Acts of the Apostles, various letters that taught doctrine and discipleship, and finally, the book of Revelation, which foretold the future of God's church and His plan of salvation. In obedience to the Great Commission, they also directed their followers to circulate what they wrote as Scripture: "I adjure you by the Lord," wrote Paul to the Thessalonian believers, "to have this letter read to all the brethren."[6]

Apostolic teaching—what the apostles and their associates preached, taught, and wrote—became the foundation of the New Testament church. It was the culmination of the Old Testament message: God has a plan of salvation offered by grace through faith in Jesus Christ. By His atoning death on the cross—confirmed by His resurrection—Jesus fulfilled the obligations of the Old Testament law for all believers, the apostles taught. Through God's grace—underserved favor—eternal life is available through personal belief in Jesus Christ as the Lord and Savior; that was the central message of the New Testament. Wrote Paul in the book of Romans: "If you confess with your mouth Jesus as Lord, and believe in your heart that God raised Him from the dead, you shall be saved; for with the heart man believes, resulting in righteousness, and with the mouth he confesses, resulting in salvation" (10:9–10). A glimpse of the New Testament church—and its devotion to apostolic teaching—is revealed in the book of Acts: "They were continually devoting themselves to the apostles' teaching and to fellowship, to the breaking of bread and to prayer. Everyone kept feeling a sense of awe; and many wonders and signs were taking place through the apostles"[7]

Depicted in an ancient mosaic astride his battle horse Bucephalus, Alexander the Great had conquered the Mediterranean basin and beyond in the fourth century BC, leaving behind the Greek language—which would be used to share the message of the Bible. Source: RuthAven/Archaeological Museum of Naples.

This era of "wonders and signs"—the apostolic age—had been predicted more than five hundred years earlier by the Old Testament prophet Joel: "I will pour out My Spirit on all mankind; and your sons and daughters will prophesy, your old men will dream dreams, your young men will see visions. Even on the male and female servants I will pour out My Spirit in those days." It was also an age of persecution, inflicted first by the Jewish leadership against the Jewish Christians—followers of "the Way" as they were initially called. The wave of persecution that originated in Jerusalem and claimed James in AD 44 eventually drove many of the first Christians out of Israel, scattering them throughout the Roman Empire. By AD 70, when Titus's Roman army destroyed Jerusalem, burned the temple, and dispersed the Jewish people, countless Christians had already been dispersed to distant regions—carrying with them the gospel of Jesus Christ. Others, such as Paul and his associates, voluntarily dispersed solely to spread the Word. "Now when they had traveled through Amphipolis and Apollonia, they came to Thessalonica, where there was a synagogue of the Jews," records the book of Acts. "And according to Paul's custom, he went to them, and for three Sabbaths reasoned with them from the Scriptures, explaining and giving evidence that the Christ had to suffer and rise again from the dead, and saying, 'This Jesus whom I am proclaiming to you is the Christ.'" Among the Jews and especially among the Gentiles, the work of the apostles and their colleagues bore dramatic fruit: "So the word of the Lord was growing mightily and prevailing"—and the New Testament message was launched on a journey through the world that continues today.[8]

"The Christian can take the whole Bible in his hand and say without fear or hesitation that he holds in it the true Word of God."

For the first time in history, the first-century Mediterranean world was united by a universal language—Greek. Established by the earlier conquests of Alexander the Great, it remained the practical language of educated peoples, and it connected a multitude of cultures. With unprecedented power, this universal communications system was combined with extraordinary mass transportation—the technologically superb system of Roman highways—to spread the Word of God. "It is the simple truth," observed William Ramsey, an internationally renowned nineteenth-century archaeologist and Bible scholar, "that traveling, whether for business or pleasure, was contemplated and performed under the Empire with an indifference and confidence, and, above all, certainty, which were unknown in [early] centuries." In what seems in hindsight to some to be an obvious act of Providence, Greek language and Roman roads delivered the gospel. Written in Greek on papyrus and parchments—and carried on reliable Roman roads—the books that became the New Testament were circulating even during the extraordinary apostolic age that they reported. The New Testament book of James appears to have been written as early as AD 46. The book of Galatians was likely written in AD 49. The earliest of the Gospels were written in the 50s. The book of Acts was apparently written around AD 61, and many of the epistles were written in the 50s and 60s. The book of Revelation—the last book of the New Testament in arrangement and chronology—was written in the 90s.[9]

Thus, the books of the New Testament were received, read, and collected by the emerging churches of the first century, and were canonized by their universal acceptance and widespread use—and, according to Scripture, by the conviction of the Holy Spirit. "Now we have received not the spirit of the world," wrote the apostle Paul, "but the Spirit who is from God, so that we may know the things freely given to us by God . . . not in words taught by human wisdom, but in those taught by the Spirit." Today, more than fifty-five hundred partial or complete New Testament manuscripts have been discovered and preserved. No other work of antiquity comes remotely close to having such a base of aged manuscripts. The earliest are called "uncials"—a reference to an ancient style of Greek writing that used capital letters. Later Greek New Testament manuscripts are called "minuscules"—a term referring to the cursive style of later Greek writing, which developed around AD 800–1000. Among the oldest existing New Testament manuscripts discovered by the early twenty-first century:

- P 52 in the JOHN RYLANDS PAPYRI—the oldest known New Testament fragment—is from John 18, dates to AD 90-150, and suggests early circulation of the Gospels;

- the New Testament portions of the CHESTER BEATTY PAPYRI dating to about AD 200, which were discovered in earthenware urns in an Egyptian Coptic Christian cemetery in 1931;

- the New Testament portion of CODEX SINAITICUS, which dates to AD 340, is presented by the British Library as "the oldest complete copy of the New Testament," and contains all of the canonical New Testament books in Koine Greek;

- the equally ancient and comparably intact text of the New Testament as recorded in the CODEX VATICANUS—the significance of which was realized by scholars in the nineteenth century after being catalogued by the Vatican Library at the time of Columbus;

- the CODEX ALEXANDRINUS, dating to about AD 425, which contains all four Gospels and much of the rest of the New Testament text, and was bequeathed to England's King Charles I by a former patriarch of the church at Alexandria, Egypt—where it may possibly have been in Alexandria's Great Library before its destruction;

- the New Testament portions of CODEX EPHRAEMI RESCRIPTUS, c. fifth century AD, have survived despite damage inflicted upon the vellum parchment when it was erased so that a twelfth century manuscript could be written over it;

- written in Greek and Latin about AD 400, CODEX BEZAE is the oldest existing bilingual New Testament manuscript, once belonged to Reformation leader Theodore Beza, and is now held by Great Britain's Cambridge University;

- also once owned by Theodore Beza and now at France's Bibliothèque Nationale, CODEX CLAROMONTANUS, c.AD 550, contains the Pauline epistles and the book of Hebrews;

- CODEX WASHINGTONIANUS, a Greek New Testament vellum manuscript dating to the fourth or fifth century AD, acquired by American art collector Charles L. Freer in Egypt and preserved in the Smithsonian Institution's Freer Gallery in Washington, D.C.[10]

Ample opportunity existed for witnesses to the events recorded in the New Testament to denounce them if they were false, and yet they have been transmitted to modern times without substantial deviation. Astonishingly, the immense collection of New Testament manuscripts has produced a transmitted text that is notable for its extremely small amount of variant readings—"one one-thousandth part of the New Testament text" according to one scholar's estimate. Through the ages—and especially since the mid-nineteenth century—New Testament scholarship has carefully and thoroughly studied and compared this unique, comprehensive body of textual evidence, which has faithfully preserved and transmitted an accurate and trustworthy text. For instance, after investing decades of research into the text and truths of the Bible, Dr. Benjamin B. Warfield, the head of Princeton Theological Seminary, who was acclaimed as "the most distinguished and learned theologian" of the late nineteenth century, concluded that "the Scriptures not only contain, but *are* the *Word of God.*"[11]

Warfield's conclusion was shared by Sir Frederic Kenyon, the long-time, highly respected director of the British Museum, who served as the president of the British Archaeology Society of Jerusalem in the early twentieth century when archaeology of biblical sites was in a golden age. Dapper, humble, and intellectually brilliant, Kenyon was a recognized expert in ancient languages, a prolific author and historian, and a leading international authority on the Bible. He was so accomplished in his studies of antiquity that the British monarchy awarded him a royal knighthood. After a lifetime of research into ancient biblical manuscripts, archaeological discoveries, and textual criticism, he confidently declared this critical fact about the textual transmission of the Bible: "The Christian can take the whole Bible in his hand and say without fear or hesitation that he holds in it the true Word of God, handed down without essential loss from generation to generation, throughout the centuries." The discoveries of the principal ancient manuscripts that convinced scholars such as Kenyon of the faithful transmission of the biblical text were in many cases marked by drama and surprise—and no manuscript discovery was more dramatic than the recovery of Codex Sinaiticus.[12]

Papal guards stand ready to protect the treasures of the Vatican, where nineteenth century Catholic scholars rediscovered the Codex Vaticanus—an ancient biblical manuscript dating to the fourth century. Source: Library of Congress.

§

There was something odd about the kindling used to set fires in the monastery fireplace. At least, that was the story reported by a nineteenth-century visitor to Saint Catherine's Monastery on Egypt's Sinai Peninsula. His name was Lobegott Friedrich Constantin von Tischendorf, and he was a twenty-nine-year-old German adventurer, travel writer, author, and Bible scholar. His driving passion was the quest to acquire and publish ancient biblical manuscripts. It had propelled him on an odyssey from London to Moscow to Cairo to Constantinople, as he searched the holdings of old libraries, monasteries, and out-of-the-way bookshops in a quest for biblical papyri and parchments. In April 1844, he arrived at the remote, isolated monastery of Saint Catherine's—a mission of the Eastern Orthodox Church built on the traditional site where Moses received the Ten Commandments. Tischendorf was welcomed by the monks into the monastery, where he encountered what he would later described as "a lofty church, rich in splendor," adorned with "many gold and silver lamps and candlesticks [that] glitter around," and—"more tasteful and more beautiful than all of these"—a ceiling mosaic depicting the burning bush of Mount Sinai, the Decalogue, and the transfiguration of Jesus before Moses, Elijah, and the three apostles.[13]

Occasionally during his visit, Tischendorf later recounted, the monks at Saint Catherine's would pull what appeared to be scrap paper from a large basket, and set it afire to kindle a new blaze in a monastery fireplace. Although monastery officials later denied the waste basket story, Tischendorf claimed that one day he retrieved a sheet of the kindling and examined it. He was stunned, he wrote, when he realized that what he held in his hands was a fifteen-hundred-year-old leaf of the Septuagint Old Testament, rendered in ancient Greek on exquisite vellum parchment. He had already discovered more than a dozen ancient manuscript fragments, and based on his findings, he had produced numerous editions of the New Testament in Greek and Latin. Financed by an influential and affluent sponsor, King Frederick Augustus of Saxony, Tischendorf had made the bone-wearying trek to Saint Catherine's to examine the monastery's ancient and extensive library.[14]

According to Tischendorf, he asked for the discarded parchments, and departed with forty-three vellum leaves that proved to include por-tions of 1 Chronicles, Jeremiah, and Lamentations, and all of the book of Esther. In the late twentieth century, a mantle of suspicion would fall over Tischendorf based on charges that he had absconded with the manuscripts—charges that eventually would be largely dispelled by new evidence supporting Tischendorf's claim that he acted appropri-ately in a complicated situation. (More material from Codex Sinaiticus would be discovered at Saint Catherine's Monastery in modern times, including a fragment of the book of Joshua found by a doctoral student in 2009.) Back home in Germany, Tischendorf donated the find to his alma mater—he held a doctorate degree in theology from Germany's Leipzig University—and in short order he oversaw its publication. He had already received professional acclaim for deciphering and publishing a version of Codex Ephraemi Rescriptus, and his accomplishments helped him obtain a professorship at the university.[15]

Despite his many projects, however, he could not keep from thinking about the amazing manuscript he had encountered at the monastery in the faraway Sinai Peninsula. Could it be the oldest copy of the Bible in existence? In 1853, he returned to Saint Catherine's to resume his quest but found little—just a small manuscript fragment from Genesis. However, that find encouraged his hopes that somewhere in the monastery lay hidden away the rest of the ancient Septuagint manuscript. Back he went in again in 1859—this time with the offi-cial backing of Czar Alexander II of Russia, who was the patron of the Eastern Orthodox Church, to which Saint Catherine's belonged. To his great disappointment, his search again appeared to be fruitless. Then, on the final evening of his stay—February 4, 1859—he took a twilight stroll with the monastery abbot, who afterward invited him to his tiny room to talk about the Scriptures. As they discussed biblical manuscripts, the steward casually remarked, "I, too, have read a Septuagint"—and from a shelf in the corner he took down a bundle wrapped in red cloth.[16]

He laid it before Tischendorf, who uncovered it to discover the ancient missing Bible manuscript he had sought for fifteen years. It dated to AD 340 and contained much of the Old Testament missing from his earlier discovery—plus an almost complete ancient Greek translation of the New Testament that would prove to be the most important New Testament manuscript ever discovered. "I could give way to the transport of joy which I felt," Tischendorf later recalled. "I knew that I held in my hand the most precious biblical treasure in existence." Rewarded by the czar, the monks of Saint Catherine's sent the ancient manuscript pages to Russia, where they were meticulously copied, and later published by Tischendorf in what twentieth-century English Bible scholar T. C. Skeat, the curator of ancient manuscripts at the British Museum, would describe as "a marvel of precise and painstaking scholarship."[17]

Constantine von Tischendorf, a twenty-nine-year-old German author, adventurer and Bible scholar, strikes a Napoleonic pose for the photographer. In the mid-nineteenth century, he made a laborious journey to an isolated Egyptian monastery in search of ancient biblical manuscripts. Source: Wikimedia Commons.

In recognition of his many achievements in biblical scholarship, Tischendorf was made a count by the Russian government, and he continued his search for ancient manuscripts. In 1867, he achieved another feat by securing permission from the Vatican to examine (and later publish) the zealously guarded Codex Vaticanus. His greatest achievement, however, would remain his discovery at Saint Catherine's Monastery, which would become internationally famous as Codex Sinaiticus—and which would be described by many authorities as "the world's oldest Bible." His country did not remain Russia, however. In 1917, Communist forces overthrew the czar, executed him and his family, and replaced Czarist Russia with the Soviet Union. In 1933, amid a financial crisis, the Soviet government—which was officially atheist—negotiated the sale of the Codex Sinaiticus to Great Britain for a price of £100,000. With the help of a nationwide fund-raising effort, the British government acquired the Codex Sinaiticus—or at least the bulk of it. By the early twenty-first century, four institutions held portions of the ancient manuscript: Saint Catherine's Monastery retained a small collection of leaves and fragments from the Codex in its library, the 43 leaves originally discovered by Count Tischendorf remained preserved at the University of Leipzig in Germany, six leaves that somehow failed to find their way to Great Britain were housed in the National Library of Russia in Saint Petersburg, but the great majority of the ancient Bible—347 leaves—came to reside at the British Library in London. In July 2009, all four institutions collaborated to visually reassemble the Codex Sinaiticus on an Internet website, accompanied by an English translation, so that scholars, students, and the general public could—cyber-style—turn the pages and intimately examine "the world's oldest complete Bible."[18]

Most of the New Testament writers composed their work in Greek. The ancient Greek of the New Testament was the ancestor of modern Greek, and was actually related to Hebrew—both had their roots in the Semitic alphabet. Tradition holds that the Greeks adopted the alphabet from seagoing Phoenicians about 1000 BC. Early Greek was written from right to left, but after about five hundred years of use, it was written left to right. By 400 BC, the Greek alphabet of twenty-four letters was firmly established. Eventually, it would influence the Etruscan and Latin alphabets, giving birth to all European languages—including English.[19]

When Alexander the Great conquered the Mediterranean world in the fourth century BC, he left it profoundly influenced by Greek culture—including the Greek language. Native tongues would continue to exist in many regions, and the prevailing Roman Empire would eventually make Latin the dominant language of the empire in the West, but at the time of Christ and in the apostolic age, the everyday language of much of the Mediterranean world was Greek, and many Latin-speakers used it also. Although written primarily in Greek, the New Testament contains a smattering of Aramaic. For instance, the words *Abba, Maranatha,* and *Cephas* are Aramaic, and so is Jesus' well-known utterance on the cross: *Eli, Eli, lama sabachthani*—which was a revealing reference to the Old Testament prophecy of the Messiah's crucifixion found in Psalm 22. However, while first-century Jews may have conversed in Aramaic, they generally wrote in Greek. Every New Testament book except Matthew is believed to have been originally written in Greek, and even Matthew—which may have been first written in Hebrew or Aramaic—was likely circulated in Greek.[20]

Greek was the perfect language for spreading the gospel in the first century AD. Unlike Hebrew—with its personal, vivid style that was perfect for communicating God's truth to the Jews—Greek was a universal language that could convey the gospel message to Jews and Gentiles alike. The Gospels were mostly written in Koine Greek, a common everyday dialect typical of fishermen, which was suitable for a wide Greek-speaking readership. Some elite early critics of Christianity reportedly ridiculed the New Testament's everyday Greek as "sailors' language," and so did later critics. "This snobbish attitude was adopted by some of the men of the Renaissance, who found the New Testament lacking in the elegance of Cicero's period and called its language Barbarian Greek," observed Sven Albert Wifstrand, an acclaimed twentieth-century Greek language authority. "The same way of looking at things lived on into the latter part of the nineteenth century." New and better research and archaeological evidence dispelled such criticism, however, and modern linguists came to praise the Greek of the New Testament as reflecting "life as it is lived" and an everyday style that was "naturally beautiful." Greek was also an intellectual language, as its use by Greek philosophers attests, and it was the ideal medium for communicating the theological truths of the New Testament. A coincidence? Not according to the New Testament book of Galatians: "But when the fullness of time came," wrote the apostle Paul, "God sent forth His Son".[21]

The English word gospel is derived from an Anglo-Saxon word—god-spell—which meant "good tidings" or "good news."

Twenty-seven books comprise the New Testament. They were written by eight or nine writers over a period of about fifty years. The first four books record the life, ministry, and message of Jesus Christ, and are called the Gospels. The English word *gospel* is derived from an Anglo-Saxon word—*god-spell*—which meant "good tidings" or "good news." The word eventually became *godspel* or "God-story"—the story of God the Son, Jesus Christ. It came to describe both the four-book account of Jesus and the salvation message the New Testament proclaims. Why four Gospels? Several reasons are likely: The four Gospels supplement and complement each other, providing a comprehensive account. Jewish law required two or more witnesses to verify events, and some scholars have advocated that fact as a reason for the four Gospels. However, the scholarly tradition is that God inspired four because each was aimed at a different primary audience.[22]

Captured in this nineteenth century photograph, Saint Catherine's Monastery stands in bleak isolation at the foot of Mount Sinai. Here, Constantine von Tischendorf "discovered" the Codex Sinaiticus—"the world's oldest Bible." Source: Library of Congress.

The Gospel of Matthew, written by the apostle Matthew—a former tax collector—appears to have been directed originally to the Jews. It emphasizes Jesus as the Messiah and King, who fulfills the prophecy and promises of the old covenant. Its Jewish tone and its many Old Testament quotations suggest an initial Jewish audience, and early church leaders, such as Papias, Irenaeus, Origen, and Jerome, reported that the book was originally written in Hebrew, although it might have been written in Aramaic. The Gospel of Mark was written by John Mark of Jerusalem, a younger companion of Paul, Barnabas, and Peter, and is believed to have been originally directed to Roman readers. Tradition holds that the book was actually the gospel as given to Peter, who may have dictated it to Mark, whom Peter called "my son." Luke, believed to be the writer of the Gospel bearing his name, was a companion of Paul and an educated doctor—"the beloved physician," Paul called him. Also the writer of the book of Acts, Luke was probably Jewish. Or, he may have been a Gentile convert to Judaism, but the book's original audience is believed to have been non-Roman Gentiles. Based on its style and its messianic focus, the Gospel of John—believed to have been written by the apostle John—appears to have been originally directed to Jews dispersed outside Israel. Matthew, Mark, and Luke are called the Synoptic Gospels—from the Greek word for "together"—because they contain so much of the same information, while much of John is unique. Some Bible scholars believe that the Gospel of Mark was written first, some think the first Gospel was Matthew, and others believe that when Luke wrote his Gospel, he referred to the works of Mark and Matthew. Some believe the Gospels were based on a lost source called Q—a view dismissed by many orthodox scholars. Others believe in a less complicated theory: that the four Gospels were inspired and written independently, based on Jesus' promise in John 14:26 that the Holy Spirit will "teach you all things and bring to your remembrance all that I said to you." While they bear the name of their human writers, the four Gospels are collectively the gospel of Jesus Christ.[23]

The Acts of the Apostles could be called the "Acts of the Holy Spirit," as this book chronicles the activities of the Spirit-directed church in the apostolic age, revealing how the gospel spread through the Greco-Roman world. Following the book of Acts are twenty-one epistles, or letters, in the New Testament arrangement of books, beginning with the book of Romans and ending with the book of Jude. Thirteen books—Romans through Philemon: the Pauline Epistles—are traditionally credited to the apostle Paul. Most were written to first-century churches, although four of the letters—1 and 2 Timothy, Titus, and Philemon—are written to individuals and (except at times for Philemon) are also called the Pastoral Epistles. The other New Testament letters are traditionally known as the General Epistles. Among them, Hebrews may have been written by Paul or one of his associates (perhaps Apollos or Barnabas), and the others—James, 1 and 2 Peter, 1–3 John, and Jude—bear the names of their human writers. The New Testament epistles—like the rest of the New Testament—teach doctrine and discipleship with a remarkable unity that Christianity historically credits to the inspiration of the Holy Spirit.[24]

The final book in the arrangement of the New Testament is the book of Revelation. Believed to have been written by the apostle John, it records the revelation of Jesus Christ to John when he was imprisoned on the island of Patmos—a revelation intended for the church. The title is derived from the Latin word *revelatio*, which means "unveiling," and the book is in a Jewish-Christian genre known as *apocalyptic literature*. The word *apocalyptic* comes from the Greek word *apokalypto*, or "uncovering"—and the genre is marked by prophecy, vivid symbolism, and a focus on the sovereignty of God. The book of Revelation, the only completely apocalyptic book in the New Testament, describes the ultimate, final victory of Jesus Christ and His people—the church. The central message of the New Testament—in fact, the central message of the Bible, from Genesis to Revelation—is summarized with powerful simplicity in the Gospel of John, chapter 3, verse 16: "For God so loved the world, that He gave His only begotten Son, that whoever believes in Him shall not perish, but have eternal life."[25]

4

HERESY, PERSECUTION, AND TRIUMPH

"For many will come in My name, saying 'I am the Christ,' and will mislead many."
—MATTHEW 24:5

SIMON MAGUS SAW POWER AND WANTED IT. He was an occult prac-
titioner—what would someday be called a psychic—and he had
developed a cult following in first-century Samaria, according to the
book of Acts. The extraordinary events of the apostolic age "amazed"
him, and he tried to buy the Holy Spirit from the apostles. Rejecting
the bribe, the apostle Peter rebuked him for being in "the bondage of
iniquity." Said Peter: "You have no part or portion in this matter, for
your heart is not right before God." Scripture is silent about Simon
afterwards, but apparently, he enriched himself with a heretical blend
of the occult, Greco-Roman mythology, and Judaism—which he tried
to popularize with traces of the gospel. According to early church
leaders, such as Justin Martyr and Irenaeus, Simon later established
himself as leader of a pagan cult, demanded worship as Messiah, and
sought to pervert the gospel for gain. He may have been the first to
do so, but he would not be the last.[1]

Anticipating the apostasy that would challenge the early church, the apostle John advised first century believers: "just as you heard that antichrist is coming, even now many antichrists have appeared." Source: Welcome Images / Wikimedia Commons.

As Christianity spread through the Roman Empire and beyond in the first three centuries, the emerging canon of the New Testament was severely threatened by heretical teaching. Cultic opposition and imitators arose—along with a flood of heretical literature that mimicked or challenged genuine Scripture. Behind the surge of fraudulent gospels and other heretical writings were a parade of cults. Among them were the Docetists, who viewed matter as evil and unfit to house the Spirit of God, believing that God merely took on the *appearance* of Christ. The Mandaeans held to an inane mix of elements from Judaism, Christianity, and paganism to profess that the soul was entrapped in the body and tortured by demons—and could be freed only by the cult. The followers of asceticism believed they could attain spiritual and moral perfection by self-flagellation and other forms of bodily punishment. Another cult was the Manichaeans, who merged bits of Christianity and Oriental dualism into a belief that only the cult leader—who claimed to be a new messiah—could liberate goodness from the evil inhabiting the body. The Marcionites were an anti-Jewish cult that rejected the Old Testament and sought to rid the Gospels of all references to it.[2]

"Children, it is the last hour;" wrote the apostle John about AD 90, "and just as you heard that antichrist is coming, even now many antichrists have appeared." The largest and most threatening of the heretical cults and philosophies that challenged the early church was Gnosticism. It swept through the Roman Empire in the second century AD, challenging the church and the Scriptures. It was a synergistic blend of Greek, Persian, Egyptian, and Indian mythology, laced with Old Testament elements and newly infused with a heretical version of Christianity. The name Gnostic was derived from the Greek *gnosis*, which meant "special knowledge." One sect of Gnosticism—the Ophites—worshipped a serpent, and taught that the "serpent of old" in the Bible was good, while God was really evil. Another, the Gnostic sect of Canaanites, believed that Moses and the prophets were sinners, while Cain, King Ahab, and the pharaoh of the Exodus were saints. Some believed that the creation of the earth occurred through the fall of a goddess-like redeemer named Sophia or "Wisdom."[3]

Mainline Gnosticism held that anything physical was evil, and that the true god was a pure being named Bythos, who ruled by dispensing *gnosis*—"special knowledge"—through a series of emanations of "aeons." These aeons, or lesser gods, included the God of the Bible, who was supposedly used by Bythos to create the earth, but who did so poorly and allowed evil to arise. According to Gnosticism, Jesus was a mere man temporarily inhabited by the brightest of all aeons or special powers, who returned to the heavenly domain of Bythos before the crucifixion. Gnosticism held that there were three classes of humanity: "hylics"—who composed the masses and were hopelessly bound for destruction; "psychics"—who were people of faith, such as the biblical prophets, but who were destined to a second-class eternity; and "pneumatics"—those Gnostic leaders and true believers who possessed enough "special knowledge" to achieve eternal salvation. The elite pneumatics would leave their bodies at death, travel through space from planet to planet in a purgatory-like state, and finally reunite with the god Bythos, who was also called "the Absolute One." Except for the power and privilege afforded the cult's leaders, Gnosticism was a religion of hopelessness compared to the embracing truth of the gospel, yet it attracted scores of followers—and produced a growing body of Gnostic literature that competed with the Scriptures for attention in the early church era.[4]

"For many will come in My name, saying, 'I am the Christ.'"

Some Gnostics were ascetic—inflicting extreme punishment or self-denial on themselves—and some were libertine, defending debauched lifestyles with claims that physical sin was irrelevant. The Gnostics produced a broad scope of literature, and some of it attempted to twist the gospel into Gnostic propaganda. As the church expanded from its Jerusalem roots—to Antioch in modern Turkey, to Alexandria in Egypt, and to Rome—Gnosticism followed. "For many will come in My name, saying, 'I am the Christ,'" warned Jesus, "and will mislead many." Finally, after about a century and a half of competing with Christianity, the Gnostics faded from history—although traces of their peculiar theology would be embraced by cult movements far into the future. Interest in Gnosticism would resurface in the late twentieth century, when a large cache of Gnostic papyri and parchments were discovered near Nag

Hammadi in Egypt in December 1945. After sensational media attention, the Nag Hammadi find proved to be nothing more than a library of fanciful Gnostic literature written in Greek and Coptic. According to antiquity authority Edward M. Blaiklock, "the collection is of interest only to students of early heresy." It was useful for the study of period culture and ancient linguistics—and beguiled the biblically illiterate for decades—but the Nag Hammadi artifacts proved valuable mainly as additional evidence of the bizarre beliefs of Gnosticism.[5]

By the end of the first century, early church fathers such as Clement of Rome—represented here by a nineteenth century stained glass image—had already quoted from all twenty-seven books of the emerging New Testament. Source: Wikimedia Commons.

As heretical cults and philosophies challenged orthodox Christianity in the first and second centuries, it was Scripture that kept the church faithful to apostolic teaching. "See to it," Paul wrote believers amid the rising flood of Gnosticism, "that no one takes you captive through philosophy and empty deception, according to the tradition of men, according to the elementary principles of the world, rather than according to Christ, for in Him all the fullness of Deity dwells in bodily form." With extraordinary efficiency, the early church progressively rejected writings that failed to meet Jewish-style standards of inspiration—a development that historic Christianity would later deem to be providential. Influenced by their Jewish roots, early Christian congregations and their leaders demanded that writings that claimed to be Scripture meet exacting standards. Canonization of the New Testament books began with the apostles. To be accepted as Scripture, a book had to have been written by an apostle or with apostolic approval—that was the primary test of early canonicity. The apostle Peter, for instance, endorsed Paul's epistles and went on record to equate them with "the rest of the Scripture." Paul, in turn, urged fledgling congregations to stand on "the foundation of the apostles and prophets, Christ Jesus being the corner stone."[6]

A selection process for Scripture based on Old Testament canonization appears to have been established by the apostles: John wrote that "many other signs therefore Jesus also performed . . . which are not written in this book"—meaning that the apostles were carefully writing and circulating only what they knew was revealed truth based on their eyewitness experiences. Luke the physician—the close colleague of Paul—wrote that his gospel account was "handed down to us by those who from the beginning were eyewitnesses," and that he had "investigated everything carefully" to record "the exact truth." A book was deemed inspired in a passive sense—it was *received* from God by an apostle or his associate, and then was received and recognized by its readers. "For this reason we constantly thank God," wrote Paul to the young church in Thessalonica, "that when you received the word of

God which you heard from us, you accepted it not as the word of men, but for what it really is, the word of God."[7]

At age seventeen, Nero Claudius Augustus Germanicus—better known as simply Nero—became emperor of the Roman Empire, and unleashed a massive, infamous persecution of Christians. Source: New York Public Library.

The apostles directed the early churches to publicly read the apostolic books and letters. "I adjure you by the Lord to have this letter read to all the brethren," Paul wrote the Thessalonian believers. The churches were also urged to collect and circulate the apostolic writings. "When this letter is read among you," Paul wrote to the Colossian Christians, "have it also read in the church of the Laodiceans."" As the apostles and their associates died, the books that composed the New Testament remained the authoritative witness for the early church. The absence of the apostles and the rise of heretical movements such as Gnosticism made application of traditional standards of canonicity even more important to the expanding church. Did a book have apostolic authority? Did it display internal evidence of divine inspiration—a depiction of God and His character that was consistent with the Old Testament? Was it widely accepted by churches that stood on the "foundation of the apostles and prophets?" Books that failed to meet those standards were either decisively rejected or were destined to be discarded eventually.[8]

At the order of Emperor Nero, Christian martyrs are set afire as human torches to illuminate a palace party. Waves of persecution claimed countless innocent lives throughout the Roman Empire, but failed to eliminate either the church or the Bible. Source: Wikimedia Commons.

By the end of the first century, that process was progressively eliminating heretical works and preserving the twenty-seven books of the New Testament in what amounted to an effective canon. Within the first half of the second century, the younger contemporaries of the apostles, such as Papias, Ignatius, and Clement of Rome—the early "church fathers"—had quoted from all twenty-seven New Testament books. The generation of church leaders who followed—men such as Polycarp, Justin Martyr, and Irenaeus—also quoted from all of them. Irenaeus, the bishop of Lyons in Gaul, wrote extensively in opposition to Gnosticism in the late second century, and quoted from twenty-three of the twenty-seven New Testament books—demonstrating that the canon was already largely developed by AD 170. By about the same time, the church at Rome had already acknowledged most of the New Testament books, according to what became known as the Muratorian fragment— a list of books named for the Italian antiquarian who discovered and published it in 1740. About AD 230, Origen cited the four Gospels, Acts, the thirteen Pauline Epistles, 1 Peter, 1 John, and Revelation as inspired Scripture universally accepted by Christians everywhere—with Hebrews, 2 Peter, 2 and 3 John, James, and Jude already accepted by most. The church fathers quoted from the twenty-seven books of the New Testament in more than thirty-six thousand citations. So extensively did they quote recognized Scripture—often to counter heresy— that the entire New Testament reportedly could be reconstructed from their writings. Instead of destroying or suppressing the gospel of Jesus Christ, Gnosticism and the other heresies of the early church age were countered by—and actually stimulated—an established foundation of truth: the emerging canon of the New Testament.[9]

While cults and heresies challenged the Scriptures in the era of the early church, another movement arose that threatened the lives of those who sought to live by the Word: deadly persecution by the Roman Empire. "If they have persecuted Me, they will also persecute you," Jesus had told His apostles, and, indeed, the first three hundred years of Christianity were marked by violent persecution. The attacks were intended to destroy Christianity and rid the empire of the Bible, but they failed. "We multiply whenever we are mown down by you," wrote the Christian author Tertullian in the late second century. "The blood of Christians is seed." He was right: Waves of persecutions claimed countless innocent lives throughout the Roman Empire and destroyed priceless copies of Scripture in untold numbers—but eliminated neither the church nor the Bible. Persecution of Christians began with Israel's Jewish leadership—Jews persecuting Jews for claiming Jesus as Messiah. As Christianity spread following the destruction of Jerusalem in AD 70, however, Gentile believers soon outnumbered Jewish Christians, and the principal persecutor was the Roman Empire.[10]

Depicted here in an ancient mosaic sculpture, Constantine the Great—emperor of the Western Roman Empire—became the first Roman Emperor to profess faith in Christ. In A.D. 313, he ended the persecution of believers, and under his influence the New Testament canon came to be revered rather than attacked. Source: Wikimedia Commons.

The first major persecution was enacted by Emperor Nero in AD 64, when he falsely blamed Christians for starting a destructive six-day fire that swept through Rome that year. "Their deaths were made farcical," wrote the Roman historian Tacitus of Nero's persecution of Christians. "Dressed in wild animals' skins, they were torn to pieces by dogs, or crucified, or made into torches to be ignited after dark as substitutes for daylight. Nero provided his Gardens for the spectacle, and exhibited displays in the Circus, as he mingled with the crowd—or stood in a chariot, dressed as a charioteer." Both Peter and Paul are believed to have perished in this persecution. Although Nero committed suicide in AD 68, the persecutions continued in waves for almost three hundred years through the reigns of other Roman emperors, including Domitian, Trajan, Marcus Aurelius, Septimius Severus, Maximus Thrax, Decius, Valerian, Aurelian, and Diocletian. Christians were persecuted by the empire because they refused emperor worship and lived differently— rejecting the debauchery that marked Roman recreation and viewing even uncultured barbarians as equals. The last persecution, ordered by Emperor Diocletian, was the worst. It began in AD 303 and continued for eight years as the full might of the Roman Empire was unleashed to destroy Christianity forever. Believers were sacrificed to wild animals in the empire's public arenas. They were tortured and starved in prisons. They were worked to death in Roman mines. Churches were destroyed, and the Bible was officially targeted for destruction. "It was in the nineteenth year of the reign of Diocletian," wrote church historian Eusebius of Caesarea, "[when] royal edicts were published everywhere, commanding that the churches be leveled to the ground and the Scriptures be destroyed by fire."[11]

"Royal edicts were published everywhere, commanding . . . that the Scriptures be destroyed by fire."

Bishop Athanasius, head of the fourth-century Christian church in Alexandria, Egypt, holds aloft the canonized Scriptures in this nineteenth century engraving. Known as the "Father of Orthodoxy," Athanasius recorded an early list of the twenty-seven books of the New Testament, which he called the "springs of salvation." Source: Wikimedia Commons.

The loss of biblical manuscripts during the periods of Roman persecution was extensive. However, the Great Persecution that began in AD 303 unintentionally reinforced the canon of New Testament books that had begun in the apostolic age. When Roman authorities showed up in the churches and homes of Christians to confiscate books, many Christians reportedly handed over everything *except* the Scriptures. The books that were worth hiding—or dying for—became even more established in the Christian community. Then—in AD 312—the unimaginable occurred: the Roman emperor professed faith in Jesus Christ. His name was Flavius Valerius Constantinus—Emperor Constantine to history—and he was a Roman general who battled his way to power after the empire was divided into eastern and western provinces by Diocletian. He assumed rule in the Western Roman Empire in 312, consolidated his power, and eventually moved the capital of the Roman Empire to a central location in the East, at Byzantium, which was renamed Constantinople. Soon after becoming emperor, he reportedly turned from worshipping *Sol Invictus*—the Roman sun god—to profess faith in Jesus Christ, and declared religious freedom throughout the Roman Empire:

> We have therefore, determined, with sound and upright purpose, that liberty is to be denied to no one, to choose and to follow the religious observances of the Christians, but that to each one freedom is to be given to devote his mind to that religion which he may think adapted to himself . . . and now that everyone who has the same desire to observe the religion of the Christians may do so without molestation.[12]

Did Constantine convert for political reasons—influenced by the unceasing growth of the empire's Christian population? Or was his conversion genuine? Historians still debate the issue. For fourth century Christians, however, there was no doubting the relief Constantine provided by his profession of faith: He ended the recurring Roman persecutions for all time. In AD 313, he formalized the end of persecution: the days of Christians slaughtered for their faith by Roman emperors thus ended. "There is no greater drama in human record," observed historian Will Durant in *The Story of Civilization,* "than the sight of a few Christians . . . fighting the sword with the Word, brutality with hope, and at last defeating the strongest state that history has known. Caesar and Christ had met in the Arena, and Christ had won."[13]

Constantine did not make Christianity the official religion of the empire, but he endorsed it and encouraged its growth—a dramatic turnaround that would eventually have mixed results, but which brought peace to the church and protection to the Scriptures. Despite all its suffering, the age of persecution had witnessed the formation of a New Testament canon—from the standards established in the apostolic age to the progressive, churchwide use of all twenty-seven books that marked the second and third centuries. By AD 250 and maybe as early as AD 175, the New Testament canon was closed—and under Constantine it was revered rather than attacked. Eusebius, the bishop of Caesarea and the famous church historian of Constantine's era, was commissioned by the emperor to have copies of the "sacred Scriptures" produced. In doing so, he acknowledged all twenty-seven New Testament books, although he noted that there were still a few books—James, 2 Peter, 2 and 3 John, and Jude—awaiting full acceptance by churches in all regions of the empire. As generations of Christians were exposed to the twenty-seven books, the canon solidified. Athanasius—known as the "father of Orthodoxy" in church history—definitively cited all twenty-seven in an Easter letter he wrote as bishop of Alexandria in AD 367. "These are springs of salvation," Athanasius called the twenty-seven books. "In these alone is the good news of the teaching of true religion proclaimed; let no one add to them or take away aught of them."[14]

In AD 325, church leaders at the Council of Nicaea, meeting near Constantinople in modern-day Turkey, acknowledged some of the New Testament books in its deliberation, but focused mainly on reinforcing orthodox doctrine and developing church government. The Council of Laodicea in AD 364 appears to have acknowledged the existence of the New Testament twenty-seven-book canon, with the the book of

Revelation alone left in abeyance. Evidence suggests that the Damasine Council in AD 382 did likewise and included Revelation. In an historically documented action in AD 393, church leaders at the Synod of Hippo—held in what is now Algeria—officially acknowledged the existing New Testament canon. The Synod's action merely verified the canon as it existed; it had been established centuries before by the widespread acceptance of the twenty-seven books of the New Testament by church congregations—an action that Christians believe occurred, in the words of Bible scholar and historian W. Donald Munson, by the "conviction of the Holy Spirit." It was also formally acknowledged by the Synod of Carthage in AD 397. By then, there was a general agreement within Christianity that the New Testament canon was closed.[15]

A remarkable agreement of opinion through individual churches had emerged over the preceding centuries, preserving and embracing the twenty-seven books and rejecting all others as noncanonical. Around the world, Christianity would be generally united in accepting the familiar books of today's New Testament—and no others—as inspired by the Holy Spirit and thus respected as authoritative and canonical. It was not a canon established by a church council, a bishop, a pope, an emperor, or a reformer. Any of those who proclaimed the New Testament canon merely acknowledged what had already emerged in the church universal, beginning in the age of the Apostles. "This was not a collection of books blown together by chance; nor was it a collection that 'forced itself' upon the church," observed twentieth-century Bible scholar John Wenham. "In the gentlest way it quietly and unhurriedly established itself in the church's life. We . . . have evidence of weight and authority, more than sufficient to justify us in humbly taking up the books that God has put into our hands and receiving their teaching as His truth."[16]

5

LIGHT IN THE DARKNESS

The Light shines in the darkness . . .
—JOHN 1:5

HE WAS AN OLD SCHOLAR NEAR THE END OF HIS DAYS. Most of his career had been invested in what he viewed as a noble scholarly quest, but the public response to his lifework was largely negative in his day. The reaction troubled him—but he dismissed his critics as "two-legged asses" who cared nothing for the truth. "If they dislike water drawn from the clear spring," he caustically observed, "let them drink of the muddy streamlet." It was AD 420, and he lived in Bethlehem. There he could debate Old Testament Scripture with his Jewish friends and continue to study the Hebrew language that was so dear to him. He would die that year, seeing little evidence at the end that his greatest work was appreciated by anyone. But his contribution to Christianity and Western civilization would prove enormous. The aged scholar's name was Eusebius Hieronymus Sophronius—better known as Jerome—and his career accomplishment would stand for a thousand years as the Vulgate: the premier translation of the Bible into Latin.[1]

Latin translations were made from the Greek as early as the second century AD for the Christian community in the Roman province of North Africa, where the early church flourished. A variety of native languages existed in North Africa, as well as the omnipresent Greek, but Latin had become the official and "civilized" language when the Romans conquered the region in 146 BC. The first Latin translations of the Bible were probably local missionary efforts, but a common Latin translation apparently emerged in North Africa as early as AD 200, and eventually became known as the "Old Latin" version. After about two centuries of Christianity, the Greek-language Bible gave way to the "Old Latin" translation in the Western Roman Empire. No complete manuscript of the Old Latin appears to have survived into modern times, but surviving fragments and quotations indicate that it was an informal translation. When peace came to the church with Emperor Constantine, church leaders and Christian scholars were free to focus on preserving and transmitting Scripture. Pleas for a uniform, accurate translation of the Bible in Latin soon arose from church leaders throughout the Western Empire. Translations of the Bible in Old Latin had been cobbled together over the decades, but an accurate, scholarly translation was needed.[2]

By the mid-fourth century AD, four centers of leadership had arisen in the organized church—in Rome, Constantinople, Alexandria, and Antioch—and their leaders all competed for the papacy. In AD 366, amid deadly riots, Damasus I, the archdeacon of the Church of Rome, emerged as head, or pope, of the church in the Western Roman Empire. Although preoccupied with preserving Rome as the seat of the Western Church, Damasus I eventually responded to the demand for an accurate Latin translation by commissioning his secretary to the task in AD 383. The pope's secretary was Jerome. Perhaps the ablest Bible scholar of his day, Jerome completed a revision of the Gospels in about one year. He then began work on a revision of the other New Testament books, but Damasus died in 384, and emerging disagreements within the church prompted Jerome to move to the faraway Mideast. He settled in Bethlehem, where he established a monastery, enticed Jewish scholars to instruct him in Hebrew and Aramaic, and began work on a Latin translation of the Old Testament.[3]

It became the Bible of the Middle Ages for countless Europeans.

His work was unique for two reasons: He established scholarly standards of translation, and he translated directly from Hebrew. By Jerome's day, the Greek Septuagint was so identified with Christianity that the Jews had abandoned it. Jerome consulted it, and apparently traveled to Israel's great library at Caesarea to consult the *Hexapla*—a massive parallel Hebrew-Greek revision of the Septuagint made more than a century earlier by the early church scholar Origen. For eighteen years Jerome labored on his Old Testament translation, meticulously rendering the Hebrew into Latin. His work was circulated book by book as it was completed, and while it would eventually earn the respect of scholars, its unfamiliar language and authentic Jewish tone alarmed many churchmen. Jerome's critics accused him of "Judaizing" the text and abandoning the beloved Septuagint. Temperamental and sensitive, Jerome wrote blistering replies to his critics, and continued his work undeterred. Although still controversial at the time of his death, his Latin translation of the Old Testament and his New Testament revision eventually became the Vulgate Bible—from the Latin *vulgata*, for "commonly accepted." It became *the* Bible of the Middle Ages for countless Europeans, and was decreed to be the official Bible of the Roman Catholic Church in 1546. Revised under Pope Sixtus V in the 1580s, it would become the first version of the Bible to be printed, and would influence modern Bible translations for centuries to come. Ironically, the scholarly knowledge of Greek would be threatened in the future because so many Bible translators would rely solely on Jerome's Vulgate.[4]

The Bible was also translated into the Syriac language. In the apostolic age, the gospel was taken eastward from Israel into Mesopotamia—which included regions of modern Iraq, Iran, and Turkey—and even into what is now India and China. When Italian adventurer Marco Polo journeyed to China in the thirteenth century, he encountered long-established churches along the way. The ancient city of Edessa in modern Turkey became the principal center of Mesopotamian Christianity, and it was apparently there that the Bible was translated in Mesopotamia's Syriac language. The Syriac Old Testament is believed to have been translated from the Hebrew by Jewish translators influenced by the Greek Septuagint, and was at one point adopted by Christians. An early Syriac translation of the New Testament—which became known as the Old Syriac translation—circulated in Mesopotamia long before the fifth century. The Old Syriac was replaced by a revised and standardized Syriac translation known as the *Peshitta,* which means "simple" in Syriac. The *Peshitta* may have been translated during the ministry of a Christian leader named Rabbula, who was bishop of Edessa from AD 411 to 435, although it may be even older. Some Bible scholars believe that a Syriac version of the New Testament predates the Vulgate, and was the first translation of the New Testament from Greek. By the middle of the sixth century AD, and perhaps earlier, all twenty-seven books of the New Testament were accepted as canonical in the *Peshitta.* In the early church age, the New Testament was also translated from the Greek into North Africa's Coptic dialects—a final form of the ancient Egyptian language—and by the fifth century into Armenian, Old Ethiopic, Georgian, and Gothic—the language of the Germanic tribes. An Arabic version of the New Testament was translated by the early eighth century, and maybe sooner. By then, however, Christianity was being forcefully erased from much of the ancient world by a militant and powerful new belief system—Islam.[5]

It began in what is now Saudi Arabia in AD 610, when Muhammad—a middle-aged Arabian in the city of Mecca—proclaimed himself a prophet of God. An orphan raised by grandparents in a tribe of Arabian merchant-traders called the Kuraish, Muhammad married a wealthy and much older widow, which enabled him to devote himself to development of a new faith. It was his practice to meditate in a mountain cave near Mecca, and at one point, he later reported, the angel Gabriel escorted him on a night journey to heaven—which he made astride a winged animal—and there, he said, he met with Adam, Abraham, Moses, Joseph, John the Baptist, Jesus, and others. According to the tenets of Islam, he was thus commissioned by *Allah* as the Messenger—a special prophet "who has knowledge of everything"—and was called to spread a unique theology that incorporated beliefs and practices from Judaism, Christianity, Persian Zoroastrianism, and Arabian traditions—all of which were eventually collected in the *Qur'an*. His call to Islam was initially rejected by the residents of Mecca, especially by the local Jewish community, and in 622, he withdrew to the city of Yathrib, which would later become known as Medina. There he built a base of support and an army capable of waging *jihad*, or holy war, and eight years later he conquered Mecca. "There is no god but Allah," claimed his growing army of followers, "and Muhammad is his prophet." Muhammad died in 632, just two years after occupying Mecca, but by then the entire Arabian Peninsula had been conquered for Islam.[6]

Zealous for their newfound faith and rewarded by the spoils of military victories, Muslim armies overwhelmed a host of other cultures in short order. Jerusalem was captured in 639. Egypt was conquered by 640. Carthage in North Africa fell in 698, and Spain was invaded in 711. Within a century of Muhammad's life, an Islamic empire stretched from Spain to India. It was checked in what is now France by the Frankish leader Charles Martel at the Battle of Tours in AD 732, and was finally halted in the East at the siege of Vienna, Austria, in 1539. Islamic civilization produced a golden age of learning, but during its violent conquests—along with countless lives—untold scores of biblical manuscripts were lost in the destruction of churches and libraries. One victim was the great Christian library at Caesarea, which was destroyed in AD 638 with a treasured collection of approximately thirty thousand manuscripts.[7]

Head down and absorbed by his studies, Jerome—the famed fourth-century Bible translator—works to render the Scriptures into Latin while his docile pet lion rests nearby. He would produce the premier Latin translation of the Bible—the Vulgate—which would be the main source for generations of Bible translations to come. Source: Library of Congress.

THE

APOCALYPSE OF
ST. JOHN THE APOSTLE.

CHAP. I.

Saint John is ordered to write to the seven churches in Asia: the manner of Christ's appearing to him.

HE Revelation of JESUS Christ, which God gave unto him, to make known to his servants the things which must shortly come to pass: and signified, sending by his Angel to his servant John,

2 Who hath given testimony to the word of God, and the testimony of JESUS Christ, what things soever he hath seen.

Elaborate artwork decorates the opening page of the New Testament book of Revelation in a nineteenth century English Bible translated from Jerome's Latin Vulgate. So many translators depended on the Latin Vulgate in the Middle Ages that the knowledge of ancient Greek was threatened. Wikimedia Commons.

By then the historic Roman Empire had ceased to exist. After Emperor Constantine died in AD 337, the Western Roman Empire grew steadily weaker as it was conquered piecemeal by barbarian invaders, such as the Vandals and the Visigoths. In 410, the Visigoths looted Rome, and in 476, the Germanic chieftain Odoacer forced Romulus Augustulus, considered to be the last Western Roman emperor, to abandon the throne. Although various European kingdoms and states arose in its place in the Middle Ages—unified by the surviving Roman Catholic Church—the historic empire of Rome was gone. The Eastern Roman Empire, headquartered in Constantinople, survived as the Byzantine Empire for another thousand years. It expanded throughout what is now Turkey and around the Mediterranean under Emperor Justinian I in the 500s, was diminished under assaults by the barbarians, rose again, and finally suffered a death-blow with the capture of Constantinople by Muslim Ottoman Turks under Mehmed the Conqueror in 1453. For centuries, it had been the outpost of Christianity and had continuously defended eastern Europe from Islamic conquest.[8]

Central to the Byzantine Empire at its peak and throughout its turbulent centuries was the Eastern Orthodox Church, which survived Mehmed's epic capture of Constantinople and the decline of the Byzantine Empire. "Yet by his victory, Mehmed had not destroyed a culture, a faith or a people," observed Byzantine authority Stephen W. Reinert. "The essential rhythms of Byzantine life would endure." At the heart of what endured from the Eastern Roman Empire was the Eastern Orthodox Church, which adopted a standardized Greek translation of the New Testament known as the Byzantine text. Although it does not appear to be based on the oldest manuscripts, it is preferred by some translators. Other text groups or families also developed, based on discoveries of older manuscripts. By the early twentieth century, Bible scholars had grouped the ancient biblical texts into four families: Alexandrian, Western, Caesarean and Byzantine. All four families have made valuable, distinctive contributions to today's reliable biblical text. Byzantine culture was distinctively artistic, and in its day produced extraordinary and unique artistic innovations—including "illuminated" New Testament manuscripts.[9]

Ornately embellished and hand colored in vivid hues, the illuminated manuscripts—known as "illuminations"—featured colorful elements, full-page color illustrations, portraits of the biblical writers, decorative covers, and a variety of artistic features. Some sixth-century manuscripts were rendered in silver or gold on dyed purple vellum. Others contained scores of illustrations—perhaps intended as evangelistic teaching tools—and all of the Byzantine-era illuminations display artistic styles that are distinctive to Byzantine art. In the Middle Ages, biblical manuscripts of the Latin Bible were also illuminated in Europe. The illuminated Latin Bibles also featured extensive illustrations, including portraits of the gospel writers. One distinctive feature of the Latin illuminations was the use of symbols for the gospel writers, who are sometimes depicted as a lion, a calf, a man, or an eagle. The lion was apparently chosen because the roaring truth of the gospel can strike fear in the hearts of heretics, the calf was intended to be a sacrificial symbol to emphasize Jesus' ultimate sacrifice on the cross, the symbol of a man emphasized the humanity of Jesus as fully God and fully man, and the eagle represented the Holy Spirit's inspiration of Scripture. Scribes usually rendered the biblical text of an illumination, while monk artists created the illustrations.[10]

Among the most remarkable Latin illuminations is the eighth-century English Codex Amiatinius, which is believed to be the oldest existing complete version of the Latin Vulgate Bible. Codex Amiatinius is large in size, contains 1,030 leaves, and weighs more than seventy-five pounds. It was one of three single-volume Bibles produced by monks at Wearmouth-Jarrow monastery in Britain, beginning in the year 692. In 716, it was carried to Rome as a gift to Pope Gregory II, and was eventually placed in the Laurentian Library in Florence. There, its origin was discovered in the nineteenth century, and today it is thought to be the sole survivor of the three monastery illuminations. Impressively illustrated, it was used in the revision of the Latin Vulgate ordered by

Pope Sixtus in the 1580s, and has been described as "one of the most important Bibles in the world." Equally impressive, but of much smaller size, is the lavishly illustrated Book of Kells, which was calligraphed and illustrated in the early ninth century. It consists of the four Gospels in Latin on 340 vellum leaves, and was probably created in Ireland. Beginning in the ninth century, it was kept for some seven hundred years at Ireland's Abbey of Kells—hence, its name—until transferred to Trinity College in Dublin. Its text is an Irish style of Latin that includes elements predating Jerome's Vulgate, and its colorful ornamentation and illustrations have earned it a reputation as "the most beautiful book of the early Middle Ages."[11]

Charles Martel and his Frankish army turn back the Muslim invasion of Western Europe at the Battle of Tours, fought in France in 732. In the centuries of warfare that established a Muslim crescent-shaped empire from Spain to India, countless Bible manuscripts perished. Source: Wikimedia Commons.

No illuminated Bible has a more unusual and dramatic history than what is known as the Lindisfarne Gospels. In 793, it was among the church treasures targeted by a murderous band of Norsemen. Better known as Vikings, the Norsemen were ferocious seafaring warriors who terrorized much of Europe in the Middle Ages. Britain's location, bordering the North Sea, and its extensive coastline made it a favorite target. Viking raiders struck the Britain's northern coast repeatedly, decade after decade, and at one point sacked Canterbury and London, and even raised a temple to Thor in nearby Ireland. In June 793, a Viking war party sailing from Denmark aboard specially crafted warships, landed on Northumbria's Holy Island on the northeast coast of England. Their target was the Lindisfarne Monastery. In the monastery were church treasures—gold and silver crucifixes, chalices, and other valuables.[12]

Like "stinging hornets" and "fearful wolves," reported a historic account, the Vikings "came to the church of Lindisfarne, laid everything to waste with grievous plundering, trampled the holy places with polluted steps, dug up the altars and seized all the treasures of the holy church. They killed some of the brothers, took some away with them in fetters, many they drove out, naked and loaded with insults, some they drowned in the sea." The monastery, it was reported, was "spattered with the blood of the priests of God [and] stripped of all its furnishings." The Vikings sailed away with an immense haul of looted valuables—but they missed Lindisfarne's greatest treasure: an illuminated manuscript that would become known as the Lindisfarne Gospels.[13]

Evidence suggests that the extraordinary illumination was the work of a monk artist named Eadfrith, who served as the bishop of Lindisfarne between 698 and 721. His artistry was superb—intricate, colorful artistic patterns; lavish colors rendered from vegetable, mineral, and animal pigments; and elaborate images and designs. It was a costly, time-rich work of art that decorated a copy of the Gospels in the Latin Vulgate. A century later—about 970—a priest named Aldred penned an Old English translation from the Latin in red ink between the lines of Latin. The addition made the manuscript even more remarkable—the New Testament Gospels rendered in both Latin and Old English. The Lindisfarne Gospels thus became the oldest example of the Scriptures in a form of the English language.[14]

It also became one of the most famous illuminated manuscripts in history. The images in the Lindisfarne Gospels—like the illustrations in other illuminated manuscripts—may have served a practical as well as an artistic purpose. They may have served as teaching tools for the monks, allowing the gospel of Jesus Christ to be shared with those who could not read. It would have been a memorable visual aid. Along with portraits of gospel writers, the artwork includes multiple geometric patterns, animal and bird images, and a wide variety of other artistic expressions—including one page that features a background pattern of more than one thousand red dots. Equally astounding is the story of its survival. In 875, fearful of more Viking raids, the Lindisfarne monks packed up the monastery belongings and fled. At sea, their ship was struck by a violent storm, and some of their cargo was washed overboard—including a box containing their beloved illuminated manuscript. According to the traditional account, the monks made landfall after the storm, and while walking along the shoreline, they discovered their manuscript—still intact and undamaged. Eventually, after escaping a Viking raid, reportedly being lost at sea, and surviving the ravages of time, the Lindisfarne illumination came to be preserved in London's British Library.[15]

Despite the historic turmoil that befell the Mideast and eastern Europe in the Byzantine era and during the Crusades of the Middle Ages, the Greek Bible of the Eastern church was not lost. Neither was the use of the Greek language for Bible translation. In fact, the fall of Constantinople and the Muslim invasion of eastern Europe drove numerous Greek-language scholars into western Europe and produced a revival of Greek-language scholarship that renewed an interest in translating Scripture from its original languages—Hebrew as well as Greek. The Latin Bible of the Western church also survived Islamic conquests, along with numerous other conflicts, floods, fires, and human tampering. Much of the work of preserving and translating Scripture occurred in Christian monasteries—particularly during the Middle Ages. The monastic movement appears to have begun with Eastern Christianity in the late third century, and was adapted in the West a century later. Monastery-dwelling monks ranged from hermit separatists, who isolated themselves in deliberate seclusion, to those who served local churches and communities from monasteries that were located in or near population centers. Some monasteries offered medical care and relief for the poor. Others were even more outwardly focused: Irish monks known as White Martyrs wandered far and wide, establishing monasteries on the European continent, evangelizing for Christ, and transporting and preserving the Scriptures as the Bible underwent attack from barbarian hordes.[16]

Despite the loss of manuscripts, the Scriptures survived.

From their earliest days, monasteries were centers of biblical study, and one of their principal focuses was the preservation and transmission of Scripture. In the mid-sixth century, a former Roman statesman and author named Flavius Magnus Aurelius Cassiodorus, after receiving Jesus Christ as Lord and Savior, established an Italian monastery called Vivarium. There he labored to save the culture and literature of Rome as it descended into the darkness of barbarian rule. In what was arguably his most important work, he collected ancient manuscripts and directed a team of monks in a translation of the Psalms and the preservation of the Latin Vulgate. Preservation of the Latin Vulgate was also enhanced in 801, when the Frankish King Charlemagne, the "father of France and Germany," commissioned the leading scholar of his court—the Anglo-Saxon theologian Alcuin of York—to produce a revised edition of the Latin Vulgate. Alcuin, who was the master of Charlemagne's scholastic center at Aachen, improved the Latin translation of the Bible in his work, which he presented to Charlemagne on Christmas Day of

801. By then, the Vulgate was the standard version of the Bible used by the Western church.[17]

An early twentieth century peasant encampment makes use of the ruins of a thousand-year-old Byzantine church in Thessalonica, located in northern Greece. Although eventually conquered by Muslim forces, the Byzantine Empire left a legacy of ornately illustrated biblical manuscripts and a Greek translation of the New Testament called the Byzantine Text. Source: Library of Congress.

The Vulgate came to Britain in the sixth century, when Pope Gregory the Great dispatched a missionary team of forty monks to bring the gospel to Britain. It was a second attempt at evangelism in British Isles. The Good News had been taken there in Roman days and had been accepted by the Britons, but fifth-century invasions by the pagan Angles, Saxons, and Jutes had weakened British Christianity. Even with Gregory's missionary team, the faith grew slowly among Britain's Anglo-Saxons. Not so among the Irish—who embraced the gospel and relished the Word. With meticulous care and a unique zeal, Irish monks established a standard for copying the Bible and preserving its text. From Ireland, they carried the Latin Bible back to the continent—to France,

Germany, and Switzerland, establishing monasteries that excelled in Bible scholarship and copying of the Scriptures. England's supply of Bibles was dealt a severe blow in the late eighth century, however, when Viking raids on targets such as the Lindisfarne monastery destroyed manuscript libraries in English monasteries and churches. Despite the loss of manuscripts, the Scriptures survived—even eventually converting and subduing the fierce Norsemen.[18]

Armed and ready, a Viking raiding party rows through heavy seas toward a coastal target. Such raids terrorized coastal inhabitants of Western Europe in the Middle Ages and destroyed unknown numbers of biblical manuscripts in attacks on monasteries. Source: Wikimedia Commons.

By the thirteenth century, the Latin Vulgate was still *the* Bible of the Middle Ages on the European continent and in England, spurred by an extraordinary era of biblical scholarship that blossomed that century in France. It was led by Bible scholars at the University of Paris, who produced a new wave of accurately rendered copies of the Latin Vulgate. It was also there at the University of Paris, in the mid-thirteenth century, that an English scholar named Stephen Langton—later the archbishop of Canterbury—introduced the formal division of chapters familiar to modern students of the Bible. Some three hundred years later, in 1551, French Bible scholar and printer Robert Estienne would publish a Greek New Testament in Switzerland with the text organized into chapters *and* verses for the first time—an idea that reportedly came to him while journeying across France on horseback. France's royal printer, Estienne embraced Protestantism and fled to Switzerland—where he published Reformer John Calvin's Bible commentaries.[19]

Despite their appreciation for the Latin Scriptures, Europeans—English-speakers included—yearned for the Bible in their native tongues. Early attempts to translate Scripture into the Anglo-Saxon tongue had yielded poetical paraphrases of Bible stories, English-language Psalters, and the Lindisfarne Gospel. An eighth-century English historian and theologian—the Venerable Bede, he was called—finished translating a portion of the gospel of John into Old English on his deathbed—which was the first translation of the gospel into English on record. For another six hundred years no English-language Bible existed—until the year 1382. That year, a Roman Catholic clergyman and scholar in England named John Wycliffe produced a new translation of the Bible in Middle English—the vernacular spoken in England between 1100 and 1500. At the time Wycliffe was a thin, bearded, aging lecturer at Oxford University. Although affable to students and colleagues, he could be temperamental and caustic, and he was an outspoken critic of church doctrines and practices that he deemed to be unbiblical. As a Roman Catholic clergyman, he had concluded that the church needed revival—and for that to happen, he believed, the common people needed to be able to read the Bible in their own language. "As the faith of the Church is contained in the Scriptures," he explained, "the more these are known . . . the better."[20]

Fearful of Viking raids, monks from the Lindisfarne Monastery on the northern coast of England fled their home in 875—and lost their precious illuminated Gospel manuscript in a storm at sea. Remarkably, the crate containing it reportedly washed ashore and it was rescued—saving the Bible and this illustrated title page from the Gospel of Matthew. Source: Wikimedia Commons.

Church leaders in Rome did not share his opinion. They believed that the Bible needed to be restricted to Latin so the church could preserve the integrity of Scripture—a position, critics would later assert, that also prevented church members from holding their leaders accountable to Scripture. For his English Bible translation—and his criticism of church doctrine—Wycliffe was denounced as a "son of the old serpent" by the church hierarchy. Even so, his English translation of the New Testament—rendered almost word for word from the Latin Vulgate—was hand-printed in 1380, four years before his death, followed by the entire Bible in 1382. Church authorities responded ferociously: His translation colleagues John Purvey and Nicholas of Hereford were arrested and imprisoned, some of his supporters were burned at the stake with Bibles tied around their necks, and later, in faraway Bohemia, Wycliffe disciple John Huss was executed. In 1428, forty-four years after Wycliffe's death, Pope Martin V ordered the Bible translator's body dug up from its churchyard grave and burned, with the ashes dumped in a nearby river. Meanwhile, the English people were forbidden to read Wycliffe's Bible, but untold numbers were willing to take the risk if they could only obtain a copy. The going rate for secretly borrowing one was an entire load of hay, and few people could ever hope to own a copy. Even so, Wycliffe's vision of a Bible in the English vernacular had launched a dream among the everyday people of England. "You could not meet two persons on the highway," recalled an Englishman of the era, "but one of them was a Wycliffe disciple." People in England and elsewhere in Europe yearned to read the Word of God in their own language—and a revival was already under way that would place readable Bibles in their hands.[21]

6

GOD'S TRUTH ABIDETH STILL

"And you will know the truth, and the truth will make you free."
—JOHN 8:32

TO SOME, JOHANN GENSFLEISCH ZUM GUTENBERG looked like a failure. He borrowed too much money, was sued by his business partner, and was swamped by competition. By the standards of business, he was hardly a success. Appearances were deceiving, however: Gutenberg made a greater mark on history than most kings, emperors, or presidents. In 1454, the middle-aged German printer advanced Western civilization with a new invention: a printing press equipped with movable and reusable type. It was state-of-the-art technology. Others were developing it too, and experimentation had occurred in ninth-century China, but it was Johann Gutenberg who really made it work. At his print shop in Mainz, Germany, sometime between 1450 and 1454, he or one of his typesetters selected individual fonts of type for the opening page of his first published work, set them in a frame on the press, and wet them with oil-based black ink from balls stuffed with horsehair. A dampened sheet of high-grade Italian paper was then placed on the press, and a pressman stamped the set type onto the paper. Modern printing was born.[1]

Johann Gutenberg and his colleagues examine a newly printed work. The Gutenberg press revolutionized the printing industry—and first off the press was the Bible. Source: Library of Congress.

No longer would books have to be handmade, tediously produced manuscripts with circulation limited to institutions, scholars, and the wealthy. The Gutenberg movable-type printing press launched a technological and cultural upheaval. Johann Gutenberg's most famous print job and the first book printed on his movable-type press was the Latin Vulgate Bible—an edition known to history as the Gutenberg Bible. It consisted of only about 180 copies. Even so, not only did the Gutenberg press revolutionize the world's printing industry—it also put the Bible in the lap of the common man. The timing was extraordinary. When he published the Gutenberg Bible, few people in Europe could read, but that was about to change. The Southern Renaissance, a rebirth of learning in southern Europe, was in full bloom, and within a half century the Northern Renaissance would blossom—and it would be much more

God-centered than the man-centered Southern Renaissance. Northern Europeans in particular would become eager readers, and movable-type presses similar to Gutenberg's would produce books on an unprecedented mass scale. Suddenly, the people of the Western world would be exposed to an array of classical and common literature—and the Bible.[2]

By Gutenberg's era hardly anyone in Europe knew what the Bible really taught—including much of the clergy. The leadership of the Church in Rome was committed to protecting the Bible from misinterpretation and controlling the reading of the Scriptures, and to achieve that goal it had outlawed the private reading of the Bible. Supporters viewed Rome's position as protective, but critics—mainly dissenting clergy within the church—believed such policies placed the Church between the Bible and the people. Meeting in France in 1229, the Fourth Council of Toulouse issued a series of rulings against heresy, which outlawed private reading of the Bible and prohibited the common people from having "in their possession any copy of the books of the Old and New Testaments." Private reading of the Bible was heresy, according to the Council, which ordered that "the house in which any heretic be discovered be destroyed," and required everyone older than age fourteen to "swear to hunt out the heretics." In 1414, an English law proclaimed that people caught reading the Bible in the "mother tongue" could be deprived of "land, cattle, life and goods." Many critics of the Roman Church—clergy and laity alike—believed such policies were grossly unbiblical.[3]

Within the late medieval Western church, countless priests, monks and nuns lived faithfully and labored mightily for the cause of Christ, and so did numerous bishops, cardinals, and popes. As Christianity continued to expand, however, some Western Church leaders engaged in political intrigue, unbiblical abuses, and scandalous lifestyles. At times, bishops, cardinals, and even popes behaved like decadent princes, wallowing in lavish self-indulgence, engaging in financial corruption and making a mockery of Christian discipleship. Pope Leo X, for instance, retained almost seven hundred servants, including a papal elephant trainer. "He would have been an ideal pope if he had had the slightest interest in religion," a future critic would charge. The church was also distracted by internal schisms: In 1054, the Eastern Church broke from the Western Church in a dispute over the authority of the pope. One pope moved the papacy to France, where it remained for seventy years, and at one point the office of pope was simultaneously claimed by three church officials.[4]

Some church leaders campaigned for replacement of the papacy by ruling councils, but the papacy remained influential, and even exercised authority over empires and nations. In the long era of the Holy Roman Empire, various popes alternately cooperated and competed with the empire's rulers. Medieval Europe meanwhile was beset by warfare, prolonged poverty, deadly plagues, and the ignorance and superstition of the Dark Ages. The Church-backed Crusades tried to permanently drive Islam from the Holy Land, but failed—and in 1204, the Fourth Crusade even made war against the Christian Byzantines, and ruthlessly conquered and sacked Constantinople. Through it all, the Word of God was often neglected, ignored, or suppressed. Despite achievements in areas such as art and architecture, medieval Europe was progressively shrouded in spiritual darkness, and countless people were left to live a grim existence.[5]

Reform-minded Catholic priests were dedicated to restoring what they believed was the Church's biblical foundation.

Meanwhile, controversial doctrines and practices that many Christian clergy and laity came to view as unbiblical developed in the medieval Church of Rome. Among them were papal infallibility, justification by faith and works, purgatory, penances, and indulgences. Emerging doctrine stated that the pope was incapable of error in his official rulings on faith and morality, and that papal edicts and church tradition carried the same authority as the Bible. On justification by faith, the Church's Council of Trent would rule in 1547: "If anyone says that the sinner is justified by faith alone…let him be anathema." Doing penance was the practice of engaging in some form of earthly self-punishment to demonstrate personal repentance. The Church's doctrine of purgatory held that despite Christ's atonement on the cross, Christians had to endure a punishing purging of sin after death before they could enter heaven. To reduce the time and punishment in purgatory, church members could obtain "indulgences" for themselves or their dead loved ones by giving a monetary donation to the Church or performing goods works, such as serving in a crusade. In the late fifteenth and early sixteenth centuries—at the same time modern nations were arising in western Europe—a reform movement arose among the clergy of the Roman Church. These reform-minded Catholic priests were dedicated to restoring what they believed was the Church's biblical foundation.[6]

Among them was a Roman Catholic priest and educator named Martin Luther. In 1517, Luther was a thirty-three-year-old theology professor at Wittenberg University, which was then a small, fledgling institution in eastern Germany. The "Reverend Father Martin Luther," as he was known to faculty and students, had grown to have deep concerns about some of the doctrines and practices that had arisen in the Roman Church over time—the same issues that troubled many Catholic clergy in the day. The difference with Martin Luther is that he decided to do something about it. To him, the troubling theological issues were very personal: He had struggled mightily with doubt about his own salvation, and with some other Church doctrines, such as purgatory, indulgences and doing penance. He finally found peace when he came to understand the biblical doctrine of justification by faith—that salvation is a gift of God's grace and comes not through works, but through personal belief in Jesus Christ as Lord and Savior. "You will know the truth," Jesus had said in John 8:32, "and the truth will make you free." No one was capable of earning his or her salvation, and neither could anyone purchase it, Luther had concluded—it was instead offered as a free gift to believers by God through His loving grace. It was a liberating revelation for the young priest: The biblical truth about salvation was clearly revealed in the Bible, he believed, and Church leaders had obscured it with a complicated, man-made theology.[7]

At Wittenberg in October 1517, Martin Luther publicly called for the church to turn back to the Bible. His action would have earth-shaking repercussions: It would forever split the Roman Church, reassert the authority of Scripture, ignite a restoration of New Testament Christianity, transform lives and nations, politically redefine the European continent, dramatically alter Western civilization, and change the course of history. But Luther's initial call sounded almost boring—it was merely a public invitation to a local academic debate of theological issues. "Out of love for the truth and a desire to bring it to light," the invitation read, "the following propositions will be discussed . . ." Luther attached it alongside other announcements on a church door, the bulletin board of the day. It would become famous as the Ninety-Five Theses—it had that many points—but read in part like a mundane academic announcement. "Wherefore, those who are unable to be present and debate orally with us," it drily noted, "may do so by letter." Posted at an obscure university in Germany by a young, unknown educator, it seemed anything but world-changing. But change the world it did.[8]

In appearance, Martin Luther was an unlikely-looking man to turn the world upside down. His bearing was anything but heroic: He was short and stocky, and, some said, was topped by a tonsured head of red hair. He was generally good-natured, loved music and the outdoors, and often bore a studious demeanor. He could also be deeply intense, coarse in his language, and at times he struggled with bouts of depression. He was personally courageous—once remaining at his post during a deadly plague when others fled so that he could minister to the stricken. He held a devout reverence for the Word of God, and professed a deep love for Jesus Christ. He apparently had no thought of starting anything new when he posted his Ninety-Five Theses—he just wanted his church to be faithful to what he believed was the truth of Scripture.[9]

One of three existing 1455 Gutenberg Bibles printed on vellum is displayed at the Library of Congress in Washington, D.C. in 1930. It was one of one-hundred-eighty copies of Gutenberg's first edition. Source: Library of Congress.

Raised by an overbearing German miner and a devout mother, he had set out to be a lawyer, but instead entered the priesthood—reportedly to keep a vow he had made while frightened by a thunderstorm. Caught in the open as lightning bolts struck nearby, he cried out to the patron saint of miners and vowed to be a clergyman. The decision infuriated his father, but Luther was ordained as a Roman Catholic priest in 1507. The next year he joined the faculty of the new Wittenberg University. There he sought to discharge his duties faithfully, but he was disillusioned by the ignorance of Scripture he found among his fellow clergymen—some of whom had never personally read the Bible. He also struggled with doubts about his own salvation, even though he did penance, bought indulgences, and whipped himself for his sins. In 1511, he was excited to make a laborious six-hundred-mile pilgrimage over the Alps to Rome. "I greet thee, Holy Rome," he exclaimed at first sight of the city.[10]

His elation turned to despair, however, as he witnessed firsthand rampant worldliness among Rome's clergy and the smug disdain some displayed for the pilgrims who flocked to the city's shrines. According to a memoir by his son Paul, Luther joined other pilgrims ascending a marble staircase called the *Scala Pilati*—reputedly the "Holy Stairs" on which Jesus stood when sentenced to crucifixion by Pontius Pilate in Jerusalem. Reverently kissing each of the twenty-eight marble steps, dutiful pilgrims climbed the *Scala Pilati* on their knees, assured by the church that their act of devotion reduced punishment in purgatory for their dead loved ones by a number of years for each step. Midway up the staircase, Luther reportedly found himself wishing his mother was already dead, so the indulgence he gained by climbing the steps could ease her punishment in purgatory. Then, he remembered a Bible passage he had been pondering: Romans 1:17, "the righteous man shall live by faith." It was the fundamental doctrine of Scripture that transformed Martin Luther: *Salvation comes from faith alone in Jesus Christ, and does not depend on good works.* Some biographers report that his transformation occurred later; others say it was immediate—that Luther stood up, reversed direction, and walked off the "Holy Stairs" a changed man.[11]

The Biblical doctrine of Justification by Faith was central to Luther's Ninety-Five Theses. So too was his opposition to the Church's selling of indulgences, which was being promoted by Church authorities to help fund construction of St. Peter's Basilica in Rome. Johann Tetzel, a worldly priest commissioned by the Church to sell indulgences in Germany, reportedly employed a sarcastic lyric to boost sales: "As soon as the coin in the coffer rings, the soul from purgatory springs." Such mockery of biblical truth aroused a righteous anger in Luther. If the pope wanted to build a spectacular cathedral in Rome, he reasoned, why not use his own money instead of soliciting poor believers to make donations in exchange for false promises of salvation? If purgatory really existed and the pope really had authority over it, he questioned in point 82 of his Theses, why should he not simply empty purgatory "for the sake of holy love" and allow its inhabitants to proceed to heaven? These and other points from Luther's list of proposed reforms gradually became known—and ignited alarm up the Church chain of command.[12]

When news of Luther's Ninety-Five Theses reached Church authorities in Rome—it produced an ominous reaction: Luther was ordered to report to Rome in sixty days. He declined and remained in Wittenberg, under the protection of a regional ruler named Frederick III of Saxony. Church authorities in Rome acted anyway: He was tried in absentia and was convicted of heresy. Defiantly, he publicly burned the papal bull issued against his writings, and appealed for support from the German people. Many of them also yearned for church reforms and sided with him, including some clergy. In 1521, however, he was formally excommunicated by Pope Leo X and was summoned to testify before a diet, or court, in the German city of Worms. There he refused to recant his beliefs, and is said to have proclaimed: "Here I stand. I can do no other. God help me. Amen." His teachings were officially condemned by the Edict of Worms, and Charles V, the emperor of the Holy Roman Empire ruling over central and western Europe at the time, sided with the pope and officially outlawed Luther.[13]

As painted by nineteenth-century Belgian artist Ferdinand Pauwels, Martin Luther posts his Ninety-Five Theses on the church door in Wittenberg, Germany in 1517. His act ignited the Protestant Reformation—and ultimately led to the printing of the Bible in a multitude of languages. Source: Wikimedia Commons.

Church authorities failed to capture Luther, but six of his supporters were rounded up and burned at the stake. For his safety, Frederick of Saxony—Luther's protector—had him kidnapped and placed in comfortable seclusion in Wartburg Castle for almost a year. It proved to be a milestone event in the history of Bible translation—for there in Wartburg Castle, Luther completed a German translation of the New Testament. The first published version of the German Bible had appeared in 1466, and others had followed, but Luther's translation of the New Testament was popularly received on a grand scale by Germany's believers—and his 1534 translation of the whole Bible earned great acclaim. He translated mainly from Latin due to limited knowledge of ancient languages, but he had a scholar's command of German, believed in the inspiration of the original Scriptures, and had an evangelist's heart for sharing the Word. "A good translation must be both true and free, faithful and idiomatic, so as to read like an original work," observed nineteenth-century church historian Philip Schaff. "This is the case with Luther's version." Luther had already translated several chapters from the book of Psalms, the Ten Commandments, the Lord's Prayer, and other Bible passages. He had a genius for poetry and music, which enabled him to faithfully render into German the flavor of Hebrew poetry and prose. Such a gift with Hebrew was ironic, for Luther at times unleashed unbiblical and anti-Semitic tirades against Germany's Jewish community for not accepting Jesus as the Messiah. Luther was also harshly critical of other Christians, such as the Anabaptists, whom he condemned. He once denounced a critic in writing as a "vulgar boor, blockhead and lout . . . that ass to cap all asses." He could also be bitterly self-critical, believing at times that he was unworthy to champion the cause of Christ. He believed that he was almost constantly engaged in spiritual warfare, and he humbly beseeched fellow believers to bolster him with prayer.[14]

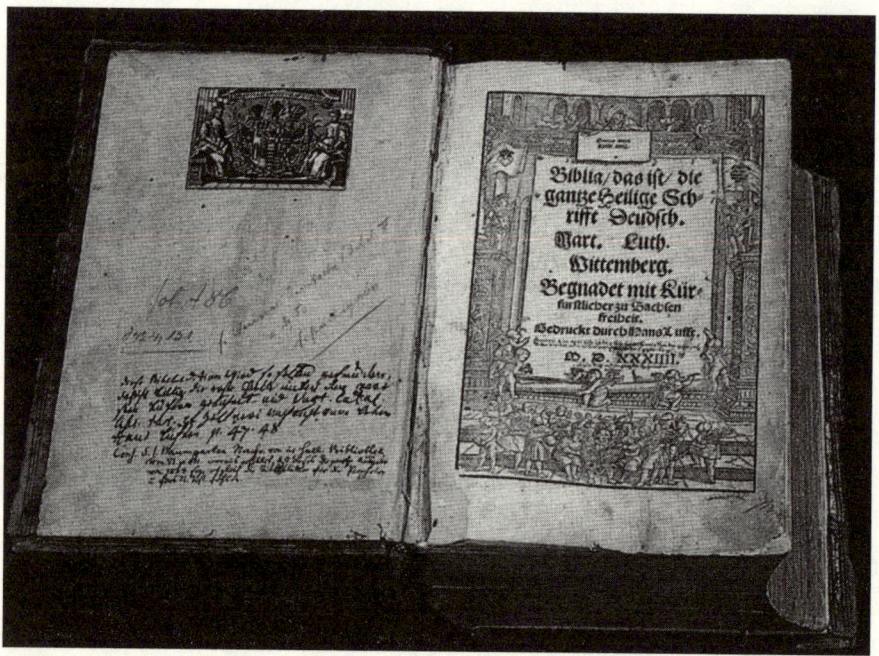

Martin Luther's German-language translation of the entire Bible was published in 1534. His first edition was published anonymously, but publishers learned that adding his name as translator increased the respect for the translation with German readers. Source: Wikimedia Commons.

He ended his seclusion at Wartburg Castle in 1522, and continued to freely write, teach, preach, and revise his Bible translations for more than two decades, until his death on February 18, 1546. Always he claimed the Bible as his primary rule of faith and practice. The first edition of his German New Testament was published anonymously, but later editions bore his name as translator—which dramatically increased their credibility with much of the German public. His linguistic command of German was unsurpassed, and his Bible translations significantly impacted the German language by efficiently combining the vernacular "Low German" with the formal "High German." Even his detractors admired the quality of his translations. Luther also wrote numerous hymns to train unlearned believers in the key truths of Scripture. The most beloved was "Eine Feste Burg Ist Unser Gott"—"A Mighty Fortress Is Our God"—which would long endure as a lyrical testimony to Martin Luther's reverence for the Bible:

> *Let goods and kindred go;*
>
> *this mortal life also;*
>
> *The body they may kill.*
>
> *God's truth abideth still.*
>
> *His kingdom is forever.*[15]

The Protestant Reformation was Bible-centered, and its guiding principles became *sola fide, solo Christo, sola gratia, sola scriptura,* and *Soli Deo Gloria*—salvation by faith alone, in Christ alone, through grace alone, by Scripture alone, and to the glory of God alone. Reformation leaders generally emphasized the authority of the Bible, including Switzerland's Huldrych Zwingli, the brilliant French-born theologian John Calvin, Theodore Beza of France and Switzerland, Philip Melanchthon in Germany, John a Lasco in Poland, Olaus and Lars Petri in Sweden,

Hans Tausen and Jørgen Sadolin in Denmark, William Tyndale and Thomas Cranmer in England, Patrick Hamilton and John Knox in Scotland, and others. When the Church divided, professing Christians faced a choice, as summarized by Reformation scholar R. C. Sproul: "Rome had said [that] through Christ's cross and his Church, salvation is possible for all who will work and suffer for it—so come to church and toil! But the Reformers said . . . through Christ's cross and his Spirit, salvation full and free, with its unlimited guarantee of eternal joy, is given once and forever to all who believe—so come to Christ, and trust and take!"[16]

The Protestant Reformation spread rapidly through Europe and swelled into a continent-wide, Bible-centered revival of New Testament Christianity. It also was accompanied by a shocking loss of life. The Church hierarchy and much of Europe's monarchy viewed the clergy and laity who embraced the Reformation as a threat to "the one true Church" and to Europe's existing political order. European rulers were generally supportive of the Roman Church and suspicious of the Reformation's emphasis on God-given rights, the value of the individual, and the belief that God's law superseded even the laws of a monarch. For religious and political reasons, Catholic monarchs at times used violence to suppress the Reformation, and at times Protestants violently retaliated. In 1524, inspired by the Reformation tenet that human rights originate with God and not with government, peasants in Germany revolted against ruling noblemen in what became known as the Peasants' War, but they were overcome, and an estimated one hundred thousand of them were killed. A century later, between 1618 and 1648, millions of Catholics and Protestants died in the political and religious fighting of the Thirty Years' War, which remade the map of Europe.[17]

Meanwhile, as the Reformation spread, it often encountered violent resistance. On Saint Bartholomew's Day of 1572, officials under France's King Charles IX launched a nationwide slaughter of French Protestants—the Huguenots—which claimed more than twenty-thousand Protestant lives. Many Catholics were horrified by the mass murder; some were not. The severed head of a Huguenot leader, Admiral Gaspard de Coligny, was presented to Church officials as a trophy, and Pope Gregory XIII ordered a medal issued to commemorate the massacre. In Portugal, meanwhile, tens of thousands of Protestants were executed between 1567 and 1573 by the Duke of Alva on behalf of Spain's Catholic King Philip II. Several thousand Protestants and Jews were executed in Spain under the Spanish Inquisition. "There were about forty people," reported an official in Barcelona, "nearly all of them Lutherans, burned along with the bones and clothes of five others who had already died; some of the books of the Lutherans were also burned." At least two thousand were killed in the Netherlands while it was under Spanish control, and several hundred were burned at the stake in England by Queen Mary Tudor in the 1550s. Although suppressed in France, Spain, and Portugal, the Reformation eventually was accepted in England, Scotland, Scandinavia, the Netherlands, northern Germany, and Switzerland. In the end, southern Europe remained predominantly Catholic, and northern Europe became largely Protestant.[18]

Generations of believers would come to view the Reformation—with all its shortcomings—as a long-overdue "cleansing of the temple." It eventually did stir reform within the Roman Catholic Church. Although retaining debated doctrines such as papal infallibility and salvation by works and faith, the Church discarded the sale of indulgences and attempted to discourage the internal financial corruption that had existed at the time of the Reformation. Protestantism, meanwhile, recorded its own history of violent excesses—though not on the scale practiced by its opponents. In various locations throughout Europe, Protestant leaders ordered the execution of Anabaptist believers; Reformers in Holland persecuted Arminian Christians; vengeful Huguenots killed Catholic priests and laymen in some regions of France; and at times Catholic clergy were executed in England and elsewhere.[19]

The illegitimate son of a Dutch priest, sixteenth century European Bible scholar Desiderius Erasmus was the first to print a Greek New Testament—which became the primary source for numerous Bible translations in the centuries to come. Source: Library of Congress.

Over the course of time, the Protestant Reformation made a dramatic impact on northern Europe and, eventually, the world at large. The refocus on New Testament Christianity produced generation after generation of new evangelists, as believers read the Bible and sought to follow the Great Commission of Christ. In northern Europe, the Reformation elevated the biblical obligations of family life and citizenship. It established precedents that would become established Western legal traditions, and it renewed an appreciation of the biblical virtues of honest work, self-sacrifice, and personal responsibility—all reflecting a biblical worldview that would become the driving force in Western civilization. Its emphasis on individual worth and God-given rights also sparked a blaze of freedom movements throughout the world. Above all, the Reformation restored the central New Testament doctrine of salvation by faith alone in Christ Jesus, and reasserted an abiding belief in the authority of Scripture as the revealed Word of God.[20]

The Protestant Reformation unleashed a flood of Bibles that eventually surged around the world.

It also unleashed a flood of Bibles that eventually surged around the world. From Germany to Britain, Christians in northern Europe were influenced by the Reformation and intellectually equipped by what would become known as the Northern Renaissance—a blossoming of the arts and learning that rivaled the renaissance that spread across southern Europe. The Northern Renaissance was particularly God-centered, and its quest for knowledge included a passion among the laity to learn for themselves what the Bible contained. The technological leap forward of the Gutenberg printing press resulted in the publication of countless Christian books and tracts—and scores of Bibles. A renewed scholarly interest in the original Hebrew and Greek languages of the Bible also emerged. It was an extraordinary convergence of events—a continent-wide spiritual revival, the renaissance of scholarship, and the impact of the printing press—and many would come to view it as providential.[21]

Already, in 1488, Jewish scholars in Soncino, Italy, had printed a complete Hebrew Old Testament. In 1525, Daniel Bomberg, a Christian printer in Venice, and Jacob ben Chayyim, a Jewish scholar, jointly published a Hebrew Old Testament called the Rabbinic Bible, which was based on Chayyim's careful consultation of a variety of aged Hebrew manuscripts. In 1517, under oversight from the Church leaders in Rome, Catholic Bible scholars in Spain had published the Bible in its original languages in a massive work called the *Complutensian Polyglot.* Before the Reformation, Catholic scholars had been allowed to produce translations of Scripture in various European languages, but these early attempts were printed in small editions and were not aimed for the laity—the Roman Church allowed them to be read only by the clergy, royalty, and university professors and students. They were also translated from the Latin Vulgate—not Hebrew and Greek—so they were translations of translations.[22]

In 1516—the year before Luther nailed his Ninety-Five Theses to the church door—the first Greek New Testament ever printed was published in Basel, Switzerland, by the leading biblical scholar of Europe—Desiderius Erasmus. Both critics and supporters alike cited his influence on the birth of the Reformation, claiming that he "laid the egg that Luther hatched." The illegitimate son of a Dutch priest, he was orphaned as a child, educated in the Roman Church, and ordained into the Catholic priesthood as a young man. He quit the priesthood, however, and became an independent Catholic scholar based in Switzerland. Erasmus was a Hebrew and Greek scholar and a superb writer, whose hugely popular books encouraged Christian discipleship. He never left the Roman Church, and used his weighty scholarly influence and a biting wit to attack church corruption and questionable doctrine. His 1516 Greek New Testament and a later parallel Greek-Latin New Testament were widely popular, despite being plagued by translation errors, which Erasmus labored mightily to correct. Even with its handicaps, Erasmus's Greek New Testament encouraged Bible translators to base their work on the original Greek of the New Testament, rather than solely on Latin. Thus, it became the Greek foundation text for Bible translations from the time of the Reformation onward and would be known as the *Textus Receptus* or "Received Text."[23]

Attired in his papal vestments, Pope Sixtus V raises his hand to bestow a blessing. His revision of the Latin Vulgate, which was further revised by Pope Clement VIII, became the Sixtus-Clementine edition—the accepted translation for generations of Catholics. Source: New York Public Library.

Protestant Reformers wanted the Bible to be made available to everyday people in their native languages. A principal doctrine of the Reformation was the "priesthood of all believers"—the belief that every Christian can directly address God in prayer, and has the right and the duty to individually read the Bible. Confident that the Bible was meant to be personally available to everyone, Reformers across northern Europe began translating and publishing the Bible in a variety of common languages. The Greek New Testament published in 1551 by the former royal French printer Robert Estienne not only established the Bible's familiar verse structure, but also improved and popularized Erasmus's Greek text. Estienne's fourth edition included a Greek translation by Reformation leader and Bible scholar Theodore Beza, and further increased the popularity of the "Received Text." In the centuries to come, the "Received Text" would be supplemented and even replaced by translations that were based on newly discovered, older manuscripts that were deemed to be more accurate. However, the "Received Text" would remain so endearing to Bible readers that—in the words of twentieth century Bible authority Bruce Metzger—"attempts to criticize or emend it have been regarded as akin to sacrilege."[24]

Meanwhile, in response to the Reformation and the surge of new Bible translations it produced, the leadership of the Roman Church engaged in what became known as the Counter-Reformation, insisting that Church members read the Bible solely in Latin. In 1546, the Council of Trent decreed the Latin Vulgate to be the church's official text and restricted Catholics to its use for centuries to come. Critics viewed the Latin-only restriction as an attempt by the Church hierarchy to control its interpretation of doctrine and access to the Bible by the laity; the Church's defenders viewed it as necessary to preserve the integrity of the Scriptures and to promote Latin as the common, worldwide language of the Church. As the Reformation spread and produced Bible translations in the languages of one nation after another, Roman Catholic scholars made Church-approved revisions to the Latin Vulgate. In 1590, Pope Sixtus V, a serious Bible scholar, rendered a version of the Vulgate text called the "Sixtine Edition," and issued a papal ruling that church members using any other text would be excommunicated. Sixtus V died soon afterwards, however, and Pope Clement VIII—who did much to restore the reputation of the papacy—had corrections made to the Sixtine Edition. Pope Clement's Bible—the Sixtine-Clementine edition of 1592—became the standard Catholic version of the Latin Vulgate.[25]

Bible-believing family members are surprised by a raid on their home by church authorities seeking forbidden Bibles. Despite the risks, Reformation-era Bible scholars throughout Europe translated the Bible into their own languages. Source: Welcome Images / Wikimedia Commons.

In Spain, Portugal, and Italy, which suppressed the Reformation, Protestant-produced Bibles in the national languages were somewhat slow to emerge, but did so. An Italian New Testament was published in Venice in 1530 by a Reform-minded Catholic layman named Antonio Brucioli. It was banned by the Catholic Church, but it would later lead to a superbly rendered Italian translation by a Swiss Protestant theologian named Giovanni Diodati that would be widely used by Italian Protestants. The first Spanish translation New Testament was published in 1543 by Francisco de Enzinas. His work resulted in his imprisonment, and his brother was burned at the stake, but Enzinas escaped and fled to Geneva, Switzerland, which was a haven for Protestants. Portugal, strictly influenced by Spain and the Roman Church, did not receive a printed version of the entire Bible in Portuguese until 1753. Unlike later Catholic versions, the Protestant Bibles typically set aside the Apocrypha from the Old and New Testaments, including it as interesting reading while emphasizing that it was not to be accepted as inspired Scripture. Eventually, the Apocrypha would be dropped from most Protestant Bibles.[26]

The Reformation spurred an outburst of Bible translations rendered from the original languages and aimed at the common people—in Dutch, Swedish, Danish, English, Hungarian, Rumanian, Slavonic-Russian, Bohemian, Lithuanian, and other languages, including even an Icelandic translation done by one of Luther's students. In the glow of the Reformation, the Bible was translated into a multitude of tongues, and everyday believers in increasing numbers were able to learn the truths of Scripture by reading a Bible translation in a language they understood. As a result, perhaps not since the days of the early church were so many Christians focused on living Bible-based lives. "Probably one of the most dynamic aspects of the Reformation," twenty-first-century Bible scholar Philip Stine would observe, "was the return to Scripture and the development of a theological method that had the study of Scripture at its center." The spread of the printed Bible to the common people in their languages did not happen easily—it was accompanied by danger, tragedy, courage and inspiration. And nowhere was the danger, tragedy, courage and inspiration greater than in England.[27]

7

LET THERE BE LIGHT

Precious in the eyes of the LORD is the death of His godly ones.
—PSALMS 116:15

WILLIAM TYNDALE STOOD FASTENED TO A POLE atop a huge pile of brush-wood, straw, and logs, all sprinkled with gunpowder. From behind, an executioner reached forward and strangled him to death with a chain garrote. Then the woodpile was set ablaze, and Tyndale's body was burned to ashes. His crimes? He supported the Reformation and published the Bible in modern English. The name of his executioner is unknown, but Tyndale was driven into his grasp by England's King Henry VIII, his key advisors, and Church officials. Known best to history for having six wives and killing two of them, Henry VIII was "the ideal standard of perfect wickedness," according to eighteenth-century British historian Sir James Mackintosh, and lived for his selfish whims and appetites. In stark contrast, William Tyndale lived and died to share the Word of God.[1]

In 1515, then in his twenties, Tyndale was ordained as a Roman Catholic priest. At the time Henry VIII was a young ruler still popular with the English people for his affability and striking figure, although he had already revealed a ruthless nature by coolly executing several prominent members of his court. As the king concentrated on expanding his prestige and power, William Tyndale became increasingly focused on a kingdom "not of this world." Like increasing numbers of Bible-believing Catholic priests, he yearned for reforms within the Church, which he believed had drifted from the principles of Scripture. He was especially troubled by the Church's restrictions on personal Bible reading, and rejected the papal argument that keeping the Scriptures from the common man protected their integrity. Instead, he believed that the Holy Spirit could open the Scriptures to any reader, and cited Psalms 119:2 as a biblical call to individual Bible study: "How blessed are those who observe his testimonies, who seek Him with all their heart." By prohibiting personal Bible reading, he boldly claimed, Church leaders were promoting "vain superstition and false doctrine, to satisfy their filthy lusts, their proud ambition, and insatiable covetousness, and to exalt their own honour." Eventually he came to believe that he had a call to translate the Bible into the English language, but he did not intend to stop there. He wanted a modern English-language translation to be published, widely distributed, and thus placed in the hands of the English people.[2]

Tyndale was supremely gifted for such a task. Born on a small farm near England's Welsh border between 1490 and 1494, he earned his bachelor's and master's degrees at Oxford, and also studied at Cambridge University. After joining the priesthood, he tutored and taught, serving as an instructor at Cambridge, and also preached for several years, earning a reputation for dynamic, Bible-based sermons. His extensive knowledge of Greek and Hebrew eventually earned him a reputation as a scholar. In 1522, he became a tutor and chaplain for one of King Henry's knights, Sir John Walsh, who lived in England's Gloucestershire region. While there, Tyndale impressed Sir John by translating a doctrinal paper by the scholar Erasmus from Latin into English. His superb translator's skills, it was said, even gained him notice within the king's court.[3]

Sixteenth-century English scholar William Tyndale was fluent in Hebrew, Greek and Latin—and felt compelled to publish the Bible in English. When condemned by a fellow clergyman, he vowed: "I will cause a boy that driveth the plow shall know more of the Scriptures than thou dost." Source: Wikimedia Commons.

> ## "I will cause a boy that driveth the plow shall know more of the Scriptures than thou dost."

His reputation with the Church and the state was soon clouded, however, by reports of his criticism of church doctrines adopted in the Middle Ages. At a dinner table debate with Tyndale in Sir John's manor, a clergyman passionately proclaimed, "We were better to be without God's law than the pope's." In response, Tyndale reportedly vowed, "I defy the Pope and all his laws. If God spare my life, ere many years I will cause a boy that driveth the plow shall know more of the Scriptures than thou dost." Obtaining permission to translate the Bible into English in the 1520s, however, was no small challenge: Church officials still did not trust laypeople to read or hear the Bible without a priest's supervision. Even so, Tyndale was hopeful that the church would finally allow a modern English translation of the Scriptures. Wycliffe's Bible had set the precedent, but it was written in Middle English, produced in few numbers, and banned from readership. As elsewhere in western Europe, the Bible was available almost exclusively in Latin, which few common people could read—and private Bible reading was discouraged by Church leaders. In 1522, Tyndale traveled to London and requested permission from Cuthbert Tunstall, the new Catholic bishop of London—but Tunstall adamantly refused.[4]

Disappointed but still determined, Tyndale took advantage of being in London to meet with some affluent cloth merchants who shared his interest in an English-language Bible—and they offered to finance his translation work outside England. So equipped, Tyndale traveled secretly to Germany in 1524, where he might have met with Martin Luther at Wittenberg—a meeting that may have sealed suspicions of Tyndale's Protestant theology within Henry VIII's court. Back in London, the king's confidant and chancellor, Sir Thomas More, was jailing and interrogating English Protestants, whom he claimed had confessed that Tyndale was engaged in a "confederacy" with the despised author of the Ninety-Five Theses. Within England's highest realm of power, William Tyndale had become a marked man. Meanwhile, working undercover in Germany, Tyndale focused on completing his English translation of the Scriptures, beginning with the New Testament. A year later he was ready to publish, and made arrangements with a printer in Cologne. Soon the long-awaited New Testament was coming off the presses—the first Bible mass-produced in the modern English language. It was also the first pocket-sized New Testament in history, and was perfectly designed to slip into the reader's clothing if necessary. While printing was under way, however, a drunken press worker revealed the project, and Catholic officials in Germany persuaded law enforcement authorities to raid the print shop. When the printing press was shut down, the translation was halted at Matthew 22:12: "And the man was speechless." Tyndale fled to the Reformation-friendly city of Worms, and there he engaged another printer. Finally, in 1526, he published the first printed English New Testament. Although he is believed to have consulted the Vulgate and Luther's German translation, Tyndale/s work was apparently done directly from the Greek—most likely from Erasmus's Greek text. It was produced in an edition of six thousand copies, and to smuggle it into England, Tyndale and his associates had it hidden in shipments of cloth.[5]

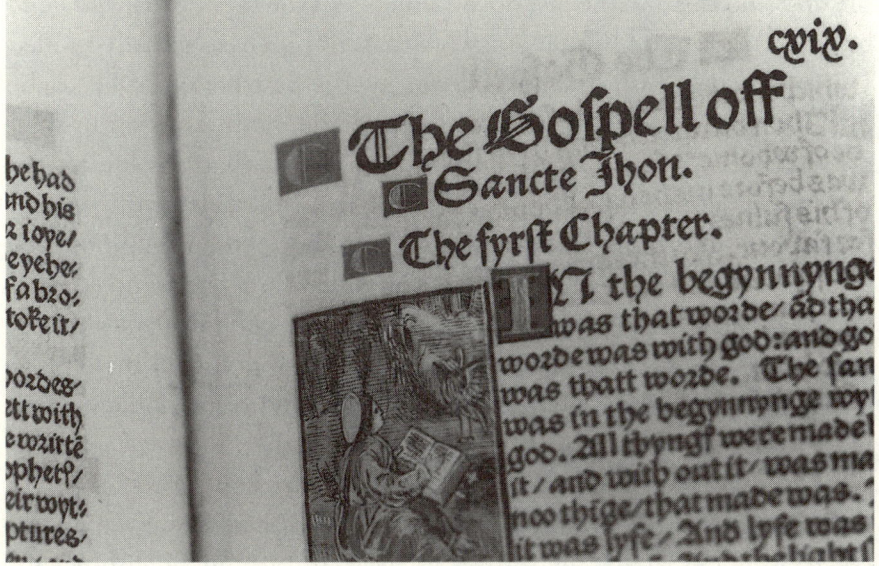

The Tyndale Bible, replicated here with the opening page of the Gospel of John, would affect English-language Bible translation for the next five centuries—and would flavor the English language with elegant and enduring phrases. Source: Kevin Rawlings/Wikimedia Commons British Library.

When the pocket-size New Testament began appearing in England, Church officials were outraged. They ardently opposed enabling the common people to read Scripture themselves, which Tyndale's Bible made possible, and they were also infuriated by the commentary in the Bible's margin notes. There—with the zeal of an Old Testament prophet—Tyndale denounced the controversial doctrines of the Roman Church. Officials of Church and state in England concurred: Tyndale and his Bible had to be silenced. Led by Thomas More and the Catholic bishop of London, Cuthbert Tunstall, a campaign was launched to track down the Bibles before most of the shipment was dispersed. Bishop Tunstall enlisted the aid of an English printer named Augustine Packington, who had connections with printers in Antwerp, and offered to buy all the Tyndale Bibles that the printer could obtain. Packington agreed—but he was secretly a friend of Tyndale's. Perhaps believing the Bibles were likely to be confiscated anyway, he rounded up a large quantity and sold them to the bishop, and then sent the money to Tyndale so he could print more Bibles. Unaware that his purchase actually funded Tyndale's work, Bishop Tunstall oversaw the destruction of his cache of Bibles in a bonfire outside St. Paul's Cathedral in London in sight of St. Paul's Cross, an open-air preaching pulpit that was located on the site. "Bishop Tunstall got [a Bible]," reported nineteenth-century British historian Eugene Stock, "took it into the open-air pulpit outside St. Paul's Cathedral, declared that it contained three thousand errors—and flung it into a fire burning nearby." Several book dealers who had been arrested for distributing Tyndale's Bible were forced by Church officials to ride to the Bible-burning sitting backwards on donkeys, with pages from the banned Bible pasted to their bodies.[6]

Although thousands of Tyndale's Bibles were consumed by flames, thousands also made it into the hands of the English people. Even if most copies were destroyed, the impact of the Scriptures in English eventually transformed England. Once unleashed in the people's language, the Word of God assumed a life of its own over time, and no king or church official could roll back the tide. It breathed life into the infant English

Reformation, which eventually swept through England as a mighty wind of revival. "Everywhere might be heard the eager conversation of minds enlightened by the truth," wrote English historian Edward B. Underhill. "The street, the tavern, the ale house, the church and every company were the scenes of earnest dispute or holy zeal. Scripture was compared to Scripture, and its sense closely scrutinized. The night of superstition retired before the morning dawn." John Strype, a seventeenth-century English historian, concurred. "Everybody that could bought the book, busily read it or got others to read it to them, and divers more elderly people learned to read on purpose," he reported. "And even little boys flocked among the rest to hear portions of the holy Scriptures read." One of those little boys was William Maldon, who—as an old man—told chronicler John Foxe how he came to hear the Bible read in English for the first time, and how it affected him. Foxe's account:

> Several poor men in the town of Chelmsford in Essex, where his father lived and where he was born, bought the New Testament and on Sundays sat reading it. . . . Many would flock about them to hear their reading, and he among the rest—being but fifteen years old—came every Sunday to hear the glad and sweet tidings of the Gospel. But his father, observing it, angrily snatched him away . . . which much grieved him. And as he returned at other times to hear the Scriptures read, his father still would fetch him away.
>
> This put him upon the thoughts of learning to read English, so he might read the New Testament himself. When this he had by diligence affected, he and his father's apprentice bought the New Testament together, and to conceal it, laid it under the bed-straw and read it at convenient times. One night his father [discovered his secret Bible-reading] and like a mad zealot, taking him by the hair of his head pulled him out of his bed and whipped him unmercifully. And when the young man, as he related, bore this beating with a kind of joy, considering it was for Christ's sake, his father was more enraged, and ran down and fetched a halter and put it about [the boy's] neck, saying he would hang him. At length, with much entreaty from the mother and a brother, he left him, almost dead. [7]

Determined to restrict the Bible to Latin and discourage personal Bible reading, church officials burn copies of Tyndale's New Testament outside St. Paul's Cathedral in London. Despite attempts to suppress it, Tyndale's Bible opened the Scriptures to the English people. Source: *The Story of the Advance of Christianity* / Wikimedia Commons.

In 1534, Tyndale revised and republished his English-language New Testament, which was again slipped into England. He appears to have published more editions in 1535 and 1536. An estimated eighteen thousand copies of Tyndale's New Testament are believed to have been printed—along with an unknown number of unauthorized copies, including a pirated version by George Joye, who was one of his assistants. In one form or another, Tyndale's New Testament spilled into England from various origins and directions, and its influence on English culture proved immeasurable. Even as his New Testament was transforming the English people, Tyndale was passionately working on a translation of the Old Testament, beginning with the Pentateuch—the first five books of the Old Testament—which was published in 1530. He followed that groundbreaking work with a translation of the book of Jonah a year later. Not only was he the first to publish an English-language version of the New Testament; he was also the first to translate the Old Testament into English directly from Hebrew, which was a milestone in the history of the Bible.[8]

His work required an impressive knowledge of Greek, Hebrew, and Latin, if not a mastery of all, and his graceful command of the English language would win praise from linguists and writers for centuries to come. "The effect," noted a twenty-first-century observer, "was the creation of an English style of Bible translation, tinged with Hebraisms, that was to serve as the model for all future English versions for nearly 400 years." He also shaped the English language, arguably, perhaps even more than William Shakespeare by translating from Greek and Hebrew into English with simple but elegant language. For instance, where Wycliffe had translated God's creative command in Genesis 1:3 as "Be made light, and made is light," Tyndale translated it as: "Let there be light: and there was light." Centuries after his epic work was first published, numerous English phrases from Tyndale's Bible would continue to be quoted, often unknowingly, by countless English speakers. Among the familiar and enduring phrases:

- "in the twinkling of an eye" (1 Corinthians 15:52)

- "apple of his eye" (Deuteronomy 32:10)

- "fell flat on his face" (Numbers 22:31)

- "nothing new under the sun" (Ecclesiastes 1:9)

- "Let my people go" (Exodus 9:1)

- "the powers that be" (Romans 13:1)

- "signs of the times" (Matthew 16:3)

- "Am I my brother's keeper?" (Genesis 4:9)

- "lick the dust" (Psalms 72:9)

- "eat, drink, and be merry" (Luke 12:19)

- "The spirit...is willing, but the flesh is weak" (Matthew 26:41)

- "and the truth shall make you free" (John 8:32)

Tyndale's single-minded focus was not crafting graceful language or establishing long-enduring English phrases; it was, instead, sharing the truth of Scripture—especially the gospel of Jesus Christ—with the English-speaking people of the world. "So now the scripture is a light and showeth us the true way, both what to do and what to hope," he wrote. "Seek therefore in the scripture as thou readest it first the law, what God commandeth us to do. And secondarily the promises, which God promiseth us again, namely in Jesus Christ our Lord." [9]

Meanwhile, back in England, the Bible-burning at St. Paul's Cathedral provoked a public outcry from the common people. Wary of rising support for the Reformation, Church authorities shifted to a different strategy to capture Tyndale: they would find him by arresting and interrogating his friends and associates. Driving the campaign were Bishop Tunstall and Catholic cardinal Thomas Wolsey. A butcher's son, Wolsey had risen to powerful positions in both the Church and the state: he was appointed archbishop by Pope Leo X and Lord Chancellor by Henry VIII. His high ecclesiastical and government posts were awarded to him despite his reputation for greed, hypocrisy, and immorality—Wolsey had amassed a measure of wealth second only to the king's, and he had also fathered two illegitimate children. Like Tunstall, Wolsey unleashed all the powers of his office to silence William Tyndale and suppress his English Bible.[10]

England's King Henry VIII appears in regal finery as painted by sixteenth-century Renaissance artist Hans Holbein. King Henry persecuted both Protestants and Catholics, but, ironically, Bible-printing flourished during his reign and fueled the English Reformation. Source: Library of Congress.

Tunstall and Wolsey were aided in their efforts by Thomas More, now King Henry's brilliant statesman, royal secretary, and powerful court advisor, who became obsessed with catching Tyndale. A prolific author and the king's chief spokesman, More was a committed Catholic. He steadfastly agreed with the leadership of the Roman Church that allowing the common man to read the Bible in his own language—and interpret it himself—threatened both the integrity of Scripture and the authority of the Church to control doctrine. "More insisted that the church could not err in one jot or tittle," according to Tyndale biographer David Daniell. "Tyndale declared, from scripture itself, that scripture belongs to the whole body of Christian people, guided by the Holy Spirit in their congregations, and the activities of the church have to be based on, and judged by, scripture." More, Wolsey, and Tunstall targeted anyone who had a connection with the Protestant Bible translator. One of Tyndale's chief benefactors was arrested for suspected heresy and was jailed in the Tower of London. Other friends were placed in stocks, tortured, and interrogated. The English reformer John Frith, a protégé of Tyndale's who helped with his translation in Germany, was imprisoned when he returned to England and was eventually burned at the stake, where winds diffused the fire and prolonged his suffering for two hours. Common people who were found with Tyndale's Bible in their possession were fined or jailed, and some suffered physical harm. Tyndale, however, remained elusive, moving from city to city in Germany. Unable to lay hands on the Bible translator, More engaged him in a published war of words in pamphlets, denouncing him as "a hell-hound in the kennel of the devil" who discharged "a filthy foam of blasphemies from his brutish beastly mouth." Tyndale countered in print with searing logic, biting wit, and powerful arguments from Scripture.[11]

As the war waged by the Church and state on Tyndale intensified, Henry VIII denounced Tyndale's English New Testament as intended to "infect the people," and earned the title "Defender of the Faith" from Pope Clement VII for opposing the "Lutheran heresy" of the rapidly spreading Reformation. The "Defender" of the Roman Church soon rebelled against it, however; but not for biblical reasons: The king wanted a divorce, and the pope did not want to grant it. Henry VIII was desperate for a male heir and determined to marry his beguiling mistress, Anne Boleyn. To do so, he needed to divorce his wife—Catherine of Aragon—who had delivered a daughter, Princess Mary, but had repeatedly miscarried without producing a son. For ecclesiastical and political reasons, the pope denied the king's request for a marriage annulment.

In response, Henry VIII broke from the Roman Church, married Anne Boleyn, and in 1534 declared himself head of the Church of England, or Anglican Church. He then turned against his Catholic advisors; first Cardinal Wolsey in 1530, then More in 1534. In a shocking turn of events, both were banished from the king's court. Wolsey died in disgrace soon afterwards, and the mercurial king ordered More beheaded in 1535, following a sham trial for treason.[12]

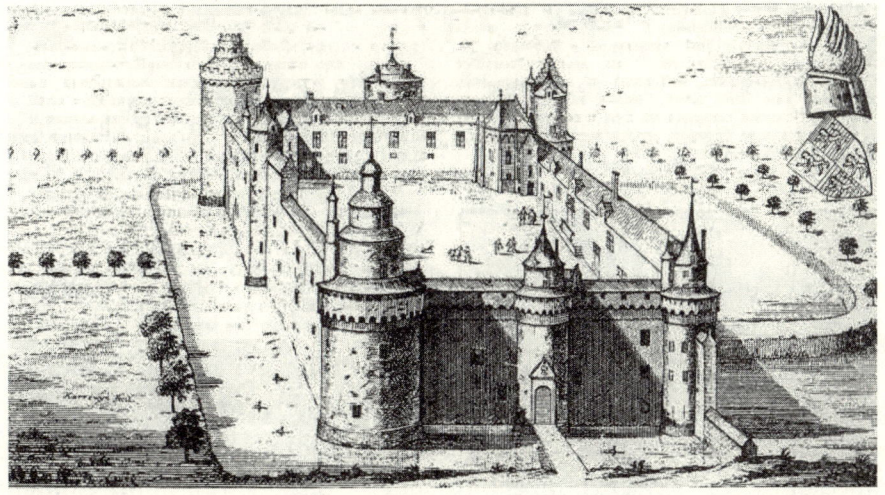

Bleak and bare, Vilvoorde Castle rises above the Belgian lowlands in this seventeenth century illustration. It was here, in gloomy, miserable conditions, that William Tyndale awaited his fate for publishing an English-language Bible. Source: Castella et Praetoria Probilium Brabantiae / Wikimedia Commons.

Tyndale, meanwhile, had moved to Antwerp in Flanders—in what would later become Belgium—and there he lived in hiding and worked on an English translation of the Old Testament. His translation of the Pentateuch—the first five books of the Bible—secretly reached England in 1530. Reading it, English believers were exposed for the first time to the famous words of the creation account—"Let there be light"—and other truths of Scripture. With Wolsey and More gone, some of Tyndale's supporters urged him to return to England. He declined. He considered many of Henry VIII's actions to be ungodly, and in a small book he boldly denounced the king's divorce as unbiblical even though it had aided the Reformation that Tyndale so passionately sought. Even so, Tyndale had the sympathies of the king's powerful new Protestant advisor, Thomas Cromwell, a former Catholic churchman and advisor to Cardinal Wolsey. Cromwell had embraced the Reformation as a means of establishing England's national sovereignty, was guiding the king in his break with the Church in Rome, and believed that Tyndale could prove useful if recruited back to England. Henry VIII, however, was incensed by Tyndale's public condemnation of his divorce as biblically groundless, and continued to view him as a menace.[13]

Even without Cardinal Wolsey and Sir Thomas More, the campaign to trap and silence Tyndale had gained momentum of its own—and a new adversary who was just as determined as More and Wolsey to capture and punish Tyndale. His name was John Stokesley, and he had succeeded Cuthbert Tunstall as the bishop of London—a former Catholic post that had become an Anglican office under King Henry's new Church of England. Known for his "cold, stern demeanor," Stokesley was ruthlessly pragmatic: he craftily supported Henry's divorce and the break from Rome, but was fanatically determined to undermine the theology of the Reformation and install Catholic doctrine in the Church of England. He died before he could succeed, but he relentlessly ordered one Protestant after another to be burned at the stake for heresy—and one of his chief targets was William Tyndale.[14]

In the spring of 1535, Tyndale was living in exile at a safe house in Antwerp, which afforded him a measure of safety because it was a free city with laws that prohibited arbitrary arrests of citizens and residents. The region was part of the gigantic Holy Roman Empire, governed by Emperor Charles V, a Catholic regent who considered Tyndale to be a heretic worthy of death. Tyndale may have underestimated the threat from the emperor because Charles was no friend of Henry VIII—it was his sister Catherine that Henry had divorced to marry Anne Boleyn. Evidence suggests that Tyndale also believed Henry VIII's self-serving decision to allow the Reformation to blossom in England reduced the dangers he faced in Antwerp. "The rigor of the laws against so-called heresy had been relaxed," observed one of Tyndale's earliest biographers, "and that great work on which Tyndale had so long labored, instead of being regarded with bitter hostility, had come to be considered as necessary and praiseworthy." However, whether originally dispatched by Wolsey, More, or Stokesley on behalf of King Henry; sent by the church hierarchy, or hired by Charles V, agents intent on capturing Tyndale were still in the field—and one of them was a money-hungry ne'er-do-well Englishman named Henry Phillips. Professing support for the Reformation, he befriended Tyndale, and at an opportune moment he lured the unsuspecting translator out of his safe house. When the two were alone on a narrow alley in Antwerp, Phillips signaled waiting accessories, who seized, bound, and kidnapped Tyndale. He was imprisoned in Belgium's Vilvoorde castle near Brussels, a gloomy, impregnable-looking fortress that lay in a region governed by magistrates hostile to the Reformation. There Tyndale waited in miserable conditions for the inevitable execution.[15]

"For Christ also suffered for us, leaving us an example that we should follow in his steps."

Henry VIII's new Protestant advisor, Thomas Cromwell, attempted to free Tyndale, writing to the appropriate authorities. However, Henry had little interest in saving the troublesome Bible translator and was preoccupied by his designs on a potential new wife and possible methods of getting rid of Anne Boleyn, his current one. Meanwhile, Tyndale was tried and convicted in an anti-Reformation local court council for "having infringed the imperial decree which forbids anyone to teach that faith alone justifies" one for salvation. Tyndale freely admitted to the "crime"—that he indeed believed in salvation by faith alone based on the truth of Scripture. "Yes," he told his accusers, "we believe, and are at peace in our consciences, because that God who cannot lie, hath promised to forgive us for Christ's sake." He was condemned by the council for heresy, and remained in prison for a year and a half, striving to demonstrate faithfulness to the Savior he served, and struggling to continue his translation work even in the cold, harsh conditions of his captivity. Surely he remembered the words he had written earlier to his friend John Frith when he was awaiting the deadly flames: "Your cause is Christ's Gospel, a light that must be fed with the blood of faith. For Christ also suffered for us, leaving us an example that we should follow in his steps, who did no sin. Hereby have we perceived love, that he laid down his life for us; therefore we ought also to lay down our lives for the brethren. Rejoice and be glad, for great is your reward in heaven."[16]

In his only surviving letter, written in Latin to the authority who oversaw his imprisonment, Tyndale noted that "it is wearisome to sit alone in the dark," and requested warm clothes, translators' tools—and the Hebrew Bible:

> I entreat your Lordship, and that by the Lord Jesus, that if I am to remain here . . . during the winter, you will request the Procurer to be kind enough to send me from my goods, which he has in his possession, a warmer cap, for I suffer extremely from cold in the head, being afflicted with a perpetual catarrh, which is considerably increased in the cell. A warmer coat also, for that which I have is very thin; also a piece of cloth to patch my leggings: my overcoat has been worn out; my shirts are also worn out. He has a woolen shirt of mine, if he will be kind enough to send it. I have also with him leggings of thicker cloth for the putting on above; he also has warmer caps for wearing at night. I wish also his permission to have a candle in the evening, for it is wearisome to sit alone in the dark.
>
> But above all, I entreat and beseech your clemency to be urgent with the Procurer that he may kindly permit me to have my Hebrew Bible, Hebrew Grammar, and Hebrew Dictionary, that I may spend my time with that study. And in return, may you obtain your dearest

wish, provided always it be consistent with the salvation of your soul. But if any other resolutions have been come to concerning me, before the conclusion of the winter, I shall be patient, abiding the will of God to the glory of the grace of my Lord Jesus Christ, whose spirit, I pray, may ever direct your heart. Amen.

Despite his plight, Tyndale remained eager to share the gospel, as chronicler John Foxe recorded: "Such was the power of his doctrine, and the sincerity of his life that during the time of his imprisonment . . . he converted his keeper, the keeper's daughter, and others of their household."[17]

No authority ever officially claimed responsibility for Tyndale's capture, but many had wanted him dead. A comment reportedly made by one of his prosecutors reflected the hostility toward the Reformation by some members of the established Church. "It is no great matter whether they that die on account of religion be guilty or innocent," the official coldly stated, "provided we terrify the people by such examples." Finally, it was Tyndale's time. One day in early October 1536, he was taken to the castle courtyard and burned at the stake. As an act of mercy, he was choked to death before the flames consumed his body. It was said that he met his death with a calm reliance on the Christ proclaimed by the Scriptures he had translated and published in English. Standing atop a cross-shaped pile of kindling, brush, and firewood, a chain garrote around his neck, William Tyndale was given an opportunity to deny his faith. Instead, he boldly pronounced his famous last words: "Lord! Open the King of England's eyes."[18]

As helpers gather fuel to burn his body, Bible translator William Tyndale is choked to death by an executioner. His last words: "Lord! Open the King of England's eyes." Source: *Story of the Advance of Christianity* / Wikimedia Commons.

8

THE HOLY BIBLE IN THEIR

MOTHER TONGUE

And . . . the sword of the Spirit . . . is the word of God.
—EPHESIANS 6:17

EVEN AS WILLIAM TYNDALE PRAYED HIS DYING PRAYER, an answer to it appeared to be unfolding in distant England. Despite all the attempts to suppress Tyndale's New Testament, thousands of copies made it into circulation in England—and in 1535, while he was still in prison, a complete English-language Bible reached the English people. It was the work of one of Tyndale's associates, Miles Coverdale, and it became known as the Coverdale Bible. It was composed of Tyndale's New Testament translation, plus an Old Testament translation drawn from the Vulgate, another Latin work, and Martin Luther's German translation. Like other Protestant translations, it distinguished the Apocrypha from the inspired Old Testament books, and thus set a precedent for future English Bibles. Coverdale was no Tyndale: he had a limited knowledge of Hebrew and Greek at best, and what he had not borrowed from Tyndale for his Bible—admittedly most of it—was translated from

Latin and German. Even so, it was the first English-language Bible to contain both the Old and New Testaments.[1]

Scripture quotations and scenes from the Bible decorate the title page of the 1535 Coverdale Bible. Published by Miles Coverdale, one of Tyndale's associates, while Tyndale was imprisoned, it was the first complete English-language Bible. Source: New York Public Library.

The new Bible had no royal backing, but Coverdale had shrewdly dedicated it to Henry VIII, and unlike Tyndale's work, it contained no provocative commentary notes. Its illustrated title page depicted King Henry as a divinely appointed monarch conveying a Bible to grateful church leaders. In contrast to the uproar and opposition from church and state that had accompanied Tyndale's New Testament, the Coverdale Bible entered England without opposition. The Church of England was now the nation's official faith, and no one—neither King Henry nor Anglican officials—attempted to suppress the new Bible. Sales were brisk, and copies soon circulated throughout the country. Even Queen Anne Boleyn was said to have been reading the Bible in English before she fell into disfavor and was beheaded by King Henry. In 1537, Coverdale published a revised edition, which stated that it was printed under "the king's most gracious license." King Henry's tacit endorsement was due in large measure to royal advisor Thomas Cromwell, who may have had mixed reasons for promoting the Bible—both political and ecclesiastical. Regardless of the motives of the self-serving king and his chief advisor, the English people in growing numbers embraced the Reformation and the English-language Bibles it produced.[2]

In 1537, another English Bible appeared in England without opposition. It became known as the Matthew Bible. It too was the work of a Tyndale associate, his close friend John Rogers, to whom the imprisoned Tyndale had bequeathed his unpublished Old Testament translations. Rogers used them to compile the new Bible's Old Testament, supplementing them with books from the Coverdale Bible—and a New Testament that was Tyndale's final revision. The Bible cited neither Rogers nor Tyndale, giving credit instead to a Thomas Matthew—which is believed to have been an alias or pen name for John Rogers. The Matthew Bible too was dedicated to the "most noble and gracious Prynce Henry the Eyght"—which may have been done to encourage the Bible's royal acceptance. To the Bible-starved English people, both the Coverdale Bible and the Matthew Bible were greatly welcome. Thus, within one year of his death, William Tyndale's Bible, in two versions and under different names, was widely dispersed and enthusiastically embraced throughout England.[3]

More Bible translations followed. While the Coverdale Bible was well received by the public, knowledgeable clergy were less enthusiastic because large parts of it were not translated from the original languages. Miles Coverdale was an editor, not a translator, and those who supported the Reformation were not as enthusiastic about the Coverdale Bible. Coverdale had rendered doctrinal terms in a manner pleasing to officials in the Church of England, many of whom still favored Catholic doctrines. For instance, he changed Tyndale's more accurate translation of angels rejoicing over "one synner that repenteth" in Luke 15:7 to "one sinner that doth pennaunce." Meanwhile, John Rogers's translation—the Matthew Bible—came to rankle some Catholic-leaning Anglican clergymen when they discovered it contained margin notes expressing Reform theology. One problem that both Bibles had in common was that knowledgeable readers could see that each reflected the work of William Tyndale—whose criticism of King Henry's conduct remained fresh in the memory of the mercurial ruler. Would clergymen who embraced the Bibles be at risk of a royal mood swing? Diplomatically, King Henry's chief advisor, Vicar General Thomas Cromwell, arranged for publication of a new, officially commissioned English Bible. He was supported by Thomas Cranmer, the Anglican archbishop of Canterbury, who would play a major role in developing the new Church of England as a Protestant church. To produce the new Bible, Cromwell and Cranmer chose Miles Coverdale.[4]

Coverdale produced a skillfully crafted pulpit Bible—so large that it became known as the Great Bible—and it was off the presses in 1539 within less than a year. "This is the Byble apoynted to the use of the churches," it officially stated. Coverdale had consulted Hebrew and Greek scholars to render a more accurate translation, The Great Bible contained no controversial margin notes, Hebrew and Greek scholars had strengthened its English text, and it had no obvious connection to William Tyndale. In reality, however, it too was a revision of William

Tyndale's superb translation—just a more elaborate version, with some notable variations. If King Henry's advisors realized that the Great Bible reflected Tyndale's work, they officially ignored that distinction. The Great Bible became the officially approved version of the Scriptures for Henry VIII's kingdom. The new Bible went through numerous editions, and English clergy were advised to display the Bible in every church—and even to encourage the people to come in and read it for themselves. The royal court officially proclaimed: "Englishmen have now in hand, in every church and place, almost every man, the Holy Bible and New Testament in their mother tongue."[5]

Voluntarily or not—the king's eyes had indeed been opened—just as Tyndale had prayed.

One of the most remarkable aspects of the Great Bible was its frontispiece, which featured elaborate artwork that depicted the glory of God the Father—along with King Henry VIII and his royal advisors Cromwell and Cranmer. King Henry was depicted twice: once in the act of kneeling with his crown on the earth before him, signifying his apparent submission to the Word of God, and again, sitting on his throne, presenting the Bible to bishops on his right and secular leaders on his left. Clearly identifiable in the artwork was Archbishop Cranmer—depicted giving the Bible to a clergyman—and Cromwell, the king's statesman, shown presenting the Bible to a commoner. Also depicted is a minister, preaching to a multitude of joyful citizens celebrating the gift of the Bible in their own tongue. Within three years of William Tyndale's execution, King Henry had recognized and submitted to the will of the English people and had transformed himself from persecutor of the English-language Bible to its protector. His motive again may have been consistently self-serving, but—voluntarily or not—the king's eyes had indeed been opened—just as Tyndale had prayed.[6]

The Great Bible was immensely popular. In England's churches, so many people crowded around the open Bible during worship services that some clergy complained of difficulty preaching. More people were interested in hearing the Bible read by a peer than hearing a sermon by a preacher. In response, King Henry issued official regulations stating that no layperson could "openly read the bible or New Testament in the English tongue in any churches or chapels, or elsewhere, with any loud our high voice, and especially during the time of divine service." In 1543, he engaged in another royal whim and pushed the English Parliament into enacting the Act for the Advancement of True Religion, which restricted personal Bible reading to the gentry because, it claimed, "many ignorant and seditious people have abused the liberty granted them for reading the Bible." By then, Henry had turned on Thomas Cromwell and had ordered his valued advisor beheaded—a rash act that he later bemoaned. The Tyndale and Coverdale Bibles were singled out and royally denounced, and once again piles of Bibles were set ablaze outside St. Paul's Cathedral in London. Henry VIII's final attempt to restrict the Bible came too late, however; it outraged the English people and was repealed after the king's death. He died a few years later, in 1547—a grossly obese, emotionally disturbed, and unpopular ruler. In the end, he was overtaken by the spiritual revival he had unintentionally allowed to ignite—the English Reformation. And it would alter the course of history.[7]

§

When Henry VIII died, his nine-year-old son, Edward VI, assumed the throne of England. He was Henry's son by third wife Jane Seymour, who had replaced Anne Boleyn when her inability to bear a son led Henry to have her beheaded on questionable charges of adultery. (Seymour died of complications soon after birthing Edward, and Henry VIII would be married thrice more.) The boy-king was Protestant, and the guardians his king-father had set up to protect him allowed the English Reformation to go forward while they engaged in power plays, financial intrigue, and infighting. By the time he reached his teen years, Edward was a mild-mannered, intellectually brilliant young king who focused on theology, foreign languages, and expanding education in his realm, while his adult advisors mishandled much of the affairs of state. He was devout, and seriously Protestant in his theology—described by one observer as "a devoted adherent to the Reformed faith." While his advisors often sought to manipulate his youth and inexperience to achieve their own self-serving ends, they were careful not to challenge his personal faith. Early in his reign, his father's turnabout restrictions on Bible reading were repealed.[8]

King Edward VI was an intellectually brilliant, mild-mannered young monarch who was passionate about theology, foreign languages and expanding education in England. He was also a devout Protestant. His death at a young age ignited deadly turmoil in England. Source: New York Public Library.

In 1553, after reigning just a few years, the boy king developed tuberculosis and died at age fifteen. A scramble for the throne immediately ensued. According to the succession tradition, the rightful heir to the throne was Princess Mary Tudor, the only surviving child of King Henry's marriage to Catherine of Aragon. In his failed attempt to obtain papal permission to divorce Catherine so he could marry Anne Boleyn, King Henry had arranged to have his marriage declared illegal in England, which officially made his daughter Mary illegitimate—and inconvenient. She was removed from court as a child, never saw her mother again, and as young adult refused to recognize her father as the head of the Church of England. After Anne Boleyn's execution, however, she was reinstated to King Henry's court and named as second in line to the throne after her younger half brother Edward VI. Mary was ardently Catholic, and when young Edward died, she prepared to assume the throne and return England to Catholicism.[9]

As Edward was dying, his court advisors encouraged him to name an heir who would keep England Protestant. Henry VIII's sixteen-year-old grandniece, Lady Jane Grey—a devout Protestant—was persuaded to claim the throne despite her reluctance to do so. Almost effortlessly, Mary Tudor and her supporters overthrew the young queen after a nine-day rule, and the new regent took throne as Queen Mary I. Most of Lady Jane Grey's advisors and family quickly switched sides, announced their allegiances to Mary, and converted to Catholicism, but young Jane refused to recant as a matter of conscience. Seven months later, on February 12, 1554, she was executed at the Tower of London, reciting the entire fifty-first Psalm aloud as she knelt before the ax.[10]

Queen Mary's rule was brief—after a five-year reign she too sickened and died—but even so, it was a deadly rule for England's Protestants. London's Smithfield execution site was kept busy and aflame. More than three hundred Protestants were executed, with most burned at the stake. Under Mary's successor, Elizabeth I, approximately two hundred Catholics would be executed as traitors and would-be assassins, but those executions would occur over the span of a long reign. So many died so quickly under "Bloody Mary," as she became known, that Queen Mary's rule would be remembered as a reign of terror. "There was no precedent in England," a modern study concluded, "for heresy executions on this scale." First to die was the Reverend John Rogers, the translator of the Matthew Bible, who was executed at Smithfield—a stone's throw from his pastorate at London's St. Sepulchre Anglican Church—leaving behind a wife and ten children. Along with little-known pastors and numerous commoners, several other prominent Anglican leaders died in the flames, including three infamously executed at Oxford: London archbishop Nicholas Ridley, Worcester bishop Hugh Latimer, and former royal advisor Thomas Cranmer, who was also the archbishop of Canterbury. Fearing for his life, Cranmer signed a document converting to Catholicism and briefly became a trophy of Queen Mary's rule. He was sentenced to be burned anyway. At the stake he surprised his executioners by publicly reasserting his Protestant beliefs. He then thrust the hand with which he had signed his recantation confession into the flames, while loudly proclaiming, "This hand hath offended."[11]

Under Mary's reign, owning or reading Protestant literature was again forbidden, Tyndale's and Coverdale's Bibles were outlawed, private homes were searched for contraband books and pamphlets, and print shops were raided for works that offended "Holy Mother the Church." Amid all the persecution and restrictions, however, King Henry's authorized Great Bible was not recalled from the churches, nor was it banned. Even so, some of Queen Mary's Catholic supporters denounced all Bibles published in English. "Even the good catholic people, which would do good and no hurt with the Bible in English, yet should not be permitted to keep it in the English tongue," a prominent Catholic clergyman proclaimed. "The well must be covered lest the younglings fall into it and be drowned." Mary may have left the Great Bible untouched because her father had authorized it or because she feared the uproar that banning it would produce among the English people. She had married Philip II, the king of Spain—another Catholic regent—making him for a time the joint sovereign of England—an action that had provoked rising discontent among the English people. While Queen Mary's deadly reign increased religious persecution in England to an unprecedented scale, it destroyed neither the English Reformation nor the English people's newfound enthusiasm for the English-language Bible.[12]

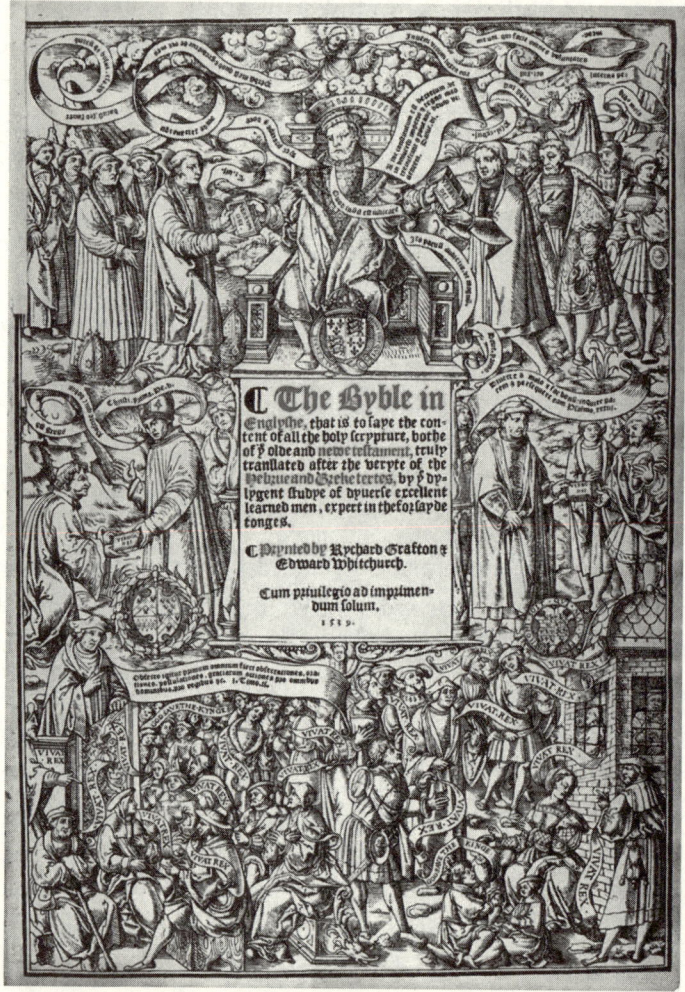

The 1539 Great Bible, which also the work of Miles Coverdale, received royal sanction by King Henry VIII, who then headed the Church of England. Its title page featured artwork of King Henry bestowing the Bible upon his clergy, who in turn pass it to the English people. Source: Wikimedia Commons.

§

To escape Queen Mary's persecution, scores of Protestant leaders, such as Miles Coverdale, fled England to Switzerland, which was an emerging Protestant stronghold. There, the city of Geneva became a safe haven for Protestant exiles—and the birthplace of a critical English-language Bible translation. Among the English exiles in Geneva was an Oxford Bible scholar named William Whittingham, who was brother-in-law to the wife of John Calvin, the brilliant, French Protestant Reformation leader who had made Geneva a center of Reformation thought and study. Born to an affluent English family, Whittingham was bright and inquisitive, and was admitted to Oxford University at age sixteen. In 1547—the year Henry VIII died—he was awarded an instructor's post at his alma mater even though he was only in his early twenties. He supported the English Reformation, and spent several years studying with Huguenot students and scholars in France, where he met and married the sister of John Calvin's wife. During the reign of Edward VI, he returned to England as a zealous Protestant who was dedicated to the English Reformation. When young King Edward died, Whittingham supported Lady Jane Grey's claim to the throne—a position that forced him to flee England when Queen Mary I began executing Protestants.[13]

He resettled in Frankfurt, Germany, where he helped administer a church pastored by the Scottish reformer John Knox, who was also a fugitive. Knox eventually moved to Geneva to pastor a Reformed church there, and—with John Calvin's encouragement—Whittingham joined him. Following the death of Queen Mary, Knox returned to Scotland, and Whittingham succeeded him as pastor of the church. While ministering in Geneva, Whittingham found himself surrounded by a community of English Protestant Bible scholars that included experts such as Coverdale, Christopher Goodman, and Anthony Gilby. It was a situation that he deemed providential, so he took the lead—with John Calvin's encouragement—in organizing a team of Bible experts to produce a new English-language translation of the Bible from the original Hebrew and Greek. The work was well under way when Queen

Mary died, and many of the translators felt free to return home, leaving Whittington to finish the translation and oversee its publication.[14]

In 1553, Queen Mary I—Henry VIII's daughter—inherited the throne of England, and unleashed the wave of executions that earned her the infamous name of "Bloody Mary." Under her reign the Tyndale Bible and Coverdale Bible were outlawed, but not the Great Bible officially authorized by her father. Source: Library of Congress.

It eventually became known as the Geneva Bible—although in its early days it was popularly known as the "Breeches Bible" because it translated Adam's and Eve's coverings in Genesis 3:7 as "breeches" instead of figleaf aprons. Printed in Geneva in 1560, the Geneva Bible was distinctive and innovative for a variety of reasons. First, it was not the work of a sole translator, but was the product of a translation team led by Whittingham. Second, while it was greatly influenced by William Tyndale's translation, the Geneva Bible featured numerous textual revisions made by the translation team. It also included the Old Testament books that Tyndale had been unable to translate and rendered them from Hebrew and Greek into English with pristine accuracy. The margin commentary notes were distinctively Calvinistic and reflected Reform theology, but were not as forceful as the notes in Tyndale's Bible. Even so, they did not spare the pope, who was identified as the beast of the end times "that cometh out of the bottomless pit" in the Book of Revelation.[14]

The Geneva Bible set other precedents for English-language Bibles: It organized the books of both the Old and New Testaments into chapters and verses—the first such structure in an English Bible—and it was first to set in italics words that were believed to have not been in the original inspired text. It was also printed in a clean, easy-to-read type font and in a smaller size that made it easier to handle. And it was affordably priced for a Bible. All of these features made the Geneva Bible tremendously popular with the English people, and it became the preferred family Bible in England. Even Anglican leaders and others who were uncomfortable with its margin commentary respected the Geneva Bible as an accurate translation of Scripture. It was the Bible most often quoted by William Shakespeare in his plays, and would become the common English-language Bible carried into the wilds of America in the opening days of English colonization. A century after it was introduced into England, it would be excerpted in a small volume entitled *The Soldier's Pocket Bible,* which would be issued to the Parliamentarian troops of Oliver Cromwell's New Model Army. Long after other English translations were available, the Geneva Bible would remain popular, and scores of editions would be published even into the twenty-first century. For many, it was *the* Bible of the English Reformation—and with so much of it influenced by Tyndale's work, the broad popularity of the Geneva Bible fulfilled his prophetic vow to the clergyman who challenged him: "If God spare my life, ere many years I will cause a boy that driveth the plow shall know more of the Scriptures than thou dost."[15]

§

By the time the Geneva Bible was ready for the printer, England had a new ruler: Queen Elizabeth I—and she was a Protestant. When Queen Mary died in 1558, Elizabeth was heir to the throne as Mary's half sister, the daughter of Henry VIII and Anne Boleyn. Until Mary's death, however, Princess Elizabeth could never be certain that her half sister would not order her killed, just as she had executed hundreds of other Protestants. In fact, as soon as she assumed the throne, Queen Mary expressed suspicions about Elizabeth, which led the twenty-year-old princess to fear that she might die much like Lady Jane Grey. On Palm Sunday of 1554, a gray and drizzly day, Elizabeth was led aboard a barge by guards and was rowed down the Thames River to the Tower of London, the imposing riverside fortress where enemies of the crown were incarcerated. Not many prisoners who entered its formidable walls ever left alive, including Elizabeth's mother, Anne. When the barge and its royal prisoner arrived at Traitors Gate—the water entrance to the prison—Elizabeth defiantly refused to get out, claiming that she was no traitor. Her guards nervously waited for orders while Elizabeth stubbornly sat in the rain—until she abruptly got up and went inside, stating aloud, "I pray you all bear me witness that I come in as no traitor." For two months, she remained imprisoned in the tower, daily pacing the walls within sight of the tower green, where her mother had been beheaded. Finally, Queen Mary decided to spare the princess's life and banished her to house arrest in a dilapidated manor.[16]

Elizabeth survived to inherit the throne, and was crowned in January 1559, amid grand pageantry that included the presentation of a Bible—which she solemnly kissed, held aloft with both hands, and then clasped above her heart. Beginning there, at age twenty-five, she would establish the Elizabethan era, in which England would dramatically increase its stature as a major world power—and a Protestant nation. She would do so with compromise and political savvy rather than the bloodshed that had tainted Queen Mary's rule, although many who conspired against her life during her long reign—Catholic and otherwise—did face the executioner. She established what would become known as the Elizabethan Religious Settlement, designed to reunite a bloodied and divided nation. The Church of England was solidly set as England's official government denomination—the state church—and it would reflect the Queen's compromise by retaining Protestant doctrine while keeping Catholic-style worship ceremony and traditions.[17]

As depicted in this seventeenth century woodcut, Bible translator and pastor John Rogers is burned at the stake at London's Smithfield execution site, within an easy walk of his church. The first to die in Queen Mary's purge, he left behind a wife and ten children. Source: *Ecclesiastical History* / Wikimedia Commons.

When Elizabeth I became queen, she hoped her compromise would mollify the nation's Catholics, but they were denied freedom to openly worship according to their consciences, and decades of religious tension continued. Adding to the conflict were several Catholic plots on the queen's life, and a Catholic-led rebellion arose in northern England. Most English Catholics refused to join the uprising, however, and those who did were harshly suppressed by royal troops. In 1570, Pope Pius V officially excommunicated Elizabeth from the Catholic Church, describing her as "the servant of wickedness," and called for Catholic nations such as Spain and France to invade England and restore it to Catholicism. A decade later, Pope Gregory XIII proclaimed that the queen's assassination would not be a sin. Elizabeth survived all assassination attempts, and England's powerful navy decisively repulsed a Spanish invasion by defeating the Spanish Armada in 1588—leaving England securely Protestant.[18]

The new translation was welcomed by Catholic leaders in Rome, who put aside decades of opposition.

All the conflict, however, resulted in a repression of Catholicism in England that would last for centuries. Over the course of five years, according to one record, eighteen Catholic priests were executed, Catholic bookstores were shut down, and the printing of Catholic literature was suppressed. Amid such tensions, many English Catholics of means fled the country, and—as happened with the Protestant exiles to Geneva in Queen Mary's reign—some of the Catholic exiles produced a new Bible translation. The effort was led by two devout Catholic scholars from Oxford University, William Allen and Gregory Martin, who had fled England for France, and together they produced an English-language New Testament in 1582. The new translation was welcomed by Catholic leaders in Rome, who put aside decades of opposition to vernacular translations so that an English-language Catholic Bible could provide an alternative to the English Bibles produced by Protestants. It was intended mainly for use by Catholic priests—but it was meant to be read aloud to worshippers during the mass. "To meet the Protestant challenge," the new Bible's preface stated, "priests must be ready to quote Scripture in the vulgar tongue since their adversaries have every favourable passage at their fingers."[19]

To escape persecution and possible death under the reign of Queen Mary I, scores of Protestants fled England. Some of them established a colony of Christian exiles in Geneva, Switzerland, where Reformation leader John Calvin had established a ministry base. Source: Wikimedia Commons.

More than twenty years later, the Old Testament was added to the Allen-Martin translation, and the work collectively became known as the Douay-Rheims Bible—named for the cities in France where the translation work was done. Like Tyndale's Bible and the Geneva Bible, it contained margin notes—although the commentary reflected the doctrinal positions of Catholicism and sharply critiqued Protestant doctrine. The Douay-Rheims Bible was based mainly on the Latin Vulgate instead of the Hebrew and Greek, making it a translation of a translation. Even so, it gained the long-lasting respect of Catholic leaders and laity, and enabled the Church's priests to present Scripture to countless English-speaking people in their own language. Despite some awkward language in the translation of Latin into English, enthusiasts of the Douay-Rheims Bible praised it for "terse, close, vigorous grand old English." In 1749, Richard Challoner, a Catholic bishop and Bible scholar in London, would revise and update the Bible's text, and the Douay-Rheims Bible would become the preferred Bible for English-speaking Catholics throughout the world until the twentieth century.[20]

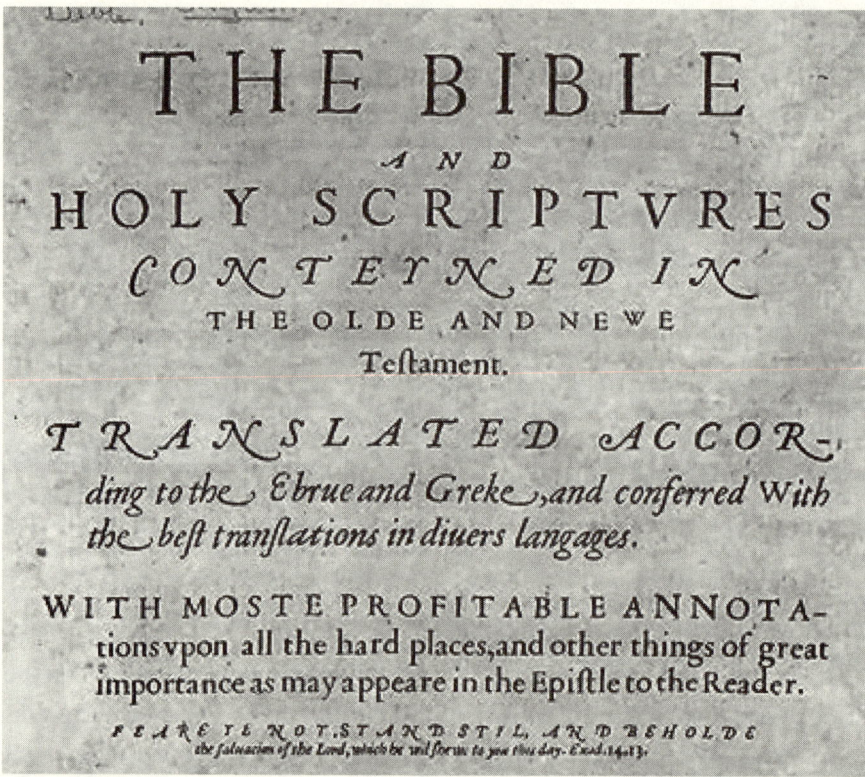

The 1560 Geneva Bible was the work of a team of English translators who had fled to Switzerland during Queen Mary's reign. Their work was directed by Oxford scholar William Whittingham, a fellow exile, and would be the preferred version of the Bible for many English Protestants for more than a century. Source: Library of Congress.

In England, meanwhile, as the Protestant movement matured, it produced two distinct lines of Bible-based believers—the mainstream Anglicans and diverging sects of Protestants who would come to be known as "Dissenters" or "Non-conformists" because they did not agree with the Church of England in all matters of doctrine and practice. As the official head of the Church of England, Queen Elizabeth I championed its doctrines and ceremonies, although she allowed a measure of dissent by other Protestants. One problem for the Church leadership, however, was the popularity of the Geneva Bible: Anglican leaders recognized its text as a superior translation to the Great Bible of 1539, but many considered its margin commentary too Calvinistic. The Church of England needed a new translation of the Bible, it was decided, and the current archbishop of Canterbury, Matthew Parker, was put in charge of producing a new English translation. Anglican bishops were asked to contribute to the work, and two years later, in 1568, the work was complete. Understandably, the new translation became known as the Bishops' Bible.[21]

Parker was a competent Bible scholar and an experienced leader. A supporter of Lady Jane Grey for the throne, he had been forced into hiding during Queen Mary's reign, but was later promoted to archbishop by Queen Elizabeth. Although he was knowledgeable and an able translator, and original languages were consulted, the bishops were equipped to the task to varying degrees. The result was a version that was reputable, and was an improvement on the Great Bible—but was not as precisely translated as the Geneva Bible. Even so, Anglican leaders preferred it over the Geneva Bible because its few margin notes were not Calvinistic. Queen Elizabeth was reportedly pleased, pronounced it the new authorized version of the Bible, and ordered it placed in all Anglican churches. The frontispiece of the Bible featured an image of the queen and figures representing hope and charity.[22]

Queen Elizabeth I, depicted here at different ages, stabilized England with the Elizabethan Religious Settlement, which established the Church of England with Protestant doctrine and Catholic ceremony. She also authorized a new English translation—the Bishops' Bible. Source: Library of Congress.

In 1568, when the Bishops' Bible was published, barely four decades had passed since the first edition of William Tyndale's English Bible had been smuggled into the country, and now the English people could freely read a variety of Bibles in their own language. In English hands somewhere in the nation were various editions of Tyndale's Bible, the Coverdale Bible, the Matthew Bible, the Great Bible, the Geneva Bible, and now the Bishops' Bible. As William Tyndale had fervently hoped, many a plow-boy in England now understood the truths of God's Word through one of the English-language Bibles. Within a few more decades, by the early 1600s, the full impact of the availability of Scripture would cause England to be awash in a flood of faith. "The whole moral effect . . . was simply amazing," renowned English historian John Richard Green would observe. "The whole nation became a church." And yet, despite the determined attempts of queens and bishops, the English people were not unified in their choice of an English-language Bible. The Bishops'

Bible was now in all the churches, but the Geneva Bible appears to have been the favorite within the home. English Protestants were anything but unified in their selection of an English-language Bible. But that would soon change.[23]

9

ENDEARED TO THE HEARTS OF MILLIONS

Let the word of Christ richly dwell within you.
—COLOSSIANS 3:16

HE DID NOT LOOK OR ACT like the fairy-tale image of a king. His smile revealed gaps between missing teeth, he was known to burp loudly even in public, and he rarely washed his hands. His family name was James Charles Stuart, but to England and the world, he was officially King James I. A man of average height, he cultivated a fashionable set of auburn whiskers, and walked with an odd gait caused by a childhood illness. He was said to be vain and was often self-indulgent, lavishing money on royal pageants while the English navy deteriorated for lack of funds and the government's debts increased. Court gossips described him as chronically worried, sometimes timid, and easily frightened. "James was singularly effeminate," claimed one critic. "He could not look at a drawn sword without shuddering." He insisted that he was endowed with godlike authority, due to his belief in the divine right of kings, and he was repeatedly embroiled in divisive controversies with the English Parliament. At times he could be politically astute, however, and sometimes he exhibited bursts of wisdom, but—as in the words of one modern biographer—he consistently demonstrated a "glaring lack of majesty."[1]

Although reportedly uncomfortable with swords, King James I posed with one for this period painting. When he was crowned monarch after Queen Elizabeth's long reign, England's Puritans hoped they had a friend on the throne—but they did not. Source: Library of Congress.

James Stuart became king of England in 1603, when Elizabeth I died at age sixty-nine after forty-five years of rule. He was then thirty-six and ruled Scotland as King James VI. As the new sovereign of England, he proclaimed himself King James I. He was the son of Mary, Queen of Scots, and her second husband, Lord Henry Stuart—but despite his royal lineage, he had been exposed to violent trauma at an early age. His father had been murdered when James was still a baby, and his mother had been executed by Queen Elizabeth for plotting her overthrow. He had grown up under the wily manipulation of court advisors, some Catholic and some Protestant, but despite his mother's Catholicism, he had become a Protestant. He understood that the line of succession potentially positioned him to be king of England someday, and had shrewdly developed an alliance with Queen Elizabeth—an alliance he had dutifully preserved even though the Queen had executed his mother.[2]

He believed that he had been called by God to unite England and Scotland, and as king of England, he managed to maintain a fragile alliance between the two throughout his reign. He was an intelligent, knowledgeable ruler who took his royal duties seriously, enthusiastically supported the arts, and loved golf, stag hunting, and archery. Keenly interested in foreign affairs, he expanded the kingdom's trade with the Far East, kept the nation out of warfare for two decades, and established the first successful English colony in America—Jamestown, in Virginia. He did not hesitate to assert his authority as the official head of the Church of England, considered himself to be a Bible scholar, and even authored a devotional on the book of Matthew and a paraphrase of the book of Revelation. His personal life, however, bordered on the bizarre.[3]

He and his wife—the former Princess Anne of Denmark—had eight children, but his marriage and his reign were marked by rumors of infidelity and immorality. A heavy drinker, he reportedly once toppled off his horse in a state of drunkenness. He was also notoriously crude and irreverent—one court observer described him as a master of "words of perfect obscenity." Another described his habitual use of profanity as almost an art form—one that "would have better befitted the mouths of bawds and ruffians." In the privacy of the royal chambers, he spent much of his time watching "pastimes and fooleries"—bawdy theatricals performed by his court jesters. According to seventeenth-century playwright Arthur Wilson, who frequented the king's court, the king's jesters once dressed a piglet in a baptism gown and staged a sacrilegious mockery of the ordinance of baptism. As the "baby" was about to be unveiled for the baptism, the pig squealed, startling the king, who declared the farce to be "blasphemy" and waved away his jesters—although Wilson claimed that James's displeasure with the skit was prompted by his dislike of pigs rather than his fear of blasphemy.[4]

Simply put, King James I was no Puritan—and ironically, that would lead him to a royal decree that would make his name known to countless Christians through the ages. Despite being head of the church, his lifestyle and worldview set him in opposition to a rising Christian movement in his day—English Puritanism. Like the Presbyterians in Scotland and England, the Huguenots in France, and the Dutch Reformed in Holland, the Puritans were followers of theologian John Calvin, whose systematic theology, they believed, faithfully reflected biblical truth. The name "Puritan" was originally a term of ridicule—applied to members of a movement that arose among faculty at Cambridge University who wanted to purify the Church of England from practices they considered to be unbiblical. Contrary to the negative stereotype with which they would be painted in the postmodern age—that of a "gaunt, lank-haired killjoy, wearing a black steeple hat"—English Puritans were generally optimistic, outgoing people who loved life and believed that God's creation was meant to be examined, explored, and enjoyed. All of life, they believed, whether it was work, play, family, government, education, law, the arts, or worship, should be approached in a manner that honored God.[5]

While acceptable for much of the English population, Queen Elizabeth's compromise of Protestant doctrine and Catholic-style ceremony deeply troubled England's Puritans. A genuine saving faith, they believed, was more than merely belonging to a church, engaging in religious practices, or intellectually accepting a belief system. They believed that salvation was an act of God's grace—an undeserved gift—bequeathed by a sovereign, loving God to those who personally surrendered their hearts and lives to Jesus Christ as Lord and Savior. Such saving faith in the life of a believer, Puritans held, was marked by spiritual fruit—repentance of sin, a desire to live as a disciple of Christ, and a belief that salvation from God is eternally secure.[6]

An English political cartoon mocks a pious-looking Puritan, who stands with Bible in hand. The mockery accuses him of the "hanging of his cat on Monday for killing of a mouse on Sunday." King James shared the sentiment, referring to Puritans as "pestes in the church." Source: Library of Congress.

It was essential Protestant doctrine and was shared in its fundamentals by the Church of England, but the Puritans dissented from Anglican practices in other ways. The rituals, trappings, and church architecture that many saw as worshipful and comforting were viewed by the

Puritans as man-centered distractions that undermined God-centered worship—and they wanted the Anglican Church to be rid of them. For instance, they opposed the requirement that Anglican ministers wear a Catholic-style priestly tunic called a surplice, which they viewed as a prideful adornment. The Anglican hierarchy disagreed, and one Church official reportedly declared that it was less sinful to have "begot seven bastards than to have preached without a surplice."[7]

Numerous Puritans were arrested and jailed, and some were even executed.

They also opposed use of the Apocrypha in the Anglican Prayer Book, arguing that the books were not inspired and were riddled with errors. Such Puritan critiques rankled the hierarchy of the Church of England. So did the Puritan belief that God viewed all people as equals whether a prince or a pauper—a notion of equality that seemed at odds with the divine right of kings, the belief that royalty should not be challenged because it was established by God. "Puritanism was not merely a religious doctrine," noted the famous nineteenth-century French observer Alexis de Tocqueville, "but corresponded in many points with the most absolute democratic and republican theories. It was this tendency which had aroused its most dangerous adversaries."[8]

Although deeply disturbed by many Church practices, mainstream Puritans did not want to replace the Church of England—they wanted to reform it. Their goal was to bring it closer to what they believed was the biblical model of the New Testament church. Queen Elizabeth I grew weary of Puritan protests about her church, however, and finally allowed church authorities to take action against the movement. They did so by rigorously enforcing England's Act of Uniformity, which required everyone to regularly attend Anglican worship services and forbade any act of worship that deviated from the Church's Book of Common Prayer. The Anglican Church's Court of High Commission ordered the arrest and imprisonment of anyone who preached without a license from the state church, and also prohibited the publication of religious literature that was deemed critical of the Church of England. It also outlawed preaching, teaching, and Bible training in private homes—a favorite practice of Puritan pastors. Numerous Puritans were arrested and jailed, and some were even executed.[9]

One was John Penry, a Welsh Puritan pastor who publicly criticized the Church of England for tardiness in supplying congregations in Wales with Welsh-language Bibles. Church officials had him imprisoned, but he resumed his public call for reform when released and separated from the church. Several years later, he was arrested again at an illegal Puritan worship service in the woods outside London. When Anglican authorities searched his home, they discovered an unpublished manuscript that criticized Queen Elizabeth's leadership as the head of the church. Penry was tried and convicted as "a seditious disturber of her Majesty's peaceable government." On May 29, 1593, at age thirty-four, he was hanged. He had a wife and four biblically named daughters—Sure-Hope, Safety, Comfort, and Deliverance—and had asked to see them before his execution, but his request was denied. Somehow, he did manage to send them and his congregation a farewell message: "[May] Jesus Christ, that great King and Prince of the kings of the earth, bless you and comfort you with his invincible Spirit, that you may be able to bear and overcome these great trials which you are yet . . . to undergo for his name's sake."[10]

England's Puritans hoped such persecution would end when James I became king, and that the new monarch would be sympathetic to their concerns. They were soon disappointed. King James, they quickly realized, was no friend to Puritans. Indeed, the new king went on record to describe Puritans as "an evill sorte" who were "pestes in the Church." He was the head of the Anglican Church, and if the Puritans did not want to obey his church, he believed, they did not want to obey him. To King James, Puritanism was a disease that threatened his rule. One of his private theatricals reflected his view of Puritans. In it, a Puritan festooned with donkey ears obnoxiously berated members of the ruling class for "making merry" while Christian dissidents in the realm were suffering persecution. To James and his court favorites, the mockery was appropriate. "I have more and more reason," he confided to a court official, "to hate and abhor all that sect, [who are] enemies to all kings." Puritan leaders were determined to make their case to the new king, however, and early in his rule they respectfully did so.[11]

In 1604, James I met with England's Puritan leaders at the one-thousand-room Hampton Court Palace. There, they petitioned the king to order reforms to the Church of England, which they believed would make church practices more biblical. Source: *The History of the Royal Residences* / Wikimedia Commons.

In the spring of 1603, King James was informed that one thousand Puritan leaders had signed a formal petition listing proposed Puritan reforms to the church. It would eventually become known as the Millenary Petition, and leading Puritan pastors asked the king for an appearance to present their protests. James agreed, and the meeting was set for a date in January 1604 at Hampton Court Palace near London—Henry VIII's thousand-room residence on the Thames—and thus it would become known as the Hampton Court Conference. Four prominent Puritan leaders—all Anglican pastors—were invited to appear before the king, the archbishop of Canterbury, eight Anglican bishops, and members of the king's court. Of the Puritan leadership, Jacobean historian John Matusiak would observe: "Most of those protesting at this time were . . . demonstrably the best educated, most zealous and conscientious of the parish clergy, the majority of whom had hitherto loyally accepted regulations of which they disapproved in the interest of Church unity." Seated in his chair of state, flanked by Anglican churchmen and officials, the king admonished the Puritan leaders with an hour-long speech designed to demonstrate his grasp of theological issues and the need for conformity to the Church of England. "Religion is the soul of a kingdom," he concluded, "and unity, the life of religion." When the royal soliloquy ended, the archbishop of Canterbury, John Whitgift, fell to his knees and proclaimed aloud that all of England should be indebted to God for "setting over us a King so wise, learned and judicious." The bishop of London, Richard Bancroft, likewise publicly declared that "such a king since Christ's time has not been."[12]

In fact, King James did little at the conference to promote unity with the Puritans. He dismissed most of their concerns about the church, some of which—the use of wedding rings in marriage ceremonies and making the sign of the cross at baptisms—seemed trivial to him. "And surely," he commented, "if these be the greatest matters you be grieved with, I need not have been troubled." One Anglican official derided the four Puritan leaders for wasting the king's time, and James himself later joked that the chief Puritan spokesman should have been treated like an errant schoolboy—with "the rod plied upon the poor boy's buttocks." At one point, another church official loudly whispered a joke about Puritan persecution. "A Puritan," he cracked, "is a Protestant flayed out of his wits." When the king ended the conference by rising and departing, he was heard to murmur an ominous comment about Puritans and other nonconformists. "I will make them conform themselves," he stated, "or else harry them out of the land, or else worse." Before leaving, however, the king did make one major concession to the Puritans. Dr. John Rainolds, a renowned Puritan Bible scholar and highly respected administrator at Oxford University, asked the king if he would consider authorizing a new English translation of the Bible—and he agreed. The proposal was discussed as almost an afterthought, but in time it would produce the most beloved English-language Bible in history: the Authorized Version. It could have been called the Puritan Bible—it was their idea—but because James I authorized it, it would be known through the ages as the King James Bible.[13]

Why did Puritan leaders propose rendering a new English translation of the Bible, and why did James I agree to it? Puritanism was deeply Bible-centered, and Puritans were keenly interested in an accurate biblical text. "So faith comes from hearing," the New Testament advised, "and hearing by the word of Christ." The Bible alone, Puritans believed, was the revealed Word of the triune God, and was therefore inerrant and authoritative. They treasured Scripture and loved deep, meaty, Bible-based sermons that were laced throughout with supporting Scripture. Even though it was now more than forty years old, the Puritans generally liked the Geneva Bible and were untroubled by its Calvinistic margin notes. However, they feared that it would someday be replaced by the newer, Bishops' Bible, which was routinely used at worship services and quoted throughout the Anglican Prayer Book. They did not consider the Bishops' Bible to be a true translation—only a revision of the Great Bible that carried forward its translation errors. Puritans scholars such as Dr. Rainolds recognized that increased knowledge of Hebrew and Greek meant that a revision of the Geneva Bible was needed—but the Bishops' Bible was not the answer. They considered it "corrupt and not answerable to the truth of the Original." Therefore, learned Puritans were interested in a new, more accurate translation that would be used in churches as well as by the family fireside—and which would replace the Bishops' Bible.[14]

Flanked by Anglican bishops, James I listens as Puritan leaders make their case for reforms to the church. In return, he lectured the Puritans for an hour and agreed to only one of their requests—royal authorization of the translation of a new English Bible. Source: Library of Congress.

King James was enthusiastic about the proposal—even though Bishop Bancroft of London had admonished the Puritans that if his majesty heeded everyone's opinion on Bible translations, "there would be no end of translating." The king ignored his bishop and ordered the new translation for a variety of reasons. As a self-styled Bible scholar, he found the idea appealing, and it was one concession he was willing to grant the Puritans. Also, the English printing industry was suffering at the time from an influx of English-language Bibles from Holland that were said to be of "better print, better bound, better paper and . . . sold cheaper." A new English translation could be a boon to the national economy. His main motivation, however, was likely his deep dislike of the Geneva Bible. He knew there were problems with the text of the Bishops' Bible and that—to the frustration of church officials—it had failed to supplant the popular the Geneva Bible. He could not deny that the Geneva Bible was a superior translation, but he loathed it. The Geneva Bible "was the worst," he declared, and he condemned the margin notes as "untrue, seditious and savouring too much of dangerous and traitorous conceits." He particularly disliked the note on Judges 9:53, which reported that a woman had crushed King Abimelech's head with a millstone. The commentary read, "Thus God by such miserable death taketh vengeance on tyrants." The Geneva Bible's notes, he believed, exhibited a decided lack of respect for the divine right of kings and for monarchy in general. Therefore, for King James, a new version of the English-language Bible offered the potential resolution of a multitude of issues.[15]

Just as the English Reformation blossomed when the opportunity was afforded by Henry VIII's self-serving actions, so was the creation of the King James Bible enabled by King James I, regardless of his reasons—an act that the Puritans no doubt deemed providential. Ironically, the project began by borrowing an innovation from the Geneva Bible the king so disliked. Like the Geneva Bible, this new English Bible would be translated by a committee composed of translation teams. The team concept might also have been inspired by the Greek Septuagint, which was reportedly translated by a committee of seventy Jewish Bible scholars. For the King James Bible, fifty-four Bible scholars were invited to participate—all of whom were said to have been selected for genuine personal faith as well as scholastic ability. The committee actually numbered forty-seven by starting time, and they were considered the best of the best—university professors from Cambridge and Oxford, Hebrew and Greek experts, and laymen who were knowledgeable in linguistics. They were organized into six translation panels, or teams—two working at Cambridge University, two at Oxford, and two at London's Westminster Abbey.[16]

Along with mainstream Anglicans, King James allowed Puritan clergy, such as Dr. Rainolds, to participate, which added some of the best Bible scholars in England to the translation teams and provided unofficial theological checks and balances to the task. The timing was also critical: The teams were organized and the work began in 1604—shortly before an assassination attempt on King James led to a crackdown on all nonconformists, including Puritans. A band of renegade Catholic conspirators managed to secretly pack the basement of Westminster Palace with more than thirty barrels of gunpowder, which they planned to explode while the king delivered a speech to Parliament. With the king dead and Parliament in chaos, they intended to seize control of the government and reinstate Catholicism as England's officially mandated faith. However, the Gunpowder Plot, as it became known, was discovered, and King James survived, but the assassination attempt spurred a royal crackdown on all Nonconformists—Catholic and Puritan alike. If the new Bible's translation teams had been organized a year or so later, after the crackdown was fully under way, the Puritan scholars might have been omitted.[17]

Each team was issued the same instructions: The translators used the Bishops' Bible as a foundation and consulted a list of other English translations, including Tyndale's version, the Great Bible, the Geneva Bible and, perhaps surprisingly, the recently published Catholic Douay-Rheims New Testament. They consulted available Hebrew and Greek sources, including the "Received Text" initiated by Erasmus. No marginal notes were added except explanations of Greek and Hebrew terms. The language needed to be easily readable and understandable by everyday people, but also needed to be dignified for public reading in churches. Each team of translators worked independently, then circulated its work among the other teams for criticism. All remaining questions or conflicting textual issues were resolved by a committee composed of two members from each team. The teams at Westminster worked on the Old Testament and the New Testament; the Cambridge teams worked on the Old Testament and the Apocrypha; and the Oxford teams rendered the Old Testament and the New Testament.[18]

THE RADCLIFFE LIBRARY.

In 1604, three teams of England's most respected Bible scholars began work on a new English translation of the Bible. One team worked at Westminster Abbey in London, one at Cambridge University, and one here—at Oxford University. Source: Welcome Images / Wikimedia Commons.

Despite their theological and political differences, the teams worked together cooperatively, focused on the common goal of creating the most accurate, most readable English-language Bible ever produced.

By some estimates, the translators based more than half of their New Testament work on William Tyndale's translation—and they kept many of his exquisite phrases, such as "in the twinkling of an eye" and "my brother's keeper." Often, one team member would read text aloud, so the other members could react to it, and so they could weigh the impact of the words in a public worship service. Some teams appear to have been more productive than others, or at least some worked more quickly than others. Regardless, they checked and rechecked each other, following the structure they had set in place to ensure accuracy of the textual rendering. The revision and translation work took approximately five years, and for some, the work was exceedingly demanding. At least two died from "too earnest study and pains about the translation," including the Bible's original promotor, Puritan academic John Rainolds, who died in May 1607 after much of the work was done.[19]

Diligently compared and revised, by his Majestie's special commandment.

Finally, in 1611—seven years after it was proposed by Dr. Rainolds—the King James Bible was published. The first edition was printed by Robert Barker, the royal printer, as a large folio work bound in two volumes, consisting of fifteen hundred pages. It used an easy-to-read Roman-type font, printed in black ink, and was organized into chapters and verses with chapter headings. Dedicated to King James I, it became formally known as the Authorized Version, although the king apparently never issued an official document stating his authorization. The title page featured elaborate artwork, which—unlike earlier English-language versions—did not depict the reigning monarch. Instead, the art depicted Moses to the left of the title, holding the Ten Commandments, and Aaron to the right, attired in his priestly vestments. The four New Testament Gospel writers were also depicted, with one placed in each corner of the artwork. Crowning the top of the page was the name of

God, rendered in Hebrew. Below His name was an image of the sacred dove, symbolizing the Holy Spirit, and centered beneath the dove was a depiction of the reigning Lamb of God, Jesus Christ. Centered in the art was an equally elaborate title, which read:

The Holy Bible,

conteyning the Old Testament and New: Newly translated out of the Original tongues: & with the former Translations diligently compared and revised, by his Majestie's special Commandment. Appointed to be read in Churches. [20]

While its original title page described it as "Newly Translated out of the Original Tongues," the King James Version kept much of the work of earlier translators, such as William Tyndale, so it was in part a revision, and not strictly a new translation directly from Hebrew and Greek in its entirety. "Truly (good Christian reader)," stated the translators in the Bible's preface, "wee neuer thought from the beginning, that we should neede to make a new Translation." The original languages were diligently rendered, however, and the text of both Testaments reflected a collective scholarship in the original languages. The first edition of the King James Bible included the Apocrypha, much to the chagrin of the Puritans and other Reformed believers, who argued that noncanonical books should not be treated the same as inspired Scripture. Over time, however, publishers began to omit the Apocrypha, and by the mid-nineteenth century it would seldom be found in new editions of the King James Bible.[21]

Of the principal ancient manuscripts that would be deemed necessary for an accurate biblical text in the twenty-first century, only one— *Codex Bezae*—was available to the King James Bible translators in the early seventeenth century. Of the five-thousand-plus New Testament manuscripts and fragments that would be available four hundred years later, no more than twenty-five were known in the early 1600s. No papyrus discoveries had occurred then, nor would they occur for another three hundred years. Even so, the King James Version set a high

standard for Bible translation in its day. The translators had also succeeded with their choice of words: The text of the King James Version
was clear, understandable, and dignified, exceedingly useful for private
study and memorization at home as well as for public reading at church.
And in places throughout both Testaments, the language of the King
James Bible almost leapt from the page with the endearing, lyrical ring
of poetry. For instance, the rendering of Psalm 23:1 is a perfect iambic
pentameter: "The LORD is my shepherd, I shall not want."[22]

An easily readable, understandable translation in the reader's language
could unlock the truth of God's Word, the translators explained in the
new Bible's preface. "[It] breaketh the shell that we may eat the kernel;
that putteth aside the curtain that we may look into the most holy place;
that removeth the cover of the well that we may come by the water, even
as Jacob rolled away the stone by the mouth of the well." The new Bible
was promptly issued to Anglican churches as expected—but unlike the
Bishops' Bible, it also proved popular with the English people, who widely
embraced it when smaller, affordable editions were printed.[23]

The new Bible did have its critics. Despite the important contributions to the King James Version by Puritan scholars such as John
Rainolds, the Geneva Bible remained the preferred version for many
Puritans—so much so that at the height of the Puritan persecution
in 1631, bishop of London William Laud ordered stacks of Geneva
Bibles set ablaze and forbade its importation. Some critics denounced
the King James Bible because it was not translated word-for-word from
the original languages. Others complained that the language of some
passages seemed to have been massaged to support James I's stance in
favor of the divine right of kings. Some wished for extensive explanatory
margin notes. One prominent critic, an irascible English Bible scholar
named Hugh Broughton—who had been passed over when the translation teams were selected—was scathing in his denunciation of the new
Bible. "Tell His Majesty that I had rather be rent in pieces with wild
horses," he stated, "than any such translation by my consent should be
urged upon poor churches."[24]

Published in 1611, the new translation might have become known as the Puritan Bible—it was their idea—but it was authorized by James I and would be known through the ages as the King James Bible—the most popular English Bible in history. Source: Wikimedia Commons.

Despite such protests, the King James Bible grew in popularity with readers, many of whom over the ages developed such a loyalty to it that they resisted the introduction of new, updated Bible translations and deemed Bible language that was different from the King James Version to be almost sacrilegious. Such steadfast loyalty by its readers enabled the King James Version to remain the English-language Bible of choice over the ages despite a series of editions known for peculiar errors. A 1631 edition became known as the "Wicked" edition because a typesetter accidentally omitted the word "not" from the seventh commandment, rendering the text of Exodus 20:14 as "Thou shalt commit adultery." A 1633 edition was called the "Unrighteous Bible" because I Corinthians 6:9 misstated that "the unrighteous shall inherit the kingdom of God." An edition printed in 1717 became known as the "Vinegar Bible" because a chapter heading of Luke 20 accidentally set the word "vinegar" for "vineyard." A 1795 edition was called the "Murderer's" edition by some because the word "filled" in Mark 7:27 was mistakenly printed as "killed," and a 1612 edition became known as the "Printer's Bible" because a typesetter intentionally or unintentionally substituted the word "printers" for "princes"—rendering Psalm 119:161 as "Printers have persecuted me without a cause." In a 1701 edition, a dating system compiled by Anglican archbishop James Ussher was added to the Bible by Anglican bishop William Lloyd, which would lead generations of readers to mistakenly believe that it was part of the original 1611 Bible.[25]

The King James Version became the best-selling, most-read book in the world. It underwent a major revision in 1629, and another in 1638. In 1768, English clergyman John Wesley, the founder of Methodism, found himself too ill to travel or preach, so he dedicated himself to revising the New Testament portion of the King James Bible. He did not merely write a paraphrase, but consulted the original Greek and rendered a translation in the common language of the eighteenth-century English marketplace. "I write chiefly for plain, unlettered men," he explained in the Bible's preface, "who understand only their mother tongue, and yet reverence and love the Word of God." Appropriately, he entitled his translation *The New Testament with Notes, for Plain Unlettered Men Who Know Only Their Mother Tongue.* Wesley's revision made more than twelve thousand changes to the King James text and provided scores of notes. Other major revisions followed, including a 1762 four-volume revision edited by a respected Bible professor at Cambridge University, and a 1769 revision by Dr. Benjamin Blayney, a Hebrew scholar at Oxford University. Produced under the reign of King George III on the eve of the American Revolution, Blayney's revision significantly updated the text; made changes to references about coinage, weights, and measures; and modernized punctuation and spelling. His work became known as the "Oxford Standard Edition" and became the basis for modern editions of the King James Version.[26]

Less than seventy years later, Great Britain's Queen Victoria would ascend to the throne and become the longest-reigning English ruler in history at the time. During her extraordinary reign, she would oversee a worldwide empire that was unmatched in scope throughout human history. Critics would fault it for imperialism and colonialism, but it undeniably spread the English language around the globe—along with the gospel. English-speaking missionaries, evangelists, and indigenous church builders would follow every step of expansion, taking the gospel of Jesus Christ to the "uttermost parts of the earth." They would carry with them—on their lips, in their hands, and into countless new languages—the King James Bible. "Its simple, majestic Anglo-Saxon tongue, its clear, sparkling style, its directness and force of utterance have made it a model in language, style and dignity," twentieth-century Bible historian Ira M. Price would conclude. "It has endeared itself to the hearts and lives of millions of Christians."[27]

-10

THE BIBLE COMES TO AMERICA

Now . . . where the Spirit of the Lord is, there is liberty.
—2 CORINTHIANS 3:17

WITH HIS LEFT HAND ON AN OPEN BIBLE and his right hand held aloft, George Washington took the oath of office as the first president of the United States. It was Thursday, April 30, 1789, and Washington stood surrounded by a handful of dignitaries on the second-floor balcony of Federal Hall in New York City, which was then the capital of the fledgling United States of America. A constitutional convention had crafted a new Constitution for the thirteen United States, establishing a three-branch federal government consisting of a congress, a federal court system, and an executive branch, or presidency. Washington was the triumphant commander in chief who had led American forces to victory in the recent Revolutionary War, and had been unanimously elected president by America's newly created electoral college. Now, with a jubilant crowd packing the street below, he stood erect in a rust-colored suit and repeated the oath of office: "I, George Washington, do solemnly swear that I will faithfully execute the Office of the President of the United States, and will to the best of my Ability, preserve, protect and defend the Constitution of the United States." Then, setting a precedent that would be followed by all American presidents to come, he deliberately added the phrase, "So help me God." With his oath thus affirmed, George Washington took his first action as president of the United States: he leaned forward over the open Bible and reverently kissed the Scriptures."[1]

Such was the respect for the Word of God in the newly established United States of America and in the thirteen English colonies that had preceded it. The English colonization of what would become the United States had begun at the peak of the English Reformation, when the English people were newly equipped with the Bible in their own language, and the English colonists who first spilled into America brought with them the biblical core values of the Judeo-Christian worldview. The first successful English colony in America—the Jamestown settlement in Virginia—was established in 1607, while the translation teams in England were working on the King James Bible. Even at rowdy, hardscrabble Jamestown, a for-profit venture in which three shiploads of men and boys hacked out a settlement in the wilds of Virginia, the Bible was the foundation. The charter of the new colony declared its mission in part to be the "propagating of the Christian Religion." Largely Anglican—at least in name—the colonists were accompanied by a chaplain, erected a cross at their landfall on Cape Henry, were called to prayer twice daily, and were expected to attend two worship services on Sundays and take regular communion. When they fumbled their way to starvation and near destruction, Captain John Smith helped save the survivors by strictly applying the New Testament admonition: "If any would not work, neither should he eat."[2]

In 1620, Plymouth Colony was established on the coast of modern Massachusetts by the people who would become known as the Pilgrims. They were led by a determined group of Separatists—a Puritan sect that believed local churches should be self-governing and had therefore illegally separated from the Anglican Church. Driven by persecution to Holland a decade earlier, they had joined with a group of non-Separatists and had endured a perilous voyage across the Atlantic aboard the *Mayflower*. Even before going ashore at Cape Cod Bay, they drafted a governing document for their colony—the Mayflower Compact—which was based on the twin pillars of faith and freedom. Its opening line—"In the name of God, Amen"—acknowledged the God of the Bible as the authority for law and culture in the Pilgrims' New World colony.[3]

With one hand on the Bible, George Washington prepares to take the oath of office as the first president of the United States at Federal Hall in New York City in 1789. He set two precedents for oath-taking in America: He added the phrase "so help me God"—and he kissed the Scriptures. Source: New York Public Library.

Ten years later, in 1630, shiploads of English Puritans began arriving on the coast of Massachusetts, inspired by the success of Plymouth Colony and fleeing the persecution unleashed by King James's son Charles I. They established the sprawling Massachusetts Bay Colony and came in such giant numbers—three thousand in a single year—that their exodus from England became known as the Great Migration. They brought with them the Judeo-Christian worldview, Puritan values, and the belief that everyone—royalty included—was subject to the higher law of God based on the Bible. Over the decades to come, others followed, establishing thirteen English colonies—each with an official charter that either openly reflected a biblical perspective or clearly stated the colony's intent to "advance the Kingdom of our Lord Jesus Christ and to enjoy the liberties of the Gospel."[4]

While officially Anglican—the Church of England was the official state denomination in English colonies too—the people of the thirteen colonies were diverse in their faith: Puritan Congregationalists in Massachusetts, New Hampshire, and Connecticut; Baptists in Rhode Island, Dutch Reformed and Lutherans in New York; Quakers in Pennsylvania; Presbyterians and Quakers in New Jersey; Lutherans in Delaware; Catholics and Congregationalists in Maryland; and Anglicans in Virginia, the Carolinas, and Georgia—with Huguenots sprinkled throughout, and small but notable Jewish communities located in New York, Philadelphia, and Charleston. It was a mix that was predominantly Protestant, but united in the Judeo-Christian worldview. Diversity reigned—but the population of the thirteen colonies was overwhelmingly composed of people of the Book.[5]

In such an atmosphere, zeal for the Scriptures flourished.

"The Christian tradition was the chief foundation stone of American intellectual development [in the Colonial Era]," renowned American historian Merle Curti would observe. "Whatever differences in ways of life and whatever conflicts of interest separated the country gentry and great merchants from the frontiersmen, poor farmers, artisans and small shopkeepers, all nominally subscribed to Christian tenets and at least in theory accepted Christianity as their guide." Twenty-first century Colonial Era expert Patricia Bonomi would agree: from Massachusetts to Georgia, she would note, "the idiom of religion penetrated all discourse, underlay all thought, marked all observances, gave meaning to every public and private crisis." And when, in the early eighteenth century, that Bible-based foundation began to weaken under the influences of prosperity, security, and a progressive culture, a revival of Christianity called the Great Awakening swept through the thirteen colonies and left colonial culture united and awash in a flood of faith on the eve of the American Revolution. "It is wonderful to see the change," observed publisher Benjamin Franklin, who was not a believer. "From being thoughtless or indifferent about religion, it seem'd as if all the world were growing religious."[6]

In such an atmosphere, zeal for the Scriptures flourished. What version of the Bible was carried to Jamestown by its first chaplain, Anglican clergyman Robert Hunt? Was it the Great Bible, the Bishops' Bible, the Geneva Bible? No one knows. The Pilgrims, however, favored the Geneva Bible, which was quoted by William Bradford, the longtime governor of Plymouth Colony, while John Winthrop, the Puritan governor of Massachusetts Bay Colony used a King James Bible. During the colonial era, publishing restrictions prohibited the King James Version from being printed in English colonies, so it had to be imported. The Puritans believed illiteracy was almost sinful because it prevented one from reading Scripture and learning God's truth, and because the Puritan movement began at Cambridge University, there was an added emphasis on education. Almost as quickly as they built homes, the Puritans of Massachusetts were built schools, and then colleges, beginning with Harvard University in 1636, which was established in newly named Cambridge, Massachusetts—so named to honor the English university dear to so many Puritans. Not surprisingly, the first book printed in North America was the work of Puritans.[7]

The full title was *The Whole Booke of Psalmes Faithfully Translated into English Metre*—commonly called the *Bay Psalm Book*—and it was published in Massachusetts Bay Colony in 1640. A common Protestant worship form that emerged from the Reformation was congregational singing, in which members of a congregation would sing praises to God as an assembly, instead of leaving musical praise and worship solely to a church choir. Congregational responses, including singing, occurred in Catholic churches in the medieval era, but was not the widespread phenomenon that became common in Protestant congregations in the sixteenth century. The Protestant practice was based at least in part on the Bible-based doctrine of the priesthood of believers that was reemphasized by the Reformation—a belief that those who receive Jesus Christ as the Lord and their personal Savior need no other intermediary, neither a pastor nor a priest, to communicate directly with God. That sense of personal freedom in prayer and worship produced innovations, including hymn singing. Martin Luther produced a psalm book in 1524, John Calvin collaborated on one in 1539, and Miles Coverdale produced an English version in 1539. In 1562, a psalm book was attached to the Anglican Book of Common Prayer.[8]

Singing the Psalms thus became a common worship practice in colonial America. Memorizing the words to a psalm so it could be sung taught Bible doctrine and also reinforced spiritual kinship in the local church. "People learned them avidly and sang them in their homes, in the field, and in their workshops," psalm book authority Zoltan Haraszti would later observe. "The communal singing especially engendered a feeling of unity." The Pilgrims brought the Anglican psalm book with them to America in 1620, and soon melodious, psalm-centered praise was drifting over the forests and fields of Plymouth Colony. Ten years later, the same psalms and psalm book were in use by mainstream Puritans at neighboring Massachusetts Bay Colony. Translation issues with the text or lyrics of the psalm book apparently did not deter the Pilgrims from using it, but when the Puritans sang psalms, they wanted to sing the most accurate translations of Scripture possible—and Puritan leaders considered the text of the Anglican psalm book to be a paraphrase and not a true translation.[9]

Equipped with their Bible, a Pilgrim couple walk to church in Plymouth Colony, which was established "in the name of God" on the coast of modern Massachusetts in 1620. Would they have carried the Geneva Bible or the newly published King James Version? Source: Library of Congress.

With typical Puritan industry and ingenuity, the leaders of the Massachusetts Bay Colony launched an effort to produce a better-translated psalm book in 1639. An imported printing press was set up in Cambridge, the home of newly established Harvard College, and an English printer's apprentice was recruited to operate it. First off the press was a legal document, and then a multiple-sheet farmer's almanac (which would allow some to assert that the *Bay Psalm Book* was actually the *second* book printed in America). The translation work was done, and the new psalm book came off the press in 1640. Deemed the first book printed in America, it would become the rarest of literary treasures by the late nineteenth century—but as a psalm book, it had many critics, even in 1640.[10]

The paper stock was heavy and durable, and the type was well inked and clearly readable, but the work was laced with inconsistent spellings, even for an era when English lacked standardization. The book's pages were unnumbered, and punctuation was woeful, with periods placed in the middle of sentences and one-syllable words needlessly hyphenated. The most lamentable problem, however, was the translation itself. The psalms were indeed translated directly from the Hebrew, but the work had been divided among thirty of the colony's most knowledgeable clergymen and Hebrew experts, and thus displayed an inconsistency in style and accuracy. Most troubling for the psalm book's users, however, was the difficulty of singing the psalms recorded on its pages—which were translated literally word for word from the Hebrew and were awkward to read and a greater challenge to sing. Puritan leader Cotton Mather went on record to explain the translators' reasoning: "If the verses are not always so elegant as some desire or expect, let them consider that God's altar needs not our polishing, we have respected rather a plain translation rather than to smooth our verses with the sweetness of any paraphrase." Later editions would be improved, and despite such problems, the *Bay Psalm Book* was a precedent-setting publication—the first book and the first work of Scripture published in America.[11]

Twenty-one years later, in 1661, the same printing press at Harvard College was used to print the first copy of the New Testament published in North America—but it was not in English. Instead it was in a Native America dialect—the Wôpanâak–Algonquin language. The translator and publisher was John Eliot, a Puritan teaching elder and linguist who had worked on the *Bay Psalm Book.* Eliot was a graduate of Cambridge University, where he had demonstrated a youthful gift for languages. He came to Massachusetts Bay Colony at the height of the Great Migration, and eventually became pastor of the Congregationalist church in Roxbury. Eliot had a heart for the Native American people of southern New England, especially those of the Massachuset and Nipmuc tribes. "I find a good measure of ability in them," he wrote a friend, "not only in prayer, wherein they exceed my expectation, but in the rehearsing of such Scriptures as I have expounded." With the encouragement of

Henry Dunster, Harvard's first president, Eliot laboriously translated the Scriptures into a phoneticized version of the Wôpanâak–Algonquin language, which he had studied for decades.[12]

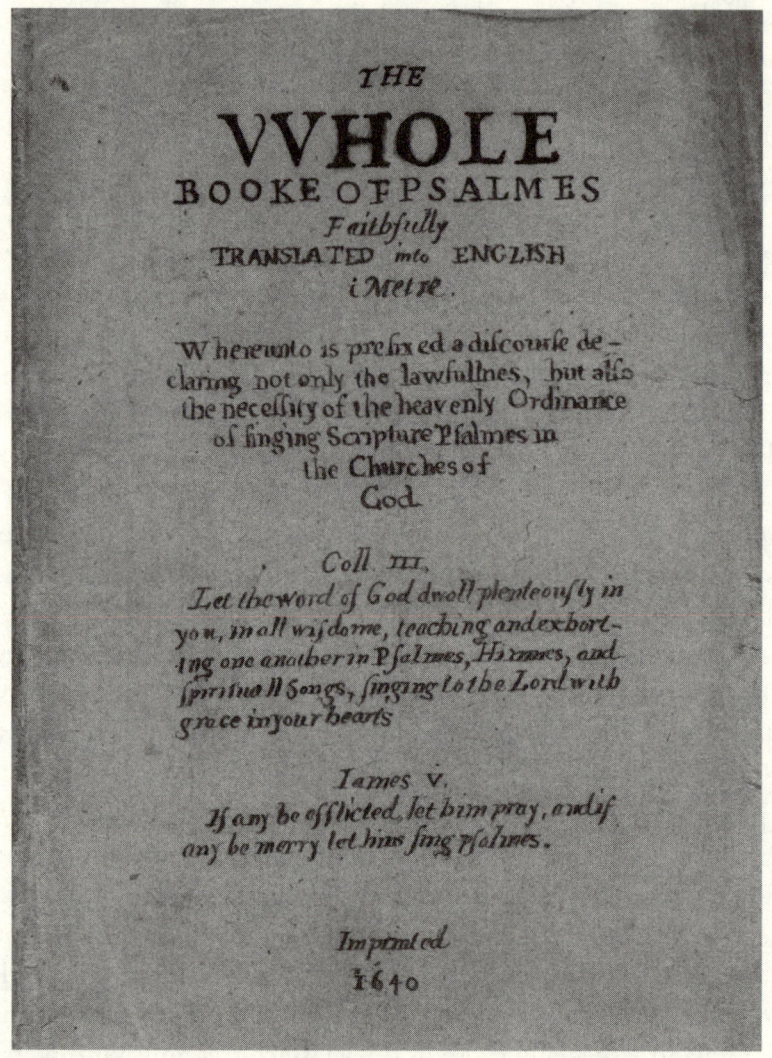

The title page from the 1640 Bay Psalm Book promises users that the Psalms inside are "Faithfully Translated into English." Published by Puritan colonists at Harvard University, it was the first book printed in America. Source: Library of Congress.

By his own admission, he did not do the work alone: he was assisted by his wife, Anne, and especially by a team of Native American interpreters and linguists, led by a young Massachuset convert named Job Nesuton. "With my care to teach the well the sounds of letters and spellings," Eliot wrote a colleague, "I trust we shall have sundry of them who shall write every man for himself so much of the Bible as God shall enable me to translate." At times, Eliot despaired of ever completing the work. "I have no hope to see the Bible translated," he wrote at one point, "much less printed in my days." But he and his team persevered, and the work was finally done. In 1661, the Algonquin New Testament was published, followed by the Old Testament in 1663. Later, both testaments were combined in a complete Bible. Although largely unknown and unappreciated outside of New England in its day, the Algonquin translation of the Bible was a unique and important collaborative accomplishment by a colonial white missionary and a team of Native Americans translators.[13]

Eliot also translated and published a series of booklets that shared the gospel in a series of dialogues, and also published the shorter catechism of the Westminster Confession of Faith—both rendered in the phoneticized Wôpanâak–Algonquin language. The Algonquin Bible became known in its day as "Eliot's Indian Bible," and Eliot used it to share the gospel message with the region's Indian peoples. Numerous Native Americans professed faith in Christ through Eliot's work and the message of his Bible, although his attempts to convert them to European ways proved ill-fated. In 1675, many of Eliot's Indian friends and converts were scattered or killed during a bloody conflict called King Philip's War, which embittered Indian-white relations in New England and permanently disrupted Eliot's mission outreach. Even so, unknown numbers of New England's Native American people made the faith of the Bible their own through the work of Eliot and his Indian translators. Remarkably, more than three hundred years later, copies of the "Indian Bible" would be used to reintroduce the Wôpanâak–Algonquin language to new generation of Native Americans. Eliot's devotion to the Indian peoples of New England earned him the name "Apostle to the Indians" and his Algonquin translation set a precedent for Bible publishing in America.[14]

Eighty years later, in 1743, another Bible was published in the thirteen colonies, but again, not in English. Christopher Sower, a printer who had immigrated to America from Germany, printed a German-language Bible in his Philadelphia print shop. It was a family business—and an innovative one. The Sowers produced their own ink, established a paper mill, set up a bindery, and constructed a foundry from which they manufactured the first metal printing type made in America. Sower's German-language Bible was a three-year project with an edition size of one thousand copies. It used Martin Luther's translation, was printed in a large format composed of 1,286 pages, and was praised as "a typographical masterpiece." His son—Christopher Jr., an ordained German Baptist minister—printed two more editions of the Bible in 1762 and 1776.[15]

American families in the colonial era generally viewed the family Bible as a cherished possession. Family Bibles were often passed from one generation to another by a last will and testament. Even if a family owned no other book, according to colonial-era probate records, it often owned a Bible. Probate records for one county in colonial Massachusetts, for instance, showed that 30 percent of families that listed no other books in property inventories, cited ownership of a Bible. Among families whose probate inventories included books, more than 75 percent owned a Bible. Relatively inexpensive copies of the Bible were available, including cheaply made editions called "common school Bibles" that were used in colonial American schools. Even so, many poor families lacked a copy of the Scriptures. "[In] multitudes of Families," lamented a New England pastor in 1673, "there is . . . no Bible, or only a torn Bible to be found. I mean but a part of the Bible." By the early eighteenth century, the Geneva Bible had been out of print since 1644. The King James Bible was the preferred version in America, but it had to be printed under royal license, which was limited to the royal printer and Oxford and Cambridge Universities. Therefore, all copies of the King James Bible sold in America had to be imported from Great Britain. One or two counterfeit editions of the King James Bible were rumored to have been printed in eighteenth-century America under the fictitious imprint of London printers, including a mysterious edition called the Baskett Bible, but no legitimately printed English-language Bible was published in colonial America—until the American Revolution.[16]

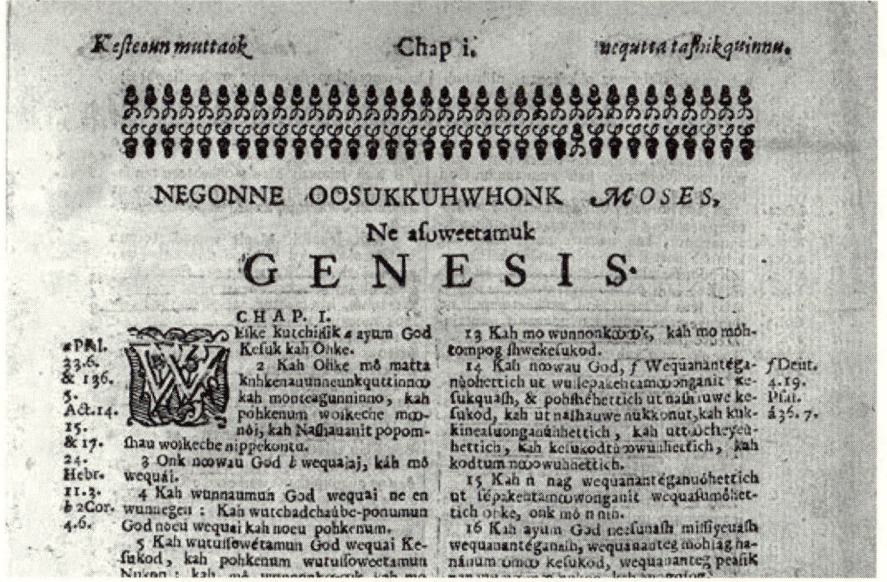

Although the title of the Old Testament's opening book bears the familiar name "Genesis," the text of the 1663 "Eliot Indian Bible" is rendered in the Wopanaak-Algonquin language. Translated by a Puritan missionary, David Eliot, and his Indian associates, it was the first Bible printed in North America. Source: Library of Congress.

In Philadelphia one day in the summer of 1777, three Presbyterian clergymen waited for news that could forever affect the use of the Bible in America. Philadelphia was the largest city in America—bigger than

New York, Boston, or Charleston. It was a major American seaport, a center of shipbuilding, crafts, and industry, and was known for its shady brick streets, busy marketplaces, and popular coffeehouses, as well as its steamy summer weather, odorous tanneries, and swarming flies. It was also the seat of the Second Continental Congress, and thus was the de facto capital of the new United States of America, which was now struggling for its survival in the midst of the Revolutionary War. The Continental Congress met in the Pennsylvania State House—an impressive brick structure topped by a lofty bell tower—and it was there, on Monday, July 7, 1777, that a formal petition from the three ministers was read before the Congress's assembled delegates. The pastors had an urgent message for the delegates: America needed more Bibles, and Congress needed to help.[17]

Although not yet three years old, the Continental Congress already had a history of officially putting the Bible to use. On the second day of deliberations, in September 1774, the First Continental Congress attempted to end a bout of bickering by voting to open future sessions with prayer and selecting a minister to do so. Their pick was the Reverend Jacob Duché, the pastor of Philadelphia's Christ Church, who would become the first congressional chaplain. The next day, Duché opened the session with prayer—and with the day's scheduled reading from the Anglican prayer book. The Scripture was Psalm 35: "Plead my cause, O Lord, with them that strive with me: fight against them that fight against me . . . . Let them be confounded and put to shame." In the face of the impending threat from the British armed forces, the passage seemed prophetic to many of the delegates. Congress resumed work with a renewed spirit of unity and purpose, according to Massachusetts delegate John Adams, who said of the devotion, "It has had an excellent Effect upon every Body here."[18]

That was just the beginning. Throughout the Revolutionary War, the Continental Congress consistently and officially expressed the Bible-based Judeo-Christian worldview in a wide variety of actions. The motivation for American independence, according to the Declaration of

Independence, was the violation of Americans' God-given "unalienable rights" to "Life, Liberty and the pursuit of Happiness" by the British king and parliament. "The general principles on which the fathers achieved independence," founder John Adams reported, "were the only principles in which that beautiful assembly of young gentlemen could unite . . . the general principles of Christianity." The Declaration was laced with biblical principles, from its preamble statement that "all men are created equal" to the closing vow by its signers: "With a firm reliance on the protection of divine Providence, we mutually pledge to each other, our Lives, our Fortunes, and our sacred Honour." Thus, the nation's founding document clearly expressed—in the words of the twentieth-century Jewish historian Abraham Katsh—"a profound sympathy with the Scriptures."[19]

During the war, the Continental Congress repeatedly proclaimed national days of "fasting, humiliation and prayer" and days of prayer and thanksgiving. "With an humble confidence in the mercies of the supreme and impartial Judge and Ruler of the Universe," Congress officially declared, "we most devoutly implore his divine goodness to protect us happily through this great conflict." The Articles of Confederation, the nation's first constitution, acknowledged the supreme authority of "the Great Governor of the world." In 1778, Congress proclaimed that "true religion and good morals are the only solid foundations of public liberty and happiness," and urged the state governments to "take the most effectual measures" to discourage "general depravity of principles and manners." Regularly, Congress assembled in Philadelphia's churches for official worship services—once attending three worship services in a single day—and adopted a design for a national seal that featured the all-seeing eye of God atop a triangle accompanied by the Latin phrase *annuit coeptis:* "He [God] has approved our beginnings." And at war's end, the Continental Congress officially urged Americans everywhere "to offer up our most fervent supplications to the God of all grace, that it may please Him to pardon our offences, and incline our hearts for the future to keep all his laws."[20]

"It is highly expedient for Congress to order a common Bible to be printed."

With such a Bible-based focus in the Continental Congress, the Presbyterian clergymen had good cause to expect a positive response when they informed the delegates of America's need for more Bibles. Plus, the three pastors were ecclesiastical heavyweights—Dr. Francis Alison, Pastor John Ewing, and the Reverend William Marshall. A Scots-Irish immigrant, Alison was the assistant pastor of Philadelphia's First Presbyterian Church, and the founder of schools that would become the Universities of Pennsylvania and Delaware. He was known in his day as "the greatest classical scholar in America," and had mentored several members of the Continental Congress. Ewing was the senior pastor at Alison's church, also Scots-Irish and a respected scholar, and was said to have hiked forty miles as a boy to borrow a book. Fluent in several languages, he was an alumnus of Princeton, and would later become provost of the University of Pennsylvania. Pastor Marshall had come to America from Scotland just twelve years earlier, and served a church in rural Pennsylvania for about seven years until he was called to the pastorate of Scots Presbyterian Church in Philadelphia, which was one of America's most prominent Reformed churches.[21]

In their petition, the pastors asked the Continental Congress to solve America's Bible shortage by doing what no one had done before— oversee the publishing of an English-language Bible in America. More than a century and a half had passed since the first successful English colony in America had been established at Jamestown, and yet no English-language Bible had been printed in the thirteen English colonies. Now the war had shut down the importation all goods from Britain— including Bibles. "[The] holy Scriptures contained in the old and new Testaments are growing so scarce and dear," the pastors' petition read, "that we greatly fear that unless timely care be used to prevent it, we shall not have bibles for our schools and families and for the publick worship of God in our churches." Such was the crisis as defined by the clergymen, who also presented their proposed solution. "We therefore, think it our Duty to our Country and to the Churches of Christ to lay this design before this honourable house," their petition continued, "humbly requesting that under your care, and by your encouragement, a Copy of the holy Bible may be printed."[22]

On September 7, 1774, delegates to the First Continental Congress open deliberations with prayer. Afterward, the Reverend Jacob Duché, America's first congressional chaplain, read to the delegates from the Bible—Psalm 35. "It seemed as if Heaven had ordained that Psalm to be read," reported one delegate. Source: National Archives.

The assembled delegates took the petition seriously, and immediately appointed a congressional committee to recommend appropriate action. It was composed of John Adams, Jonathan Bayard Smith, and Daniel Roberdeau. Adams, the future second president of the United States, was an influential delegate from Massachusetts, and a key leader in the independence movement within the Congress that had produced the Declaration of Independence in the summer of the previous

year. Known to be serious about his faith, Adams had considered the
ministry as a young man, and was a lifelong student of the Bible. A
Princeton graduate, Jonathan Smith was a Presbyterian layman, a leader
of the independence movement in Philadelphia, and an officer in the
Pennsylvania militia. He was also a prominent Philadelphia businessman
who knew the city's printers. Daniel Roberdeau was a second-generation
American from a family of Huguenots who had fled France to escape
persecution. A successful Philadelphia merchant and a general in the
state militia, he too was a devout Presbyterian who served as a ruling
elder in his church.[24]

While a member of the Continental Congress, founding father John Adams and other leaders made an
official recommendation for "Congress to order a common Bible to be printed under their Inspection for
Use of the United States of America." Source: Library of Congress.

On the same day that the petition was presented, the committee dispatched a letter to five Philadelphia printers, inquiring what would be necessary for the Continental Congress to publish thirty thousand American-made Bibles. "The Congress desire to have a bible printed under their care and by their encouragement," the letter stated, "and request you to inform them." The letter included a list of questions. How much time would be required for such a Bible to be printed? How much type would be needed? Did ample paper stock exist in America, or would paper have to be imported? How should the Bible be priced? While the printers developed job specifications, the three-man committee—Adams, Roberdeau, and Smith—went to work devising plans for a congressional Bible that would be comparable to the Authorized King James Version—but without an endorsement by the British king. Instead, as they envisioned it, the American Bible would be endorsed by the Continental Congress. The committee even provided the official congressional endorsement for the Bible's title page: "That instead of the Words, *newly translated out of the original Tongues, & by his Majesty's special Command*, in the title page of our Bibles, it be said, *translated from the original Tongues and Printed by Order of Congress*." [24]

Adams, Roberdeau, and Smith pushed the congressional Bible proposal forward and delivered a report to the full Congress. "As the Price of Bibles for the Use of Families and Schools is greatly advanced beyond what was formerly given for them, thro their Scarcity and Difficulty in importing them from Europe," the committee advised, "it is highly expedient for Congress to order a common Bible to be printed under their Inspection for Use of the United States of America." The committee members estimated that there were approximately a half million families in the United States, and observed that each one was "standing in Need of one or more Bibles." Therefore, they calculated, "many Thousand copies of the holy Scriptures are immediately wanted." They were equally concerned that the congressional Bible be an accurate translation. Whichever printer won the bid should be provided with "the most Correct copy of the Bible that can be found," they advised, and should be "bound by solemn Oath not to vary from it knowingly in his Edition, even in a single Iota."[25]

Then, just when the movement for a congressional Bible appeared to be gaining momentum, it collapsed. The Philadelphia printers reported that the paper stock necessary for the giant printing project probably could not be found in wartime America, and importing the metal type and other necessary tools would be too costly. Unwilling to give up, the committee members presented an alternative to Congress: buy thousands of Bibles abroad and import them into the United States. In an official recommendation, the committee members stated that "use of the Bible is so universal, and its importance so great" that Congress should take action to "import 20,000 Bibles from Holland, Scotland, or elsewhere into the different ports of the states of the Union." It was September 11, 1777, and the Continental Congress promptly moved to vote on the recommendation—not just because of the urgent need for Bibles, but because the British army was bearing down on Philadelphia.[26]

Fifteen thousand British troops under the command of General William Howe were advancing on Philadelphia in a new offensive to seize the American capital. General George Washington's Continental Army tried to block the enemy advance, but was pushed aside, and on September 26, 1777, victorious British troops marched into Philadelphia with their regimental bands playing "God Save the King." The British army would be forced to withdraw from Philadelphia the following summer, but its advance on Philadelphia spurred a rush of panicky refugees from the city, and forced the members of the Continental Congress to hurriedly pack up their papers and evacuate the city. Enough delegates for a quorum were still at their seats when the Bible proposal came to a vote on September 11—and it passed. In the face of the immediate emergency, however, final action was postponed as the delegates fled the city. The twenty-thousand imported Bibles were never bought, and America's first complete English-language Bible would not be published by the Continental Congress. It *would* become a reality, however, and soon.[27]

A NEW NATION EMBRACES AN OLD BOOK

Blessed is the nation whose God is the LORD.
—PSALMS 33:12

ROBERT AITKEN HAD TAKEN RISKS BEFORE, but none more challenging than this one, which he knew could cost him everything he owned. In 1781, Aitken was a middle-aged printer in Philadelphia, where he operated a well-known print shop, bindery, and bookstore near the popular London Coffee Shop at Market and Front Streets. He had learned his trade in his homeland of Scotland, and had achieved a measure of success since setting up his business in Philadelphia a decade earlier. He was skilled at his craft and was known to be innovative—among the first in America to print pocket-sized calendars—but he was best known as the printer for the *Pennsylvania Magazine,* a popular journal of the day, and for successfully bidding on works from the Continental Congress, including the *Journal of the Continental Congress.* He was a devout believer, serving as a ruling elder at Philadelphia's Associate Presbyterian Church, and was respected for his forbearance and ability to deal with all sorts of personalities in Philadelphia's sometimes rough-and-tumble business community. For instance, one of his regular freelance writers was Thomas Paine, who had become famous for his best-selling pro-independence booklet, *Common Sense,* but who was also a notoriously irascible, irreverent rum-guzzler. To get the famous author to meet deadline during one of his binges, it was said, Aitken would sit Paine down in his print shop and stand over him until his article was written and ready for the press.[1]

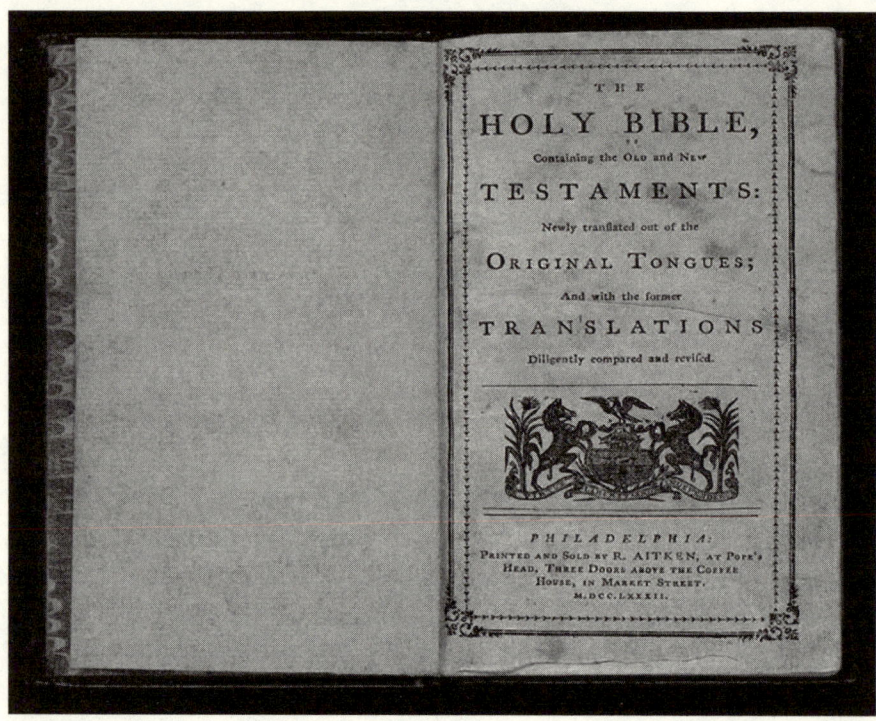

The title page of the Aitken Bible bears nothing to show its historical significance, but it was the first complete English-language Bible published in America—and the only Bible to be officially authorized by the United States Congress. Source: Library of Congress.

Aitken was one of the Philadelphia printers who had been contacted by the Continental Congress about printing a congressional Bible in 1777. When the British occupation of Philadelphia forced Congress to abandon the Bible proposal, Aitken took the initiative himself and printed a copy of the New Testament. Printing a Bible, even the New Testament alone, was a formidable print job for a small-shop printer, but Aitken did what no one before him had ever done. He printed the first known English-language New Testament published in the United States with an American imprint. It was a 353-page, small-sized New Testament, priced at twenty-five dollars. The title page artwork depicted a scroll held by two children and garnished with the image of a dove holding an olive branch. The translation was the King James Version. Amid the Revolutionary War, the license required by the British Crown could be ignored—if the United States successfully earned its independence. Centered in the scroll on the New Testament's title page was the following declaration, which had obviously been lifted from the title page of the Authorized Version:

> The New Testament of our Lord and Saviour Jesus Christ; Newly translated out of the Original Greek; And with the former Translations Diligently compared and revised. Appointed to be read in Churches.

Beneath this was the printer's imprint—the first ever to bear the name of an American printer on an English-language Bible:

> Philadelphia: Printed and sold by R. Aitken, Printer and Bookseller, Front Street. 1777. *Spectamur Agendo*.[2]

Aitken's use of the Latin motto at the end of his imprint indicates that he fully understood the significance of his achievement. Translated into English, it read, "Let us be judged by our acts." Ironically, the motto acquired an ominous meaning when the British army occupied Philadelphia. Knowing that the British might indeed judge him for some of his publications and especially for his close association with the Continental Congress, Aitken had his precious supply of metal type secretly hauled into the countryside outside Philadelphia and hidden in a barn. There it stayed, undiscovered, until the British high command—alarmed at news that France was joining the war on the side of the United States—ordered British forces to evacuate Philadelphia and retreat back to New York in the spring of 1778. Soon Patriot exiles were streaming back into Philadelphia, including the delegates to the

Continental Congress, which eventually resumed deliberations in the Pennsylvania State House.[3]

With the British gone, Aitken soon had his presses running again, and began specializing in artistic engravings of the war's notable battlefields, producing some of the first printed works of military operations in the Revolutionary War. But Aitken—who was known as "a man of truth, and of an irreproachable character"—wanted to do something even more important. By the beginning of the new year begun in 1781, he was committed to take on the task that the Continental Congress had been unable to accomplish—to publish the first complete Bible printed in America. His New Testament had successfully sold through several editions, and he had reason to hope that the Continental Congress would back his plans to print the entire Bible. Earlier in 1780, interest in promoting an American Bible had resurfaced in Congress: A resolution had been proposed to encourage the state governments to "take proper measures" to promote the printing of "new and correct editions of the old and new testaments." So, on Sunday, January 21, 1781—one day before his forty-seventh birthday—Aitken drafted a petition, or "memorial," to the Continental Congress, asking for an official endorsement and financial support for his bold venture.[4]

He made the case that in "every well regulated Government in Christendom" it was the role of the government to protect and publish the "Sacred Books of the Old and New Testaments, commonly called the Holy Bible," so that Christianity would not suffer "alarming Injuries" from "spurious and erroneous Editions of Divine Revelation." He reported that his work on publishing the Bible was well underway, and asked that Congress officially authorize and commission his work "so that the same may be published under the Authority of Congress [and] that he may be Commissioned and otherwise appointed & Authorized to print and vend Editions of, the Sacred Scriptures." Five days later, his appeal was read to the full Continental Congress, which referred it to a three-man committee for study and a recommendation to Congress.[5]

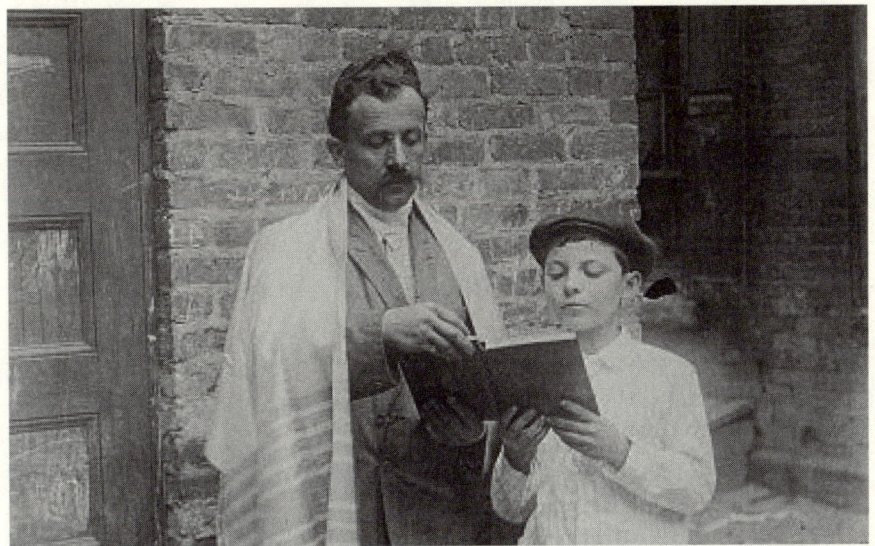

A Jewish father instructs his son in the Scriptures at the dawn of twentieth century America. Earlier, another American milestone work in Bible translation occurred when Jewish scholar Isaac Leeser rendered an original translation of the Old Testament into English as the Leeser Bible. Source: Library of Congress.

"Resolved, That the United States in Congress assembled...recommend this edition of the Bible to the inhabitants of the United States...."

The committee was composed of Thomas McKean of Delaware, a signer of the Declaration of Independence and a current congressional leader; James Duane, a New York lawyer and longtime member of Congress; and John Witherspoon, a Presbyterian minister from New Jersey, who had been president of Princeton University and a signer of the Declaration of Independence. The war was still underway, and while the committee apparently continued to consult with the printer, it did not make a recommendation to Congress for more than a year.

By then it was September 1782. The British army had been forced into a humiliating surrender by American and French forces under General George Washington at Yorktown, Virginia the previous October, and peace negotiations now were underway in Paris. It was obvious to all that the war was ending in victory and nationhood for the United States. A spirit of relief, celebration, and optimism was sweeping America, and to Robert Aitken, it surely seemed that the time was right for the first full Bible published in America.[6]

Joyful worshippers at a rural camp meeting reflect the exuberance of the Second Great Awakening, a revival of Christianity that swept through the nation in the early nineteenth century. Among its achievements: an explosion of Bible-reading among Americans. Source: Library of Congress.

On September 1, 1782, the congressional committee requested an evaluation of Aitken's Bible from the ministers who were jointly serving as congressional chaplains—the Reverend George Duffield and the Reverend William White, who were provided with a printer's copy of Aitken's Bible. Both were known for knowledge of the Bible. Duffield was a former frontier preacher now pastoring at Scots Presbyterian

Church in Philadelphia, and White was the pastor of St. Peter's Church—an Anglican church attended by General Washington when he was in the city. Both gave Aitken's Bible an enthusiastic ecclesiastical endorsement, declaring it to be "executed with great accuracy as to the sense, and with as few grammatical and typographical errors as could be expected in an undertaking of such magnitude." They too hoped its printing would help alleviate the shortage of Bibles in America. "Being ourselves witnesses for the demand for this invaluable book," they wrote, "we rejoice in the present prospect of a supply, hoping it will prove as advantageous as it is honorable to the gentleman, who has exerted himself to furnish it at the evident risk of private fortune."[7]

Despite the chaplains' enthusiasm, Congress did not attempt to fund Robert Aitken's Bible. The American economy was in shambles, the national government was near bankruptcy, and Congress owed years of back pay to American troops. But Congress did endorse it. On September 12, 1782, Congress passed an official resolution recommending the Bible "to the inhabitants of the United States." About two weeks later, Aitken publicly announced that he was publishing the new Bible. When it was printed, bound, and presented to the public for sale, the Aitken Bible—as it became known—featured the Congressional resolution on one of its opening pages:

> Whereupon, Resolved, That the United States in Congress assembled, highly approve the pious and laudable undertaking of Mr. Aitken, as subservient to the interest of religion as well as an instance of the progress of arts in this country, and being satisfied from the above report, of his care and accuracy in the execution of the work, they recommend this edition of the Bible to the inhabitants of the United States, and hereby authorise him to publish this recommendation in the manner he shall think proper.[8]

Aitken printed ten thousand copies in a small-sized, two-volume edition bound in calfskin, although he also printed some single-volume copies. It was the King James Version, and—probably to conserve paper—it contained no margin notes. Along with the congressional endorsement and the date 1782 in Roman numerals, the Bible also carried a statement on its title page that was a standard feature of all King James Bibles published in Britain: "The Holy Bible, Containing the Old and New Testaments: Newly translated out of the Original Tongues, And with the former Translations Diligently compared and revised." Aitken's Bible was unique, however, in that it also bore the printer's imprint—"Printed and Sold by R. Aitken"—with the place of publication cited not as London, Cambridge, or Oxford, but as Philadelphia, distinguishing the Aitken Bible as the first complete Bible printed in America. It also carried the less lofty, but very practical information stating where the new Bible could be purchased in Philadelphia: "Three doors above the Coffee House, in Market Street." [9]

Aitken's Bible was an extraordinary achievement—and a financial disaster. The end of the Revolutionary War did indeed provide opportunities for innovation and investments—but it did so for many and not just a solitary printer in Philadelphia. Competition in the printing industry arose quickly, including the publication of the Bible. Cheaper, imported Bibles from England and Scotland flooded America and undercut the sales of Aitken's new Bible. He tried various innovative sales methods: he placed copies on consignment with other printers and booksellers, unsuccessfully petitioned Congress to purchase a portion of his inventory for public distribution, and tried in vain to obtain funding to distribute the Bible to America's Revolutionary War veterans. He did eventually receive some financial assistance from the local Presbyterian synod, which purchased a quantity of Aitken Bibles to give to the city's poor. Aitken accepted his losses and continued his printer's trade in Philadelphia until his death at age sixty-eight in 1802. The Aitken Bible was the peak of his work as a printer—although it did not provide financial success for Aitken. Even so, wrote a contemporary, "he acquired the respect of those who became acquainted with him," and Robert Aitken entered history as the man who published the first complete American Bible—the Aitken Bible. [10]

A mid-nineteenth century American clergyman happily holds his Bible for the photographer. In the nineteenth century, the Bible solidly remained the bedrock foundation of American culture, law and government. Source: Library of Congress.

§

The Aitken Bible was the first of many American Bibles that would follow. In 1790, eight years after Aitken Bible was published, a Philadelphia printer named Matthew Carey published an edition of the Catholic Douay-Rheims Bible. A fiery Irishman with a gift for languages and a love for printing, Carey had been forced to flee Ireland disguised as a woman because a newspaper he published was deemed traitorous by the British Parliament. He landed in Philadelphia almost penniless at age twenty-four, but through hard work and influential connections, he established another newspaper, a print shop and a bookstore, prospering despite a serious wound suffered in a duel with a rival newspaper editor. Like Aitken, Carey was disappointed with the sales of his Douay-Rheims Bible. It was skillfully printed but sold slowly, perhaps because early-nineteenth-century American Catholics still preferred to hear the Scriptures read aloud in church rather than read the Bible themselves. But also like Aitken, Carey was a risk-taker—and he decided that he would try again.[11]

This time, in 1801, he reluctantly printed the King James Bible, and directed his sales efforts at Protestants. Carey's King James Version was larger and cheaper than Aitken's Bible; it was also expertly bound by a professional binder, and included numerous illustrations, reference materials, and other features. Americans loved it. "Bible after Bible issued from his presses," observed nineteenth-century American Bible scholar John Wright, "and many of the editions were embellished with engravings executed in the best style of the day." Assisting Carey's publishing efforts was a colorful, controversial Anglican minister-turned-author-and-book-salesman named Mason Locke Weems. As an author, Weems was shamelessly prone to embellishment and literary invention: he concocted numerous tall tales, including the familiar legend of young George Washington chopping down a cherry tree, which he recorded in an immensely popular biography of Washington he published with Carey. "You have a great deal of money lying in the bones of old George," he callously advised Carey, "if you will exert yourself to extract it." As a book salesman, however, Weems was gifted with a remarkable ability to gauge the interests of the American reading public, and in the opening years of the nineteenth century, Americans wanted Bibles.[12]

REV. MASON L. WEEMS.[1]

With hand in coat, Mason Locke Weems strikes a Napoleonic pose. Although colorful and controversial, he was the emperor of Bible sales in America's early national era. Thus assisted, Matthew Carey—Weems' employer—became the largest Bible publisher in early America. Source: New York Public Library.

Weems conveyed that demand to Carey in letter after letter as the publisher weighed the risks of losing another fortune after the poor sales of his Douay-Rheims Bible. "I would as soon set my property on fire, as engage in such a work," Carey declared at one point—but Weems was relentless in his assurances that the American public was hungry for the

Scriptures. "You hear nothing here now," Weems advised Cary from the field, "but printing the Bible." His advice proved true: Carey printed more King James Bibles, many more, and eventually became the leading Bible publisher in America in the early nineteenth century. He was also the first to offer Bible readers a variety of choices on a grand scale—plain Bibles printed with text alone; elaborate Bibles featuring illustrations, charts, and commentary; Bibles that were handsomely bound or plainly bound; Bibles for school, home, teaching, and preaching. Some people wanted inexpensive Bibles; others were willing to invest, as Weems put it, "in but one bible, as one Wife, in their lifetime." Carey made a fortune printing Bibles; put much of his profits in charitable causes, such as the first Sunday school society; and became a respected entrepreneur, economist, and philanthropist. America's other Bible publishers followed his example, producing a variety of King James Bibles in an array of editions and styles. By the mid-nineteenth century, William Carey—the brash, dueling, Irish immigrant-turned-publisher—had forever changed Bible publishing in America.[13]

Meanwhile, as Carey was struggling to blaze a path toward successful Bible publishing in America, other American printers brought early Bibles off their presses in various edition sizes. One of them, William Young, a Philadelphia printer who was a contemporary of Robert Aitken, published a King James New Testament in 1790, and a year later reprinted it with the addition of the book of Psalms—the first New Testament of its kind to be printed in America. Also in 1791, Isaac Collins, a newspaper and book publisher in Trenton, New Jersey, printed a popular, large-sized Bible that would become known as the first "family Bible" published in America. Collins reportedly used his children to proof the text, and remarkably, the only error said to be found when the Bible was published was a single incorrect punctuation mark. In December 1791, Isaiah Thomas, a printer in Worcester, Massachusetts, also published a large-sized Bible. During the American

Revolution, Thomas had gained fame as the editor of the *Massachusetts Spy*, an influential, pro-independence newspaper. The Thomas Bible, as it became known, was distinctive for the quality of its typography and binding—and also because Thomas allowed early purchasers to partially pay for a Bible with "wheat, rye, Indian corn, butter or pork."[14]

The early nineteenth century also saw the first direct translation of the Septuagint into English, the first translation of the New Testament by an American, and the first Bible published by a female printer—all of which were accomplished with one Bible. It was the Thomson Bible—the work of Charles Thomson, who was the former secretary of the Continental Congress and a codesigner of the official seal of the United States, with its biblically based imagery and motto. He was also a Greek and Latin scholar, and in 1808, his English translation of the Bible was published by Philadelphia printer Jane Aitken, the daughter of Robert Aitken, who had taken over her father's printing business. The large, four-volume Thomson Bible was not a home Bible—it was the Scriptures for scholars. It translated the Old Testament directly from the Septuagint, and earned wide praise from the Bible scholars of the day. Thomson not only attempted to produce a translation from the oldest and most reliable sources in the Bible's original languages; he also sought to use words according to their historic meaning. "I have sought for truth with the utmost ingenuity," he wrote, "and endeavored to give a just and true representation of the sense and meaning of the sacred Scriptures." His Bible would be read by few other than scholars, but it would set a standard for translation in the early nineteenth century.[15]

Ignited by the Second Great Awakening, a revival of Christianity that began in the 1790s and continued into the 1840s, the nineteenth century witnessed an explosion in Bible reading by Americans, accompanied by a flood of faith reminiscent of the Great Awakening in the colonial era. In contrast to the rise of secular humanism in Europe, the Judeo-Christian worldview was reinforced as the bedrock of American culture, law, and government, and Christianity specifically expanded so pervasively that the nineteenth century would be dubbed "the Christian Century" by

American believers. "Under all our institutions rest the Bible and the schoolhouse," enthused American educator George Edward Reed, a minister and the president of Dickinson College, as he surveyed the nineteenth century from the pinnacle of 1899. "America is a land of churches . . . ," he wrote, "[and] that we are a religious, a Christian people, may be argued from the steady and enormous increase during this century of the spiritual and material forces of the church of Christ, an increase phenomenal even amid the wonders of a phenomenal century."[16]

The twin towers of Westminster Abbey rise above the bustle of Parliament Square in late nineteenth century London. In 1870, a team of Bible translators at Westminster Abbey began work on a major revision of the King James Bible—which would be published fifteen years later as the English Revised Version. Source: Library of Congress.

Bible societies blossomed throughout the land—the Ladies Auxiliary Bible Society, the Marine Bible Society, the Young Men's Bible Society, and countless others. In 1809, the International Bible Society was established in New York City, modeled after the British and Foreign Bible Society, founded five years earlier in Britain. Seven years later, the American Bible Society was established, also in New York, and was headed by Elias Boudinot, the former president of the Continental Congress, who was both devout and a Bible scholar. Both U.S. Bible societies actively supported Bible translation efforts and the distribution of the Scriptures—including widespread distribution to U.S. military forces. In 1815, the International Bible Society sponsored a French translation for newly acquired French-speaking Louisiana, while the American Bible Society translated New Testament books into the language of the Delaware Indian tribe. In 1835, Samuel G. Howe produced a New Testament for the blind using a raised-letter alphabet with the help of the American Bible Society. So inspired, wives of plantation owners in the South broke the law and taught house slaves how to read so they could study the Bible.[17]

Meanwhile, Bible revisions and translations continued. In 1814, the first complete version of the Old Testament in Hebrew was published by a Scots-American printer named William Dobson in Philadelphia. Although it *was* the Hebrew Bible, it did not follow the Masoretic text, and its principal readership was Christians who wished to read the Old Testament in its original language. Father Francis Kenrick, an American Catholic scholar, worked on a revised version of the Douay-Rheims Bible, which was published in parts beginning in 1849. The Vatican still considered itself the only "divinely appointed custodian and interpreter" of the Scriptures, but Kenrick's work was followed by a parade of revised editions of the Bible for use by Catholics. Between 1839 and 1884, translations of the Old Testament into English by Jewish scholars such as Salid Neuman, Abraham Benish, and Michael Friedlander were introduced to Jewish homes and synagogues in America. A milestone work was Jewish scholar Isaac Leeser's original translation of the entire

Hebrew Bible—the Old Testament—into English, which was published in 1853 and became known as the "Leeser Bible" within America's Jewish community. It was revised in the late nineteenth century by the Jewish Publication Society.[18]

§

The discovery and study of early biblical manuscripts in the nineteenth century—especially Codex Sinaiticus and Codex Vaticanus—encouraged demand for revision of the King James Version in the United States as well as in Great Britain. By 1870, approximately six dozen other versions of the English Bible had been published, but none approached the King James in popularity. That year—almost 260 years after the first printing of the Authorized Version—work on a full revision of the King James Bible was begun. It was called the English Revised Version, and it originated in 1870, when Anglican Bishop Samuel Wilberforce—son of British antislavery crusader William Wilberforce—officially recommended that the Church of England sponsor a revision of the King James New Testament. Church leaders agreed, and invited Bible experts from other denominations to join Anglican scholars for the task. A revision committee of fifty-four members was selected and divided into two groups—one to work on the New Testament, and the other to translate the Old Testament. The revisers volunteered their work, and Oxford and Cambridge University Presses agreed to bear the printing costs in exchange for a fourteen-year copyright. The New Testament committee began first, starting its work at London's Westminster Abbey on June 22, 1870.[19]

It took eleven years to complete the Revised New Testament, which was published in London on May 17, 1881, and a few days later in the United States. It sold two million copies in a single week in Britain. In the United States, more than 200,000 copies were sold within one week in New York City alone. It was a major national event in the United States, with several newspapers printing the entire New Testament for their readers. The Revised Old Testament was finished four years later, and the complete work was published in 1885 as the English Revised

Version. The new translation benefited from advances made in the scholarly understanding of the Hebrew language over the centuries; and the New Testament was believed to be a more accurate English expression of the Greek than what could have been done in 1611.[20]

It was a major national event in the United States, with several newspapers printing the entire New Testament for their readers.

The Revised Version also substituted modern terms for obsolete English words, such as "smooth" for "peeled," "falsehood" for "leasing," and most notably, "the Holy Spirit" for "the Holy Ghost." Even so, many readers did not like the unadorned style of English used in the translation, especially in the New Testament. The average reader—including many Americans—missed the elegant, poetic language of the King James Version, and even scholars admitted that the new English of the English Revised Version, like the text in original languages, was noticeably plain. "It is strong in Greek, weak in English," observed Charles Spurgeon, who was the most celebrated English preacher of the day. In 1898, the complete English Revised Version—Old and New Testaments—was released with new cross-references. The English Revised Version gradually became the preferred version for countless English-speaking Bible readers, but much time would pass before it would equal the popularity of the time-honored King James Version.[21]

An American edition of the Revised Version enjoyed greater success, however, due to changes implemented by its publisher and Bible scholars in the United States. The British revisers and publishers had agreed to an American edition of the Bible with modifications made by an American translation committee, but required fourteen years to pass before the American Bible could be published. In 1901, it was released by New York publisher Thomas Nelson and Sons as the

American Standard Version. In translation and style, many reviewers and readers in the United States considered it superior to the English Revised Version. It replaced even more antiquated English terms—such as "holpen," "strowed," "bewray" and "hough"—and used Americanized words and phrases such as "turned away" instead of "eschewed" and "patched" instead of "clouted." It also reduced the number of marginal notes found in the British edition, restored section headlines, included convenient cross references, and improved the structure of paragraphs and the use of punctuation.[22]

An elderly American farmer reads the Word on his front porch at the close of the nineteenth century. Ahead, a new century was dawning—and with it would come an astonishing wave of English-language Bible translations and revisions. Source: Library of Congress.

The American Standard Version did have its critics—and not just those who preferred the familiarity of the King James Version. It was criticized for doctrinal lapses and textual inconsistency, for instance, because it referred to the Holy Spirit as "it" in some places and "he" in others. Adding to the criticism it received, the Revised Version almost immediately had to surrender its claim to being the most accurate available biblical text. Although its text indeed benefited from the use of Codex Sinaiticus and Codex Alexandrinus, many other papyri manuscripts had been discovered in the three decades that passed between when the research began on the Revised Version and the publication of the American Standard Version. Its strength was therefore its weakness as well. "The ASV represented the best scholarship and biblical learning of its time," observed twentieth-century Bible authority Jack P. Lewis. "It is not, however, the final word in Bible translation."[23]

At the opening of the twentieth century, the King James Version remained the most beloved Bible translation in American history—and first choice for many people—but the American Standard Version did set precedents for future Bible translations and revisions. Its emphasis on a scholarly, accurate text would be followed by other important Bible translations in the future, and the impact of its less-successful attempt to produce elegant or at least very readable English would not go unnoticed by Bible translators and publishers. The discussion and debate surrounding the American Standard Version marked what respected twentieth-century Bible scholar Paul Wegner described as "a significant upsurge in interest for modern-speech versions" of the Bible. Equally significant, the widespread national attention garnered by its publication also reflected the continued importance of the Bible in American culture. The twentieth century was dawning, and with it would come an astonishing wave of English-language Bible translations and revisions.[24]

12

THE WORD OF OUR GOD STANDS FOREVER

The grass withers, the flower fades, but the word of our God stands forever.
—ISAIAH 40:8

THIRTY-ONE-YEAR-OLD THOMAS KUTLUK knew he only had moments to live as he struggled in the freezing water. An Inuit man living on the western shore of Canada's Hudson Bay, he was a seasoned arctic traveler, but he had made a grave mistake. It was the spring of 1983, and the ice on the bay was melting into a thin layer. He was driving a dogsled led by a team of huskies across the white-draped wilderness when he let his team veer too close to thin ice. It cracked and collapsed, dumping the sled and its driver into the subzero water of Hudson's Bay. Kutluk could not swim— and he knew that within fleeting minutes the deadly cold water would kill him. Stifling his panic, he struggled to pull himself up on the ice, but it fell off in chunks. The water current beneath the bay's icy surface was powerful, and he felt himself being sucked under. "With my body tilted and my face toward heaven, I cried out to God," he later recalled. "I had no words—just a voice from deep within me—a desperate cry to the Lord God." Immediately, he remembered his father's words: "If you ever fall into the water, hang on to the ice and kick your feet." He immediately did so—and in a moment he slid out onto the ice, alive.[1]

Thomas Kutluk was a nominal Christian at the time of his near-death accident. He belonged to a Bible-centered church, but seldom attended and never seemed to find time to read the Scriptures. His survival prompted him to refocus his priorities on what God expected of him. As a believer, he wanted to grow in discipleship, so he began to read the Bible seriously. As was the case for many Inuit, Yupik, Eskimo, and other indigenous people of the arctic regions of North America, English was his second language, and awaiting him as he began his walk of faith was a unique English-language Bible designed for him and his people. It was called the New Life New Testament, and it was the work of a Christian missionary named Gleason H. Ledyard. In 1946, Ledyard followed his call and fulfilled a personal life's dream when he founded a small church in the village of Arviat on the isolated western shore of Hudson Bay. He was accompanied by his wife, Kathryn. She established a school for Inuit children, and Ledyard ministered to the indigenous people of Canada's Northwest Territories, traveling by dogsled or flying a lightweight ski-plane. Often, the Ledyards found themselves sharing God's Word with Inuit or Yupkit people who spoke different indigenous languages, but shared a common ability to read and understand limited English. If only a Bible translation existed in basic, simple English, they reasoned, millions of people around the world would not have to wait for translations in their native language.[2]

After fifteen years of ministering in the Northwest Territories, Gleason Ledyard set out to produce that simple English Bible translation himself. He and Kathryn placed their mission post in the hands of the Christian and Missionary Alliance, and retired to Oregon, where Ledyard began work on what would become the New Life Bible. Like John Eliot, who had translated his "Indian Bible" three hundred years earlier, Ledyard was assisted by his wife and by indigenous interpreters. Also like Eliot, he began with the New Testament, which was published in 1969, followed by the complete Bible in 1986. Ledyard and his team approached the work as a new translation, not a paraphrase, and limited the vocabulary to about 850 words. The brevity of the Bible's language gave the New Life Version, as it eventually came to be called, a simple, easy-to-comprehend text, as evidenced by its rendering of John 3:16: "For God so loved the world that He gave His only Son. Whoever puts his trust in God's Son will not be lost but will have life that lasts forever." The New Life New Testament, published by Christian Literature International, quickly became a favorite in mission fields where English was a second language, and within little more than twenty-five years, it had sold more than five million copies.[3]

Inuit dogsleds prepare for a run amid thinning ice within the arctic circle. In the twentieth century, Bible translations were available even for indigenous peoples in the world's remotest corners. Source: NOAA Photo Library/Wikimedia Commons

The challenge to all Bible translators through the ages has been to accurately and respectfully render the words and message.

The New Life Version was among scores of new Bible translations and revisions that marketed the explosion of American Bible publishing in the twentieth century and the early decades of the following century. Dozens of new English translations were produced. Some were paraphrases, in which English translations were rewritten for easier reading but were not newly translated. Those that were newly translated from the original languages followed one of two translation styles. They were either a literal, word-for-word translation—called "formal equivalence"—or they focused on translating the thought or message of a passage and were thus message-for-message translations—called "dynamic equivalence." A few translations attempted to combine the two styles—a translation method called the "ideolectical technique." Translating words and messages from Hebrew, Greek, and Aramaic into English or any other language has never been an easy task. Message-for-message translations faced the dangers of omitting a key word from the original language and obscuring the intent of the inspired text. Literal translations that focused solely on words faced the danger of obscuring the intent of the inspired text through awkward language that was difficult to read. One rare truly literal translation, for instance, was Robert Young's 1862 Bible—Young's Literal Translation—which rendered the familiar verse of Galatians 2:20 word for word from the Greek thus: "With Christ I have been crucified, and live no more do I, and Christ doth live in me; and that which I now live in the flesh—in the faith I live of the Son of God, who did love me and did give himself for me." The challenge to all Bible translators through the ages has been to accurately and respectfully render the words and message of Scripture as the inspired, authoritative Word of God—as directed by 2 Timothy 2:15:

"Be diligent to present yourself approved to God as a workman who does not need to be ashamed, accurately handling the word of truth." Major Bible translations and paraphrases published in the twentieth and early twenty-first centuries included the following:[4]

- REVISED STANDARD VERSION. A multi-denomination group called the International Council of Religious Education acquired the copyright to the 1901 American Standard Bible in 1928, but could not raise the funds to publish a new revision during the Great Depression. In 1946, a revision of the New Testament was published, followed by the complete Revised Standard Version of the Bible in 1952. The RSV, as it became known, was heralded as a model of scholarship and the modernized use of the English language. It was viewed as a literal translation, received wide sales, and was updated with a 1952 edition—but it also stirred criticism because its copyright was connected to the National Council of Churches, which held theologically liberal positions that were troubling to many Christians. Numerous Bible readers were also alarmed that the Revised Version used the word "maiden" instead of the term "virgin" in the messianic prophecy of Isaiah 7:14. In 1973, what was billed as an "ecumenical edition" of the RSV was released. It became known as the Common Bible, included the Apocrypha in appendices, and was designed to appeal to Catholic, Protestant, and Eastern Orthodox readers. The Revised Standard Version continued to be updated and republished, including the New Revised Standard Version, a 1990 revision directed by the National Council of Churches, that became the preferred Bible for many in the English-speaking world, despite concerns that it eliminated "masculine-oriented language" from the text.[5]

- JERUSALEM BIBLE. Originally published in 1966, the Jerusalem Bible was the first Roman Catholic Bible to be translated directly from the original Hebrew, Greek, and Aramaic instead of depending primarily on Jerome's Latin Vulgate. About forty French Catholic scholars at L'Ecole Biblique de Jerusalem (the School of Biblical and Archaeological Studies) produced a French translation and commentary in 1948. That was followed by an English translation rendered by a team of British Catholic scholars. Questions about the text, including Catholic–Protestant interpretations and terminology in passages such as Isaiah 7:14, were addressed by scholarly notes. The original edition has been revised, and as in the RSV, masculine pronouns from the original languages have been altered in places because, in the words of the Bible's preface, they are "now found so offensive by some people."[6]

A tent revival service in California attracts a full house in the mid-twentieth century. A 1927 tent revival dramatically changed the life of a California citrus grower named Dewey Lockman—and eventually led to the publishing of the New American Standard Bible. Source: Mennonite Church USA Archives.

- NEW ENGLISH BIBLE. Less than a year after World War II ended, the general assembly of the Church of Scotland was asked by two local presbyteries to take the lead in developing a new English translation of the Bible to replace the King James Version. As a result, the New Testament portion of the New English Bible, or NEB, was published fifteen years later, in 1961, followed by the complete Bible in 1970. It was an entirely new English translation produced by leading English Bible scholars and jointly published by the university presses of Oxford and Cambridge. Although initially praised for its scholarship, the NEB was bemoaned by some critics for such a free, message-for-message translation in places that some deemed it a paraphrase. It was updated in 1989 as the Revised English Bible (the REB), but its modernized language still troubled some readers, and others were disappointed to find "gender-inclusive" changes to masculine pronouns in ancient texts. The British flavor of its English vernacular reduced its popularity in the United States, and it failed to replace the King James Bible in sales.[7]

- THE LIVING BIBLE. When Kenneth Taylor was a child in Oregon, he saw his father accidentally drop the Bible on the floor. His dad, a Presbyterian pastor, stooped over and picked it up—gently and reverently. Young Taylor was impressed by the respect his father displayed toward the Bible, and he too grew to revere it as the Word of God. But he had difficulty reading the seventeenth-century vernacular of the King James Version. Many years later, as an adult and the father of ten children, he struggled again with his beloved KJV as he tried to read it to his children. By then, Taylor was an alumnus of Wheaton College and Dallas Theological Seminary, and was an editor of Christian literature at Moody Bible Institute in Chicago. He prayerfully began writing a careful paraphrase of the Bible, working on it as he rode the train home from the city, and even consulting a poet to develop simple but elegant English language that anyone, children and immigrants alike, could read and understand. Unable to find a publisher for his work, Taylor established his own publishing firm, Tyndale House Publishing—named for his Bible translator hero—which eventually became one of the world's leading Christian publishing firms. Released in 1971, the Living Bible eventually sold more than forty million copies in North America alone. In 1996, Tyndale House published an extensively updated version of the Living Bible—the NEW LIVING TRANSLATION—which employed 90 Bible scholars and translators "to render the message of the original texts of Scripture into clear, contemporary English." Described by the publisher as "an authoritative Bible translation . . . both faithful to the ancient texts and eminently readable," the New Living Translation has proven to be immensely popular with contemporary Bible readers.[8]

- NEW AMERICAN STANDARD BIBLE. When Dewey Lockman attended a tent revival in California in 1927, he had no idea how much his life was about to change. It did—and so did countless other lives as a result. He underwent what he called "a miraculous conversion," surrendering his life to Jesus Christ as Lord and Savior. Four years later, he felt convicted to become a serious tither based on his reading of Malachi 3:10 in the Old Testament. Lockman and his wife, Minna, were not wealthy— they were California citrus farmers—but they began to increase the amount they tithed to God's work, even when times were difficult. Eventually, their farm became prosperous, and in 1942, they used the proceeds from sales of their farmland to create the nonprofit Lockman Foundation for "the established purpose to promote Christian evangelism, education and benevolence."[9]

   In 1959, Lockman focused his foundation on replacing the ASV with an even more accurate, readable English translation based on the latest scholarship and study of ancient manuscripts. A team of Hebrew and Greek scholars, educators, and pastors was assembled to "produce a translation that would"—in their words—"adhere as closely as possible to the original language of the Holy Scriptures and to make the translation in a fluent and readable style." It was published in 1971 as the New American Standard Bible, or NASB. It was a literal translation, but substituted a "current English idiom" where a word-for-word rendering was difficult to comprehend. Thus, it was viewed by many evangelicals and theological conservatives as a vastly improved version that combined a literal translation with enhanced readability—based on superior scholarship. "Since they are the eternal Word of God," stated the NASB's foreword, "the Holy Scriptures speak with fresh power to each generation, to give wisdom that leads to salvation, that men may serve Christ to the glory of God." Dewey Lockman died in 1974, several years after his wife's passing. A few years later, according to the Christian Booksellers Association, the New American Standard Bible was for a time the best-selling Bible in the United States.[10]

• GOOD NEWS BIBLE/TODAY'S ENGLISH VERSION. While the Lockman Foundation's translators were laboring to produce the word-for-word NASB, the American Bible Society successfully captured the attention of English-language Bible readers around the world with publication of a remarkable work that would be internationally famous as the Good News Bible. Formally entitled *Good News for Modern Man: The New Testament in Today's English Version*, it would become popularly known as the Good News Bible or the TEV—Today's English Version. It was not a paraphrase: it was the first modern-style message-for-message Bible translation. The TEV was born from the experiences of Bible translators in the Third World, and was translated from the original languages into simple, common, sixth-grade American English. It was a language style, American Bible Society leaders believed, that accurately conveyed Scripture with the power of the Bible's original languages. Critics complained, however, that its language was too simplistic, even childlike, and diminished the elegance of language that had been a hallmark of many English-language Bibles dating to William Tyndale's work. "Not everyone prefers a God who talks like a pal or a guidance counselor," one critic suggested. Others asserted that its unadorned choice of words fell flat when it attempted to convey Old Testament poetry. Even so, tens of millions of readers loved it. It was endorsed by the revered American evangelist Billy Graham and accepted by the Roman Catholic Church. Mass-published in paperback, the TEV was embraced by scores of new Christians, children, and indigenous people in the mission fields whose second language was English. In the decades to come, it would be updated and revised—inspiring the Contemporary English Version of 1995—but no new edition could be expected to match its early popularly: In its first decade, the Good News Bible sold an astonishing fifty-two million copies.[11]

Fresh from the ship, newly arrived immigrants at New York's Ellis Island receive a New Testament in their language in 1911—courtesy of the International Bible Society. Later renamed Biblica, it and the American Bible Society ceaselessly promoted Bible-reading.

- NEW INTERNATIONAL VERSION. The NIV, as the New International Version is popularly called, traces its origins to a Seattle engineer named Howard Long, who considered himself to be "a lifelong devotee" to the King James Bible, but who struggled with its seventeenth-century English language when sharing his faith with others. Long belonged to a local body of the Christian Reformed Church in the mid-1950s, and he enlisted his pastor in a campaign to launch a new, accurate, and readable English-language translation of the Bible. Eventually, their denomination joined the effort, and so did the National Association of Evangelicals, which assembled a team of Bible scholars to discuss the proposal. The movement for a new translation became serious in the mid-1960s, when it received funding from the International Bible Society—originally the New York Bible Society and later renamed Biblica.[12]

  A team of more than one hundred evangelical Bible translators was organized from more than thirty Protestant denominations, went to work on the new translation, and produced a New Testament that was published in 1971 as the New International Version. In 1978, the complete Bible was published. Anticipation was high in America's evangelical community, and the new Bible was enthusiastically received. Its translation style was ideolectical and attempted to blend both a word-for-word translation with a message-for-message translation. In the new Bible's preface, its translators stated their intention to produce "an accurate translation and one that would have clarity and literary quality." The NIV featured a moderate contemporary form of English, contained more than thirty-five hundred footnotes explaining content and textual issues, and was based on the broad range of ancient textual sources available in the late twentieth century. It was heralded as a "monument of Christian scholarship" and was embraced by Bible readers in the United States, Britain, and elsewhere in the English-speaking world. Sales soared, and by the dawn of the twenty-first century, the NIV was the top-selling Bible in America.[13]

It did have critics, including some who were concerned that its easy-reading style camouflaged a tendency to be too free with the translation in some places. But critics were few in number—until 1997. That year a revision of the NIV was published in the United States as Today's New International Version—promptly known as the TNIV—and it ignited a firestorm of criticism. The main controversy was the revised Bible's "gender accurate" format, which eliminated numerous masculine pronouns in both the Old and New Testaments. *World* magazine, a popular evangelical news journal, described the TNIV as a "Stealth Bible" that was quietly spearheading a "feminist seduction of the evangelical Church." Pastors, laity, and several denominations expressed deep concerns. In response, the TNIV publishers openly invited criticism from the Christian community, and in 2011 published a revised NIV Bible to replace both the original NIV and the TNIV. Some evangelical leaders still expressed lingering concerns, but Biblica (International Bible Society) stood by the revised NIV, stating that its translators "don't just translate the Bible. They believe the Bible. They're united by the conviction that what they translate isn't just any book: it's the inspired Word of God." Six decades after its initial publication, the NIV Bible had sold more than sixty million copies.[14]

- NEW KING JAMES VERSION. What has made the King James Version so popular year after year? Pollsters and others asked that same question year after year, as new data continued to show a widespread affection for the King James Version among American Bible readers despite the availability of a growing number of accurate and carefully rendered English-language translations. Typical perhaps was a 2014 nationwide study by the Center for Religion and American Culture, which found that approximately 55 percent of Bible readers in America still preferred the

King James Version, compared to 19 percent who used the NIV, 7 percent who read the New Revised Standard Version, and the remaining percentage who preferred a variety of translations. Study researchers found that many people believed they could depend on the King James Version for a faithfully transmitted, literal word-for-word text of the Scriptures. Even the antiquated seventeenth-century language of the KJV, with its "thees" and "thous," was preferable to many Bible readers, leading some pollsters to conclude that the language of the King James Bible had become the language of things sacred for many people. It was also reassuringly familiar. Noted one lifetime reader of the KJV, "It was the Bible I was raised with."[15]

In response to this national trend, Thomas Nelson Inc.—a leading American Bible publisher—released a revised KJV New Testament in 1979, followed by a revision of the complete King James Bible in 1982. The New King James Version, or NKJV, was the work of more than 130 Bible scholars. "The purpose of this most recent revision of the King James Version," the translators stated in the new Bible's preface, "is in harmony with the purpose of the original King James scholars: Not to make a new translation. . . . but to make a good one better." Accordingly, the New King James Version attempted to maintain the text of the 1611 King James Bible (as revised over the ages) while modernizing its language and reinforcing the text with the knowledge gained from manuscript discoveries made over the course of almost four hundred years. It was an attempt, the translators stated, to continue "the labors of the earlier translators, thus unlocking for today's readers the spiritual treasures found especially in the Authorized Version."[16]

The NKJV's translators followed the 1881 revision of the King James Bible and retained familiar terms such as *behold* while eliminating seventeenth-century English words such as *thee* and *thou*. They were also required by the publisher to sign a statement affirming their belief in verbal, plenary inspiration—that the original Scripture writings were fully inspired by God, even to the selection of words. Unlike the 1611 King James Bible, the NKJV did not include the Apocrypha, and it was complemented by extensive textual notes that reflected "the scholarship of the past 150 years and will assist the reader to observe the variations between the different manuscript traditions." It was published in a variety of styles, ranging from children's Bibles to study Bibles. The New King James Bible immediately proved popular with American Bible readers, and continued so into the twenty-first century. Ironically, the King James Version also outsold the New King James Version.[17]

- THE MESSAGE. When the members of Pastor Eugene Peterson's Sunday school class stopped stirring their coffee and began listening to him, he knew that he was onto something. Almost every Sunday for decades, he had explained the Scriptures to his congregation, but often they just did not seem to get it. Then one Sunday, as he spoke to his class, he began to informally translate into everyday English "the rhythms and idioms" straight from the Greek. As later stated, "Peterson's congregation quit stirring their coffee and felt stirred themselves." Years afterward, Peterson thought about the moment and was inspired. Why not do the same in a Bible? By then he was a bearded, bespectacled professor of spiritual theology at Canada's Regent College, and he went to work to complete and publish what would be a unique addition to the growing number of English-language Bibles. It was entitled *The Message*—a fresh, message-for-message rendering of the Greek into everyday English. In some ways it resembled Kenneth Taylor's Living Bible paraphrase, but the English was even more colloquial and not as simple. The Bible, Peterson explained in the introduction to *The Message*, was written "in the street language of the day, the idiom of the playground and marketplace." Likewise, the everyday English that Peterson translated from the Greek made *The Message* bold, dynamic, and attention-getting for the modern reader. His unique translation, published in 1993, proved popular with American Bible readers. It was revised and republished in 2002.[18]

- CHRISTIAN STANDARD BIBLE. In 2004, Holman Bible Publishers, a ministry of Lifeway Christian Resources and one of the oldest Bible publishers in America, released the Holman Christian Standard Bible. Produced by a team of more than one hundred evangelical Bible experts from seventeen denominations, the Bible was an ideolectical translation that attempted to combine word-for-word and message-for-message techniques. The end result was—in the words of the American Bible Society—a translation that was "as close to the original wording as possible while emphasizing clarity for modern English readers." The new Bible rendered the English language at a seventh-grade reading level to ensure readability for a wide range of users. "For a Bible translation to be trustworthy in modern English," the translators stated, "it must faithfully communicate the authority and urgency understood by its original audience." In 2017, it was republished as the updated Christian Standard Bible.[19]

- THE ENGLISH STANDARD VERSION. At the dawn of the twenty-first century, there were still countless English-speaking Bible readers who yearned for a new English translation of the Bible— "something more readable than the NASB and more literal than the NIV." In 2001, Crossway Books published the English Standard Version to meet that demand. Launched in their spare bedroom by a Minneapolis printer and his wife—Clyde and Muriel Dennis—Crossway Books was established in 1938 with the family savings of twenty dollars. By the beginning of the twenty-first century, it was a major Christian publishing house still openly proclaiming its mission to "publish gospel-centered, Bible-based content aimed at honoring our Savior and serving his church." In the 1990s, Crossway acquired the rights to the

1971 editions of the Revised Standard Version and put together a sixty-person team of evangelical Bible scholars to update and revise it. The team updated the RSV, replaced its dated language with modern English, made textual corrections, and restored the traditional majority-view translation to key texts, such as restoring the word "virgin" to Isaiah 7:14. It was a word-for-word revision—an "essentially literal" translation—that also emphasized modern, easily readable language.[20]

"The English Standard Version (ESV) stands in the classic mainstream of English Bible translations over the past half-millennium," the translators stated in the new Bible's preface. "The fountainhead of that stream was William Tyndale's New Testament of 1526; marking its course were the King James Version of 1611 (KJV), the English Revised Version of 1885 (RV), the American Standard Version of 1901 (ASV), and the Revised Standard Version of 1952 and 1971 (RSV). . . . Our goal has been to carry forward this legacy for a new century." The general editor of the ESV's translation oversight committee was evangelical scholar and theologian J. I. Packer. "I find myself suspecting very strongly that this was the most important thing that I have ever done for the Kingdom," Packer said of his work with the ESV, "and that the product of our labors is perhaps the biggest milestone in Bible translation in certainly the last half century at least, and perhaps more." Crossway's hope in publishing the ESV was that it would become the English-language Bible of choice for English-speaking congregations and readers.[21]

Other Bibles available to twenty-first-century American Bible readers included:

- THE COMMON ENGLISH BIBLE (CEB), which was published in 1995 and revised in 2011, and was translated by a team composed of Bible scholars from mainline Protestant denominations

- THE CONTEMPORARY ENGLISH VERSION (CEV), which was directed at new Bible readers, children, and young Bible readers, and featured a simple, easy-to-comprehend vernacular designed to be read aloud as well as privately

- THE CATHOLIC NEW AMERICAN BIBLE, REVISED EDITION (NABRE), which was published in 2011 as a revision of the 1970 edition, containing the Apocrypha and scholarly margin notes, and which reflected the Second Vatican Council's call to Catholics everywhere to embrace to the Bible "as teaching solidly, faithfully and without error"

- THE NEW GENEVA STUDY BIBLE, published in 1995 and republished in 1998 as the Reformation Study Bible, which reintroduced the original Geneva Bible under the direction of Reform scholar R. C. Sproul, and featured commentary, catechisms, creeds, and doctrinal documents related to the Protestant Reformed churches

- THE COMPLETE JEWISH STUDY BIBLE, a 2016 study version designed to introduce Christians, Jews, and others to the Jewishness of the Old and New Testaments, it includes extensive commentary by Messianic Jews and Christian theologians, with a foreword that praises God for "the good news of salvation to his people Isra'el and to all the peoples through his son Yeshua the Messiah, our Lord."[22]

As Bible publishing flourished amid the freedom of faith enjoyed by twentieth- and twenty-first-century Americans, Bible-based beliefs and even simply owning a Bible resulted in imprisonment, torture, or death in other cultures around the globe. In the Soviet Union, the Communist dictator Joseph Stalin unleashed the government's League of Militant Atheists against Christians, Jews, and others in 1929. Within a decade visible religious life had largest ceased to exist in the Soviet Union and "distributing religious literature" could result in imprisonment and death—and did so untold numbers of the sixty-million people who died under Stalin. In Nazi Germany, Adolf Hitler established the National Reich Church to replace Christianity; ordered that "the Christian Cross must be removed from all churches, cathedrals and chapels" so it could be replaced by the Nazi swastika; and imprisoned scores of Christian pastors who opposed the Third Reich on biblical grounds. From 1949 until his death in 1976, Mao Zedong, the dictator of the Communist People's Republic of China, oversaw the mass murder of an estimated sixty-five million Chinese, including countless Christians whose "crimes" were owning a Bible and seeking to worship. Stalin, Hitler, and Mao perished, while the Bible persevered in their lands—but attempts to suppress the Bible and its readers continued worldwide.[23]

The Bible has a tendency to outlast all would-be pallbearers.

In the early twenty-first century, the deadliest place in the world to own a Bible was North Korea, a totalitarian socialist state where possession of a Bible could result in almost certain death. "A person caught carrying a Bible is doomed," reported a North Korean refugee, "and the whole family disappears." The Open Door World Watch List, produced annually by a ministry to persecuted Christians, listed the top fifty nations persecuting the people of the book in 2017—from North Korea, Somalia, Afghanistan, and Pakistan to Uzbekistan and the Maldives. "The Bible is a revolutionary book," explained Roy Peterson, president of the American Bible Society in 2017. "Christians open the pages of the Bible and read about loving one's enemies, standing up for the oppressed and worshipping God alone. Totalitarian regimes and those who hope to bring a society into unquestioned obedience to a particular doctrine must see the Bible as a threat to their control."[24]

In contemporary America, the Bible remains the nation's most popular book—based on ownership. According to various polling sources, approximately 90 percent of American households own a Bible. The version of choice? Recent survey data from the American Bible Society found that 31 percent of Americans still prefer the King James Version; 13 percent favor the New International Version; nine percent prefer the English Standard Version; 7 percent prefer the New King James Version; and the rest prefer a scattering of versions ranging from the New American Standard Bible to the New Living Translation. Never in the history of America and the English-speaking world have so many Bible versions been available—more than a hundred. Bibles can be found in a remarkable array of styles and formats: study Bibles; large-print Bibles; youth editions; Bibles on a variety of electronic devices; Bible blogs and websites; audio and Braille Bibles; paraphrased Scriptures; BibleZines, which resemble girls' teen magazines; outdoor Bibles on fold-up plastic that resemble maps; story Bibles that read like a novel; superhero Bibles; and an array of conventional Bibles featuring scholarly commentaries, informative margin notes, detailed charts, colorful maps, extensive indexes, and lengthy appendices. Never in American history has the Bible been so handy.[25]

And yet, while twenty-first-century Americans overwhelmingly view the Bible with respect, relatively few are actually reading it frequently. In a survey conducted in 2014 by the Pew Research Center, 71 percent of adult Americans identified themselves as Christians, and 75 percent of them said they considered the Bible to be "the word of God"—with opinions about evenly divided on whether it should always be interpreted literally. According to the Pew data, however, only 37 percent of Americans regularly read the Bible more than once or twice a month even though a Bible can be found in 90 percent of American homes. A 2017 survey for the American Bible Society conducted by the Barna Group showed a higher level of readership: 58 percent of Americans reported reading or listening to the Bible at least once a week; however, only 20 percent reported reading or listening to it four times a week or more. Among those reading the Bible once a week, 78 percent noted that they "wished they read or listened to the Bible more." In the American Bible Society study, the group reading the Bible frequently—at least four times a week—was largely composed of evangelical Christians, black Protestants, older Americans, Southerners, women, married couples, and households with young children.[26]

If the number of twenty-first-century Americans reading the Bible frequently—four times a week or more—appears low, it is extraordinarily high compared to Bible readership in Great Britain, where the English-language Bible was born. There, twenty-first-century surveys have revealed that household Bible ownership declined from 90 percent in 1953 to 52 percent in 2010. In the land of John Wycliffe, William Tyndale, Miles Coverdale, and countless everyday Christians who were martyred for a Bible-based faith, a mere nine percent of twenty-first-century Britons reported personally reading the Bible once a week or more. Among professing Christians in Britain, 62 percent admitted that they seldom or never personally read the Bible. Only about 10 percent could identify the phrase "eat, drink and be merry" from Luke 12:19 as a quote from the Bible, and five times as many thought it originated with William Shakespeare. Among the Britons questioned about the source of the Bible-based phrase "the writing on the wall" from Daniel 5, just as many believed it came from the Beatles as thought it originated with the Bible. And fewer than half of Britons surveyed in the first decade of the twenty-first century understood that Easter was connected to the resurrection of Jesus.[27]

While the overwhelming majority of Americans today still identify themselves as professing Christians who believe the Bible is the Word of God, the American Bible Society recently noted rising challenges to the Bible's influence in America. "The steady rise of skepticism," the ABS survey concluded, "is creating a cultural atmosphere that is becoming unfriendly to claims of faith." In 2017, for the first time in its polling history, the American Bible Society added the category "Bible Hostile" to its State of the Bible survey as a subset of its "Bible Skeptic" category.

The "Bible Hostile" respondents—who believed "the Bible was written to manipulate or control other people"—were few in number, but their numbers are rising. How did a nation with a founding document declaring that "all men are created equal, that they are endowed by their Creator with certain unalienable rights" develop a postmodern culture that is "unfriendly to claims of faith"? The answer, according to some Christian leaders, lies in an underreported but critical change in the national worldview—the way Americans look at life and their surrounding culture.[28]

An African-American woman in Washington, D.C. faithfully reads the Scriptures to her children in 1942. Modern surveys of Bible readership ranked black American Protestants as among the most faithful Bible readers. Source: Library of Congress.

In the late twentieth century, some American Christian leaders began to identify a shift in the national worldview from the historic Judeo-Christian or biblical worldview that was traditional to Western civilization to something radically different—a secular humanistic worldview. If true, America is in the midst of a seismic shift in the national consensus. Over the course of about half a century, many Christian leaders believe, many Americans consciously or unconsciously began to view humanity, not God, as the rightful authority over all things and as the foundation of human thought and action. "There is, without question, an absolutely new philosophy, a philosophy of secularism, of humanism—or, as it is called, 'secular humanism,'" observed evangelical Christian leader D. James Kennedy. "Humanism is not to be confused with humanitarianism, which is doing good for humanity. Humanism is trust in man, in opposition to God." Such thinking, evangelical leaders warn, is nothing less than self-worship, and yet studies indicate that the humanistic worldview has quickly grown to challenge the historic biblical worldview of Western culture. "In our time," concluded twentieth-century author and thinker Francis Schaeffer, "humanism has replaced Christianity as the consensus of the West." Evangelist Billy Graham concurred. "In this view," he wrote, "the Bible . . . was not the inspired Word of God or the objective standard of truth for our faith and practice. Instead, it was a book of human origin, to be approached the same way any other human book was approached."[29]

By the dawn of the twenty-first century, according to Kennedy and other Christian leaders, secular humanism was steadily replacing the traditional Judeo-Christian or biblical worldview as the prevailing philosophy of America's institutions, including law, government, education, health care, media, popular culture—and even the church. "Much of the church no longer holds that the Bible is God's Word in all that it teaches," Schaeffer observed. "It simply blends with the current thought-forms rather than being the 'salt' that judges and preserves the life of its culture." Such a shift might explain why a 2017 Barna poll found that a large percentage of American "practicing Christians" were dabbling in doctrines contrary to biblical teachings: 61 percent agreed with some aspects of pantheism, 54 percent agreed with postmodernist views, and 36 percent accepted "ideas associated with Marxism" even though Marxist movements had historically persecuted Christians.[30]

A shift from a biblical worldview to a humanistic worldview may also explain the controversies within the American church over doctrinal and cultural issues—and the late-twentieth-century move by some denominations to question Christianity's historic belief in the authority and inerrancy of the Bible. So pervasive was the shift away from Bible-based instruction among some denominations of the mainline American Protestant church that in 1978, an assembly of more than three hundred prominent American evangelical Christian leaders felt compelled to reassert the historic Christian position in what became known as the Chicago Statement on Biblical Inerrancy, which read in part, "Holy Scripture, being God's own Word, written by men and prepared and superintended by His Spirit, is of infallible divine authority in all matters upon which it touches: It is to be believed, as God's instruction, in all that it affirms; obeyed, as God's command, in all that it requires; embraced, as God's pledge, in all that it promises . . . being wholly and verbally God-given."[31]

In the twenty-first century, the drift from the historic view of biblical authority by much of the mainline Protestant church in America has dramatically affected the people in its pews. Bible-based evangelical churches and denominations are expanding in membership, while mainline Protestant denominations that have strayed from their biblical foundations appear to be declining in numbers. Such shrinkage in numbers and influence—in the words of Bible scholar J.I. Packer—is due to "uncertainty as to whether Bible teaching is God's truth." According to Packer, much of the contemporary American church has abandoned biblical truth and Christianity's historic belief in the authority of the Bible—which has undermined preaching, uundercut teaching, weakened faith and discouraged lay Bible reading. "Fifthly, and saddest of all," he concluded, "skepticism about the Bible has hidden Christ from view. . . . No wonder, then, that relatively few in our churches seem to know . . . Jesus as their Saviour and Lord."[32]

Packer's grave concern—shared by many evangelicals in postmodern America—is that the shift to a humanistic worldview has produced an American culture that resembles ancient Israel as described in the last line of the Book of Judges: "In those days . . . every man did what was right in his own eyes." A national "famine" of the knowledge of and respect for the Word of God in America, according to Packer, will eventually result in a cultural catastrophe—much as that reported in the Old Testament Book of Amos:

"Behold, days are coming," declares the Lord GOD,

"When I will send a famine on the land,

"Not a famine of bread or a thirst for water,

"But rather for hearing the words of the LORD.

"People will stagger from sea to sea

And from the north even to the east;

They will go to and fro to seek the word of the LORD,

But they will not find it."[33]

As the third decade of the twenty-first century approached, only 45 percent of Americans surveyed by the Pew Research Center could identify the first four books of the New Testament, and even fewer could identify the figure of Job from the Old Testament. As the lack of biblical knowledge in Western culture declined, disregard for the Bible appeared to increase. Typical perhaps was the opinion of a pair of secular-minded writers in a progressive online news journal, who suggested that if Christianity is to survive and thrive in postmodern culture, it might need to abandon the Bible as antiquated and unpopular. History has demonstrated, however, that the Bible has a tendency to outlive all would-be pallbearers. Even as biblical illiteracy increased in the United States and western Europe, the Bible was and is making an enormous impact in what the King James Version describes as "the uttermost part of the earth." Beginning in the late twentieth century, Christianity's center of gravity began shifting from North America and western Europe to the world's Southern Hemisphere, and was growing steadily. By 2017, one-fourth of the world's Christians lived in Africa, and Asia's Christian population was projected to top 460 million by 2025. In China alone, the Christian community may exceed 200 million by 2025, despite persecution by the nation's Communist government. Throughout much of the Third World where the Bible was introduced by Western missionaries, the twenty-first century Church is dramatically expanding on its own, and is even evangelizing in the West. And as the church of Christ expands around the globe today, it continues to be propelled by the revelation of the Bible.[34]

An African evangelist and his family stand at the entrance to their church in Kenya. By the opening decades of the twenty-first century, the Bible's life-changing message had been dispersed throughout the world by Western missionaries—and was being renewed in the West and elsewhere by Third World Bible believers. Source: Center for the Study of World Christianity.

In the postmodern United States, meanwhile, Christian leaders continue to urge American believers to pray for a Bible-based revival and a return to a biblically-based culture in obedience to 2 Chronicles 7:14:

"If . . . my people who are called by my name humble themselves and pray and seek my face and turn from their wicked ways, then I will hear from heaven, will forgive their sins and heal their land."

"If we ever needed guidance, if we ever needed stability, if we ever needed strength, if we ever needed faith, if we ever needed integrity, if we ever needed righteousness, if we ever needed a Heaven-sent revival, it is at the present hour," stated evangelist Billy Graham in 2017 at age 98. "And God has told us in His Word, time after time, that we need to repent of our sins, and we're to turn to Him and He will bless us." Timothy Keller, pastor of New York City's Redeemer Presbyterian Church, agreed. "Throughout the Old Testament, the people of God fall into periods of spiritual stagnation and then cultural accommodation," he observed. "Then there is a turning to God, the raising up of new leaders, then a 'covenant renewal'—a restoration of spiritual vision and vitality." Meanwhile, in the twenty-first century, the Bible has continued to transform the world:

- Gideons International, a Bible distribution ministry birthed by two Bible-believing American businessmen in 1908, reported in 2017 that it had placed more than two billion Bibles in two hundred countries and in almost a hundred languages.

- Wycliffe Bible Translators, established by a Third World missionary in 1942, had translated the Bible into more than five hundred languages by its seventieth anniversary, with a goal of translating it into sixteen hundred more by 2025.

- Biblica, or the International Bible Society, in Colorado Springs, Colorado, the sponsoring publisher of the NIV Bible, reported in 2017 that sixty million copies of the NIV had been sold to date around the world.

- In the Communist-ruled People's Republic of China—fueled in modern times by government-backed capitalism, and home to sixty-seven million Christians—Bible possession was once a capital crime, and Bibles were still limited in supply for Chinese believers in 2008. Yet in that same year, a printing facility jointly run by the Chinese government's China Christian Council and Great Britain's United Bible Societies reportedly became the largest Bible publisher in the world, printing more than 100 million Bibles in more than ninety languages.

- In 2018, the newly opened Museum of the Bible in Washington, D.C., was drawing huge crowds of visitors to its 430,000-square-foot facility, located three blocks from the U.S. Capitol. Established at a cost of a half billion dollars, the nonprofit museum documented, exposed, and celebrated the Book of books, proclaiming that its mission was "to invite all people to engage with the Bible."[35]

A towering stack of five thousand Bibles awaits distribution to hotels in the nation's capital by the Gideons, a Bible distribution ministry established by two Bible-believing American businessmen in 1908. By 2017, the Gideons had placed two-billion Bibles in two hundred countries. Source: Library of Congress.

And so the Bible stands—sixty-six books compiled over a span of more than fifteen hundred years in three ancient languages by scribes, priests, kings, poets, scholars, fishermen and others. Through the ages, books, and multiple writers, a unified theme cumulates in a single verse: "For God so loved the world, that He gave His only begotten Son, that whoever believes in Him shall not perish, but have eternal life." As foretold ages ago in Scripture: "The grass withers, the flower fades, but the word of our God stands forever."[36]

Acknowledgments

NO AUTHOR WRITES A BOOK ALONE, and that's especially true of this one. I'm grateful to WND Books' chief executives, Joseph and Elizabeth Farah, for publishing this work, and to editors Geoffrey Stone and Felicia Dionisio for their important suggestions and invaluable editorial direction. I'm also thankful to my literary agent, Steve Laube, for his sage advice and capable representation. Many thanks, too, are due Renee Chavez, for her editorial insights and elegant copy-editing, and to designer Mark Karis and production manager Federico Lines—all of whom contributed significantly to the production of this book. Thanks also to my longtime friend and former editor Larry Stone, who long ago encouraged me to research and write on this topic. I'm especially grateful to my mentor, friend, and Bible teacher, the Reverend J. R. "Randy" Riddle, for his years of encouragement and counsel—and to his wife, Judy, for her support and friendship. Over time, many knowledgeable experts at a variety of institutions made major contributions to this work. I'm indebted to the British Library, the British Museum, the Library of Congress, the National Archives, Kimbel Library at Coastal Carolina University, Dallas Theological Seminary, Perkins Library at Duke University, Columbia International University, and others.

ACKNOWLEDGMENTS

As always, I'm deeply grateful for the prayerful support from my friends Mark Roach, Stovall Witte, David Frost, and all the members of our weekly Bible Study. Many thanks to my pastor, Rick Atkins, and others at Carolina Forest Community Church, as well as friends and colleagues at Conway Christian School. Many thanks, too, are due my brother, Ted Gragg; his wife, Connie; my cousin-brothers, Charles Lunsford and Bob Melton; and Bob's wife, Sandra. Thanks also to "Aunty" Delores, Deborah Outlaw, Joe and Margaret Outlaw, Doug and Jackie Rutt, John and Tina Outlaw, Jimmy and Gail Outlaw, Newt Outlaw, and "Mama-O."

I'm grateful for my always-supportive family: Skip, Mary, Matt, Miranda, Elizabeth, Jon, Rachel, Jay, Faith, Troy, Joni, and Penny. And I'm blessed by my outstanding grandchildren: Leyton, Ty, Ashlyn, Jate, Gracie, Jaxon, Cody, Sophia and Kylah. I'm ever grateful to my parents, Skip and Lib Gragg, for walking the walk and introducing me to the Word, and to my mentor grandfather, the Reverend T. O. Lunsford. Always, I am deeply grateful to my Proverbs 31 wife, Cindy, who loves the Lord and His Word. And, I remain eternally thankful for the promises of Romans 10:9–11 and Psalms 119:18.

—ROD GRAGG

Notes

INTRODUCTION: THE KING TORE HIS CLOTHES

1. 2 Kings 21-23:25; 2 Chronicles 34-35; Heinrich Ewald, *The History of Israel* (London: Longmans Green, 1871), 4:231–46; Thomas H. Gallaudet, *The History of Josiah: The Young King of Judah* (New York: American Tract Society, 1837), 83–91.

2. Lawrence Mykytiuk, "Archaeology Confirms 50 Real People in the Bible," *Biblical Archaeology Review* 40, no. 2 (March–April 2014): 42–43; Lester L. Grabbe, *Good Kings and Bad Kings: The Kingdom of Judah in the Seventh Century BCE* (London: T&T Clark, 2005), 78–79; J.D. Douglas, ed., *The Illustrated Bible Dictionary*, (Leicester, UK: Inter-Varsity Press, 1980), 1:131, 2:943.

3. 2 Kings 22:2; 2 Chronicles 34:2; Ewald, *History of Israel*, 4:231-35; *Illustrated New Bible Dictionary*, 1:131; Gallaudet, *History of Josiah*, 83-86.

4. Ewald, *History of Israel*, 4:231-35; Gallaudet, *History of Josiah*, 83-86.

5. 2 Kings 22:10; *Illustrated Bible Dictionary*, 2:650; Ewald, *History of Israel*, 239-46; Gallaudet, *History of Josiah*, 87-91.

6. Deuteronomy 6:4–7; *Illustrated Bible Dictionary*, 2:819-20.

7. Deuteronomy 5:7–9; *Illustrated Bible Dictionary*, 2: 819-20.

8. Deuteronomy 28:1–2; Adele Berlin, ed., *The Oxford Dictionary of the Jewish Religion*, (New York: Oxford University Press, 2011), 411.

9. 2 Kings 23:2.

10. 2 Kings 23:3; Isaiah 55:11.

11. 2 Kings 23:24. John J. Rosseau and Rami Arav, *Jesus and His World: An Archaeological and Cultural Dictionary* (Minneapolis: Fortress Press, 1995), 144–45; Paul S. Evans, *The Invasion of Sennacherib in the Book of Kings: A Source-Critical and Rhetorical Study of II Kings 18–19* (Leiden: E.J. Brill, 2009), 50.

12. 2 Kings 23:25; Erik Eynikel, *The Reform of King Josiah and the Composition of the Deuteronomistic History*, (Leiden: E.J. Brill, 1996), 17; Rosseau and Arav, *Jesus and His World*, 145.

13. *Oxford Dictionary of the Jewish Religion*, 411; 2 Kings 23:25.

14. Isaiah 40:8; Francis Schaeffer, *He Is There and He Is Not Silent* (Carol Stream, IL: Tyndale House, 1972), 17.

CHAPTER 1: INSPIRED BY GOD

1. Sidney Lee, ed., *Dictionary of National Biography* (London: Smith Elder, 1909), 19:1355; Magna Saebo, ed., *Hebrew Bible Old Testament: The History of Its Interpretation* (Göttingen: Vandenhoeck & Ruprecht, 2008), 2:546; Timothy George, *The Theology of the Reformers* (Nashville: B&H, 2013), 373; David Daniell, *William Tyndale: A Biography* (New Haven, CT: Yale University Press, 1994), 379; F. F. Bruce, *The Books and the Parchments* (Westwood, NJ: Fleming H. Revell, 1963), 9–10; Ira Maurice Price, *The Ancestry of Our English Bible: An Account of Manuscripts, Texts and Versions of the Bible* (New York: Harper & Bros., 1956), 249–51; Norman L. Geisler and William E. Nix, *A General Introduction to the Bible* (Chicago: Moody Press, 1986), 550–51; 2 Timothy 4:13.

2. Charles Francis Adams, ed., John Adams, *The Works of John Adams: Second President of the United States* (Boston: Little, Brown, 1850–1856), 10:105 (hereafter cited as *WJA); WJA* 2:6–7, 22–23; "Gladstone's Latest Tribute to the Bible," *Literary Digest* 10, no. 26 (April 27, 1895): 18; Noah Webster, *History of the United States* (New Haven, CT: Durrie and Peck, 1832), 339; Sarah Ogilve, *Words of the World: A Global History of the Oxford English Dictionary* (Cambridge: Cambridge University Press, 2013), 87; Joshua Kendall, *The Forgotten Founding Father: Noah Webster's Obsession and the Creation of an American Culture* (New York: G. P. Putnam's Sons, 2011), 297–303; James E. Force and Richard H. Popkin, *Essays on the Context, Nature and Influence of Isaac Newton's Theology* (London: Kluwer Academic, 1990), 1033; *Annual Report of the American Bible Society* (New York: American Bible Society, 1936), 120:21; Schaeffer, *He Is There and He Is Not Silent*, 17 (see introduction, n. 1).

3. James Strong, *Strong's Exhaustive Concordance of the Bible* (Peabody, MA: Hendrickson, 2007), 1613; David Ewert, *From Ancient Tablets to Modern Translations: A General Introduction to the Bible* (Grand Rapids: Zondervan, 1983), 19–21; T. K. Lim, *Edible Medicinal and Non-Medicinal Plants* (New York: Springer Science and Business Media, 2016) 10:172; G. S. Wegner, *6,000 Years of the Bible* (New York: Harper and Bros., 1963), 56–58; "The World of Papyrus," Duke Papyrus Archive, Special Collections Library, Duke University.

4. David Carvelho, *Forty Centuries of Ink* (Seattle: The Worldwide School, 1999), 2–8; *Nelson's New Dictionary of the English Language* (New York: Thomas Nelson & Sons, 1922), 356; Revelation 5:1; Ewert, *From Ancient Tablets,* 19–21; Bruce, *Books and Parchments,* 11–12; Isaiah 34:4 KJV; "The World of Papyrus," Duke Papyrus Archive; Geisler and Nix, *Introduction to the Bible,* 21; Revelation 6:14 KJV.

5. Wegener, *6,000 Years of the Bible,* 60; Ewert, *From Ancient Tablets,* 20; Michael D. Coogan, ed., *The Oxford Encyclopedia of the Books of the Bible* (Oxford: Oxford University Press, 2011), 75; Robinson Ellis, *A Commentary on Catullus* (Oxford: Clarendon Press, 1889), 72; James E. Bowley, ed., *Living Traditions of the Bible: Scripture in Jewish, Christian and Muslim Practice* (St. Louis: Chalice, 1999: 10–11).

6. Jean-Jacques Glassner, *The Invention of Cuneiform Writing in Sumer* (Baltimore: Johns Hopkins Press, 2003), 6–7, 45–48; John Gaudet, *Papyrus: The Plant that Changed the World* (New York: Pegasus Books, 2014), 22–27; E. M. Blaiklock and R. K. Harrison, eds., *The New International Dictionary of Biblical Archaeology* (Grand Rapids: Zondervan, 1983), 142–43; Lily Kahn, *The Routledge Introductory Course in Biblical Hebrew* (London: Routledge, 2014), 2–3; Ilan Stavans, *Resurrecting Hebrew* (New York: Random House, 2008), 17–20.

7. J. B. Poole and R. Reed, "The Preparation of Leather and Parchment by the Dead Sea Scrolls Community," *Technology and Culture* 3, no. 1:1–26; "Classic Vagaries," *American Literary Magazine,* July 1847, 32–33; Wegner, *6,000 Years of the Bible,* 59–60; *New International Dictionary of Biblical Archaeology,* 353–54; Bruce, *Books and Parchments,* 11–12; J. F. Kennedy, *Illustrated Sketches of the Countries and Places Mentioned in Bible History* (Philadelphia: American Sunday School Union, 1847), 340.

8.   Norman Geisler, *Christian Apologetics* (Grand Rapids: Baker Book House, 1976), 305–28; Rene Pache, *The Inspiration and Authority of Scripture* (Chicago: Moody Press, 1969), 111–19.

9.   Carl F. Henry, ed., *Revelation and the Bible* (Grand Rapids: Baker Book House, 1958), 389–401; Pache, *Inspiration and Authority of Scripture,* 111–19; Geisler, *Christian Apologetics:* 305–28.

10. Geisler and Nix, *Introduction to the Bible,* 21; Pache, *Inspiration and Authority of Scripture:* 16–20; Norman Geisler and Peter Bocchino, *Unshakable Foundations: Contemporary Answers to Crucial Questions about the Christian Faith* (Grand Rapids: Bloomington, 2001), 277; Charles C. Ryrie, "The Inspiration of the Bible," Supplement to the *Ryrie Study Bible* (Chicago: Moody Press, 1994, 2078).

11. Genesis 10:10, 11:2; Gerald A. Larue, "Ancient Jewish History: Who Were the Hebrews?," Jewish Virtual Library, jewishvirtuallibrary.org /who-were-the-hebrews; Craig A. Lockard, *Societies, Networks and Transitions: A Global History* (Stamford: Cengage Learning, 2015), 1:31–35; Leonard Woolly, *Ur: The First Phases* (New York: Penguin Books, 1946), 7–11; Anthony Lyle, *Ancient History: A Revised Chronology* (Bloomington: Authorhouse, 2012), 1:197; J. D. Douglas, ed., *The New Bible Dictionary* (Wheaton, IL: Tyndale House, 1982), 4–6, 1231; Henry M. Morris, *The Genesis Record: A Scientific and Devotional Commentary on the Book of Beginnings* (Grand Rapids: Baker Book House, 1982), 253, 307–8; *Dictionary of Biblical Archaeology:* 462–63; George Aaron Barton, *Archaeology and the Bible* (Philadelphia: American Sunday School Union, 1916), 290–98, 400.

12. George Henry Ewald, *A Grammar of the Hebrew Language of the Old Testament* (London: Williams and Norgate, 1836), 2–4; Larue, "Ancient Jewish History"; Woolly, *Ur: The First Phases,* 7–11; *Dictionary of Biblical Archaeology,* 462–3; *New Bible Dictionary,* 1231; Genesis 12:1-2.

13. Kenyon, *Story of the Bible,* 9–10; Ewert, *Ancient Tablets to Modern Translations,* 54; Bruce, *Books and Parchment,* 15–16, 31; Ira Spar, *Cuneiform Texts in the Metropolitan Museum of Art* (New York: Metropolitan Museum of Art, 1988), 172; *Dictionary of Biblical Archaeology,* 425, 478–77; Karen Radner and Eleanor Robson, eds., *The Oxford Handbook of Cuneiform Culture* (New York: Oxford University Press, 2011), 82–84; Flavius Josephus and William Whiston, *The Genuine Works of Flavius Josephus, the Jewish Historian* (New York: William Borradaile, 1823), 1:26–27.

14. Jean-Jacques Glassner, *The Invention of Cuneiform: Early Writing in Sumer* (Baltimore: Johns Hopkins University Press, 2003), 4–7; Ewald, *Grammar of the Hebrew Language:* 2–4; Adele Berlin, ed., *The Oxford Dictionary of the Jewish Religion* (New York: Oxford University Press, 2001), 336; F. L. Cross, ed., *The Oxford Dictionary of the Christian Church* (Oxford: Oxford University Press, 1997), 741–42; *Dictionary of Biblical Archaeology,* 183–84; Bruce, *The Books and the Parchments,* 18–27; Ewert, *Ancient Tablets to Modern Translations,* 54–61; F. F. Bruce, "The Origin of the Alphabet," *Faith and Thought: The Journal of the Transactions of the Victoria Institute* 80 (1948): 10.

15. Ronald H. Isaacs, *Why Hebrew Goes from Right to Left* (Jersey City: KTAV, 1992), 2–4; Bruce, *The Books and the Parchments,* 31; Ewald, *Grammar of the Hebrew Language,* 55–57; Ewert, *Ancient Tablets to Modern Translations,* 39–45; Joseph Addison Alexander, *Commentary on Isaiah* (Grand Rapids: Kregel Classics, 1992), 356; Ewald, *Grammar of the Hebrew Language,* 38–42; *Oxford Dictionary of the Jewish Religion,* 336; *New Bible Dictionary,* 675–77.

16.   Jeremiah 7:24; William Ewing and John Ebenezer Thomson, eds., *The Temple Dictionary of the Bible* (London: J. M. Dent, 1910), 378, 909; Ewert, *Ancient Tablets to Modern Translations,* 39–45; *Oxford Dictionary of the Jewish Religion,* 336; Ewald, *Grammar of the Hebrew Language,* 38–42; *New Bible Dictionary,* 675–77.

17. *Oxford Dictionary of the Jewish Religion,* 336, 741–42; Bruce, *The Books and the Parchments,* 34–37; *Eerdmans Handbook to the Bible,* 153; Ewald, *Grammar of the Hebrew Language,* 39–42; *New Bible Dictionary,* 675–77; Ewert, *Ancient Tablets to Modern Translations,* 39–45.

18. Isadore Singer, ed. *The Jewish Encyclopedia, The History, Religion, Literature and Customs of the Jewish People* (New York: Funk and Wagnalls, 1902), 2:69–72; William D. Davies, Louis Finkelstein, and Stephen T. Katz, eds., *The Cambridge History of Judaism* (Cambridge: Cambridge University Press, 2006), 4:457–59; Angel Sáenz-Badillos, *A History of the Hebrew Language* (Cambridge: Cambridge University Press, 1993), 50–51, 111–12; Lazer Gurkhow, "Purim: When Hebrews Became Jews," *Israel National News*, June 11, 2017; *Eerdmans Handbook to the Bible*, 153; Ewald, *Grammar of the Hebrew Language*, 39–42; Bruce, *The Books and the Parchments*, 34–37; *New Bible Dictionary*, 675–77; Ewert, *Ancient Tablets to Modern Translations*, 39–45; *Oxford Dictionary of the Jewish Religion*, 336.

19. *Oxford Dictionary of the Jewish Religion*, 2:69–72; *Jewish Encyclopedia*, 4:457–59; Cross, *Oxford Dictionary of the Christian Church*, 96; *Eerdmans Handbook to the Bible*, 153; Ewald, *Grammar of the Hebrew Language*, 39–42; Bruce, *The Books and the Parchments*, 34–37; *Oxford Dictionary of the Jewish Religion*, 336; *New Bible Dictionary*, 675–77; Ewert, *Ancient Tablets to Modern Translations*, 39–45.

20. Genesis 31:47–38; H. C. O. Lanchester, *The Book of Genesis* (Cambridge: Cambridge University Press, 1924), 43; Stepan Reif, "Impact on Jewish Studies of a Century of Genizah Research," *Jewish Studies at the Turn of the 20th Century: Biblical, Rabbinical, and Medieval Studies:* ed. Judit T. Borras and Angel Saenz-Badillos (Leiden: Brill, 1999), 1:580; *Oxford Dictionary of the Jewish Religion*, 2:69–72; Wegener, *6,000 Years of the Bible*, 54–55; *Temple Bible Dictionary*,: lix; *Jewish Encyclopedia*, 4:457–59; *New Bible Dictionary*, 407; Bruce, *The Books and the Parchments*, 53, 133.

21. Jennifer M. Dines, *The Septuagint* (London: T & T Clark, 2004), 41–44; Bruce, *Books and Parchments*, 48–60; Cross, *Oxford Dictionary of the Christian Church*, 95–96; Price, *The Ancestry of Our English Bible* (New York: Harper & Bros., 1956), 16–18 (see chap. 1, n. 1); Liel Leibovitz, "Should Hebrew Be Israel's Official Language?" *Tablet*, September 12, 2014; Malka Muchnik, Marina Miznik, and Tania Gluzman, *Elective Language Learning and Policy in Israel* (London: Palgrave Macmillan UK), 2016: 4.

CHAPTER 2: THE OLD TESTAMENT

1. Geza Vermes, *An Introduction to the Complete Dead Sea Scrolls* (Minneapolis: Fortress Press, 1999), 1–7: James Vanderkam and Peter Flint, *The Meaning of the Dead Sea Scrolls* (London: T&T Clark, 2005), 34–43; Norman Golb, "Who Hid the Dead Sea Scrolls?" *Biblical Archaeological Review* 48 (1985): 68–82; Norman Golb, *Who Wrote the Dead Sea Scrolls? The Search for the Secret of Qumran* (New York: Scribners, 1995), 5–46; James A. Sanders, *The Dead Sea Psalms Scrolls* (Ithaca, NY: Cornell University Press, 1967), 4–9; Edwin Yamauchi, *The Stones and the Scriptures: An Introduction to Biblical Archaeology* (Grand Rapids: Baker Book House, 1972), 126–28; *Dictionary of Biblical Archaeology*, 156, 379; P. R. Ackroyd and C. F. Evans, eds., *The Cambridge History of the Bible* (Cambridge: Cambridge University Press, 1970), 1:183.

2. Edward M. Blaiklock, *The Archaeology of the New Testament* (Nashville: Thomas Nelson, 1984), 139–52; "The Four Dead Sea Scrolls," *Wall Street Journal*, June 1, 1954; Yamauchi, *Stones and Scriptures*, 127–28; Yigael Yadin, *The Message of the Scrolls* (New York: Grosset and Dunlap, 1961), 41, 126–28; Sanders, *Dead Sea Psalms Scroll*, 4–9; *Dictionary of Biblical Archaeology*, 156, 379.

3. Hava Katz, "The Dead Sea Scrolls Exhibition," Israel Antiquities Authority, http://www.antiquities.org.il/scroll_eng_new.aspx (accessed October 23, 2017); Yamauchi, *Stones and Scriptures*, 128–45; *Archaeology of the New Testament*, 139–52, 379; *Dictionary of Biblical Archaeology*, 154–57; Adolfo Roitman, "The History, Architecture, and Symbolism of the Shrine of the Book," *Israel Museum Journal* 15 (1997): 15.

4. Yamauchi, *Stones and Scriptures,* 127–28; Yadin, *Message of the Scrolls,* 41, 126–28; Sanders, *Dead Sea Psalms Scroll,* 4–9; *Dictionary of Biblical Archaeology,* 156, 379; "Scrolls from the Dead Sea: The Ancient Library of Qumran and Modern Scholarship," U.S. Library of Congress, https://www.loc.gov/exhibits/scrolls/ (accessed October 23, 2017).

5. Cross, *Oxford Dictionary of the Christian Church,* 741–42 (see chap. 1, n. 14); Bruce, *The Books and the Parchments,* 48–60 (see chap. 1, n. 1); Price, *Ancestry of Our English Bible:* 16–18; Sidnie White Crawford, "The Rewritten Bible at Qumran" in *Scripture and the Scrolls: The Bible and the Dead Sea Scrolls,* ed. James H. Charlesworth (Waco: Baylor University Press, 2006), 1:131.

6. Cross, *Oxford Dictionary of the Christian Church,* 741–42; Bruce, *Books and Parchments,* 34–37; *Eerdmans Handbook to the Bible,* 153; Blaiklock, *Archaeology of the New Testament,* 139–52; Ewert, *Ancient Tablets to Modern Translations,* 55–56; *Dictionary of Biblical Archaeology,* 155–57, 379–80; Marilyn J. Lunberg, commentator, "The Discovery of the Dead Sea Scrolls," West Semitic Research Project, http://wsrp.usc.edu/educational_site/dead_sea_scrolls/discovery.shtml (accessed October 23, 2017).

7. R. A. Stewart Macalister, *The Excavation of Gezer, 1902–05 and 1907–09* (London: John Murray, 1912), 1:25–28; R. A. Stewart Macalister, *Bible Side-Lights from the Mound of Gezer: A Record of Excavation and Discovery in Palestine* (London: Hodder and Stoughton, 1907), 7–37; *Dictionary of Biblical Archaeology,* 142–43; Israel Ministry of Foreign Affairs, "Gezer—A Canaanite City and Royal Solomonic City," *Ministry of Foreign Affairs Newsletter,* November 26, 2003; W. F. Albright, "The Gezer Calendar," *Bulletin of the American Schools of Oriental Research* 92, no. 16: 26; Seymour Gitin, ed., *Confronting the Past: Archaeological and Historical Essays on Ancient Israel in Honor of William G. Dever* (Winona Lake, IN: Eisenbrauns, 2006), 338; William G. Dever, "The Middle Bronze Age 'High Place' at Gezer," *Bulletin of the American Schools of Oriental Research,* no. 371 (May 2014): 17–57; Robin Ngo, "The 'High Place' at Tel Gezer," *Bible History Daily,* August 13, 2016.

8. Genesis 28:14; Kahn, *Routledge Introductory Course in Biblical Hebrew:* 2–3; Stavans, *Resurrecting Hebrew:* 17–20; Nadav Naaman, "A New Appraisal of the Silver Amulets from Ketef Hinnom," *Israel Exploration Journal* 61, no. 2 (2001): 187–92; *New Bible Dictionary,* 167; Bruce, *Books and Parchment:* 34–37, 89–91; Ewert, *Ancient Tablets to Modern Translations,* 55–56, 66–67; *Eerdmans Handbook to the Bible,* 71–72, 153; Cross, *Oxford Dictionary of the Christian Church,* 741–42; *Dictionary of Biblical Archaeology* 17, no. 14: 155–57, 284, 319, 396, 379–80, 414–15.

9. Pache, *Inspiration and Authority of Scripture,* 186–87; Geisler and Nix, *A General Introduction to the Bible,* 603 (see chap. 1, n. 1); Ewert, *Ancient Tablets to Modern Translations,* 39–45; Nehemiah 13:25.

10. 2 Peter 1:19–20; Kenneth A. Kitchen, *On the Reliability of the Old Testament* (Grand Rapids: Eerdmans, 2003), 2–8; Katz, "The Dead Sea Scrolls Exhibition"; Wegner, *Journey from Texts to Translations,* 31; *New Bible Dictionary,* 240–43, 763–72; Bruce, *Books and Parchment,* 75–76; Ewert, *Ancient Tablets to Modern Translations,* 22-24; Ex. 24:8; 2 Kings 23:2; Matt. 26:28.

11. Wegner, *From Text to Translation:* 101; *The Complete Jewish Study Bible: Illuminating the Jewishness of God's Word* (Peabody, MA: Hendrickson, 2016): *xxxi-xxxiv;* John D. Davis, *A Dictionary of the Bible* (Philadelphia: Westminster Press, 1917), 227; Everett Jenkins Jr., *The Creation: Secular, Jewish, Catholic, Protestant and Muslim Perspectives Analyzed* (Jefferson, NC: McFarland Publishing, 2003), 115–16; Kitchen, *Reliability of the Old Testament:* 2.

12. Geisler and Nix, *A General Introduction to the Bible,* 29; *Eerdmans Handbook to the Bible,* 66–67; *Complete Jewish Study Bible,* xxxii–xxxiii. See also Gen. 1:26; Ps. 22; Isaiah 53; Matt. 28:29; Luke 3:21–22.

13. *Complete Jewish Study Bible,* xxxi–xxxix; *New Bible Dictionary,* 167; Bruce, *Books and Parchment,* 89–91; Ewert, *Ancient Tablets to Modern Translations,* 66–67; *Eerdmans Handbook to the Bible,* 71–72; Ex. 17:14.

14. Jeremiah 36:2; Flavius Josephus, *The Jewish War,* trans. Martin Hammond (Oxford: Oxford University Press, 2017), xiii, 21, 234; Jacob Neusner, *A Life of Rabban Yohanan ben Zakkai* (Leiden: E.J. Brill, 1977), 175–88; Wegner, *From Text to Translation,* 101, 114–15; Jack P. Lewis, "What Do We Mean by Javneh?" *Journal of the Bible and Religion* 32, no. 2 (April 1964):125–32; Publius Cornelius Tacitus, *The Histories of Tacitus* (London: Macmillan, 1907), 5:12; Everett Ferguson. *Encyclopedia of Early Christianity* (London: Garland, 1998), 1:856; Bill T. Arnold, *Introduction to the Old Testament* (Cambridge: Cambridge University Press, 2014), 21–22; Price, *Ancestry of Our English Bible,* 140–49; Bruce, *The Books and the Parchments,* 163–75; Ewert, *Ancient Tablets to Modern Translations,* 73–82; Bleddyn J. Roberts, *The Old Testament Text and Versions: The Hebrew Text in Transmissions and the History of the Ancient Versions* (Cardiff: University of Wales Press, 1951), 60.

15. Stephen J. Vacchio, *Job in the Ancient World* (Eugene: Wipf & Stock: 2006), 59–60; Ralph Terry, ed., *Reader's Guide to Judiasim* (London: Routledge, 2000), 550; Ernst Werthwein, *The Text of the Old Testament: An Introduction to Biblia Hebraica,* trans. Erroll F. Rhodes (Grand Rapids: Eerdmans, 2014), 15–25; Wegner, *From Text to Translation,* 173–75; Arnold, *Introduction to the Old Testament,* 26.

16. Wegner, *From Text to Translation,* 171–72; *Complete Jewish Study Bible,* xxxviii–xxxii; *New Bible Dictionary,* 166–71; Price, *Ancestry of Our English Bible,* 140–49; Bruce, *The Books and the Parchments,* 163–75; Ewert, *Ancient Tablets to Modern Translations,* 73–82.

17. *New Bible Dictionary,* 166–71; Price, *Ancestry of Our English Bible,* 140–49; Bruce, The Books and the Parchments, 163–75; Ewert, Ancient Tablets to Modern Translations, 73–82; Wegner, From Text to Translation, 171–72.

18. Deuteronomy 18:20; Isaiah 18:14; Jeremiah 1:2; Ezekiel 6:1; Hosea 1:1; Jeremiah 2:5; Ezekiel 3:11; Hosea 2:21; Isaiah 37:22; Exodus 24:7; *New Bible Dictionary,* 166–71; Price, *Ancestry of Our English Bible,* 140–49; Bruce, *The Books and the Parchments,* 163–75; Ewert, *Ancient Tablets to Modern Translations,* 73–82; Karel Van Der Toorn, *Scribal Culture and the Making of the Hebrew Bible* (Cambridge: Harvard University Press, 2007), 124–27; Wegner, *From Texts to Translations,* 117, 165–69; Pache, *Inspiration and Authority of Scripture,* 186–87; Geisler and Nix, *A General Introduction to the Bible,* 603; Ewert, *Ancient Tablets to Modern Translations,* 223–26.

19. Milton Spencer Terry, *Biblical Hermeneutics: A Treatise on the Interpretation of the Old and New Testaments* (New York: Phillips & Hunt, 1983), 2:656; Pache, *Inspiration and Authority of Scripture,* 186–87; Geisler and Nix, *A General Introduction to the Bible,* 550–51, 603; Ewert, *Ancient Tablets to Modern Translations,* 223–26; Van Der Toorn, *Scribal Culture and the Making of the Hebrew Bible:* 124–27; Wegner, *From Texts to Translations,* 165–69.

20. Donald K. McKim, ed. *The Cambridge Companion to Martin Luther* (Cambridge: Cambridge University Press, 2005), 46–48, 65–66; George W. Nicklesburg, *Jewish Literature Between the Bible and the Mishnah: A Historical and Literary Introduction* (Minneapolis: Fortress Press, 2005), 4–5; *Encyclopedia of Early Christianity,* 1:77–78; Kevin Killeen, Helen Smith, and Rachel Willie, eds., *The Oxford Handbook to the Bible in Early Modern England, 1530–1700* (Oxford: Oxford University Press, 2015), 40–41; *New Bible Dictionary,* 166–71; Price, *Ancestry of Our English Bible,* 140–49; Bruce, *The Books and the Parchments,* 163–75; Ewert, *Ancient Tablets to Modern Translations,* 73–82.

21. Gary D. Martin, *Multiple Originals: New Approaches to Hebrew Bible Textual Criticism* (Atlanta: Society of Biblical Literature, 2010), 219–20; Ed Stetzer, "A Closer Look: The Historical Reliability of the Old Testament," *Christianity Today*, February 22, 2012, http://www.christianitytoday.com/edstetzer/2012/february/closer-look-historical-reliability-of-old-testament.html; Ewert, *Ancient Tablets to Modern Translations*, 65-71,

22. C. Edmund Bosworth, ed., *A Century of British Orientalists. 1903–2001* (Oxford: Oxford University Press, 2001), 191–93, 147; W. Andrew Smith, *A Study of the Gospels in the Codex Vaticanus* (Leiden: Brill, 2014), 1–4; David C. Parker, *Codex Sinaiticus: The Story of the World's Oldest Bible* (London: British Library, 2010), 31–45; W. Andrew Smith, *A Study of the Gospels in the Codex Alexandrinus* (Leiden: Brill, 2014), 10–13; Leo Deuel, *Testaments of Time: The Search for Lost Manuscripts and Records* (New York: Alfred A. Knopf, 1965), 264–65; Ronen Berman, "A Holy High Whodunit," *New York Times*, July 25, 2012; Matti Friedman, *The Aleppo Codex: In Pursuit of One of the World's Most Coveted, Sacred and Mysterious Books* (Chapel Hill: Algonquin Books, 2013), 145–47; Hayim Tawil and Bernard Schneider, *Crown of Aleppo: The Mystery of the Oldest Hebrew Bible Codex* (Philadelphia: Jewish Publication Society, 2010), 3–5, 16–23, 45–49; Joel Hoffman, *In the Beginning: A Short History of the Hebrew Language* (New York: New York University Press, 2004), 176–78; William E. Barton, *The Samaritan Pentateuch: The Story of a Survival Among the Sects* (Oberlin: Bibliotecha Sacra: 1903), 13–26.

23. Kenyon, *Story of the Bible*, 14–16, 56, 124; Bruce, *Books and Parchment*, 128–29; 147–51, 162, 182, 188; Ewert, *Ancient Tablets to Modern Translations*, 92–93, 99–101, 144–45; Price, *Ancestry of Our English Bible*, 56–68; Pache, *Inspiration and Authority of Scripture*, 186–98; Geisler and Nix, *A General Introduction to the Bible*, 447.

CHAPTER 3: THE NEW TESTAMENT

1. Stephen Dando-Collins, *Legions of Rome: The Definitive History of Every Imperial Roman Legion* (New York: St. Martin's Press, 2012), 318, 351, 439–41; Jim Bishop, *The Day Christ Was Born and the Day Christ Died* (New York: Galahad Books, 1993), 419; Jungwha Choi, *Jewish Leadership in Roman Palestine, 70 C.E. to 130 C.E.* (Leiden: Brill, 2013), 28, 131; Mark A. Chancey, *Greco-Roman Culture and the Galilee of Jesus* (Cambridge: Cambridge University Press, 2005), 45–49; Yann Le Bohec, *The Imperial Roman Army* (London: B. T. Batsford 2013), 41–53, 83; Gary M. Burge, Lynn Cohick, and Gene L. Green, *The New Testament in Antiquity: A Survey of the New Testament within its Cultural Context* (Grand Rapids: Zondervan, 2009), 48–53; 145, 206–7; *New Bible Dictionary*, 1082; Elizabeth Bloch-Smith, *Judahite Burial Practices and Beliefs about the Dead* (Sheffield: Sheffield Academic Press, 1992), 236; Matt. 27:62-66.

2. Matthew 28:2-4; Publius Cornelius Tacitus, *Annals of Imperial Rome* (New York: Penguin Books, 1956), 15:44; Flavius Josephus, *Jewish Antiquities*, trans. William Whiston (London: Wordsworth Editions, 2006), 780.

3. Acts 1:9; F. F. Bruce, *New Testament History* (New York: Doubleday, 1969), 205; Wegner, *From Texts to Translations*, 132; John C. Lambert, ed., *Dictionary of the Bible: Dealing with Language, Literature and Contents* (New York: Charles Scribner's 1902), 4:488–89; George L. Miller, *The Shekinah Glory* (Maitland: Xolon Press, 2007), 70; John Hastings, John Selbie, and John C. Lambert, eds., *Dictionary of Christ and the Gospels* (Edinburgh: T&T Clark, 1908), 2:620–21.

4. Matthew 28:19–20;Josephus, *Jewish Antiquities*, 877; *Davis Dictionary of the Bible*, 37, 81, 369, 424, 446, 505–6, 627, 633, 820; Herbert Lockyer, *All the Apostles of the Bible* (Grand Rapids: Zondervan, 1972), 51–55, 58, 75–78, 159–60, 166–67, 171–72, 175–77, 269–72; John W. Wayland, *The Apostles: Who They Were and What They Did* (Elgin: Brethren, 1907), 162–63, 209–11, 219, 227, 231–33, 248.

5. 2 Peter 1:16; John 14:26; Acts 1:8; Jack Cottrell, *The Holy Spirit: A Biblical Study* (Joplin: College Press, 2006), 22–23; *New Bible Dictionary,* 916–90; Wayland, *The Apostles,* 162–63, 209–11, 219, 227, 231–33; 2 Peter 1:20–21.

6. Amos 9:11–12: Archibald A. Hodge and Benjamin B. Warfield, "Inspiration," *British and Foreign Evangelical Review* 117, no. 30 (July 1881): 583; *New Bible Dictionary,* 32; Bruce, *New Testament History,* 285–87, 369–75; *Complete Jewish Study Bible,* lii-lv; Craig L. Bloomberg, *The Historical Reliability of the Gospels* (Downers Grove, IL: Intervarsity Press, 2007), 60–61; Hebrews 1:1–2; 1 Thessalonians 5:27.

7. Henry R. Boer, *A Short History of the Early Church* (Grand Rapids: Eerdmans, 1976), 19–24; Wegner, *From Texts to Translations,* 131–32; Bruce, *New Testament History,* 206; Acts 2:42–43.

8. Joel 2:28–29; Acts 9:2; Wegner, *From Texts to Translations,* 131–24; Boer, *Short History of the Early Church,* 19–24; *New Bible Dictionary,* 600–01; Bruce, *New Testament History,* 212, 369–75; Acts 17:1-3; Acts 19:20.

9. 1 Corinthians 2:12-13; L.D. Twilley, *The Origin and Transmission of the New Testament* (Grand Rapids: Eerdmans, 1957), 9–34; George Milligan, *The New Testament Documents: Their Origin and History* (London: Macmillan, 1913), 175; Price, *Ancestry of Our English Bible,* 154; Geisler and Nix, *Introduction to the Bible,* 387, 395–98; *Davis Dictionary of the Bible,* 562; Ewert, *From Ancient Tablets to Modern Translations,* 136–37.

10. Martin, *Multiple Originals,* 219–20; Twilley, *Origin and Transmission of the New Testament,* 9–34; Price, *Ancestry of Our English Bible,* 154; Geisler and Nix, *Introduction to the Bible,* 387, 395–98; Davis, *Dictionary of the Bible,* 562; Ewert, *From Ancient Tablets to Modern Translations,* 136–37; *Century of British Orientalists,* 191–93, 147; Parker, *Codex Sinaiticus,* 31–45; The Codes Sinaiticus Project, "Codex Sinaiticus," http://www.codexsinaiticus.org/en/, accessed October 24, 2017; Smith, *Codex Vaticanus,* 1–4; Smith, *Codex Alexandrinus,* 10–13; "Codex Alexandrinus," http://www.bl.uk/onlinegallery/sacredtexts/codexalex.html, accessed October 24, 2017; Deuel, *Testaments of Time,* 264–65; Geisler and Nix, *Introduction to the Bible,* 387, 395–98; Ewert, *From Ancient Tablets to Modern Translations,* 141–43; C. C. Parker, *Codex Bezae* (Cambridge: Cambridge University Press, 1996), 7–10; Wegner, *From Text to Translations,* 311–15, 269; Larry W. Hurtado, ed., *The Freer Biblical Manuscripts: Fresh Studies of an American Treasure Trove* (Atlanta: Society of Biblical Literature, 2006), 167.

11. Pache, *Inspiration and Authority of Scripture,* 157, 196–98; Benjamin B. Warfield, *The Inspiration and Authority of the Bible* (Phillipsburg: Presbyterian and Reformed Publishing, 1948), 419–42; John A. T. Robinson, *Redating the New Testament* (Eugene: Wipf and Stock, 1976), 13–18, 335–43; E. Earle Ellis, *History and Interpretation in New Testament Perspective* (Leiden: Brill, 2001), 39–45; Archibald A. Hodge and Benjamin B. Warfield, "Inspiration," *British and Foreign Evangelical Review* 117, no. 30 (April 1881): 583.

12. "Obituary: Sir Frederic George Kenyon," *Scripture: The Quarterly of the Catholic Biblical Association* 5, no. 5 (January–March 1953):110; Miriam C. Davis, *Dame Kathleen Kenyon: Digging Up the Holy Land* (Walnut Creek: Left Coast Press, 2008), 15; Frederic George Kenyon, *The Bible and Archaeology* (New York: Harper Bros., 1940), 286; Kenyon, *Story of the Bible,* 41, 113; Frederic George Kenyon, *The Reading of the Bible: As History, as Literature and as Religion* (London: J. Murray, 1944), 32; Frederic George Kenyon, *Our Bible and the Ancient Manuscripts* (Eugene: Wipf and Stock, 2011), 23.

13. Stanley E. Porter, *Constantine Tischendorf: The Life and Work of a 19th Century Bible Hunter* (London: Bloomsbury, 2015), 53–60; Constantin von Tischendorf, *Travels in the East* (London: Longman, Brown and Green, 1851), 95–98; Stanley E. Porter, "Hero or Thief: Constantine Tischendorf Turns Two Hundred," *Biblical Archaeology Review* 41, no. 5 (September–October 2015), 41–53; Daniel Gurtner, Juan Hernandez Jr., and Paul Foster, *Studies on the Texts of the*

*New Testament and Early Christianity: Essay*s by (New York: Doran Books, 1926), 15–21; Scot McKendrick et al., *Codex Sinaiticus, New Perspectives on the Ancient Biblical Manuscript* (London: British Library, 2015), 53–89.

14. Porter, *Constantine Tischendorf,* 12–18, 26–32, 46–58; Tischendorf, *Travels in the East,* 98–102; Porter, "Hero or Thief," 41–53; A. T. Robertson, *Studies on the Texts of the New Testament* (New York: Doran Books, 1926), 15–21; *Codex Sinaiticus, New Perspectives on the Ancient Biblical Manuscript,* 53–89.

15. Anatoly Kholodiuk, "Exhibition: 'Tischendorf, in Search of the Oldest Bible in the World,' Opens in Leipzig Library," *Orthodox Christianity,* February 18, 2011; Porter, *Constantine Tischendorf,* 40–48, 60–67; Theodore Cressy Skeat, *The Collected Biblical Writings of T. C. Skeat,* ed. J. K. Elliott (Leiden: Brill, 2004), 109–10; Jerome Taylor, "Fragment of World's Oldest Bible Found Hidden at Egyptian Monastery," *Independent,* September 1, 2009.

16. Leobegott Friedrich Constantine von Tischendorf, *The Revised Versions of the New Testament: With a History of the Revision* (St. Louis: Scammel, 1881), 27–31; Kholodiuk, "Exhibition: 'Tischendorf," *Orthodox Christianity;* Porter, *Constantine Tischendorf,* 42–58; Taylor, "Fragment of World's Oldest Bible."

17. Tischendorf, *Revised Version of the New Testament,* 29–33; Kholodiuk, "Exhibition: 'Tischendorf," Porter, *Constantine Tischendorf,* 41, 60–64; Taylor, "Fragment of World's Oldest Bible."

18. Porter, *Constantine Tischendorf,* 51; John Wolfenden, *Treasures of the British Museum* (New York: Viking Press, 1972), 174; Taylor, "Fragment of World's Oldest Bible"; Tischendorf, *Revised Version of the New Testament,* 29-33; "*Codex Sinaiticus,*" http://www.codexsinaiticus.org/en/project/webdevelopment.aspx, accessed October 24, 2017.

19. Wegner, *From Text to Translation,* 87; *Cambridge History of the Bible,* 1:7–8; Geisler and Nix, *Introduction to the Bible,* 323–30; Ewert, *From Ancient Tables to Modern Translation*s, 57–60; *New Bible Dictionary,* 678–80; Rodney J. Decker, *Koine Greek Reader: Selections from the New Testament, the Septuagint, and Early Christian Writer*s (Grand Rapids: Kregel Academic, 2007), 18–24.

20. Debra Skelton and Pamela Dell, *Empire of Alexander the Great* (New York: Chelsea House, 2009), 109–10; *Cambridge History of the Bible,* 1:7–8; Geisler and Nix, *Introduction to the Bible,* 323–30; Ewert, *From Ancient Tables to Modern Translation*s, 57–60; Wegner, *From Text to Translation,* 87.

21. Albert Wifstrand, *Epochs and Styles: Selected Writings on the New Testament, Greek Language and Greek Culture in the Post-Classical Era,* ed. Lars Rydbeck and Stanley E. Porter, trans. Denis Searby (Tubingen: Mohrs Siebeck, 2005), 71–72; *Cambridge History of the Bible,* 1:7–8; Geisler and Nix, *Introduction to the Bible,* 323–30; Ewert, *From Ancient Tables to Modern Translation*s, 57–60; Wegner, *From Text to Translation,* 87; Galatians 4:4.

22. Joseph Bosworth, *An Anglo-Saxon Dictionary,* ed. T. Northcote Toller (Oxford: Clarendon Press, 1882), 484; D. S. Gregory, *Why Four Gospels?* (New York: Sheldon, 1876), 85–88, 150–63, 207–21, 271–79; Wegner, *From Texts to Translations,* 56–59, 63–65, 147; *Davis Dictionary of the Bible,* 279, 496–98; 505–6; Walter M. Chandler, *The Trial of Jesus: From a Lawyer's Standpoint* (Norcross, GA: Harrison, 1976), 64–65; Geisler and Nix, *Introduction to the Bible,* 392–94, 470–72; Price, *Ancestry of Our English Bible,* 60–81; Kenyon, *Story of the Bible,* 74–75.

23. Gleason Archer, *Encyclopedia of Bible Difficultie*s (Grand Rapids: Zondervan, 1982), 311–15; Gregory, *Why Four Gospels?:* 85–88, 150–63, 207–21, 271–79; Wegner, *From Texts to Translations,* 56–59, 63–65, 147; James R. Edwards, *The Gospel According to Luke* (Grand Rapids: Eerdmans, 2015), 19; Geisler and Nix, *Introduction to the Bible,* 392–94, 470–72; Charles B. Herbermann, ed., *The Catholic Encyclopedia* (New York: Encyclopedia Press, 1911), 58–59; Price, *Ancestry of*

Our English Bible, 60–81; Kenyon, Story of the Bible, 74–75; Davis Dictionary of the Bible, 279, 496–98; 505–6, 481–83; New Bible Dictionary, 606–8, 713–16, 737–38, 749–52; 1 Peter 5:13; Colossians 4:14.

24. F. F. Bruce, The Book of Acts (Grand Rapids: Eerdmans, 1988), 28–32; Thomas R. Schreiner, Interpreting the Pauline Epistles (Grand Rapids: Baker Academic, 1990), 11–39; H. A. Ironsides, I and II Timothy, Titus and Philemon (Grand Rapids: Kregel, 2007), 9, 100–01; Wegner, From Texts to Translations, 58–60; New Bible Dictionary, 11–12; Davis Dictionary of the Bible, 226–27, 561–63; New Bible Dictionary, 11–12, 340–41; Eerdmans Handbook to the Bible, 549–50, 574–80; Warfield, Inspiration and Authority of the Bible: 424–25.

25. Matthew Henry, Revelation, ed. Alister McGrath and J. I. Packer (Wheaton, IL: Crossway Books, 1999), 13–22; Joseph A. Seiss, The Apocalypse: Lectures on the Book of Revelation (New York: Cosimo Classics, 2007), 15–24, 521–29; Eerdmans Handbook to the Bible, 549–50, 574–80; Davis Dictionary of the Bible, 561–63; New Bible Dictionary, 54–56; New Bible Dictionary; 1025–27.

CHAPTER 4: HERESY, PERSECUTION, AND TRIUMPH

1. Acts 8:9–24; Bill R. Austin, Austin's Topical History of Christianity (Wheaton, IL: Tyndale House, 1983), 272; Pheme Perkins, Gnosticism and the New Testament (Minneapolis: Ausburg Fortress, 1993), 4–12; Tim Dowley, ed., Eerdmans History of Christianity (Grand Rapids: Eerdmans, 1977), 99–100; New Bible Dictionary, 1115–16.

2. Adrian Hastings, Alistar Mason, and Hugh Pyper, eds., The Oxford Companion to Christian Thought: Intellectual, Spiritual and Moral Horizons (Oxford: Oxford University Press, 2000), 193, 268–69; Robert Martin Pope, An Introduction to Early Church History: A Survey of the Relations Between Christianity and Paganism in the Early Roman Empire (London: Macmillan, 1918), 36–48; Walter A. Ewell, ed., The Evangelical Dictionary of Theology (Grand Rapids: Baker Academic, 2007), 485–86.

3. 1 John 2:18; The Oxford Companion to Christian Thought, 268–69; Pope, Introduction to Early Church History, 36–48; Perkins, Gnosticism and the New Testament, 6–12; Dowley, ed., Eerdmans History of Christianity, 77–86: Bruce, Books and Parchment, 112: Austin, History of Christianity, 60–66, 85; Perkins, Gnosticism and the New Testament, 79–84.

4. Paul R. Gilliam, Ignatius of Antioch and the Arian Conspiracy (Leiden: Brill, 2017), 31; Alexander Souter, The Text and Canon of the New Testament (New York: Scribner's Sons, 1913), 177, 195–97, 215; Bruce, Books and Parchment, 112–13; Pope, Early Church History, 39–41; Adolph Harnack, History of Dogma, trans. Neil Buchanan (Boston: Little & Brown, 1905), 1:262–63; Edward Burton, An Inquiry into the Heresies of the Apostolic Age (Oxford: Oxford University Press, 1829), 561–63; Geisler and Nix, Introduction to the Bible, 282, 292–93; Ewert, From Ancient Tablets to Modern Translations, 134; John W. Wenhan, Christ and the Bible (Downers Grove, IL: InterVarsity Press, 1973), 163.

5. Will and Aerial Durant, The Story of Civilization: Caesar and Christ (New York: Simon and Schuster, 1944), 502, 604–5; Souter, Text and Canon of the New Testament, 177, 195–97, 215: Wegner, From Texts to Translations, 157–58; Dictionary of Biblical Archaeology, 327; Bruce, Books and Parchment, 112–13; Geisler and Nix, Introduction to the Bible, 282, 292–93; Ewert, From Ancient Tablets to Modern Translations, 134; Wenhan, Christ and the Bible, 163.

6. Colossians 2: 8-9: Henry C. Thiessen, Introduction to the New Testament (Grand Rapids: Eerdmans, 1954), 3–12; Wenhan, Christ and the Bible, 163; Bruce, The Books and the Parchments, 104–10 (see chap. 1, n. 1); Bruce, New Testament History, 415–30; Dowley, ed., Eerdmans History of Christianity, 75–78, 101–26; Wegner, From Text to Translations, 148–51; Peter 3:16; Ephesians 2:20.

7. John 20:30; Bruce, The Books and the Parchments, 104–10; Wegner, From Texts to Translations,

148–50; Bruce, *New Testament History,* 415–30; Thiessen, *Introduction to the New Testament,* 10; Luke 1:2-14; 1 Thessalonians 2:13.

8. 1 Thessalonians 5:27; Colossians 4:16; Bruce, *The Books and the Parchments,* 109; Geisler and Nix, *Introduction to the New Testament,* 292, 430–31; Thiessen, *Introduction to the New Testament,* 9–12; Wegner, *From Texts to Translations,* 149–50; Ephesians 2:20.

9. Everett Ferguson, David Scholer, and Paul C. Finey, eds., *Personalities of the Early Church* (London: Routledge, 1993), 351; Burton, *An Inquiry into the Heresies of the Apostolic Age,* 534–40; Thiessen, *Introduction to the New Testament,* 12–24; C. E. Hill, "The Debate over the Muratorian Fragment and the Development of the Canon," *Westminster Theological Journal* 57, no. 2 (Fall 1995):437–52; Bruce Metzger, *The Canon of the New Testament: Its Origin, Development and Significance* (Oxford: Oxford University Press, 1987), 19–20; Wegner, *From Texts to Translations,* 140–48; Pope, *Introduction to Early Church History,* 90–101.

10. John 15:20; Ralph Martin Novak, *Christianity and the Roman Empire: The Texts* (Harrisburg: Trinity Press, 2001); Quentus Septimius Tertullian, *Apology De Spectaculis,* trans. T. R. Glover (Cambridge: Harvard University Press, 1931), 227; Herbert B. Workman, *Persecution in the Early Church* (Manchester: Epworth Press, 1923), 29–40; Bruce, *The Books and the Parchments* 104–10; James J. Burke, *Characteristics of the Early Church* (Milwaukee: M. H. Wiltzius, 1899), 101–2; Martin Goodman, *The Roman World: 44 B.C. to 190 A.D.* (London: Routledge, 1997), 55–57, 327–28; Tacitus, *Annals of Rome,* 15:44; Edward Champlin, *Nero* (Cambridge: Harvard University Press, 2003), 17–21, 122–28; Christopher A. Mackay, *Ancient Rome: A Military and Political History* (Cambridge: Cambridge University Press, 2004), 300–02; Henry Wace and Philip Schaff, eds., *A Select Library of Nicene and Post-Nicene Fathers of the Christian Church* (Oxford: Parker, 1890), 1:324; Sandra Sweeney Silver, *Footprints in Parchment: Rome Verses Christianity, 30–313 A.D.* (Bloomington: Authorhouse, 2013), 503–4.

11. David Potter, *Constantine the Emperor* (Oxford: Oxford University Press, 2013), 149–57; Mackay, *Ancient Rome,* 300–02; Silver, *Footprints in Parchment,* 503–4; Wace and Schaff, *Select Library of Nicene and Post-Nicene Fathers,* 1:325–66.

12. Potter, *Constantine the Emperor*: 149–57; Mackay, *Ancient Rome,* 300–02; Silver, *Footprints in Parchment,* 503–4; Wace and Schaff, *Select Library of Nicene and Post-Nicene Fathers,* 1:375.

13. Potter, *Constantine the Emperor,* 149–57; Mackay, *Ancient Rome,* 300–02; Silver, *Footprints in Parchment,* 503–4; Wace and Schaff, *Select Library of Nicene and Post-Nicene Fathers,* 1:375; Durant, *The Story of Civilization,* 654.

14. Milligan, *New Testament Documents,* 299; Souter, *Text and Canon of the New Testament,* 210–15; Eusebius, *Eusebius: The Church History,* ed. Paul L. Maier (Grand Rapids: Kregel, 1999), 334–37; James D. Ernest, *The Bible in Athanasius of Alexandria* (Leiden: Brill Academic, 2004), 343; Khaled Anatolis, *Athanasius* (London: Routledge, 2004), 88–91.

15. Charles J. Hefele, *A History of the Christian Councils to the Close of the Council of Nicaea in A.D. 325,* trans. William R. Clark (Edinburgh: T&T Clark, 1871), 1:2–6, 368–73; W. Donald Munson Jr., Bible lecture, Montreat-Anderson College, April 17, 1978; Tom Streeter, *The Church and Western Culture: An Introduction to Church History* (Bloomington: Authorhouse, 2008), 73–79; Dean Dudley, *The First Council of Nice* (New York; Cosimo, 2007), 78–84.

16. Streeter, *The Church and Western Culture,* 73–79; Dudley, *First Council of Nice,* 78–84; Hefele, *History of the Christian Councils,* 1:2–6, 368–73; Souter, *Text and Canon,* 195–97, 277; Arthur J. Bellinzoni, *The New Testament: An Introduction to Biblical Scholarship* (Eugene: Wipf and Stock, 2016), 428; Souter, *Canon of the New Testament,* 177, 195–97, 215: Bruce, *Books and Parchment,*

112–13; Geisler and Nix, *Introduction to the Bible,* 282, 292–93; Ewert, *From Ancient Tablets to Modern Translations,* 134; Wenhan, *Christ and the Bible,* 163–68.

CHAPTER 5: LIGHT IN THE DARKNESS

1.   John D. Kelly, *Jerome: His Life, Writings and Controversies* (New York: Harper & Row, 1975), 88–91, 127–30, 223–25; Finley Hooper and Matthew Schwartz, *Roman Letters: History from a Personal Point of View* (Detroit: Wayne State University Press, 1991), 213; William Smith, ed., *Dictionary of Greek and Roman Biography and Mythology* (London: Taylor and Walton, 1846), 2:459–61; Price, *Ancestry of Our English Bible,* 86–90; Neil R. Lightfoot, *How We Got the Bible* (Grand Rapids: Baker Book House, 1963), 71–74; Dowley, ed., *Eerdmans History of Christianity,* 188–89; *Austin's History of Christianity,* 100.

2.   Cynthia White, *The Emergence of Christianity: Classical Traditions in Contemporary Perspective* (Minneapolis: Fortress Press, 2011), 108; John 18:36; Kelly, *Jerome,* 127–30, 223–25; *Dictionary of Greek and Roman Biography and Mythology,* 2:459–61; Price, *Ancestry of Our English Bible,* 86–87; Philip Wesley Comfort, ed., *The Origin of the Bible* (Carol Stream, IL: Tyndale House, 1992), 322–23; Dowley, ed., *Eerdmans History of Christianity,* 188–89; Bruce, *Books and Parchment,* 202–3; Craig A. Evans, *Ancient Texts for New Testament Studies: A Guide to Background Studies* (Peabody, MA: Hendrickson, 2015), 162.

3.   Raymond Davis, ed., *The Book of Pontiffs: The Ancient Biographies of the First Ninety Roman Bishops to A.D. 75* (Liverpool: Liverpool University Press, 1989), 6:30; Dennis Trout, *Damasus of Rome: The Epigraphic Poetry* (Oxford: Oxford University Press, 2015), 1–2; Cross, *The Oxford Dictionary of the Christian Church,* 451 (see chap. 1, n. 14); White, *Emergence of Christianity,* 108; Kelly, *Jerome,* 127–30, 223–25; *Dictionary of Greek and Roman Biography and Mythology,* 2:459–61; Price, *Ancestry of Our English Bible,* 86–87; *Origin of the Bible,* 322–23.

4.   C. T. R. Hayward, *Saint Jerome's Hebrew Questions on Genesis* (Oxford: Oxford University Press, 1995), 1–6; Timothy M. Law, *Origenes Orientalis: The Preservation of Origin's Hexapla in the Syrohexapla* (Gottingen: Vandenhoeck and Ruprecht, 2011), 16–18; Blackford Condit, *The History of the English Bible, Extending from the Earliest Saxon Translations to the Present Anglo-American Revision* (New York: A. S. Barnes, 1882), 313–15; *Origin of the Bible,* 322–23; Price, *Ancestry of the English Bible,* 86–89; Bruce, *The Books and the Parchments,* 202–6 (see chap. 1, n. 1); Lightfoot, *How We Got the Bible,* 71–74; Geisler and Nix. *General Introduction to the Bible,* 529–38 (see chap. 1, n. 1); J. B. Lightfoot, *On a Fresh Translation of the English New Testament* (London: Macmillan, 1871), 225.

5.   T. S. Greenslade, ed., *The Cambridge History of the Bible, The West from the Reformation to the Present* (Cambridge: Cambridge University Press, 1963), 3:73–75; Julius A. Bewer, *The History of the New Testament Canon in the Syrian Church* (Chicago: University of Chicago Press, 1900), 3–6; Hugh Murray, *The Travels of Marco Polo* (New York: Harper Bros., 1851), 67, 163–64; Marco Polo, *The Book of Marco Polo the Venetian,* trans. and ed. Henry Yule (New York: Charles Scribner's, 1903), 2:358; Lee Martin McDonald, *The Formation of the Biblical Canon: The Old Testament* (London: Bloomsbury, 2017), 1:xvi, 455–66; Gerald O. West, *The Stolen Bible: From the Tool of Imperialism to African Icon* (Leiden: Brill, 2016), 13–16; Ewert, *Ancient Tablets to Modern Translations,* 167–68; Lightfoot, *How We Got the Bible,* 67–68; *Origin of the Bible,* 325–26; Price, *Ancestry of Our English Bible,* 95–97; Bruce, *The Books and the Parchments,* 192–95.

6.   F. E. Peters, *Muhammad and the Origins of Islam* (Albany: State University of New York Press, 1994), 34–43, 144–47, 288–90; Thomas Houtsman, ed., *Brill's First Encyclopedia of Islam* (Leiden:

Brill, 1993), 4:1121–24; Juan E. Campo, ed., *Encyclopedia of Islam* (New York: Facts on File, 2009), 491–96; Crane Brinton, John B. Christopher, and Robert Lee Wolfe, *A History of Civilization* (Englewood Cliffs, NJ: Prentice-Hall, 1955), 1:183, 243–47, 361; Dowley, ed., *Eerdmans History of Christianity*, 224–26; Price, *Ancestry of the English Bible*, 77–78.

7. William Montgomery Watt, *Muhammad: Prophet and Statesman* (Oxford: Oxford University Press, 1961), 8–16; Peters, *Muhammad and the Origins of Islam*, 34–36, 216–24, 237–43; Hugh Kennedy, *The Great Arab Conquests: How the Spread of Islam Changed the World We Live In* (Philadelphia: Da Capo Press, 2007), 154–57, 201–15, 308–14, 321–26; Christopher and Wolfe, *History of Civilization*, 1:183, 243–247, 361; Dowley, ed., *Eerdmans History of Christianity*, 224–26; Price, *Ancestry of the English Bible*, 77–78; Robert Grant, "The Textual Tradition of Theophilus of Antioch," *Vigiliae Christianae* 6, no. 3 (July 1952):146–59; Harry Y. Gamble, *Books and Readers in the Early Church: A History of Early Christian Texts* (New Haven, CT: Yale University Press, 1995), 132, 154–57.

8. Peter Heather, *The Fall of the Roman Empire: A New History of Rome and the Barbarians* (Oxford: Oxford University Press, 2006), 367–73, 431–43, 454–64; Jack L. Swartzwald, *The Collapse and Recovery of Europe, A.D. 476–1648* (Jefferson, NC: McFarland, 2016), 3–5; Carl Waldman and Catherine Mason, eds., *Encyclopedia of European People* (New York: Facts on File, 2006), 2:699; Brinton, Christopher, and Wolfe, *History of Civilization*, 335–37; Price, *Ancestry of Our English Bible*, 206; Dowley, ed., *Eerdmans History of Christianity*, 226; Bruce, *The Books and the Parchments*, 186–87; Franz Babinger, *Mehmed the Conqueror and His Time* (Princeton: Princeton University Press, 1978), 89–94; Steven Ruciman, *The Fall of Constantinople, 1453* (Cambridge: Cambridge University Press, 1965), 133–47.

9. Cyril Mango, ed., *The Oxford History of Byzantium* (Oxford: Oxford University Press, 2002), 283; Robert F. Hull, *The Story of the New Testament Text: Movers, Materials, Motives, and Models* (Atlanta: Society of Biblical Literature, 2010), 150; Roger E. Olson, *The Story of Christian Theology: Twenty Centuries of Tradition and Reform* (Downers Grove, IL: Intervarsity Press, 1999), 142–43; D. S. Wallace-Hadrill, *Christian Antioch: A Study of Early Christian Thought in the East* (Cambridge: Cambridge University Press, 1982), 82; Lightfoot, *How We Got the Bible*, 77–85; Price, *Ancestry of the English Bible*, 73–75, 228; Ewert, *Ancient Tablets to Modern Translations*, 83.

10. Bruce M. Metzger, *Manuscripts of the Greek Bible: An Introduction to Palaeography* (New York: Oxford University Press, 1981), 44–46; Stephen M. Miller and Robert V. Huber, *The Bible: A History* (Oxford: Lion Books, 2015), 213–15; Thomas Aquinas, *Catena Aurea: Commentary on Matthew's Gospel* (Old Chelsea Station: Cosimo, 2007), 1:2.13–15; *Cambridge History of the Bible*, 2:117, 326.

11. Richard Marsden, *The Text of the Old Testament in Anglo-Saxon England* (Cambridge: Cambridge University Press, 1995), 107–8; Celia Chazelle, "Ceolfrith's Gift to St. Peter: The First Quire of the *Codex Amiatinus* and the Evidence of Its Roman Destination," *Early Medieval Europe* 12, no. 2 (July 2003): 129–30; "Codex Amiatinus Bible Returns to Its Home in Jarrow," BBC News, May 15, 2014; *Cambridge History of the Bible*, 2:117; Wegner, *From Texts to Translations*, 256–57; Blanche Cirker, ed., *The Book of Kells: Selected Plates in Full Color* (Mineola: Dover, 1982), 2–4; Edward Sullivan, *The Book of Kells* (London: The Studio, 1920), 4–6, 23–24.

12. Charles R. Dodwell, *The Pictorial Arts of the West, 800–1200* (New Haven, CT: Yale University Press, 1993), 85–86; John Haywood, *Northmen: The Viking Saga, AD 793–1241* (New York: St. Martin's Press, 2015), 42–46; Dorothy Whitelock, *English Historical Documents, 500–1042* (London: Routledge, 1996), 271; Gwyn Jones, *A History of the Vikings* (Oxford: Oxford University Press, 1968), 195–96.

13. Haywood, *Northmen*, 42–46; *English Historical Documents*, 271; Jones, *History of the Vikings*, 28–30, 195–96.

14.   George P. Marsh, *The Origin and History of the English Language* (New York: Charles Scribner's Sons, 1892), 75–78; Julia Fernandez Cuesta and Sara M. Pon-Sans, eds., *The Old English Gloss to the Lindisfarne Gospels: Language, Author and Context* (Berlin: Walter de Gruyter, 2016), 3–5; Simpson, *Lindisfarne Gospels*, 28–30.

15.   Marsh, *Origin and History of the English Language*, 75–78; *Old English Gloss to the Lindisfarne Gospels*, 3–5; Simpson, *Lindisfarne Gospels*, 28–30; Haywood, *Northmen*, 42–46; Christopher De Hamel, *A History of Illuminated Manuscripts* (London: Phaidon Press, 1994), 30–31; "Manuscripts in the British Library: Lindisfarne Gospels," British Library, https://www.bl.uk/collection-items/lindisfarne-gospels, October 24, 2017.

16.   Adrian Hastings, ed., *A World History of Christianity* (Grand Rapids: Eerdmans, 1999), 42–45; Henry Barker, *English Bible Versions: A Tercenteary Memorial to the King James Version, from the New York Bible and the Common Prayer Book Society* (Cambridge: Cambridge University Press, 1911), 82–83; Adolf von Harnack, *Monasticism: Its Ideals and Its History,* trans. Charles R. Gillet (New York: Christian Literature Company, 1895), 27–30; Thomas Cahill, *How the Irish Saved Civilization: The Untold Story of Ireland's Heroic Role from the Fall of Rome to the Rise of Medieval Europe* (New York: Doubleday, 1995), 193–94.

17.   P. G. Walsh, trans., *Cassiodorus: Explanation of the Psalms* (New York: Paulist Press, 1990), 1:1–19; Cassiodorus, *Cassiodorus: Variae,* trans. S. J. D. Barnish (Liverpool: Liverpool University Press, 1992), 12: xxix–liv; Peter Hunter Blair, *The World of Bede* (Cambridge: Cambridge University Press, 1970), 127–29; Rene Lauret, *France and Germany: The Legacy of Charlemagne* (Chicago: Henry Regnery, 1964), 147, 258; Urban T. Holmes and Alexander H. Schultz, *A History of the French Language* (New York: Biblio and Tannen, 1928), 27–28.

18.   Robert Benedetto, ed., *The New Westminster Dictionary of Church History: The Early, Medieval and Reformation Eras* (London: Westminster John Knox Press, 2008), 1:171; Price, *Ancestry of the English Bible,* 181–92, 225–26; Bruce, *The Books and the Parchments,* 219–21; Dowley, ed., *Eerdmans History of Christianity,* 205–16; Anders Winworth, *The Conversion of Scandinavia: Vikings, Merchants and Missionaries in the Remaking of Europe* (New Haven, CT: Yale University Press, 2012), 102–8, 132–40.

19.   Lori Anne Ferrell, *The Bible and the People* (New Haven, CT: Yale University Press, 2008), 259; Bruce M. Metzger and Michael D. Coogan, eds., *The Oxford Guide to Ideas and Issues of the Bible* (Oxford: Oxford University Press, 2001), 89; Elizabeth Armstrong, *Robert Estienne: Royal Printer* (Cambridge: Cambridge University, 1954), 33–34, 72–76; John Edwin Sandys, *A History of Classical Scholarship: From the Revival of Learning to the Eighteenth Century* (Cambridge: Cambridge University Press, 1908), 173–74.

20.   Blair, *World of Bede*, 235; John C. Bruce, *Old Newcastle: Lectures* (Newcastle-Upon-Tyne, Andrew Reid, 1904), 26–27; J. D. Penrose, *An Outline of Christianity: The Story of Our Civilization* (New York: Bethlehem, 1926), 2:204, 230; Sidney Lee, ed., *Dictionary of National Biography* (London: Smith and Elder, 1900), 63:202–21: Lewis Sergeant, *John Wyclif: Last of the Schoolmen and First of the English Reformers* (Harrington: Delmarva, 2013), 214–27; Benson Bobrick, *Wide as the Waters: The Story of the English Bible and the Revolution It Inspired* (New York; Simon and Schuster, 2001), 43–46, 51–57, 74–76; Matthew McMahon, *The Life and Times of John Wycliffe: Morning Star of the Reformation* (London: Religious Tract Society, 1884), 117.

21.   Gillian Rosemary Evans, *John Wyclif: Myth and Reality* (Downers Grove, IL: Intervarsity Press, 2005), 13–15, 230–33; David Fountain, *John Wycliffe and the Dawn of the Reformation* (Southampton: Mayflower Christian Books, 1984), 38–39, 90–92; McMahon, *Life and Times of*

John Wycliffe, 115–19, 122–27; Wegner, *From Text to Translations*, 282–84; *Oxford Guide to Ideas and Issues in the Bible*, 506.

CHAPTER 6: GOD'S TRUTH ABIDETH STILL

1. John Man, *Gutenberg: How One Man Remade the World with Words* (New York: John Wiley & Sons, 2002), 84–95; Diana Childress, *Johannes Gutenberg: Inventor of the Printing Press* (Minneapolis: Twenty-First Century Books, 2008), 71; Wegner, *From Texts to Translations*, 263–64; "From Script to Print," Ball State, http://cms.bsu.edu/academics/libraries/collectionsanddept/archives/collections/rarebooks/exhibits/fromscripttoprint, accessed October 24, 2017; Brinton, Christopher, and Wolff, *History of Civilization,* 1:449–50.

2. Janet Inge, *Johann Gutenberg and His Bible: A Study* (New York: Typophiles, 1988), 65–66, 89–91; Brinton, Christopher, and Wolff, *History of Civilization,* 1:449–50; Man, *Gutenberg,* 71; Paul A. Winkler, ed., *History of Books and Printing* (Engelwood: Information Handling Services, 1978), 271–74; Bruce C. Metzger, *The Bible in Translation: Ancient and English Versions* (Grand Rapids: Baker Academic, 2006), 9.

3. Edward H. Landon, ed., *Manual of Councils of the Holy Catholic Church* (London: Francis & John Rivington, 1846), 593–94; John Mclintock and James Strong, eds., *Cyclopedia of Biblical, Theological and Ecclesiastical Literature* (New York: Harper & Bros., 1891), 499–500; Brinton, Christopher, and Wolff, *History of Civilization*, 1:203–9, 298–304.

4. Chambers, *Popes, Cardinals and War*, 134–45; E. R. Chamberlin, *The Bad Popes* (New York: Barnes & Noble Books, 1993), 210–31; Austin, *Austin's. History of Christianity,* 199–205, 222; John W. O'Malley, *A History of the Popes: From Peter to the Present* (New York: Rowan & Littlefield, 2010), 179; Roger Collins, *Keeper of the Keys to Heaven: A History of the Papacy* (New York: Basic Books, 2009), 350–54; E. Glenn Hinson, *The Church Triumphant: A History of Christianity Up to 1300* (Mercer: Mercer University Press, 1995), 367, 430; Andrew Louth, *Greek East and Latin West: The Church AD 681–1071* (Crestwood: St. Vladimer's Seminary Press, 2007), 3: 271; Michael J. Angold, *The Fourth Crusade: Event and Context* (London: Routledge, 2003), 100–03.

5. Chambers, *Popes, Cardinals and War,* 134–45; Chamberlin, *The Bad Popes,* 210–31; Austin, *Austin's History of Christianity,* 199–205, 222; O'Malley, *A History of the Popes,* 179; Collins, *Keeper of the Keys to Heaven,* 350–54; Hinson, *Church Triumphant,* 367, 430; Louth, *Greek East and Latin West,* 3: 271; Angold, *The Fourth Crusade,* 100–03.

6. Alan F. Johnson and Robert E. Webber, *What Christians Believe: A Biblical and Historical Summary* (Grand Rapids: Zondervan, 1993), 306–12; *Baker's Dictionary of Theology,* 283–84, 303–7, 399–400, 410, 430; Francis Schaeffer, *How Should We Then Live: The Rise and Fall of Western Thought and Culture* (Wheaton, IL: Crossway Books, 1976), 88; Brian Tierny, *Origins of Papal Infallibility, 1150–1350* (Leiden: E. J. Brill, 1972), 31–38; James Montgomery Boice, *Foundations of the Christian Faith* (Downers Grove, IL: Intervarsity Press, 1986), 416–26; Lawrence G. Duggan, *Encyclopedia Britannica,* s.v., "indulgence," accessed October 24, 2017, https://www.britannica.com/topic/indulgences; Luke 23:43; John 3:16; 10:28; Rom. 3:23; 6:23; 10:9–11; Eph. 2:8–9; Heb. 9:27; 1 John 5:11–12.

7. Roland H. Bainton, *Here I Stand: A Life of Martin Luther* (Nashville: Abingdon Press, 1978), 4–12; Brinton, Christopher, and Wolff, *History of Civilization,* 1:203–09; Maurice Price, "The Hebrew Text of the Old Testament," *The Biblical World* 37, no. 4: 247–48; Bruce, *The Books and the Parchments,* 207–9, 230 (see chap. 1, n. 1); Price, *Ancestry of Our English Bible,* 185–87; Metzger,

Canon *of the New Testament,* 102–5; Dowley, ed., *Eerdmans History of Christianity,* 366–68, 373–74, 382; *Baker's Dictionary of Theology,* 419–20; Paul Althaus, *The Theology of Martin Luther,* trans. Robert C. Schultz (Philadelphia: Fortress Press, 1966), 121–22, 180–83, 226.

8.   Martin Luther, *Martin Luther's 95 Theses: With the Pertinent Documents from the History of the Reformation* (St. Louis: Concordia, 2004), 55–64; Marvin Perry, *Western Civilization: Ideas, Politics and Society* (Boston: Cengage Learning, 2009), 1:322; Austin, *Austin's History of Christianity,* 426–40.

9.   Bainton, *Here I Stand,* 4–12; Austin, *Austin's History of Christianity,* 227–38; Brinton, Christopher, and Wolff, *History of Civilization,* 1: 461–91; Cross, *The Oxford Dictionary of the Christian Church,* 1007–9 (see chap. 1, n. 14); J. I. Packer, "Sola Fide: The Reformed Doctrine of Justification," http://www.ligonier.org/learn/articles/sola-fide-the-reformed-doctrine-of-justification/, accessed October 25, 2017; Wegener, *6,000 Years of the Bible,* 213–15; Geisler and Nix, *A General Introduction to the Bible,* 264–75 (see chap. 1, n. 1).

10.   Bainton, *Here I Stand,* 5–16; Ludwig Hausser, *The Period of the Reformation, 1517–1648,* ed. Wilhelm Oncken (New York: American Tact Society, 1873). 15–16; Austin, *Austin's History of Christianity,* 303–10; Brinton, Christopher, and Wolff, *History of Civilization,* 1: 485–88, 515–17; M. Reu, "Luther's Journey to Rome," *Lutheran Church Review* 36, no. 2 (February 1917): 47–49, 100; Dowley, ed., *Eerdmans History of Christianity,* 373–92; Hans J. Hillerbrand, ed., *The Oxford Encyclopedia of the Reformation* (New York: Oxford University Press, 1996), 3:31, 469–70.

11.   Ernst Bruegemann, *The Life of Dr. Martin Luther,* 19–21; Reu, "Luther's Journey to Rome," 36:2:47–48; Thomas Lindsey, *A History of the Reformation* (New York: Charles Scribner's Sons, 1906), 207; Carol Glatz, "Scala Santa Chapel: Under Soot and Grime, a Visual Treasure," Catholic News Service, June15, 2007; H. V. Morton, *Travels in Rome* (New York: Da Capo Press, 1957), 7; Charles Spurgeon, "Scala Santa," *Sword and Trowel,* January 1874; Adolph Spaeth, ed., *The Works of Martin Luther* (Philadelphia: A. J. Holman, 1915), 29–38.

12.   Henry Loewin, *Ink Against the Devil: Luther's and His Opponents* (Waterloo: Wilfrid Laurier University Press, 2015), 11–14; William R. Estep, *Renaissance and Reformation* (Cedar Rapids: Eerdmans, 1986), 118–19; Brinton, Christopher, and Wolff, *History of Civilization,* 1: 486–91.

13.   Scott A. Hendrix, *Martin Luther: Visionary Reformer* (New Haven, CT: Yale University Press, 2015), 300; Loewin, *Ink Against the Devil,* 11–14; Estep, *Renaissance and Reformation,* 118–19; Brinton, Christopher, and Wolff, *History of Civilization,* 1: 486–91.

14.   Hendrix, *Martin Luther,* 193; Philip Schaff, *History of the Christian Church* (New York: Charles Scribner's Sons, 1910), 7:61; Lowen, *Ink Against the Devil,* 9, 33, 87; Robert Turnbull, *Christ in History* (Boston: Phillips, Sampson, 1854), 467; Brooks Schramm and Kirsi I. Stjerna, eds., *Martin Luther, the Bible and the Jewish People: A Reader* (Minneapolis: Fortress Press, 2012), 9–16; Berhard Lohse, *Martin Luther: An Introduction to His Life and Work* (Philadelphia: Fortress Press, 1986), 88; Bruce, *The Books and the Parchments,* 207–9; Price, *Ancestry of the English Bible,* 186–88; Austin, *Austin's History of Christianity,* 214–15; Metzger, *Canon of the New Testament,* 98–102.

15.   Lowen, *Ink Against the Devil,* 42; Kenneth A. Strand, *Early Low-German Bibles* (Grand Rapids: Eerdmans, 1967), 27–31; Lohse, *Martin Luther,* 106, 118–22; Martin Luther, "A Mighty Fortress is Our God," trans. Thomas Carlyle, *The Lutheran Hymnal* (St. Louis: Concordia., 1958), 193.

16.   David W. King, *The Bible in History: How the Texts Have Shaped the Times* (Oxford: Oxford University Press, 2004), 142–47; Cross, *The Oxford Dictionary of the Christian Church,* 1007–9 (see chap. 1, n. 14); John Tulloch, *Leaders of the Reformation: Luther, Calvin, Latimer and Knox* (London: William Blackwood: 1859, 2–4, 92–94, 187–90, 257–61; Lindsey, *History of Reformation,* 207;

Austin, *Austin's History of Christianity,* 230–45; Robert Turnbull, *Christ in History* (Boston: Phillips, Sampson, 1854), 467; R. C. Sproul, *Soli Deo Gloria: Essays in Reformed Theology* (Phillipsburg: Presbyterian and Reformed Publishing, 1976), 12.

17. William Fleming, *The True Church of the Bible* (London: Washburn, 1895), 10–18; *History of the Christian Church,* 7:61; Peter Marshall, ed., *The Oxford Illustrated History of the Reformation* (Oxford: Oxford University Press, 2015), 148–51, 192–93; James M. Stayer, *The German Peasants' War and Anabaptist Community of Goods* (Montreal: McGill-Queens University Press, 1991), 20, 42.

18. R. J. Knecht, *Catherine D'Medici* (London: Routledge, 1998), 158–60; Edward Peters, *Inquisition* (Berkeley: University of California Press, 1989), 97–99; Peter Grell and Bob Scribner, eds., *Tolerance and Intolerance in the European Reformation* (Cambridge: Cambridge University Press, 1986), 48–52; William Monter, *Judging the French Reformation, Heresy Trials by Sixteenth Century Parliaments* (Cambridge: Harvard University Press, 1999), 52.

19. Marshall, ed., *Oxford Illustrated History of the Reformation,* 129–31; Christine Kooi, *Calvinists and Catholics During Holland's Golden Age: Heretics and Idolaters* (Cambridge: Cambridge University Press, 2002), 23–24; Monter, *Judging the French Reformation,* 231–35; Darrel Hart, *Calvinism: A History* (New Haven, CT: Yale University Press, 2013), 1525, 1548–56; George Anderson, "The Doctrines of Calvin and the Theology of the Congregational Churches," *The Evangelical Repository: A Quarterly Magazine of Theological Literature* 7, no. 1 (1879): 96.

20. Andrew Johnston, *The Protestant Reformation in Europe* (London: Routledge, 1991), 76–77; Harold J. Berman, *Law and Revolution, The Impact of the Protestant Reformation on Western Legal Tradition* (Cambridge: Harvard University Press, 2003), xii, 28–29; Schaeffer, *How Should We Then Live?,* 108.

21. Johnston, *The Protestant Reformation,* 76–77; Berman, *Law and Revolution,* 28–29; Schaeffer, *How Should We Then Live?* 87; Jeremy Jackson, *No Other Foundation* (Westchester: Cornerstone Books, 1980), 153–54.

22. Sue Vander Hook, *Johannes Gutenberg: Printing Press Inovator* (Edina: ABDO, 2010), 92–94; Christian D. Ginsburg, *The Rabbinic Bible: Hebrew and English* (London: Longmans, Green, Reader and Dyer, 1867), 4–12; John C. Olin, *Catholic Reform: From Cardinal Ximenes to the Council of Trent, 1495–1563* (New York: Fordham University Press, 1990), 61; J. N. D. Kelly, *Early Christian Creeds* (London: Continuum, 1960), 368–71; John McClintock and James Strong, eds., *Cyclopaedia of Biblical, Theological and Ecclesiastical Literature* (New York: Harper Bros., 1894), 10:833; Alexander Monro, *The Paper Trail: An Unexpected History of a Revolutionary Invention* (New York: Alfred A. Knopf, 2016), 261.

23. Erika Rummel, ed., *The Erasmus Reader* (Toronto: University of Toronto Press, 1990), 195; Cornelis Augustijn, *Erasmus: His Life, Works and Influence,* trans. J. C. Grayson (Toronto: University of Toronto, 1991), 21–27, 89–91; McClintock and Strong, eds., *Cyclopaedia of Biblical, Theological and Ecclesiastical Literature,* 10: 833.

24. Cyril Eastwood, *The Priesthood of All Believers: An Examination of the Doctrine from the Reformation to the Present Day* (Eugene: Wipf & Stock, 1960), 244; McClintock and Strong, eds., *Cyclopaedia of Biblical, Theological and Ecclesiastical Literature,* 10:833; Ginsburg, *The Rabbinic Bible,* 4–12; Olin, *Catholic Reform,* 61; Kelly, *Early Christian Creeds,* 368–71; McKim, ed., *The Cambridge Companion to Martin Luther* (Cambridge: Cambridge University Press, 2003), 65–66 (see chap. 2, n. 19).

25. J. Gordon Melton, *Encyclopedia of Protestantism* (New York: Facts on File, 2005), 232; Philip A. Noss, *A History of Bible Translation* (New York: American Bible Society, 2007), 100–02, 134–38; M. Lamberigts and Den Hollander, eds., *Lay Bibles in Europe, 1450–1800* (Leuven: Leuven University Press, 2006), 134–35; Jaroslav Pelikan, *The Reformation of the Bible; The Bible of the Reformation* (New Haven, CT: Yale University Press, 1996), 156–57; Henry E. Jacobs, ed., *The*

Lutheran Cyclopedia (New York: Charles Scribner's Sons, 1899), 450–51; Wegner, *From Text to Translations,* 305; McClintock and Strong, *Cyclopaedia of Biblical, Theological and Ecclesiastical Literature,* 10: 833.

26. Melton, *Encyclopedia of Protestantism,* 232; Noss, *History of Bible Translation,* 100–02, 134–38; Lamberigts and Hollander, *Lay Bibles in Europe,* 134–35; Pelikan, *Reformation of the Bible,* 156–57; *Lutheran Cyclopedia,* 450–51; Eastwood, *Priesthood of All Believers,* 244; *Cambridge Companion to Martin Luther,* 65–66.

27. Philip C. Stine, *Bible Translations and the Spread of the Church* (Leiden: E. J. Brill, 1990), 85; Noss, *History of Bible Translation,* 100–02, 134–38; Lamberigts and Hollander, *Lay Bibles in Europe,* 134–35; Pelikan, *Reformation of the Bible,* 156–57; *Lutheran Cyclopedia,* 450–51.

CHAPTER 7: LET THERE BE LIGHT

1. Christopher Anderson, *The Annals of the English Bible* (London: William Pickering, 1845), 2:515–19, 587–94; Daniell, *William Tyndale,* 107–9, 207–10, 383 (see chap. 1, n. 1); James Mackintosh, *The History of England* (London: Longman, Orme, Brown and Green, 1838), 2:205; John Leeman, trans., *More Than A Memory: The Discourse of Martyrdom and the Construction of Christian Identity in the History of Christianity* (Leuven: Uitgeverij Peeters, 2005), 318; Alison Weir, *Henry VIII: The King and His Court* (New York: Ballantine Books, 2009), 638.

2. Dewey M. Beegle, *God's Word into English: The Adventure of Bible Translation* (New York: Harper and Row, 1960), 65–70; Daniell, *William Tyndale,* 51–58; Wegener, *6,000 Years of the Bible,* 226–33; Ralph S. Werrell, *The Roots of William Tyndale's Theology* (Cambridge: James Clark, 2013), 43; William Tyndale, *Doctrinal Treatises and Introductions to Different Portions of the Holy Scriptures,* ed. Henry Walter (Cambridge: Cambridge University Press, 1848), 42:393; John F. A. Sawyer, ed., *The Blackwell Companion to the Bible and Culture* (Oxford: John A. Wiley and Sons, 2012), 60.

3. Brian Moynahan, *God's Bestseller: William Tyndale, Thomas More and the Writing of the English Bible—A Story of Martyrdom and Betrayal* (New York: St. Martin's Press: 2002), 2–15; David Teems, *Tyndale: The Man Who Gave God an English Voice* (Nashville: Thomas Nelson, 2012), 30–36; Price, *Ancestry of the English Bible,* 240–51; Anderson, *Annals of the English Bible,* 2:515–19; Dowley, *Eerdmans History of Christianity,* 370; Wegener, *6,000 Years of the Bible,* 226–33.

4. Moynahan, *God's Bestseller,* 4–18; John Foxe, *Book of Martyrs: A History of the Lives, Sufferings and Triumphant Deaths of the Primitive as Well as Protestant Martyrs* (Hartford: Philemon Canfield, 1830), 253; Cross, *The Oxford Dictionary of the Christian Church,* 752–54 (see chap. 1, n. 14); Gotthard V. Lechler, *John Wycliffe and His English Precursors* (London: Religious Tract Society, 1904), 504–5; Teems, *Tyndale:* 41; *Blackwell Companion to the Bible:* 57.

5. Moynahan, *God's Bestseller,* 168; Dowley, *Eerdmans History of Christianity,* 370; Price, *Ancestry of the English Bible,* 240–51; Anderson, *Annals of the English Bible,* 2:510–20, 585–96; Teems, *Tyndale,* 44; Brinton, Christopher, and Wolff, *History of Civilization,* 1:470–72.

6. Teems, *Tyndale,* 44–45, 76–78; John Schofield, *Philip Melanchthon and the English Reformation* (Burlington: Ashgate, 2006), 88; Richard W. Dixon, *History of the Church of England: Henry VIII, 1529–1537* (Oxford: Oxford University Press, 1895), 1:448; Price, *Ancestry of Our English Bible,* 240–51; Eugene Stock, *The Story of the Bible* (New York: E. P. Dutton, 1906), 103; George Stokes, *The Lives of the English Reformers* (Philadelphia: Presbyterian Board of Publication, 1870), 80.

7. Material from this block quote and the preceding paragraph was taken from: William Tyndale, trans., *Tyndale's New Testament* (New Haven, CT: Yale University Press, 1989), ix; Henry Bean

Underhill, *The Struggles and Triumphs of Religious Liberty* (New York: Lewis Colby, 1851), 58; John Strype, *Memorials of Thomas Cranmer: Wherein the History of the Church and the Reformation of It* (Oxford: Oxford University Press, 1840), 2:90–92.

8. Charles Harold Williams, *William Tyndale* (Nashville: Thomas Nelson, 1969), 111–14; David Price and Charles C. Ryrie, *Let It Go Among Our People: An Illustrated History of the English Bible from John Wyclif to the King James Version* (Cambridge: Lutterworth Press, 2004), 45–47; Underhill, *Struggles and Triumphs of Religious Liberty*, 57–60; Strype, *Memorials of Thomas Cranmer*, 2:88–94.

9. Williams, *William Tyndale*, 69–70; Daniell, *William Tyndale*, 297–300 (see chap. 1, n. 1); *The New Encyclopaedia Britannica* (Chicago: Encyclopaedia Britannica, 1974), 2:890; *The Holy Bible, King James Authorized Version* (New York: American Bible Society: 1865); Alexander Monro, *The Paper Trail: The History of an Unexpected Revolution* (New York: Alfred A. Knopf: 2016), 258.

10. Henry Friedman, *The Murderous History of Bible Translations: Power, Conflict and the Quest for Meaning* (New York: Bloomberg Books, 2016), 107–8; Alison Findley, *Illegitimate Power: Bastards in Renaissance Drama* (Manchester: Manchester University Press, 1994), 41; Henry Peacham, *Peacham's Compleat Gentleman, 1634* (Oxford: Clarendon Press, 1904), 9; Teems, *Tyndale*, 44–45, 76–78; Stokes, *Lives of the English Reformers*, 80–83; G. R. Elton, *England under the Tutors* (London: Routledge, 1991), 102.

11. Friedman, *Murderous History of Bible Translations*, 107–8; Teems, *Tyndale*, 44–45, 76–78; Stokes, *Lives of the English Reformers*, 80–83; Dan Graves, "John Frith Burned for Beliefs," Christianity. com, http://www.christianity.com/church/church-history/timeline/1501-1600/john-frith-burned-for-beliefs-11629954.html, accessed October 25, 2017; David Lowenstein, *Treacherous Faith: The Spectre of Heresy in Early Modern English Literature and Culture* (Oxford: Oxford University Press, 2013), 90–91; William Tyndale, *The Obedience of a Christian Man* (London: Penguin, 2000), xi–xvii; Andrew Atherstone, *Reformation: A World in Turmoil* (Oxford: Lion Books, 2005), 114; Elton, *England under the Tutors*, 111.

12. Robert Demaus, *William Tyndale: A Biography* (Boston: Religious Tract Society, 1886): 284; John Brown, "Defender of the Faith," *American Bibliopolist* 7, no. 73 (February 1875): 16–17; Anne Murphy, *Thomas More* (Chicago: Triumph, 1997), 91; Christopher Hibbert, *Tower of London* (New York: Newsweek Books, 1971), 47–65; Joanna Denny, *Anne Boleyn: A New Life of England's Tragic Queen* (Philadelphia: Da Capo Press, 2006), 68–73, 313–18; Brinton, Christopher, and Wolff, *History of Civilization*, 1:470–72; Anderson, *Annals of the English Bible*, 2:160; 510–20; 585–96; Cross, *The Oxford Dictionary of the Christian Church*, 752–54; Price, *Ancestry of Our English Bible*, 240–51; Bruce, *Books and Parchment*, 222–26; Daniell, *William Tyndale*: 203–04.

13. Dixon, *History of the Church of England*: 1:47–65; Daniell, *William Tyndale*: 208–09; 283–87; 297–99; Brinton, Christopher, and Wolff, *History of Civilization*, 1:470–472; Anderson, *Annals of the English Bible*, 2:160; 510–20; 585–96; Cross, *The Oxford Dictionary of the Christian Church*, 433, 752–54; Underhill, *Struggles and Triumphs of Religious Liberty*, 16–24; Michael Everett, *The Rise of Thomas Cromwell: Power and Politics in the Reign of Henry VIII* (New Haven, CT: Yale University Press, 2015), 232–33; Theodore Maynard, *The Crown and the Cross: A Biography of Thomas Cromwell* (New York: McGraw-Hill, 1950), 75.

14. Daniell, *William Tyndale*, 26–27 (see chap. 1, n. 1); Henry Hart Milman, *Annals of St. Paul's Cathedral* (London: John Murray, 1868), 197; Dixon, *History of the Church of England*, 30–31, 534–26; Underhill, *Struggles and Triumphs of Religious Liberty*, 43; Geisler and Nix, *Introduction to the Bible*, 551–53; Price, *Ancestry of Our English Bible*, 252–60; Cross, *The Oxford Dictionary of the Christian Church*, 433.

15. Demaus, *William Tyndale*, 382–83; Merle D'Aubigne, *History of the Reformation in the Time of*

Calvin (New York: Robert Carter and Bros., 1867), 1:103–04; F. L. Clarke, *The Life of William Tyndale* (London: Swan Sonnenschien, 1883), 103, 121–23; Daniell, *William Tyndale*, 370–71; Foxe, *Acts and Monuments*, 5:127.

16. Thomas Russell, ed., *The Works of the English Reformers: William Tyndale and John Frith* (London: Ebenezer Palmer, 1831), 1:329; Price, *Ancestry of Our English Bible*, 260–67; Cross, *The Oxford Dictionary of the Christian Church*, 433; Bruce, *The Books and the Parchments*, 222–26; Foxe, *Acts and Monuments*, 131.

17. Daniell, *William Tyndale*, 381–82; Barker, *English Bible Versions*, 96–97 (see chap. 5, n. 16); Price, *Ancestry of Our English Bible*, 260–67; Cross, *The Oxford Dictionary of the Christian Church*, 433; Bruce, *The Books and the Parchments*, 222–26; Foxe, *Acts and Monuments*, 5:127; Clarke, *Life of William Tyndale*, 101, 121-23.

18. Henrico Tulse, *History of the Church of Great Britain: From the Birth of Our Saviour to Until the Year of Our Lord 1667* (London: Philip Chetwin, 1674), 150; Thomas Cahill, *Heretics and Heroes: How Renaissance Artists and Reformation Priests Created Our World* (New York: Anchor Books, 2013), 229–30; Gerard Brandt, *A History of the Reformation in the Low Countries* (London: T. Wood, 1720), 1:1219; Foxe, *Acts and Monuments*, 5:127; Daniell, *William Tyndale*, 380–82; Clarke, *Life of William Tyndale*, 124–27; Bruce, *History of the Bible in English*, 52.

CHAPTER 8: THE HOLY BIBLE IN THEIR MOTHER TONGUE

1. J. J. Lowndes, *Memorials of Miles Coverdale* (London: Samuel Bagster, 1838), 74; Barker, *English Bible Versions*, 100–02 (see chap. 5, n. 16); Clarke, *Life of William Tyndale*, 94 (see chap. 7, n. 15); Geisler and Nix, *Introduction to the Bible*, 550–55; Price, Ancestry of Our English Bible, 252–60.

2. Roland H. Worth, *Church, Monarch and Bible in Sixteenth Century England* (Jefferson, NC: McFarland, 2000), 48–49; Barker, *English Bible Versions*, 101; Lowndes, *Memorials of Miles Coverdale*, 75–78; Cross, *The Oxford Dictionary of the Christian Church*, 433, 752–54 (see chap. 1, n. 14).

3. Joseph Elkington, "The Divine Library: An Historical Sketch," *The Friend: A Religious and Literary Journal* 85, no. 25 (March 1, 1912): 109–11; Barker, *English Bible Versions*, 110; Clarke, *Life of William Tyndale*, 135; John C. Greider, *The English Bible Translations and History* (Bloomington: Xlibris, 2013), 268; J. F. Mozley, *Coverdale and His Bibles* (Cambridge: James Clarke, 2004), 201.

4. Blackford Condit, *The History of the English Bible: Extending from the Earliest Saxon Translations to the Present Anglo-American Revision* (New York: A. S. Barnes, 1882), 199–206; Wegner, *From Texts to Translations*, 296–99; "Coverdale Bible 1535," *Textus Receptus Bibles*, "Luke 15:7," http://www.textusreceptusbibles.com/Interlinear/42015007, accessed October 25, 2017; Worth, *Church, Monarch and Bible*, 84–88; James Orri, ed., *The International Standard Bible Encyclopedia* (Chicago: Howard-Severance, 1915), 2:949.

5. Condit, *History of the English Bible*, 204; Worth, *Church, Monarch and Bible*, 84–88; *International Standard Bible Encyclopedia*, 2:949; Wegner, *From Texts to Translations*, 296–99; "Biographical Description of the First Edition of Cranmer's or the Great Bible," Government Office of Royal Collections for a History of the English Bible, 1525–1539, British Library; Henry Hamilton-Hoare, *The Evolution of the English Bible* (London: John Murray, 1902), 194; Jeremy Collier, ed., "A Declaration of the Faith, and a Justification of the Proceedings of King Henry the Eighth in Matters of Religion," *An Ecclesiastical History of Great Britain* (London: Samuel Keele, 1714), 2:47:36.

6. Worth, *Church, Monarch and Bible*, 84–88; *International Standard Bible Encyclopedia*, 2:949;

Wegner, *From Texts to Translations*, 296–99; Condit, *History of the English Bible*, 204; Peter Ackroyd, *Tudors: The History of England from Henry VIII to Elizabeth I* (New York: St. Martin's Press: 2012), 131–35.

7.   Charles MacFarlane, *The Cabinet History of England* (London: Charles Knight, 1845), 130; Ackroyd, *Tudors*, 75–78; *The Parliamentary History of England: From the Earliest Period to the Year 1803* (London: T. C. Hansard, 1806), 1:1556; David Lowentstein and Janel Mueller, eds., *The Cambridge History of Early Modern English Literature* (Cambridge: Cambridge University Press, 2002), 288; Weir, *Henry VII*, 484.

8.   Dixon, *History of the Church of England*, 459; Stewart Mottram, *Empire and Nation in Early English Renaissance Literature* (Cambridge: D. S. Brewer, 2008), 170; D. E. Hoak, *The King's Council in the Reign of Edward VI* (Cambridge: Cambridge University Press, 1976), 244; Worth, *Church, Monarch and Bible*, 140–46.

9.   David Loades, *Mary Tudor* (London: Amberly, 2012), 56–62; A. G. Dickens, *The English Reformation* (University Park: University of Pennsylvania Press, 1964), 187–96; Eamon Duffy, *Fires of Faith: Catholic England Under Mary Tudor* (New Haven, CT: Yale University Press, 2009), 24–38; Leada De Lisle, *The Sisters Who Would Be Queen: Mary, Katherine and Lady Jane Grey* (New York: HarperCollins, 2008), 98–112; 154–68; Ackroyd, *Tudors*, 275; Hibbert, *Tower of London*, 66–74; Brinton, Christopher, and Wolff, *History of Civilization*, 1:470–72; Cross, *The Oxford Dictionary of the Christian Church*, 1051, 1511.

10. Dairmaid MacCulloch, *The Boy King: Edward VI and the Protestant Reformation* (Berkeley: University of Californias Press, 2002), 126–28; James D. Taylor, *Documents of Lady Jane Grey: Nine Day Queen of England, 1553* (New York: Algora, 2004), 12; Nicholas H. Nicolas, *The Literary Remains of Lady Jame Grey* (London: Harding and Triphook, 1825), 91; Worth, *Church, Monarch and Bible*, 61–63.

11. Carolly Erickson, *Bloody Mary* (New York: St. Martin's Press, 1978), 410, 435–36; Susan Doran and Thomas S. Freeman, eds., *Mary Tudor: Old and New Perspectives* (Basingstoke: Palgrave Macmillan, 2011), 179–80, 189–90; John Foxe, *Foxe's Book of Martyrs: Select Narratives*, ed. John N. King (Oxford: Oxford University Press, 2009), 35–38, 151–55; St. Sepulchre's, "History," http://stsepulchres.org/our-community/history/, accessed October 25, 2017; Hugh Latimer, *Selected Sermons of Hugh Latimer*, ed. Allan Chester (Charlottesville: University of Virginia Press, 1968), xxxiii–iv; Edward Tagart, *Sketches of the Lives of the Leading Reformers of the Sixteenth Century* (London: John Green, 1843). 114–16; Oxford History, Broad Street, Oxford, "The Martyrs' Cross," http://www.oxfordhistory.org.uk/broad/buildings/martyrs.html, accessed October 25, 2017; Dairmaid MacCulloch, *Thomas Cranmer: A Life* (New Haven, CT: Yale University Press, 1996), 601–3.

12. Erickson, *Bloody Mary*, 332–36, 370–77; Roland Worth, *Bible Translations: A History Through Source Documents* (Jefferson: MacFarland, 1992), 79; John Foxe, *A Select History of the Lives and Sufferings of the Principal English Protestant Martyrs* (London: T. Gardner, 1746), 245; Henry Kamen, *Philip of Spain* (New Haven, CT: Yale University Press, 1997), 55–57.

13. William Cooke Taylor, ed., *Romantic Biography of the Age of Elizabeth* (London: Richard Bentley, 1842), 2:72–79; Wegner, *From Texts to Translations*, 301–2; Mary Anne Greene, ed., *Life of William Whittingham* (Westminster: J. B. Nichols, 1870), 1–10; Vivienne Westbrook, *Long Travail and Great Paynes: The Politics of Reformation Revision* (London: Kluwer Academic, 2001), xxxviii.

14. Taylor, *Romantic Biography of the Age of Elizabeth*, 78–79; Greene, *Life of William Whittingham*, 9–10; Westbrook, *Long Travail and Great Paynes*, 127–29; Lewis F. Lufton, *A History of the Geneva Bible: Welcome Joy* (Providence: Fauconberg Press, 1966), 37–39; Bruce M. Metzger, "The Geneva

Bible of 1560," *Theology Today* 17, no. 3 (October 1, 1960): 339; *The Geneva Bible; A Facsimile of the 1560 Edition* (Peabody, MA: Hendrickson, 2007), 5–6; Wegner, *From Texts to Translations,* 301–2; Revelation 11:7 (Geneva Bible).

15. Greene, *Life of William Whittingham,* 9–10; Taylor, *Romantic Biography of the Age of Elizabeth,* 78–79; Westbrook, *Long Travail and Great Paynes,* 128–30; Wegner, *From Texts to Translations,* 301–2; F.F. Bruce, *History of the Bible in English,* Canbridge: Lutterworth Press: 1979: 92; Lightfoot, *How We Got the Bible,* 181; *The Geneva Bible: A Fasimile,* 19–20; Hannibal Hamlin, *The Bible in Shakespeare* (Oxford: Oxford University Press, 2013), 10–11, 34–35; *Cromwell's Soldier's Bible: Being a Reprint, in Facsimile, of the Soldier's Bible, 1643* (London: Elliot Stock, 1895), 2–3.

16. J. E. Neale, *Queen Elizabeth I* (Chicago: Academy Chicago, 1992), 35–41, 59–68; Jane Resh Thomas, *Behind the Mask: The Life of Elizabeth I* (New York: Clarion Books, 1998), 62–68, 74–77.

17. Anne Somerset, *Elizabeth I* (London: Wiedenfeld and Nicholson, 1993), 71–72; Thomas, *Behind the Mask,* 74–77; Neale, *Queen Elizabeth I,* 59–68; Daniel Neal, *The History of the Puritans or Protestant Non-Conformists* (Boston: Charles Ewer, 1817), 179–80; Jackson, *No Other Foundation,* 127–29; *The Prayer Book of Queen Elizabeth, 1559* (Edinburgh: Grant, 1911), 1–3.

18. Jeremy Collier, *An Ecclesiastical History of Great Britain* (London: Samuel Keele, 1714), 2:520; Stephen Alford, *The Watchers: A Secret History of the Reign of Queen Elizabeth I* (New York: Bloomsbury Press, 2012), 45–46; James C. Bryant, *Tudor Drama and Religious Controversy* (Macon: Mercer University Press, 1984), 39–40; Somerset, *Elizabeth* I, 245, 457; Colin Martin and Geoffrey Parker, *The Spanish Armada* (New York: Penguin, 1989), 243–46.

19. Collier, *Ecclesiastical History of Great Britain,* 2:523; Paul Hilliam, *Elizabeth I: Queen of England's Golden Age* (New York: Rosen, 2005), 45–48; Swift Edgar, ed., *The Vulgate Bible: Douay-Rheims Translation* (Cambridge: Harvard University Press, 2011), viii–xii; "The English Translation of the Bible," *Catholic World* 12, no. 68 (October 1870–March 1871): 155–64.

20. *The Vulgate Bible: Douay-Rheims Translation,* viii–xii; "The English Translation of the Bible," 155–64; Richard Challoner, *A Specimen of the Spirit of the Dissenting Preachers* (London: Thomas Meighan, 1736), 29–36, 125–32; Wegner, *From Texts to Translations,* 304–5.

21. Jeremy Morris, ed., *The Oxford History of Anglicanism* (Oxford: Oxford University Press, 2017), 4:xiv; Jack P. Lewis, *The Day after Doomsday: The Making of the Bishops' Bible* (Eugene, OR: Wipf & Stock, 2016), 125–30; Wegner, *From Texts to Translations,* 303–4.

22. Lewis, *The Day after Doomsday,* 28–31, 125–30; John Strype, *The Life and Acts of Matthew Parker* (Oxford: Clarendon Press, 1830), 2:212–24; Collier, *Ecclesiastical History of Great Britain,* 2:542; Wegner, *From Texts to Translations,* 303–4; Bruce, *The Books and the Parchments,* 218.

23. Wegner, *From Texts to Translations,* 282; Lewis, *The Day after Doomsday,* 28–31, 125–30; Strype, *The Life and Acts of Matthew Parker,* 2:212–24; Collier, *Ecclesiastical History of Great Britain,* 2:542; Bruce, *The Books and the Parchments,* 218; Edward B. Underhill, ed., *Tracts on Liberty of Conscience and Persecution, 1614–1661* (London: J. Haddon, 1846), lii; John Richard Green, *History of the English People* (London: Macmillan, 1885), 4:191.

CHAPTER 9: ENDEARED TO THE HEARTS OF MILLIONS

1. Pauline Croft, *James I* (London: Palgrave Macmillan, 2003), 100–03, 156–69; Joseph R. Tanner, ed., *Constitutional Documents of the Reign of James I* (London: Bentley House, 1930), 58–65; Ralph Anthony Houlbrook, ed., *James I and VI: Ideas, Authority and Government* (Hampshire: Ashgate, 2006), 77–78, 87–91; Cross, *The Oxford Dictionary of the Christian Church,* 859–60 (see chap. 1,

n. 14); Isaac Disraeli, *Curiosities of Literature* (London: Routledge, Warnes and Routledge, 1859), 3:464–66; John Matusiak, *James I: Scotland's King of England* (Strand: History Press, 2015), 205–8, 285; Michael A. Lacombe, *Political Gastronomy: Food and Authority in the English Atlantic World* (Philadelphia: University of Pennsylvania Press, 2002), 158.

2.   John Guy, *Mary Queen of Scots: The True Life of Mary Stuart* (Boston: Houghton-Mifflin, 2005), 356–59, 371–74, 462–63, Houlbrook, *James I and VI*, 77–78, 87–91; Matusiak, *James I*, 197–98. Croft, *James I*, 100–03, 156–69; Tanner, *Constitutional Documents of the Reign of James I*, 58–65; Cross, *The Oxford Dictionary of the Christian Church*, 859–60.

3.   Matusiak, *James I*, 104, 119, 295; Guy, *Mary Queen of Scots*, 462–63, Houlbrook, *James I and VI*, 87–91; Disraeli, *Curiosities of Literature*, 3:463–66; Croft, *James I*, 100–03, 156–69; Tanner, *Constitutional Documents of the Reign of James I*, 58–65; Cross, *The Oxford Dictionary of the Christian Church*, 859–60; James Stuart, *James VI and I: Political Writings*, ed. Johann P. Sommerville (Cambridge: Cambridge University Press, 1994), xviii–xxi.

4.   Eileen Reeves, *Evening News: Optics, Astronomy and Journalism in Early Modern Europe* (Philadelphia: University of Pennsylvania Press, 2014), 211; Disraeli, *Curiosities of Literature*, 3:463; Anthony Weldon, *The Court and Character of King James* (London: John Wright, 1650), 24; Anne MacDonald, ed., *Letters to King James VI* (Edinburgh: Maitland Club, 1835), 23–25; Matusiak, *James I*, 285; Anthony Weldon, ed., *The Court and Times of James I* (London: Henry Colburn, 1849), 1:227–28.

5.   Daniel Neal, *The History of the Puritans or Protestant Non-Conformists* (Boston: Charles Ewer, 1817), 2:179–80, 232; Perry Miller and Thomas H. Johnson, eds., *The Puritans: A Sourcebook of Their Writings* (New York: Harper & Row, 1963), 1:2; Francis J. Bremer and Tom Webster, eds., *Puritans and Puritanism in Europe and America: A Comprehensive Encyclopedia* (Santa Barbara: Clio, 2006), 419; Lindsey, *History of the Reformation*, 207.

6.   Henry Gee and William J. Hardy, eds., *Documents Illustrative of English Church History* (New York: Macmillan, 1896), 460–61; John Hastings, ed., *The Encyclopedia of Religion and Ethics* (New York: Charles Scribner's Sons, 1919), 10:507.

7.   Killeen, Smith, and Willie, *Oxford Handbook to the Bible in Early Modern England*, 142 (see chap. 2, n. 19): Perry Miller, *The New England Mind: From Colony to Province* (Cambridge: Belknap Press, 1953), 3; Benjamin Brook, *The Lives of the Puritans* (London: James Black, 1813), 1:153.

8.   Christopher Durston and Jacqueline Eales, *The Culture of the English Puritans, 1560–1700* (New York: Macmillan, 1996), 8–11; Dickens, *English Reformation*, 324; Alexis de Tocqueville, *Democracy in America* (London: Colonial Press, 1900), 1:31.

9.   Gerald Bray, *Documents of the English Reformationy* (Cambridge: James Clarke, 1994), 550–53; Samuel R. Gardiner, ed., *Reports of Cases in the Star Chamber and the Court of High Commission* (Westminster: Nichols and Sons, 1886), 222, 236.

10.   Benjamin Hanbury, *Historical Memorials Relating to the Independents or Congregationalists* (London: Fisher and Son, 1839), 1:86; John Waddington, *John Penry: The Pilgrim Martyr, 1553–1593* (London: W. F. G. Cash, 1854), 427–28; John Penry, *The Notebook of John Penry, 1593* (London: Royal Historical Society, 1944), xix, 18–19; Rod Gragg, *The Pilgrim Chronicles: An Eyewitness History of the Pilgrims and the Founding of Plymouth Colony* (Washington, D.C.: Regnery History, 2014), 26–32.

11.   James Doelman, *King James I and the Religious Culture of England* (Cambridge: D.S. Brewer, 2000), 15–17; Henry Morley, *A Miscellany Containing Richard of Bury's Prohibition, the Basilikon Doron of James I* (London: George Routledge, 1888). 118; Tim Harris, *Rebellion, England's First Stuart Kings* (Oxford: Oxford University Press, 2014), 193; Matusiak, *James I*, 226.

12.   "Hampton Court Conference," Manuscripts Collection, Mss Eu F89/102, Box 5A, British Library;

William Barlow, *Sum and Substance of the Hampton Court Conference* (London: Vance, 1604), 3–4, 7–10, 21–30; Harris, *Rebellion*, 70–72; Matusiak, *James I*, 221; Doelman, *King James I and the Religious Culture of England*, 7–8; Joseph Hammond, "Christian Disunity," *The Church of England Pulpit and Ecclesiastical Review* 48, no. 1227 (July 1899): 207.

13. Ernest P. Law, *Hampton Court: A Short History of the Royal Manor and Palace* (London: George Bell and Sons, 1900), 178–80; Matusiak, *James I*, 220–23; W. B. Patterson, *James VI and I and the Reunion of Christendom* (Cambridge: Cambridge University Press, 1997), 43–46; Edwin Hall, *The Puritans and Their Principles* (New York: Baker and Scribner's, 1846), 143; Barlow, *Sum and Substance*: 71, 83; Robert Baird, *Religion in America* (New York: Harper and Bros., 1856), 95; *Dictionary of National Biography*: 1:1082; Wegner, *From Texts to Translations*, 308.

14. Romans 10:17; Richard Baker, comp. *A Chronicle of the Kings of England: From the Times of Roman Government to the Death of King James* (London: George Sawbridge, 1670), 441; John J. Taylor, *A Retrospect of the Religious Life of England: The Church, Puritanism and Free Inquiry* (London: Trubner, 1876), 38; Matusiak, *James I*, 227; T. B. Howell, comp., *A Complete Collection of State Trials and Proceedings for High Treason and Other Crimes and Misdemeanors* (London: Longman and Brown, 1816), 4:492; Derek Wilson, *The Peoples' Bible: The Remarkable History of the King James Version* (Oxford: Lion Hudson, 2010), 86–87.

15. Baker, *A Chronicle of the Kings of England*, 441; Taylor, *Retrospect of the Religious Life of England*, 38; Matusiak, *James I*, 227; Barlow, *Sum and Substance of the Hampton Court Conference*, 71–80; Alan Stewart, *The Cradle King: The Life of King James VI and I—the First King of a United Britain* (New York: St. Martin's, 2003), 206; Thomas P. Power, ed., *Change and Transition: Essays in Anglican History* (Eugene: Wipf and Stock, 2013), 36; Christopher Hill, *The English Bible and the Seventeenth Century Revolution* (London: Allen Lane, 1993), 63–64.

16. Adam Nicholson, *God's Secretaries: The Making of the King James Bible* (New York: HarperCollins, 2003), 80–99; Stewart, *The Cradle King*, 201–2; Geisler and Nix, *Introduction to the Bible*, 564–68; Wegener, *6,000 Years of the Bible*, 241–46; Price, *Ancestry of Our English Bible*, 268–77; Bruce, *The Books and the Parchments*, 227–30 (see chap. 1, n. 1); Austin's *History of Christianity*, 280–83.

17. Green, *History of the English People*, 3:49–53; Alan Haynes, *The Gunpowder Plot: Faith in Rebellion* (Dover: Alan Sutton, 1994), 10, 85, 92; Mark Nicholls, *Investigating the Gunpowder Plot* (Manchester: University of Manchester Press, 1991), 21, 41; "Civil and Religious Liberty Not Obtained by the Reformation," *Catholic Monthly Intelligencer* 5, no. 44 (January 1817): 3–5; Patrick Collinson, *Richard Bancroft and Elizabethan Anti-Puritanism* (Cambridge: Cambridge University Press, 2013), 6–10.

18. David Norton, *A Textual History of the King James Bible* (Cambridge: Cambridge University Press, 2005), 11–20, 25–27, 30–35; The King James Bible, 1611–2011, Tibor Fabiny and Sara Toth, eds., *Prehistory and Afterlife* (Budapest: L'Harmattan, 2016), 20; John Bois, *Translating for King James: Notes Made by a Translator of the King James Bible*, ed. Ward Allen (Nashville: Vanderbilt University Press, 1989), 16–18; Francis Peck, comp., *Desiderata Curiosa: Collection of Divers Scarce and Curious Pieces of English History* (London: Thomas Evans, 1779), 2:333–35; Power, *Change and Transition*, 41.

19. 1 Corinthians 15:52; Genesis 4:9; Cross, *The Oxford Dictionary of the Christian Church*, 135; Melvyn Bragg, *The Book of Books: The Radical Impact of the King James Bible*, 1611–2011 (Berkley: Counterpoint, 2011), 43; Norton, *A Textual History of the King James Bible*, 12; John Rainolds, *John Rainolds' Oxford Lectures on Aristotle's Rhetoric*, ed. Lawrence Green (Newark: University of Delaware Press, 1986), 39–40.

20. *The Holy Bible: Containing the Old and New Testaments, Translated out of the Original Tongues and*

with the Former Translations Diligently Compared and Revised by His Majesty's Special Command, AD 1611 (London: British and Foreign Bible Society, 1967), frontispiece; *Oxford Handbook of the Bible*, 692; Ewert, *From Ancient Tablets to Modern Translations*, 197–204; Cross, *The Oxford Dictionary of the Christian Church*, 135.

21. Alistar E. McGrath, *In the Beginning: The Story of the King James Bible and How It Changed a Nation, a Language and a Culture* (New York: Anchor Books, 2012), 223–27; Alfred W. Pollard, ed., *Records of the English Bible, 1525–1611* (London: Oxford University Press, 1911), 369; Peck, *Desiderata Curiosa*, 2:333–35; Geisler and Nix, *A General Introduction to the Bible*, 420 (see chap. 1, n. 1); Wegner, *From Texts to Translations*, 309–11; "Additions to the Library," *Bulletin of the John Rylands Library* 1, no. 5 (April–October 1907): 272–73.

22. McGrath, *In the Beginning*, 225–27; Jack P. Lewis, *The English Bible: From the KJV to the NIV* (Grand Rapids: Baker Book House, 1991), 41–42; Wegner, *From Texts to Translations*, 308–11; Geisler and Nix, *Introduction to the Bible*, 564–68; Bruce, *The Books and the Parchments*, 227–30; Fabiny and Toth, *Prehistory and Afterlife*, 20; Norton, *A Textual History of the King James Bible*, 159–61.

23. Massomiliano Morini, *Tudor Translation in Theory and Practice* (London: Routledge, 2017), 50–51; *King James Bible, 1611–2011*, Fabiny and Toth, *Prehistory and Afterlife*, 24–25; Wegner, *From Texts to Translations*, 313; Lewis, *The English Bible*, 29–32.

24. *International Standard Bible Encyclopedia*, 2:89–90; Avner Shamir, *English Bibles on Trial: Bible Burning and the Desecration of Bibles, 1640–1800* (London: Routledge, 2017), 5–6; Lewis F. Lupton, *Welcome Joy: A History of the Geneva Bible* (Riverside: Olive Tree, 1975), 211; David North, *A Short History of the King James Bible: From Tyndale to Today* (Cambridge: Cambridge University Press, 2011), 135; Herbraeolus, "To Mr. A.P. on His Proposal and Translation of the 68 Psalm," *The Gentleman's Magazine and Historical Chronicle* 6 (1736): 322.

25. John Patterson Smyth, *How We Got Our Bible* (New York: James Pott, 1909), 12; Norton, *A Textual History of the King James Bible*; Brooke F. Wescott, *A General View of the History of the English Bible* (London: Macmillan, 1905) Cross, *The Oxford Dictionary of the Christian Church*, 135.

26. Mark Weeter, *John Wesley's View and Use of Scripture* (Eugene: Wipf and Stock, 2007), 137; John Wesley, *The New Testament with Explanatory Notes* (Halifax: William Morrison, 1869), 4–5; William E. Paul, *English Language Bible Translators* (Jefferson, NC: McFarland, 2003), 32; John Brown, *The History of the English Bible* (Cambridge: Cambridge University Press, 1912), 111; Wegner, *From Texts to Translations*, 313–15; Norton, *A Textual History of the King James Bible*, 166–67.

27. Edward N. Nolan, *A History of India and the British Empire of the East* (London: Viscount and Clark, 1878), 57–63; Julia Baird, *Victoria the Queen: An Intimate Biography of the Woman Who Ruled an Empire* (New York: Random House, 2016), xiv; Sidney Lee, *Queen Victoria: A Biography* (New York: Macmillan, 1908), 393; James S. Olson and Robert Shadle, eds., *Historical Dictionary of the British Empire* (Westport: Greenwood Press, 1996), 1:298–99; Price, *Ancestry of Our English Bible*, 282; Psalm 2:8.

CHAPTER 10: THE BIBLE COMES TO AMERICA

1. Douglas Southall Freeman, *George Washington: A Biography* (New York: Charles Scribner's Sons, 1948), 6:191–92; Jared Sparks, *The Life of George Washington* (London: Henry Colburn, 1839), 1:440; James D. Richardson, ed., *A Compilation of Messages and Papers of the Presidents* (New York:

Bureau of National Literature, 1897),1:50; Gordon DenBoer, *The Documentary History of the First Federal Elections, 1778–1790* (Madison: University of Wisconsin Press, 1989), 4:268–69; Rod Gragg, *By the Hand of Providence: How Faith Shaped the American Revolution* (New York: Simon and Schuster, 2011), 217–18.

2. Clarence L. Ver Steeg, *The Formative Years, 1607–1763* (New York: Hill and Wang, 1965), 21–24; First Charter of Virginia, April 10, 1606, Avalon Project, Lillian Goldman Law Library, Yale University; George Percy, "A Trewe Relacyon: Virginia from 1608–1612," *Tyler's Historical and Genealogical Magazine,* ed. Leon G. Tyler, 1922), 3:627; John Smith, *Travels and Works of Captain John Smith, President of Virginia and Admiral of New England, 1580–1631,* ed. Edward Arber (Edinburgh: John Grant, 1910), 2:474, 498–99; 2 Thessalonians 3:10.

3. Roland G. Usher, *The Pilgrims and Their History* (New York: Macmillan, 1918),75; William Bradford, *Bradford's History of Plymouth Plantation* (Boston: Wright and Porter, 1899), 59–60; Nathaniel Philbrick, *Mayflower: A Story of Courage, Community, and War* (New York: Viking Penguin, 2006), 31–42; Nick Bunker, *Making Haste from Babylon: The Mayflower Pilgrims and Their World* (New York: Alfred A. Knopf, 2010), 53–55; Gragg, *The Pilgrim Chronicles,* 181–85, 188–91.

4. John Winthrop, *Life and Letters of John Winthrop,* ed. Robert C. Winthrop (Boston: Little and Brown, 1869), 2:19–20; Perry Miller, *An Errand into the Wilderness* (Cambridge: Harvard University Press, 1956), 8, 113; Leland Ryken, *Worldly Saints: The Puritans as They Really Were* (Grand Rapids: Zondervan, 1991), 24–25.

5. Francis N. Thorpe, *The Federal and State Constitutions, Colonial Charters and Organic Laws* (Washington, D.C.: U.S. Government Printing Office, 1909), 1:77, 1:249–52, 1:529, 1:577, 2:765, 3:1677, 3:1841, 5:2753, 6:3047–3070, 7:3783; Rod Gragg, *Forged in Faith: How Faith Shaped the Birth of the Nation* (New York: Simon and Schuster, 2010), 89–94; Charles Z. Lincoln, William H. Johnson, and Ansul J. Northrup, eds., *Colonial Laws of New York from the Year 1664 to the Revolution* (Albany: J. B. Llyon 1894), 1: xii, 20.

6. Merle Curti, *The Growth of American Democracy* (New York: Harper and Row, 1943), 24:3; Patricia U. Bonomi, *Under the Cape of Heaven: Religion, Society, and Politics in Colonial America* (New York: Oxford University Press, 1986), 3, 188, 209–11; Abraham Isaac Katsh, *The Biblical Heritage of American Democracy* (New York: KATV, 1977), 116; Cedric B. Cowling, *The Great Awakening and the American Revolution: Colonial Thought in the 18th Century* (Chicago: Rand McNally, 1971), 67–69; Benjamin Franklin, *The Autobiography of Benjamin Franklin* (New York: Henry Holt, 1916), 101–2, 253.

7. John A. Goodwin, *The Pilgrim Republic: A Historical Review of the Colony of New Plymouth* (Boston: Tichnor, 1888). 44; Perry D. Westbrook, *William Bradford* (Detroit: Thomson Gale, 1978), 35, 97; Francis J. Bremer, *John Winthrop: America's Forgotten Founding Father* (Oxford: Oxford University Press, 2003), 238; Perry Miller, *The New England Mind: The Seventeenth Century* (New York: Macmillan, 1939), 463; Gragg, *Forged in Faith,* 54–55.

8. Joseph Herl, *Worship Wars in Early Lutheranism: Choir, Congregation and Three Centuries of Conflict* (Oxford: Oxford University Press, 2004), 33–34, 54–56; Zoltan Haraszti, *The Bay Psalm Book: The First Book Printed in British North American, 1640* (Mineola: Dover: 2016), 3–5; D. W. Krummell, *The Bay Psalm Book Tencentenary, 1698–1998* (London: Bibliographical Society, 1975), 75–77.

9. Haraszti, *Bay Psalm Book,* 3: Krummell, *Bay Psalm Book,* 75–77; Isaac Thomas, *The History of Printing in America* (Albany: Joel Munsell, 1874), 1; 46–47.

10. Alice Morse Earl, *The Sabbath in Puritan New England* (New York: Charles Scribner's Sons, 1891), 144–50; Cotton Mather, *Magnalia Christi Ameicana: The Ecclesiastical History of New England*

(Hartford: Silas Andrus, 1855), 1: 407–8.

11. Earl, *Sabbath in Puritan New England,* 148–50; Mather, *Magnalia Christi Americana,* 1:408; Haraszti, *Bay Psalm Book,* 3–5; John Winthrop, *Winthrop's Journal, 1630–1649,* ed. James K. Hosmer (New York: Charles Scribner's Sons, 1908), 2:v; Krummell, *Bay Psalm Book,* 76–77.

12. Jared Sparks, ed., *The Library of American Biography* (Boston: Hilliard and Gray, 1836), 5:237–40; Pelikan, *Reformation of the Bible,* 156; Timothy L. Hall, *American Religious Leaders* (New York: Facts on File, 2003), 120; John Carne, "Life of the Rev. John Eliot," *The Missionary Register* 3, no. 28 (April 1815): 177–79.

13. Margaret Connell Szasz, *Indian Education in the American Colonies, 1607–1783* (Lincoln: Bison Books, 2007), 113–15; Philip Goff, ed., *The Bible in America* (Oxford: Oxford University Press, 2017), 38–41; 171–72; Bruce E. Johansen and Barry M. Pritzker, eds., *Encyclopedia of American Indian History* (Oxford: ABC-CLIO, 2008), 1: 719–720.

14. Pelikan, *Reformation of the Bible,* 156; Hall, *American Religious Leaders,* 120; Neal Salisbury, "Red Puritans: 'The Praying Indians' of Massachusetts Bay and John Eliot," *The William and Mary Quarterly* 31, no. 1 (January 1974): 27–31; Hughes Oliphant Old, *The Reading and the Preaching of the Scriptures in the Worship of the Christian Church* (Grand Rapids: Eerdmans, 2004), 5:189–90; *The Bible in America,* 38–41; Szasz, *Indian Education in the American Colonies,* 113–15.

15. Edwin T. Freedley, *Philadelphia and its Manufactures* (Philadelphia: Edward Young, 1867), 142; Felix Reichman, comp., *Christopher Sower Senior* (Philadelphia: Carl Schurz Memorial Foundation, 1944), 3–6; Allen Kent, ed., *Encyclopedia of Library and Information Science* (New York: Marcel Dekker, 1978), 29–31.

16. Hugh Amory and David D. Hall, eds., *A History of the Book in America: The Colonial Book in the Atlantic World* (Chapel Hill: University of North Carolina Press, 2010), 1:124; Francis J. Bremer and Lynn A. Bohtelo, eds., *The World of John Winthrop: Essays on England and New England, 1588–1649* (Boston: Massachusetts Historical Society, 2005), 345; James Ciment, ed., *Colonial America: An Encyclopedia of Social, Political, Cultural, and Economic History* (New York: Taylor and Francis, 2006), 147; Barbara E. Lacy, *From Sacred to Secular: Visual Images in Early American Publications* (Newark: University of Delaware Press, 2007), 80; *The Geneva Bible: A Facsimile of the 1560 Edition* (Peabody, MA: Hendrickson, 2007), v; Ernest S. Frerichs, *The Bible and Bibles in America* (Atlanta: Scholars Press, 1988), 14; Barker, *English Bible Versions,* 251–53 (see chap. 5, n. 16); Charles Lemuel Nichols, *Isaiah Thomas: Printer, Writer and Collector* (Boston: Club of Old Volumes, 1912), 4–6.

17. Worthington C. Ford, ed., *Journals of the Continental Congress, 1774–1789* (Washington, D.C.: U.S. Government Printing Office, 1906), JCC 8: 536, 733–735 (hereafter cited as JCC) John P. Butler, ed., *The Papers of the Continental Congress, 1774–1789* (Washington, D.C.: National Archives and Records Administration, 1978), 42:1:35 (hereafter cited as PCC); William H. Gaines Jr., "The Continental Congress Considers Publication of a Bible," *Studies in Bibliography: Papers of the Bibliographical Society of the University of Virginia,* (1950) 3:274–78; Struthers Burt, *Philadelphia: The Holy Experiment* (New York: Doubleday, 1945), 122–23; Rod Gragg, *The Declaration of Independence: The Story Behind America's Founding Document and the Men Who Created It* (Nashville: Thomas Nelson, 2005), 6, 22; Paul H. Smith, ed., *Letters of Delegates to Congress, 1774–1789* (Washington, D.C.: Library of Congress, 1931), 25:549–52 (hereafter cited as LDC); WJA: 2:370–73.

18. JCC 1:13–28; 18:979–80; LDC 1: 31, 34–36, 45, 55; 24:549–50; WJA 2:368–73, 386; Jerilynn Green Marston, *King and Congress: The Transfer of Political Legitimacy, 1774–1776* (Princeton:

Princeton University Press, 1987), 76–78.

19. JCC 5:510–15; Gragg, *By the Hand of Providence*, 46–49; Bonomi, *Under the Cope of Heaven*, 213–16; Thomas Jefferson, *The Writings of Thomas Jefferson*, ed. Paul Leicester Ford (New York: G. P. Putnam's Sons, 1904), 10:268; Katsh, *Biblical Heritage of American Democracy*, 116.

20. JCC 2:87–88, 154–57, 192; 4:208–9; 8:733–35; 12:1001; 21:1074–76; 22:339–40; Moses Coit Tyler, *The Literary History of the American Revolution 1763–1783* (New York: G. P. Putnam's Sons, 1897), 2:284–86; Caleb Haskell, *Caleb Haskell's Diary, May 5, 1775–May 30, 1776*, ed. Lothrop Withington (Newburyport: 1881), 8; William D. Love, *The Fast and Thanksgiving Days of New England* (Boston: Houghton Mifflin, 1895), 345, 442; John and Abigail Adams, *The Letters of John and Abigail Adams*, ed. Frank Shuffleton (New York: Penguin Books, 2004), 64; Gaillard Hunt, *The Seal of the United States: How It Was Developed and Adopted* (Washington, D.C.: U.S. Department of State, 1892), 24–25; Gragg, *By the Hand of Providence*, 127–34.

21. Allen Johnson and Dumas Malone, eds., *Dictionary of American Biorgraphy*, (New York: Charles Scribner's Sons, 1928) 36:181–182; 6:236–237; James Price, "Memorable Places Within the Bounds of the United Presbyterian Presbytery," *Journal of Presbyterian History* 6 (1911–1912): 236; Scharf, *History of Philadelphia* 2:1274–75; Benjamin Franklin, *The Writings of Benjamin Franklin*, ed. Albert H. Smyth (New York: Macmillan 1907), 6:15; "Abstract of Church Records," Box 3031, Scots Presbyterian Church Records, Historical Society of Pennsylvania.

22. JCC 8:536; LDC 7: 312–13; PCC 42:1:34 (hereafter cited as PCC); PCC 46:1:155–73; Gaines, "Continental Congress Considers Publication of a Bible," 41: 274–78; Thomas C. Pears, "The Story of the Aitken Bible," *Journal of the Presbyterian Historical Society* 18, no. 6 (June 1939): 225–41; Margaret T. Hills, ed., *The English Bible in America: A Bibliography of Editions of the Bible and New Testament Published in America, 1777–1957* (New York: American Bible Society, 1961), 13–16.

23. JCC 8: 734; PCC 1: 163–64; PCC 46:1:155–73; LDC 7: 312–13; Gaines, "Continental Congress Considers Publication of a Bible," 3: 274–76, 280–81; Hills, *The English Bible in America*, 13–16.

24. LDC 7:312; JCC 8:536; PCC 42:1:35; Gaines, "Continental Congress Considers Publication of a Bible," 3:274–76, 280–81; WJA 2: 6–7, 22–23; 10:104–5; Allen Johnson and Dumas Malone, eds., *Dictionary of American Biography* (New York: Charles Scribner's Sons, 1928–36), 15:646–47; 17: 308–9; Gragg, *By the Hand of Providence*, 200.

25. JCC 8:536, 734; LDC 1:34–36, 75; 7:312–13; PCC 1:163–64; Gaines, "Continental Congress Considers Publication of a Bible," 3:274–78, 280–81.

26. JCC 8:733–35; Hills, *The English Bible in America*, 13–16; Gaines, "Continental Congress Considers Publication of a Bible" 3:274–78, 280–81.

27. Robert Middlekauff, *The Glorious Cause: The American Revolution, 1763–1789* (New York: Oxford University Press, 1982), 391–95; George Otto Trevelyan, *The American Revolution* (New York: Longman and Green, 1922), 4:242–49; Edmund C. Burnett, *The Continental Congress: A Definitive History of the Continental Congress from Its Inception in 1774 to March 1789* (New York: W. W. Norton, 1941), 662; JCC 8:733–35; Hills, *The English Bible in America*, 13–16; Gaines, "Continental Congress Considers Publication of a Bible," 3:274–78, 280–81.

CHAPTER 11: A NEW NATION EMBRACES AN OLD BOOK

1. Johnson and Malone, *Dictionary of American Biography*, 1:131–32 (see chap. 10, n. 24); Robert E. Thompson, *A History of the Presbyterian Churches in the United States* (New York: Charles Scribner's, 1895), 60; Robert Aitken, *R. Aitken, Printer, Book-binder, and Bookseller, Opposite the Coffee-house, Front-Street, Philadelphia* (Philadelphia: R. Aitken, 1779), frontispiece; Joseph Jackson, *Market*

Street, Philadelphia: The Most Historic Street in America (Philadelphia: Joseph Jackson, 1918), 13–15; Benjamin B. Warfield, *The Printing of the Westminster Confession of Faith* (Philadelphia: MacCalla, 1901), 1:81; John T. Scharf and Thomas Westcott, *History of Philadelphia, 1609–1884* (Philadelphia: L. H. Wescott, 1884), 2:1274; Gerald Newman, ed., *Britain in the Hanoverian Age, 1714–1837* (London: Garland, 1997), 206.

2. Pears, "Story of the Aitken Bible," 18: 225–41 (see chap. 10, n. 22); Paul C. Gutjahr, *An American Bible: A History of the Good Book in the United States, 1777–1880* (Stanford: Stanford University Press, 1999), 20–21; John Wright, *Early Bibles of America: Being a Descriptive Account of Bibles Published in the United States, Mexico and Canada* (New York: Thomas Whitaker, 1894), 385.

3. "Congress Bible," *The American Stationer* 69, no. 16 (April 22, 1911):30; 87–90; Hills, *The English Bible in America*, 13–16 (see chap. 10, n. 22); Gaines, "The Continental Congress Considers Publication of a Bible," 3:280–81 (see chap. 10, n. 17); Trevelyan, *American Revolution,* 4:376–79 (see chap. 10, n. 27).

4. Pears, "Story of the Aitken Bible," 18:224–441; "Congress Bible," 30; Johnson and Malone, *Dictionary of American Biography,* 1:131–32; Gutjahr, *An American Bible,* 20–21; Wright, *Early Bibles of America,* 385.

5. JCC 19:91; PCC 4:1:63; LDC 7:312–313; Pears, "Story of the Aitken Bible," 18:224–441; Hills, *The English Bible in America,* 13–16; Gaines, "Continental Congress Considers Publication of a Bible," 3:274–78, 280–81.

6. JCC 19:91; PCC 4:1:63; Gutjahr, *An American Bible,* 20–21; Wright, *Early Bibles of America,* 385; Gaines, "Continental Congress Considers Publication of a Bible," 3:274–78; Hills, *The English Bible in America,* 13–16; Gragg, *By the Hand of Providence,* 178–83.

7. JCC 8:733–35; 16:656; 18:979–80; 19:91; 23:572–74; LCD 7:311–12; 19:119; PCC 19:1:59, 63–64; 78:1:421–22, 425–28; Bird Wilson, *Memoir of the Life of the Right Reverend William White* (Philadelphia: James Kay, 1839), 51; Alice L. George, *Philadelphia: A Pictorial Celebration* (New York: Sterling, 2006), 26.

8. JCC 8:733–35; JCC 16:656; 18:979–80; 19:91; 23:572–74; LCD 7:311–12; 19:119; PCC 19:1:59, 63–64; 78:1:421–22, 425–28; Wilson, *Memoir of the Life of the Right Reverend William White,* 51; George *Philadelphia,* 26; Matthew L. Harris and Thomas S. Kidd, eds., *The Founding Fathers and the Debate Over Religion in Revolutionary America: A History in Documents* (New York: Oxford University Press, 2012), 33–36; Wright, *Early Bibles of America,* 385; Gaines, "Continental Congress Considers Publication of a Bible," 3:274–78; Gutjahr, *An American Bible,* 20–21; Hills, *The English Bible in America,* 13–16; Gragg, *By the Hand of Providence,* 178–83.

9. Aitken Bible, call number BS185 1782, Rare Book and Special Collections Division, Library of Congress; Wright, *Early Bibles of America,* 59; Gaines, "Continental Congress Considers Publication of a Bible," 3:274–78; Barker, *English Bible Versions,* 256 (see chap. 5, n. 16); Gutjahr, *An American Bible,* 20–21; Hills, *The English Bible in America,* 13–16.

10. Johnson and Malone, *Dictionary of American Biography,* 1:132; Wright, *Early Bibles of America,* 59; Gaines, "Continental Congress Considers Publication of a Bible," 3:274–78; Barker, *English Bible Versions,* 256; Gutjahr, *An American Bible,* 20–21; Hills, *The English Bible in America,* 13–16.

11. Johnson and Malone, *Dictionary of American Biography,* 4:90–91; Gutjahr, *An American Bible,* 25–27; Wright, *Early Bibles of America,* 70–73; Barker, *English Bible Versions,* 257.

12. Johnson and Malone, *Dictionary of American Biography,* 4:90–91; Wright, *Early Bibles of America,* 73; Lewis Gaston Leary, *The Book-Peddling Parson: An Account of the Life and Times of Mason Locke Weems* (Chapel Hill: Algonquin Books, 1984), 21–23; Daniel J. Boorstein, *The Americans: The National Experience* (New York: Knopf Doubleday 2010), 343; Steven Watts, *The Republic Reborn:*

War and the Making of Liberal America (Baltimore: John Hopkins Press, 1987), 141.

13.   Wright, *Early Bibles of America,* 70–73; Johnson and Malone, *Dictionary of American Biography,* 3:490–91; Gutjahr, *An American Bible,* 24, 26; Emily E. Ford Skeel, ed., *Mason Locke Weems: His Works and Ways* (New York: Plimpton Press, 1929), 2:137, 143, 153; 3:75, 148, 210, 359; Barker, *English Bible Versions,* 257.

14.   Wright, *Early Bibles of America,* 87, 323; Thomas, *The History of Printing in America,* 401–3; Nichols, *Isaiah Thomas,* 100; Gutjahr, *An American Bible,* 90; Barker, *English Bible Versions,* 259.

15.   Lewis R. Harley, *The Life of Charles Thomas, Secretary of the Continental Congress and Translator of the Bible from the Greek* (Philadelphia: George Jacobs, 1900), 163.

16.   Andrew K. Frank, ed., *Early Republic: People and Perspectives* (Oxford: ABC-CLIO, 2009), 155; Elesha J. Coffman, *The Christian Century and the Rise of Protestant Mainline* (Oxford: Oxford University Press, 2013), 5–6, 66; James P. Boyd, ed., *Triumphs and Wonders of the 19ᵗʰ Century* (Philadelphia: A.J. Holman, 1899), 147-58; "George Edward Reed, 1846–1930," Archives and Special Collections, Dickinson University.

17.   Alexander Watson, *History of the New York Bible Society* (New York: Anson Randolph, 1858), 10–11; George A. Boyd, *Elias Boudinot: Patriot and Statesman* (Westport: Greenwood Press, 1969), 250; Johnson and Malone, *Dictionary of American Biography,* 4:477–78; John Fea, *The Bible Cause: A History of the American Bible Society* (Oxford: Oxford University Press, 2016), 171; Charles Joyner, *Down by the Riverside: A South Carolina Slave Community* (Urbana: University of Illinois Press, 1984), 216.

18.   Paul, *English Language Bible Translators,* 124–35 (see chap. 9, n. 26); Eitan P. Fishbane and Jonathan D. Sarna, eds., *Jewish Renaissance and Revival in America* (Lebanon: University Press of New England, 2011), 73: James Cardinal Gibbons, *The Faith of Our Fathers: Being a Plain Exposition and Vindication of the Church Founded by Our Lord Jesus Christ* (New York: P. J. Kennedy: 1917), 63; Lance J. Sussman, *Isaac Leesman and the Making of American Judaism* (Detroit: Wayne State University, 1995), 151.

19.   Philip Schaff, *The Revision of the English Version of the Holy Scriptures* (New York: Harper and Bros., 1875), viii-xv; Glen Butterfield, *Bible Unity* (Bloomington: WestBow Press, 2013), 39–40.

20.   V. George Shillington, *Reading the Sacred Text: An Introduction to Biblical Studies* (London: T & T Clark: 2002), 191–92; Lewis, *The English Bible,* 105 (see chap. 10, n. 22).

21.   Shillington, *Reading the Sacred Text,* 191–92; Lewis, *The English Bible,* 105: Balmer H. Kelly, *The Laymen's Bible Commentary* (Louisville: John Knox: 1959), 1:136–37; Wegner, *From Text to Translations,* 319–20; Price, *Ancestry of Our English Bible,* 300.

22.   Wegner, *From Text to Translations,* 319–20; Lewis, *The English Bible,* 105; Price, *Ancestry of Our English Bible,* 300.

23.   Wegner, *From Texts to Translations,* 320; Lewis, *The English Bible,* 105; Price, *Ancestry of Our English Bible,* 103.

24.   Matthew B. Riddle, *The Story of the Revised New Testament, American Standard Version* (Philadelphia: Sunday School Times, 1908), 67–72; Price, *Ancestry of Our English Bible,* 103; Wegner, *From Texts to Translations,* 320.

CHAPTER 12: THE WORD OF OUR GOD STANDS FOREVER

1.   Thomas Kutluk "Breakthrough at Eskimo Point: God Used an Icy Plunge to Redirect this Eskimo's Life," *Alliance Witness* 120, no. 1 (January 2, 1985): 6–7; Frederic Laugrand and Jarich Oosten, "Reconnecting People and Healing the Land: Inuit Pentecostal and Evangelical Movements in the Canadian Eastern Arctic," *Numen* 54 (2007): 234.

2.   Kutluk, "Breakthrough at Eskimo Point," 7; Gerald H. Anderson, ed., *Biographical Dictionary of*

Christian Missions (Grand Rapids: Eerdmans, 1999), 391; Wilson E. Paul, *English Language Bible Translators* (Jefferson, NC: McFarland, 2009), 140.

3. Anderson, *Biographical Dictionary of Christian Missions*, 391; Paul, *English Language Bible Translators* (2009), 140; Laugrand and Oosten, "Reconnecting People and Healing the Land," 234; Frederic Laugrand and Jarich G. Oosten, *Inuit Shamanism and Christianity* (Montreal: McGill-Queens University Press, 2010), 344.

4. Eugene A. Nida and Charles R. Taber, *The Theory and Practice of Translation* (Leiden: Brill, 2003), 28–31; Athalya Brenner and Jan Willem van Henten, eds., *Bible Translation on the Threshold of the Twenty-First Century: Authority, Reception, Culture and Religion* (London: Sheffield Academic, 2002), 108; Dave Brunn, *One Bible, Many Versions: Are All Created Equal?* (Downers Grove: IVP Academic, 2013), 132.

5. Bruce, *History of the Bible in English*, 258; Wegner, *From Texts to Translations*, 321; Bruce M. Metzger, *The Bible in Translation: Ancient and English Versions* (Grand Rapids: Baker Academic, 2001), 151.

6. Ava Bar-Am, "St. Stephen's Monastery: The Bros.' Work," *Jerusalem Post*, September 14, 2009; Metzger, *The Bible in Translation*, 151; James Krukel, "On the Bible and Literary Criticism," *Journal of Biblical Literature* 105, no. 3 (September 1986): 189.

7. A. P. Salom, "The New English Bible: A Preliminary Critique," *Ministry* 61, no. 10 (October 1961): 13–15, 168; David Dewey, *A User's Guide to Bible Translations: Making the Most of Different Versions* (Downers Grove, IL: Intervarsity Press, 2004), 147–48; Metzger, *The Bible in Translations*, 133–36, 153.

8. "Ken Taylor, "Translator of *The Living Bible*, Dies at 88," *Christianity Today*, June 10, 2005, http://www.christianitytoday.com/ct/2005/juneweb-only/55.0a.html; Dewey, *A User's Guide to Bible Translations*, 178; Glen G. Scorgie, Mark L. Strauss, and Steven M. Voth, *The Challenge of Bible Translation: Communicating God's Word to the World* (Grand Rapids: Zondervan, 2003), 189; https://www.tyndale.com/nlt; https://www.biblegateway.com/versions/New-Living-Translation-NLT-Bible/#vinfo; http://www.newlivingtranslation.com/05discoverthenlt/nltintro.asp, (accessed November 25, 2017).

9. "About the Lockman Foundation," Lockman Foundation, http://www.lockman.org/tlf/tlfhistory.php (accessed October 27, 2017); Bruce, *History of the Bible in English*, 258–59.

10. John J. Pilch, *Choosing a Bible Translation* (Collegeville: Liturgical Press, 2000), 5; Bruce, *History of the Bible in English*, 258–59; *The Ryrie Study Bible: New American Standard Translation*, commentary by Charles C. Ryrie (Chicago: Moody Press, 1978), viii–ix.

11. Dewey, *A User's Guide to Bible Translations*, 157; Bruce, *History of the Bible in English*, 262; *The Challenge of Bible Translation*, 189; Larry Stone, *The Story of the Bible: The Fascinating History of Its Writing, Translation and Effect on Civilization* (Nashville: Thomas Nelson, 2010), 93; Charles McGrath, "Why the King James Bible Endures," *New York Times*, April 23, 2011.

12. Wegner, *From Texts to Translations*, 379–83; Leland Ryken, *Understanding English Bible Translations: The Case for an Essentially Literal Approach* (Wheaton, IL: Crossway, 2009), 65; *The Challenge of Bible Translation*, 188; Dewey, *A User's Guide to Bible Translations*, 161; Robert G. Hoerber, ed., *Concordia Self-Study Bible: New International Version* (St. Louis: Concordia, 1986), x–xi.

13. Ted Olsen, "Correcting the 'Mistakes' of the TNIV and Inclusive NIV, Translators will Revise NIV in 2011," *Christianity Today*, September 1, 2009, http://www.christianitytoday.com/news/2009/september/correcting-mistakes-of-tniv-and-inclusive-niv-translators.html; Sarah E. Zylstra, "The Most Popular and Fastest-Growing Bible Translation Isn't What You Think It Is," *Christianity Today*, March 13, 2014, http://www.christianitytoday.com/news/2014/march/most-popular-and-

fastest-growing-bible-translation-niv-kjv.html.

14. Susan Olasky, "Femme Fatale," *World*, March 29, 1997, https://world.wng.org/1997/03/femme_ fatale; William Combs, "History of the NIV Translation Controversy," *Detroit Baptist Seminary Journal* 17, no. 3 (2012): 3–34; "The NIV's Commitment to Accuracy," Biblica: The International Bible Society, https://www.biblica.com/niv-bible/niv-bible-translation-accuracy/ (accessed October 27, 2017).

15. Hannibal Hamlin and Norman W. Jones, eds., *The King James Bible After 400 Years: Literary, Linguistic and Cultural Influence*s (Cambridge: Cambridge University Press, 2010), 164; Arthur Goff, Phillip E. Farnsley II, and Peter J. Theusen, *The Bible in American Life* (Indianapolis: Center for the Study of Religion and American Culture, 2017), 12–14; *The Challenge of Bible Translation*, 188; Ronnie Todd, conversation with author, August 31, 2017.

16. Wegner, *From Texts to Translations*, 329–31; Richard G. Lee, ed., *The American Patriot's Bible: New King James Version* (Nashville: Thomas Nelson, 2009), *x; The Challenge of Bible Translation*, 188; Earl D. Radmacher, ed., *The Nelson Study Bible: New King James Version* (Nashville: Thomas Nelson, 1997), xiii.

17. *The Challenge of Bible Translations*, 188; Radmacher, *Nelson Study Bible*, xiii–xii; Wegner, *From Texts to Translations*, 329–31; Zylstra, "The Most Popular and Fastest-Growing Bible Translation Isn't What You Think It Is."

18. "What Is *The Message*,"NavPress, https://www.navpress.com/what-is-the-message, (accessed October 27, 2017); *The Message: The Bible in Contemporary Language* (Colorado Springs: NavPress, 2002), 6–7; Wegner, *From Texts to Translations,* 386–87; Dewey, *User's Guide to Bible Translations*, 36.

19. B&H, "Point Your Heart to True North," Holman Bibles, http://www.bhpublishinggroup.com/ category/bibles (accessed October 27, 2017); Gordon D. Fee and Mark L. Strauss, *How to Choose a Translation for All Its Worth* (Grand Rapids: Zondervan, 2007), 99–100; "Christian Standard Bible," American Bible Society, "A Brief Description of Popular Bible Translations," http://bibleresources. americanbible.org/resource/a-brief-description-of-popular-bible-translations (accessed October 27, 2017).

20. Crossway Books, "Ministry," Crossway, https://www.crossway.org/ministry/ (accessed October 27, 2017); William Combs, "History of the NIV Translation Controversy," 12–13; *The Challenge of Bible Translations*, 48–49.

21. Fee and Strauss, *How to Choose a Translation for All Its Worth,* 99–100; William Combs, "History of the NIV Translation Controversy," 12–13; *The Challenge of Bible Translation*, 48–49; Crossway, "Preface to the English Standard Version," ESV.org, www.esv.org/resources/esv-global-study-bible/ preface-to-the-english-standard-version (accessed October 27, 2017).

22. American Bible Society, "A Brief Description of Popular Bible Translations"; John Riches *The New Cambridge History of the Bible, From 1750 to the Present* (New York: Cambridge University Press, 2015), 4:556; Ligonier Ministries, "The Reformation Study Bible (ESV)," http://www.ligonier. org/store/the-reformation-study-bible-esv-hardcover (accessed October 27, 2017); *The Complete Jewish Study Bible, Insights for Jews and Christian*s (Peabody, MA: Hendrickson, 2016), vi, xvii–xviii.

23. Salerna Petra Ramet, ed., *Religious Policy in the Soviet Union* (Cambridge: Cambridge University Press, 1993), 13–16; Perry L. Glazner, *The Quest for the Russian Soul: Evangelicals and Moral Education in Post-Communist Russia* (Waco: Baylor University Press, 2002), 81; Michael Novak, *Taking Glasnost Seriously: Toward an Open Soviet Union* (Washington, D.C.: American Enterprise Institute, 1988), 114–15; Steven Rosefielde, *Red Holocaust* (London: Routledge, 2010), 8, 250; Gragg, *My Brother's Keeper*, 14; William L. Shirer, *The Rise and Fall of the Third Reich: A History of Nazi Germany* (New York: Simon & Schuster, 1960), 240–41; Arthur C. Cochrane, *The Church's*

Confession Under Hitler (Philadelphia: Westminster Press, 1962), 237–42; Gerda Wielander, *Christian Values in Communist China* (London: Routledge, 2013), Timothy Snyder, "Hitler v. Stalin: Who Killed More?" *New York Review of Books*, March 30, 2011, http://www.nybooks. com/articles/2011/03/10/hitler-vs-stalin-who-killed-more/; Lee Edwards, "The Heritage of Mao Zedong Is Mass Murder," Heritage Foundation, February 2, 2010, http://www.heritage.org/asia/ commentary/the-legacy-mao-zedong-mass-murder.

24. Paul A. Marshall, Lela Gilbert, and Nina Shea, *Persecuted: The Global Assault on Christians* (Nashville; Thomas Nelson, 2013), 54–57, 175; John L. Allen Jr., *The Global War on Christians: Dispatches from the Front Lines of Anti-Christian Persecution* (New York: Image, 2016), 40, 90, 159, 169; Roy Peterson, "The Forbidden Bible," Fox News, January 29, 2015, http://www.foxnews. com/opinion/2015/01/27/forbidden-bible.html; "Open Doors World Watch List, 2017," Open Doors USA, https://www.opendoorsusa.org/christian-persecution/world-watch-list/ (accessed October 27, 2017).

25. The Barna team, "State of the Bible 2017: Top Findings," Barna, April 4, 2017, https://www.barna. com/research/state-bible-2017-top-findings/; "The Bible in American Life," Center for the Study of Religion in American Culture," March 6, 2014, https://raac.iupui.edu/files/2713/9413/8354/ Bible_in_American_Life_Report_March_6_2014.pdf, no longer accessible; Arthur Goff, Phillip E. Farnsley II, and Peter J. Theusen, *The Bible in American Life* (Oxford: Oxford University Press, 2017), 10; Daniel Radosh, "The Good Book Business," *New Yorker,* December 18, 2006, https:// www.newyorker.com/magazine/2006/12/18/the-good-book-business.

26. Pew Research Center, "Religious Landscape Study," Pew Research Center on Religion and Public Life, http://www.pewforum.org/religious-landscape-study/ (accessed October 27, 2017); Abigail Geiger, "5 Facts on How Americans View the Bible and Other Religious Texts," *Fact Tank*, April 14, 2017, http://www.pewresearch.org/fact-tank/2017/04/14/5-facts-on-how-americans-view-the-bible-and-other-religious-texts/; Barna Team, "State of the Bible 2017; American Bible Society, "2017 State of the Bible," available online at https://www.americanbible.org/state-of-the-bible; Barna, "The Bible in America, 6-Year Trends," Barna Group, June 15, 2016, https://www.barna. com/research/the-bible-in-america-6-year-trends/.

27. Evangelical Alliance, "Attitudes to the Bible," Evangelical Alliance of Great Britain, www.eauk. org/church/research-and-statistics/attitudes-to-the-bible.cfm (accessed October 27, 2017); Clive D. Field, "Is the Bible Becoming a Closed Book?," *Journal of Contemporary Religion* 29, no. 3 (2014): 503–28; Raj Persaud and Peter Bruggan, "British Opinion Polls Reveal a Dramatic Decline in the Impact of the Bible on the UK," *HuffPost*, updated November 23, 2014, http://www.huffingtonpost. co.uk/dr-raj-persaud/british-opinion-polls-rev_b_5870786.html; Luke 12:19.

28. Lydia Saad, "Three in Four in U.S. Still See the Bible as the Word of God," Gallup, June 4, 2014, Gallup News, http://news.gallup.com/poll/170834/three-four-bible-word-god.aspx; Barna, "The Bible in America," Geiger, "5 Facts on How Americans View the Bible and Other Religious Texts"; Barna team, "State of the Bible 2017, Declaration of Independence, July 6, 1776, National Archives and Records Administration.

29. Barna, "The Bible in America," Geiger, "5 Facts on How Americans View the Bible and Other Religious Texts"; Barna team, "State of the Bible 2017; American Bible Society, "2017 State of the Bible"; D. James Kennedy, "The Threat of Humanism," D. James Kennedy Ministries, https://www. djameskennedy.org/devotional-detail/20160701-the-threat-of-humanism, (accessed November 26, 2017); C. Everett Koop and Francis Schaeffer, *Whatever Happened to the Human Race?* (Wheaton: Crossway, 1978), 4; Billy Graham, *Just as I Am: The Autobiography of Billy Graham* (New York: HarperColllins, 1997), 578.

30. Koop and Schaeffer, *Whatever Happened to the Human Race?* 4; Morgan Lee, "Many Practicing Christians Agree with Marxism," *Christianity Today,* May 10, 2017, http://www.christianitytoday.com/news/2017/may/many-practicing-christians-agree-marxism-worldviews-barna.html.

31. R. Dale Tedder Jr., "United Methodist Authority and the Question of Inerrancy," Florida Confessing Association, http://ucmpage.org/fa_cm/cmfa_3.htm (accessed October 27, 2017); see in particular n. 1; Jonathan Merritt, "Mega-Church Pastor's Scandalous Take on Scripture," Religious News Service, May 1, 2014; Barna Organization, "The State of the Church, 2016," September 15, 2016, https://www.barna.com/research/state-church-2016/; Ed Stetzer, "If It Doesn't Stem Its Decline, Mainline Protestantism Has Just 23 Easters Left," *Washington Post,* April 28, 2017, "Chicago Statement on Biblical Inerrancy," International Council on Biblical Inerrancy, Archives, Dallas Theological Seminary.

32. Barna, "The Bible in America," Geiger, "5 Facts on How Americans View the Bible and Other Religious Texts"; Barna team, "State of the Bible 2017; David Haskell, "Liberal Churches Are Dying. But Conservative Churches are Thriving," *Washington Post,* January 4, 2017, Paula R. Kincaid, "Three Presbyterian Denominations Experience Growth in the Number of Churches in 2014," *Presbyterian News and Analysis,* June 5, 2015; J. I. Packer, *God Has Spoken: Revelation and the Bible* (Grand Rapids: Baker Book House, 2000), 22-23, 31–35.

33. Judges 17:6; Packer, *God Has Spoken,* 21-35; Ivan Mesa, "J.I. Packer, 89, On Losing Sight But Seeing Christ," The Gospel Coalition, https://www.thegospelcoalition.org/article/j-i-packer-89-on-losing-sight-but-seeing-christ/ (accessed November 27, 2017); Amos 8:11.

34. Geiger, "5 Facts on How Americans View the Bible and Other Religious Texts"; Persaud and Bruggan, "British Opinion Polls Reveal a Dramatic Decline in the Impact of the Bible on the UK"; Acts 1:8; Wes Granberg-Michaelson, "Think Christianity Is Dying? No, Christianity is Shifting Dramatically," *Washington Post, May 20, 2015; Brandon Showalter, "China on Track to Have World's Largest Christian Population by 2030," Christian Post, July 21, 2016;* George Thomas Kurian and Mark A. Lamport, eds., *Encyclopedia of Christianity in the United States* (New York: Loman and Littlefield, 2016), 5:1913.

35. Anne Graham Lotz, "Trusting Him Completely," Billy Graham Evangelistic Association, https://billygraham.org/decision-magazine/july-august-2012/trusting-him-completely/, (accessed November 26, 2017); D. James Kennedy, "Trust in the Lord," D. James Kennedy Ministries, https://djameskennedy.org/devotional-detail/trust-in-the-lord, (accessed November 26, 2017); Billy Graham, "We Need a Heaven-Sent Revival," *Decision Magazine,* July 17, 2017, *https://billygraham.org/decision-magazine/july-2017/56832-2/ (*accessed November 27, 2017; Graham, *Just as I Am,* 753; Timothy Keller, "Kingdom Centered Prayer," Gospel in Life, http://www.gospelinlife.com/kingdom-centered-prayer-7753 (accessed October 27, 2017); "Disciples of All Nations," Gideons International website, https://www2.gideons.org/ (accessed October 27, 2017); "The History of Wycliffe," Wycliffe Bible Translators, https://www.wycliffe.org/about (accessed October 27, 2017); Biblica, "Our History," Biblica: The International Bible Society, https://www.biblica.com/about/history/, (accessed October 27, 2017); "Exporting Bibles: In the Beginning Was the Ideogram," *Economist,* March 30, 2013, https://www.economist.com/news/china/21574529-china-has-become-one-largest-producers-bibles-world-beginning-was; Jennifer Harper, "Museum of the Bible to Open Near U.S. Capitol," *Washington Times,* July 10, 2017, http://www.washingtontimes.com/news/2017/jul/10/museum-of-the-bible-gears-up-to-open-unique-430000/; Museum of the Bible, https://www.museumofthebible.org/museum (accessed October 27, 2017) .

36. John 3:16; Isaiah 40:8.

Bibliography

"About the Lockman Foundation." Lockman Foundation. www.lockman.org/tlf/tlfhistory.php.

Abstract of Church Records. Box 3031. Scots Presbyterian Church Records. Historical Society of Pennsylvania.

Ackroyd, Peter. *Tudors: The History of England from Henry VIII to Elizabeth I.* New York: St. Martin's Press: 2012.

Adams, John. *The Works of John Adams: Second President of the United States.* Charles Francis Adams, editor. Boston: Little, Brown, 1850-56.

Adams, John and Abigail. *The Letters of John and Abigail Adams.* Frank Shuffleton, editor. New York: Penguin Books, 2004.

"Additions to the Library." *Bulletin of the John Rylands Library.* Vol. 1. No. 5. (April – October 1907).

Aitken Bible. Call number BS185 1782. Rare Book and Special Collections Division. Library of Congress.

Aitken, Robert. *R. Aitken, Printer, Book-binder, and Bookseller, Opposite the Coffee-house, Front-Street, Philadelphia,* Philadelphia: R. Aitken, 1779.

Albright, W.F. "The Gezer Calendar." *Bulletin of the American Schools of Oriental Research.* Vol. 92. No. 16. (December 1943).

Alexander, Joseph Addison. *Commentary on Isaiah.* Grand Rapids: Kregel Cassics, 1992.

Alford, Stephen. *The Watchers: A Secret History of the Reign of Queen Elizabeth I.* New York: Bloomsbury, 2012.

Allen, John L. Jr. *The Global War on Christians: Dispatches from the Front Lines of Anti-Christian Persecution.* New York: Image, 2016.

Althaus, Paul. *The Theology of Martin Luther.* Robert C. Schultz, translator. Philadelphia: Fortress Press, 1966.

The American Patriot's Bible: New King James Version. Richard G. Lee, editor. Nashville: Thomas Nelson, 2009.

Anatolis, Khaled. *Athanasius,* London: Routledge Publishing, 2004.

Anderson, Christopher. *The Annals of the English Bible.* London: William Pickering, 1845.

Anderson, George. "The Doctrines of Calvin and the Theology of the Congregational Churches." *The Evangelical Repository: A Quarterly Magazine of Theological Literature,* 1879.

Angold, Michael J. *The Fourth Crusade: Event and Context.* London: Routledge Publishing, 2003.

Annual Report of the American Bible Society. New York: American Bible Society. Vol. 120. (1936).

Aquinas, Thomas. *Catena Aurea: Commentary on Matthew's Gospel.* Old Chelsea Station: Cosimo, 2007.

Archer, Gleason. *Encyclopedia of Bible Difficulties.* Grand Rapids: Zondervan Corporation, 1982.

Armstrong, Elizabeth. *Robert Estienne: Royal Printer.* Cambridge: Cambridge University, 1954.

Arnold, Bill T. *Introduction to the Old Testament.* Cambridge: Cambridge University Press, 2014.

Atherstone, Andrew. *Reformation: A World in Turmoil.* Oxford: Lion Books, 2005.

"Attitudes to the Bible." Evangelical Alliance of Great Britain. www.eauk.org/church/research-and-statistics/attitudes-to-the-bible.cfm.

Austin, Bill R. *Austin's Topical History of Christianity.* Wheaton, Illinois: Tyndale House Publishers, 1983.

Babinger, Franz. *Mehmed the Conqueror and His Time.* Princeton: Princeton University Press, 1978.

Bainton, Roland H. *Here I Stand: A Life of Martin Luther.* Nashville: Abingdon Press, 1978.

Baird, Julia. *Victoria the Queen: An Intimate Biography of the Woman Who Ruled an Empire.* New York: Random House, 2018.

Baird, Robert. *Religion in America.* New York: Harper and Brothers, 1856.

Bar-Am, Ava. "St. Stephen's Monastery: The Brothers' Work." *The Jerusalem Post,* 14 September 2009.

Barker, Henry. *English Bible Versions: A Tercenteary Memorial to the King James Version, from the New York Bible and the Common Prayer Book Society.* Cambridge: Cambridge University Press, 1911.

Barlow, William. *Sum and Substance of the Hampton Court Conference.* London: Vance, 1604.

Barton, George Aaron. *Archaeology and the Bible.* Philadelphia: American Sunday School Union, 1916.

Barton, William E. *The Samaritan Pentateuch: The Story of a Survival Among the Sects.* Oberlin: Bibliotecha Sacra: 1903.

Beegle, Dewey M. *God's Word into English: The Adventure of Bible Translation.* New York: Harper and Row, 1960.

Bellinsoni, Arthur J. *The New Testament: An Introduction to Biblical Scholarship.* Eugene: Wipf and Stock, 2016.

Berman, Harold J. *Law and Revolution: The Impact of the Protestant Reformation on Western Legal Tradition.* Cambridge: Harvard University Press, 2003.

Berman, Ronen. "A Holy High Whodunit." *New York Times.* 25 July 2012.

The Bible in America. Philip Goff, editor. Oxford: Oxford University Press, 2017.

"The Bible in America: Six Year Trends." Barna Group. 15 June 2016. www.barna.com/research/the-bible-in-america-6-year-trends.

"The Bible in American Life," The Center for the Study of Religion in American Culture. 6 March 2014. www.raac.iupui.edu/files/2713/9413/8354/Bible_in_American_Life_Report_March_6_2014.pdf.

Bible Translation on the Threshold of the Twenty-First Century: Authority, Reception, Culture and Religion. Athalya Brenner and Jan Willem van Henten, editors. London: Sheffield Academic, 2002.

"Biographical Description of the First Edition of Cranmer's or the Great Bible." Government Office of Royal Collections for a History of the English Bible, 1525-1539. British Library.

Biographical Dictionary of Christian Missions. Gerald H. Anderson, editor. Grand Rapids: William B. Eerdmans, 1999.

Bishop, Jim. *The Day Christ Was Born and the Day Christ Died.* New York: Galahad Books, 1993.

The Blackwell Companion to the Bible and Culture. John F.A. Sawyer, editor. Oxford: John A. Wiley and Sons, 2012.

Blaiklock, Edward M. *The Archaeology of the New Testament.* Nashville: Thomas Nelson, 1984.

Blair, Peter Hunter. *The World of Bede.* Cambridge: Cambridge University Press, 1970.

Bloch-Smith, Elizabeth. *Judahite Burial Practices and Beliefs about the Dead.* Sheffield: Sheffield Academic Press, 1992.

Bloomberg, Craig L. *The Historical Reliability of the Gospels.* Downers Grove: Intervarsity Press, 2007.

Bobrick, Benson. *Wide as the Waters: The Story of the English Bible and the Revolution It Inspired.* New York; Simon and Schuster, 2001.

Boer, Henry R. *A Short History of the Early Church.* Grand Rapids: William B. Eerdmans Publishing, 1976.

Bohec, Yann Le. *The Imperial Roman Army.* London: B.T. Batsford, 2013.

Boice, James Montgomery. *Foundations of the Christian Faith.* Downers Grove: Intervarsity Press, 1986.

Bois, John. *Translating for King James: Notes Made by a Translator of the King James Bible.* Ward Allen, editor. Nashville: Vanderbilt University Press, 1989.

Bonomi, Patricia U. *Under the Cape of Heaven: Religion, Society, and Politics in Colonial America.* New York: Oxford University Press, 1986.

The Book of Kells: Selected Plates in Full Color. Blanche Cirker, editor. Mineola: Dover Publications, 1982.

The Book of Pontiffs: The Ancient Biographies of the First Ninety Roman Bishops to A.D. 75. Raymond Davis, editor. Liverpool: Liverpool University Press, 1989.

Boorstein, Daniel J. *The Americans: The National Experience.* New York: Knopf Doubleday 2010.

Bosworth, Joseph. *An Anglo-Saxon Dictionary.* T. Northcote Toller. Oxford: Clarendon Press, 1882.

Boyd, George A. *Elias Boudinot: Patriot and Statesman.* Westport: Greenwood Press, 1969.

Boyd, James P. Boyd, *Triumphs and Wonders of the 19th Century,* Philadelphia: A.J. Holman, 1899

Bradford, William. *Bradford's History of Plymouth Plantation.* Boston: Wright and Porter, 1899.

Bragg, Melvyn. *The Book of Books: The Radical Impact of the King James Bible, 1611-2011.* Berkley: Counterpoint, 2011.

Brandt, Gerard. *A History of the Reformation in the Low Countries.* London: T. Wood, 1720.

Bremer, Francis J. *John Winthrop: America's Forgotten Founding Father.* Oxford: Oxford University Press, 2003.

Brewer, Julius A. *The History of the New Testament Canon in the Syrian Church.* Chicago: University of Chicago Press, 1900.

"A Brief Description of Popular Bible Translations." American Bible Society. http://bibleresources. americanbible.org/resource/a-brief-description-of-popular-bible-translations.

Brill's First Encyclopedia of Islam. Thomas Houtsman. Leiden: E.J. Bill, 1993.

Brinton, Crane, John B. Christopher and Robert Lee Wolfe. *A History of Civilization.* Englewood Cliffs, New Jersey: Prentice-Hall, 1955.

Britain in the Hanoverian Age, 1714-1837. Gerald Newman, editor. London: Garland, 1997.

Brook, Benjamin. *The Lives of the Puritans.* London: James Black, 1813.

Brown, John. "Defender of the Faith." *The American Bibliopolist.* Vol. 7. No. 73. (February 1875).

_____. *The History of the English Bible.* Cambridge: Cambridge University Press, 1912.

Bruce, F.F. *The Book of Acts.* Grand Rapids: William B. Eerdmans, 1988.

_____. *The Books and the Parchments.* Westwood: Fleming H. Revell Company, 1963.

_____. *History of the Bible in English.* Cambridge: Lutterworth Press, 1961.

_____. *New Testament History.* New York: Doubleday, 1969.

_____. "Origin of the Alphabet." *Faith and Thought: The Journal of the Transactions of the Victoria Institute.* Vol. 80. (1948).

Bruce, John C. *Old Newcastle: Lectures.* Newcastle-Upon-Tyne: Andrew Reid Publishers, 1904.

Brunn, Dave. *One Bible, Many Versions: Are All Created Equal?* Downers Grove: IVP Academic, 2013.

Bryant, James C. *Tudor Drama and Religious Controversy.* Macon: Mercer University Press, 1984.

Bunker, Nick. *Making Haste from Babylon: The Mayflower Pilgrims and Their World.* New York: Alfred A. Knopf, 2010.

Burge, Gary M., Lynn Cohick, and Gene L. Green. *The New Testament in Antiquity: A Survey of the New Testament within its Cultural Context.* Grand Rapids: Zondervan Publishing, 2009.

Burke, James J. *Characteristics of the Early Church*. Milwaukee: M.H. Wiltzius, 1899.

Burnett, Edmund C. *The Continental Congress: A Definitive History of the Continental Congress from Its Inception in 1774 to March 1789*. New York: W.W. Norton, 1941.

Burt, Struthers. *Philadelphia: The Holy Experiment*. New York: Doubleday, 1945.

Burton, Edward. *An Inquiry into the Heresies of the Apostolic Age*. Oxford: Oxford University Press, 1829.

Butterfield, Glen. *Bible Unity*. Bloomington: WestBow Press, 2013.

Cahill, Thomas. *Heretics and Heroes: How Renaissance Artists and Reformation Priests Created Our World*. New York: Anchor Books, 2013.

_____. *How the Irish Saved Civilization: The Untold Story of Ireland's Heroic Role from the Fall of Rome to the Rise of Medieval Europe*. New York: Doubleday, 1995.

The Cambridge Companion to Martin Luther. Donald K. McKim, editor. Cambridge: Cambridge University Press, 2005.

The Cambridge History of the Bible: From the Beginnings to Jerome. P.R. Ackroyd and C.F. Evans, editors. Cambridge: Cambridge University Press, 1970.

The Cambridge History of the Bible: The West from the Reformation to the Present. T.S. Greenslade, editor. Cambridge: Cambridge University Press, 1963.

The Cambridge History of Early Modern English Literature. David Lowentstein and Janel Mueller, editors. Cambridge: Cambridge University Press, 2002.

The Cambridge History of Judaism. William D. Davies, Louis Finkelstein and Stephen T. Katz, editors. Cambridge: Cambridge University Press, 2006.

Carne, John. "Life of the Rev. John Eliot." *The Missionary Register*. Vol. 3. (April 1815).

Carvelho, David. *Forty Centuries of Ink*. Seattle: The Worldwide School, 1999.

Cassiodorus. *Variae*. S.J.D. Barnish, translator. Liverpool: Liverpool University Press, 1992.

Cassiodorus. *Explanation of the Psalms*. P.G. Walsh, translator. New York: Paulist Press, 1990.

The Catholic Encyclopedia. Charles B. Herbermann. New York: Encyclopedia Press, 1911.

A Century of British Orientalists. 1903-2001. C. Edmund Bosworth, editor. Oxford: Oxford University Press, 2001.

The Challenge of Bible Translation: Communicating God's Word to the World. Glen G. Scorgie, Mark L. Strauss and Steven M. Voth, editors. Grand Rapids: Zondervan, 2003.

Challoner, Richard. *A Specimen of the Spirit of the Dissenting Preachers*. London: Thomas Meighan, 1736.

Chamberlin, E.R. *The Bad Popes*. New York: Barnes & Noble Books, 1993.

Chambers, D.S. *Popes, Cardinals and War: The Military Church in Renaissance and Early Modern Europe*. London: I.B. Taurus, 2006.

Champlin, Edward. *Nero*. Cambridge: Harvard University Press, 2003.

Chancey, Mark A. *Greco-Roman Culture and the Galilee of Jesus*. Cambridge: Cambridge University Press, 2005.

Chandler, Walter M. *The Trial of Jesus: From a Lawyer's Standpoint*. Norcross, Georgia: The Harrison Company, 1976.

Change and Transition: Essays in Anglican History. Thomas P. Power, editor. Eugene: Wipf and Stock, 2013.

Chazelle, Celia. "Ceolfrith's Gift to St. Peter: The First Quire of the *Codex Amiatinus* and the Evidence of Its Roman Destination." *Early Medieval Europe*. Vol. 12. No. 2. (December 2003).

"Chicago Statement on Biblical Inerrancy." International Council on Biblical Inerrancy. Archives. Dallas Theological Seminary.

Childress, Diana. *Johannes Gutenberg: Inventor of the Printing Press*. Minneapolis: Twenty-first Century Books, 2008.

Choi, Jungwha. *Jewish Leadership in Roman Palestine, 70 C.E. to 130 C.E.* Leiden: Brill Publishing, 2013.

"Christian Standard Bible." American Bible Society. http://bibleresources.americanbible.org/resource/a-brief-description-of-popular-bible-translations.

Christopher Sower Senior. Felix Reichman, editor. Philadelphia: Carl Schurz Memorial Foundation, 1944.

A Chronicle of the Kings of England: From the Times of Roman Government to the Death of King James. Richard Baker, compiler. London: George Sawbridge: 1670.

"Civil and Religious Liberty Not Obtained by the Reformation." *Catholic Monthly Intelligencer.* Vol. 5. No. 44. (January 1817).

Clarke, F.L. *The Life of William Tyndale.* London: Swan Sonnenschien, 1883.

"Classic Vagaries." *The American Literary Magazine.* T. Dwight Sprague, editor. vol. 1, no.1. (July 1847).

Cochrane, Arthur C. *The Church's Confession Under Hitler.* Philadelphia: Westminster Press, 1962.

"Codex Alexandrinus." www.bl.uk/onlinegallery/sacredtexts/codexalex.html.

"Codex Amiatinus Bible Returns to Its Home in Jarrow." BBC News. 15 May 2014.

"Codex Sinaiticus: Experience the Oldest Bible." www.codexsinaiticus.org.

Codex Sinaiticus: New Perspectives on the Ancient Biblical Manuscript. Scot McKendrick, David Parker, Amy Myshrall and Cillian O'Hogan. London: The British Library, 2015.

Codex Sinaticus. www.codexsinaiticus.org/en/project/webdevelopment.aspx.

Coffman, Elesha J. *The Christian Century and the Rise of Protestant Mainline.* Oxford: Oxford University Press, 2013.

Collier, Jeremy. *An Ecclesiastical History of Great Britain.* London: Samuel Keele, 1714.

Collins, Roger. *Keeper of the Keys to Heaven: A History of the Papacy.* New York: Basic Books, 2009.

Collinson, Patrick. *Richard Bancroft and Elizabethan Anti-Puritanism.* Cambridge: Cambridge University Press, 2013.

Colonial America: An Encyclopedia of Social, Political, Cultural, and Economic History. James Ciment, editor. New York: Taylor and Francis, 2006.

Colonial Laws of New York from the Year 1664 to the Revolution. Charles Z. Lincoln, editor. William H. Johnson, and Ansul J. Northrup. Albany: J.B. Llyon, 1894.

Combs, William. "History of the NIV Translation Controversy." *Detroit Baptist Seminary Journal.* Vol. 17. (2012).

A Compilation of Messages and Papers of the Presidents. James D. Richardson, editor. New York: Bureau of National Literature, 1897.

A Complete Collection of State Trials and Proceedings for High Treason and Other Crimes and Misdemeanors. T.B. Howell, compiler. London: Longman and Brown, 1816.

The Complete Jewish Study Bible: Illuminating the Jewishness of God's Word. Peabody: Hendrickson Publishers, 2016.

Concordia Self-Study Bible: New International Version. Robert G. Hoerber, editor. St. Louis: Concordia Publishing House, 1986.

Condit, Blackford. *The History of the English Bible: Extending from the Earliest Saxon Translations to the Present Anglo-American Revision.* New York: A.S. Barnes, 1882.

Confronting the Past: Archaeological and Historical Essays on Ancient Israel in Honor of William G. Dever. Seymour Gitin, editor. Winona Lake: Eisenbrauns, 2006.

"Congress Bible." *The American Stationer.* Vol. 69. No. 16. (April 22, 1911).

Constitutional Documents of the Reign of James I. Joseph R. Tanner, editor. London: Bentley House, 1930.

Cottrell, Jack. *The Holy Spirit: A Biblical Study.* Joplin: College Press Publishing, 2006.

Cowling, Cedric B. *The Great Awakening and the American Revolution: Colonial Thought in the 18th Century.* Chicago: Rand McNally, 1971.

The Court and Times of James I. Anthony Weldon, editor. London: Henry Colburn, 1849.

Croft, Pauline. *James I.* London: Palgrave Macmillan, 2003.

Cromwell's Soldier's Bible: Being a Reprint, in Facsimile, of the Soldier's Bible, 1643. London: Elliot Stock, 1895.

Curti, Merle. *The Growth of American Democracy.* New York: Harper and Row, 1943.

Cyclopedia of Biblical, Theological and Ecclesiastical Literature. John Mclintock and James Strong, editors. New York: Harper & Brothers, 1891.

D'Aubigne, Merle. *History of the Reformation in the Time of Calvin.* New York: Robert Carter and Brothers, 1867.

Dando-Collins, Stephen. *Legions of Rome: The Definitive History of Every Imperial Roman Legion.* New York: St. Martin's Press, 2012.

Daniell, David. *William Tyndale: A Biography.* New Haven: Yale University Press, 1994.

Davis, John D. *A Dictionary of the Bible.* Philadelphia: Westminster Press, 1917.

Davis, Miriam C. *Dame Kathleen Kenyon: Digging Up the Holy Land.* Walnut Creek: Left Coast Press, 2008.

"A Declaration of the Faith, and a Justification of the Proceedings of King Henry the Eighth in Matters of Religion." *An Ecclesiastical History of Great Britain.* Jeremy Collier, editor. London: Samuel Keele, 1714.

DenBoer, Gordon. *The Documentary History of the First Federal Elections, 1778-1790.* Madison: University of Wisconsin Press, 1989.

Declaration of Independence, 6 July 1776. Washington, D.C.: National Archives and Records Administration.

De Hamel, Christopher. *A History of Illuminated Manuscripts.* London: Phaidon Press, 1994.

De Lisle, Leada. *The Sisters Who Would Be Queen: Mary, Katherine and Lady Jane Grey.* New York: HarperCollins, 2008.

De Tocqueville, Alexis. *Democracy in America.* London: Colonial Press, 1900.

Decker, Rodney J. *Koine Greek Reader: Selections from the New Testament, the Septuagint, and Early Christian Writers.* Grand Rapids: Kregel Academic, 2007.

Demaus, Robert. *William Tyndale: A Biography.* Boston: Religious Tract Society, 1886.

Denny, Joanna. *Anne Boleyn: A New Life of England's Tragic Queen.* Philadelphia: Da Capo Press, 2006.

Desiderata Curiosa: Collection of Divers Scarce and Curious Pieces of English History. Francis Peck, editor. London: Thomas Evans, 1779.

Deuel, Leo. Testaments of Time: The Search for Lost Manuscripts and Records. New York: Alfred A. Knopf, 1965.

Dewey, David. *A User's Guide to Bible Translations: Making the Most of Different Versions.* Downers Grove: InterVarsity Press, 2004.

Dickens, Arthur G. *The English Reformation.* University Park: University of Pennsylvania Press, 1964.

Dictionary of American Biography. Allen Johnson and Dumas Malone, editors. New York: Charles Scribner's Sons, 1928-1936.

Dictionary of Christ and the Gospels. John Hastings, John Selbie and John C. Lambert, editors. Edinburgh: T&T Clark, 1908.

Dictionary of Greek and Roman Biography and Mythology. William Smith, editor. Taylor & Walton Publishers, 1846.

Dictionary of National Biography. Sidney Lee, editor. London: Smith Elder Publishing, 1909.

Dictionary of the Bible: Dealing with Language, Literature and Contents. John C. Lambert, editor. New York: Charles Scribner's, 1902.

"Disciples of All Nations." The Gideons International. www2.gideons.org.

Disraeli, Isaac. *Curiosities of Literature.* London: Routledge, Warnes and Routledge, 1859.

Dixon, Richard W. *History of the Church of England: Henry VIII, 1529-1537.* Oxford: Oxford University Press, 1895.

Documents Illustrative of English Church History. Henry Gee and William J. Hardy, editors. New York; Macmillan, 1896.

Documents of the English Reformation. Gerald Bray, editor. Cambridge: James Clarke, 1994.

Dodwell, Charles R. *The Pictorial Arts of the West, 800-1200.* New Haven: Yale University Press, 1993.

Doelman, James. *King James I and the Religious Culture of England.* Cambridge: D.S. Brewer, 2000.

Dudley, Dean. *The First Council of Nice.* New York; Cosimo Publishing, 2007.

Duffy, Eamon. *Fires of Faith: Catholic England Under Mary Tudor.* New Haven: Yale University Press, 2009.

Duggan, Lawrence. "Indulgence." *Encyclopedia Britannica.* www.britannica.com/topic/indulgence.

Duke Papyrus Archive. Special Collections Library. Duke University.

Durant, Will and Aerial. *The Story of Civilization: Caesar and Christ.* New York: Simon and Schuster, 1944.

Durston, Christopher and Jacqueline Eales. *The Culture of the English Puritans, 1560-1700.* New York: Macmillan, 1996.

Earl, Alice Morse. *The Sabbath in Puritan New England.* New York: Charles Scribner's Sons, 1891.

Early Republic: People and Perspectives. Andrew K. Frank, editor. Oxford: ABC-CLIO, 2009.

Edwards, James R. *The Gospel According to Luke.* Grand Rapids: William B. Eerdmans, 2015.

Edwards, Lee. "The Heritage of Mao Zedong is Mass Murder." Heritage Foundation. 2 February 2010. www.heritage.org/asia/commentary/the-legacy-mao-zedong-mass-murder.

Eerdmans History of Christianity. Tim Dowley, editor. Grand Rapids: Eerdmans Publishing, 1977.

Elkington, Joseph. "The Divine Library: An Historical Sketch." *The Friend: A Religious and Literary Journal.* Vol. 85. No. 25. (March 1, 1912).

Ellis, Earle. *History and Interpretation in New Testament Perspective.* Leiden: Brill Publishing, 2001.

Elton, G.R. *England Under the Tutors.* London: Routledge Publishing, 1991.

Encyclopedia of American Indian History. Bruce E. Johansen and Barry M. Pritzker, editor. Santa Barbara: ABC-CLIO, 2008.

Encyclopedia of Christianity in the United States. George Thomas Kurian and Mark A. Lamport, editors. New York: Loman and Littlefield, 2016.

Encyclopedia of Early Christianity. Everett Ferguson, editor. London: Garland Publishing, 1998.

Encyclopedia of European People. Carl Waldman and Catherine Mason, editors. New York: Facts on File, 2006.

Encyclopedia of Islam. Juan E. Campo, editor. New York: Facts on File, 2009.

Encyclopedia of Library and Information Science. Allen Kent, editor. New York: Marcel Dekker, 1978.

The Encyclopedia of Religion and Ethics. John Hastings, editor. New York: Charles Scribner's Sons, 1919.

The English Bible in America: A Bibliography of Editions of the Bible and New Testament Published in America, 1777-1957. Margaret T. Hills, editor. New York: American Bible Society, 1961.

English Historical Documents, 500-1042. Dorothy Whitelock, editor. London: Routledge Publishing, 1996.

"The English Translation of the Bible." *The Catholic World.* Vol. 12. No. 68. (October 1870-March 1871).

Erickson, Carolly. *Bloody Mary.* New York: St. Martin's Press, 1978.

Ernest, James D. *The Bible in Athanasius of Alexandria.* Leiden: Brill Academic Publishing 2004.

Estep, William R. *Renaissance and Reformation.* Cedar Rapids: William B. Eerdmans Publishing, 1986.

Eusebius. *Eusebius: The Church History.* Paul L. Maier, editor. Grand Rapids: Kreger Publishing, 1999.

Evans, Craig A. *Ancient Texts for New Testament Studies: A Guide to Background Studies.* Peabody: Hendrickson Publishers, 2015.

Evans, Gillian Rosemary. *John Wyclif: Myth and Reality.* Downers Grove: Intervarsity Press, 2005.

Evans, Paul S. *The Invasion of Sennacherib in the Book of Kings: A Source-Critical and Rhetorical Study of II Kings 18-19.* Leiden: Brill Publishing, 2009.

The Evangelical Dictionary of Theology. Walter A. Ewell, editor. Grand Rapids: Baker Academic Publishing, 2007.

Everett, Michael. *The Rise of Thomas Cromwell: Power and Politics in the Reign of Henry VIII.* New Haven: Yale University Press, 2015.

Ewald, George Henry. *A Grammar of the Hebrew Language of the Old Testament.* London: Williams and Norgate, 1836.

Ewald, Heinrich. *The History of Israel.* London: Longmans Green Publishing, 1871.

Ewert, David. *From Ancient Tablets to Modern Translations: A General Introduction to the Bible.* Grand Rapids: Zondervan Publishing, 1983.

"Exporting Bibles: In the Beginning Was the Ideogram." *The Economist.* 30 March 2013.

Eynikel, Erik. *The Reform of King Josiah and the Composition of the Deuteronomistic History.* Leiden: E.J. Brill, 1996.

Fea, John. *The Bible Cause: A History of the American Bible Society.* Oxford: Oxford University Press, 2016.

Fee, Gordon D. and Mark L. Strauss. *How to Choose a Translation for All Its Worth.* Grand Rapids: Zondervan, 2007.

Ferrell, Lori Anne. *The Bible and the People.* New Haven: Yale University Press, 2008.

Field, Clive D. "Is the Bible Becoming a Closed Book?" *Journal of Contemporary Religion.* Vol. 29. No. 3. (2014).

Findley, Alison. *Illegitimate Power: Bastards in Renaissance Drama.* Manchester: Manchester University Press, 1994.

First Charter of Virginia, 10 April 1606. Avalon Project. Lillian Goldman Law Library. Yale University.

Fleming, William. *The True Church of the Bible.* London: Washburn Publishing, 1895.

Force, James E. and Richard H. Popkin. *Essays on the Context, Nature and Influence of Isaac Newton's Theology.* London: Kluwer Academic Publishers, 1990.

The Founding Fathers and the Debate Over Religion in Revolutionary America: A History in Documents. Matthew L. Harris and Thomas S. Kidd. New York: Oxford University Press, 2012.

Fountain, David. *John Wycliffe and the Dawn of the Reformation.* Southampton: Mayflower Christian Books, 1984.

"The Four Dead Sea Scrolls." *The Wall Street Journal.* 1 June 1954.

Foxe, John. *Book of Martyrs: A History of the Lives, Sufferings and Triumphant Deaths of the Primitive as Well as Protestant Martyrs.* Hartford: Philemon Canfield, 1830.

Foxe, John. *Foxe's Book of Martyrs: Select Narratives.* John N. King, editor. Oxford: Oxford University Press, 2009.

Franklin, Benjamin. *The Autobiography of Benjamin Franklin.* New York: Henry Holt, 1916.

_____. *The Writings of Benjamin Franklin.* Albert H. Smyth, editor. New York: Macmillan, 1907.

Freedley, Edwin T. *Philadelphia and its Manufactures.* Philadelphia: Edward Young, 1867.

Freeman, Douglas Southall. *George Washington: A Biography.* New York: Charles Scribner's Sons, 1948.

The Freer Biblical Manuscripts: Fresh Studies of an American Treasure Trove. Larry W. Hurtado, editor. Atlanta: Society of Biblical Literature, 2006.

Frerichs, Ernest S. *The Bible and Bibles in America.* Atlanta: Scholars Press, 1988.

Friedman, Henry. *The Murderous History of Bible Translations: Power, Conflict and the Quest for Meaning.* New York: Bloomberg Books, 2016.

Friedman, Matti. *The Aleppo Codex: In Pursuit of One of the World's Most Coveted, Sacred and Mysterious Books.* Chapel Hill: Algonquin Books, 2013.

"From Script to Print: The Transformation of Medieval and Renaissance Documents," www.cms.bsu.edu/academics/libraries/collectionsanddept/archives/collections/rarebooks/exhibits/fromscripttoprint.

Gaines, William H. Jr. "The Continental Congress Considers Publication of a Bible." *Studies in Bibliography: Papers of the Bibliographical Society of the University of Virginia.* Vol. 3. (1950).

Gallaudet, Thomas H. *The History of Josiah: The Young King of Judah.* New York: American Tract Society, 1837.

Gamble, Harry Y. *Books and Readers in the Early Church: A History of Early Christian Texts.* New Haven: Yale University Press, 1995.

Gaudet, John. *Papyrus: The Plant that Changed the World.* New York: Pegasus Books, 2014.

Geiger, Abigail. "Five Facts on How Americans View the Bible and Other Religious Texts." 14 April 2017. www.pewresearch.org/fact-tank/2017/04/14/5-facts-on-how-americans-view-the-bible-and-other-religious-texts.

Geisler, Norman. *Christian Apologetics.* Grand Rapids: Baker Book House, 1976.

Geisler, Norman and Peter Bocchino. *Unshakable Foundations: Contemporary Answers to Crucial Questions about the Christian Faith.* Grand Rapids: Bloomington, 2001.

Geisler, Norman and William E. Nix. *A General Introduction to the Bible.* Chicago: Moody Press, 1986.

The Geneva Bible; A Facsimile of the 1560 Edition. Introduction by Lloyd E. Berry. Peabody: Hendrickson Publishers, 2007.

George, Alice L. *Philadelphia: A Pictorial Celebration.* New York: Sterling, 2006.

"George Edward Reed, 1846-1930." Archives and Special Collections. Dickinson University.

George, Timothy. *The Theology of the Reformers.* Nashville: Broadman & Holdman, 2013.

"Gezer – A Canaanite City and Royal Solomonic City." *Ministry of Foreign Affairs Newsletter.* Israel Ministry of Foreign Affairs. 26 November 2003.

Gibbons, James Cardinal. *The Faith of Our Fathers: Being a Plain Exposition and Vindication of the Church Founded by Our Lord Jesus Christ.* New York: P.J. Kennedy: 1917.

Gilliam, Paul R. *Ignatius of Antioch and the Arian Conspiracy.* Leiden: Brill Publishing, 2017.

"Gladstone's Latest Tribute to the Bible." *The Literary Digest.* Edward Jewitt Wheeler, editor. Vol. 10, No. 26, (27 April 1895).

Glassner, Jean-Jacques. *The Invention of Cuneiform Writing in Sumer.* Baltimore: Johns Hopkins Press, 2003.

Glatz, Carol. "Scala Santa Chapel: Under Soot and Grime, a Visual Treasure." Catholic News Service, 15 June 2007.

Goff, Arthur, Phillip E. Farnsley II, and Peter J. Theusen. *The Bible in American Life.* Indianapolis: The Center for the Study of Religion and American Culture, 2017.

_____. *The Bible in American Life,* Oxford: Oxford University Press, 2017.

Golb, Norman. "Who Hid the Dead Sea Scrolls?" *Biblical Archaeological Review*. Vol. 48. (1985).

_____. *Who Wrote the Dead Sea Scrolls? The Search for the Secret of Qumran*. New York: Scribners, 1995.

Goodman, Martin. *The Roman World: 44 B.C. to 190 A.D.* London: Routledge Publishing, 1997.

Goodwin, John A. *The Pilgrim Republic: A Historical Review of the Colony of New Plymouth*. Boston: Tichnor, 1888.

Grabbe, Lester L. *Good Kings and Bad Kings: The Kingdom of Judah in the Seventh Century BCE*. London: T&T Clark Publishing: 2005.

Gragg, Rod. *By the Hand of Providence: How Faith Shaped the American Revolution*. New York: Simon and Schuster, 2011.

_____. *The Declaration of Independence: The Story Behind America's Founding Document and the Men Who Created It*. Nashville: Thomas Nelson, 2005.

_____. *Forged in Faith: How Faith Shaped the Birth of the Nation*. New York: Simon and Schuster, 2010.

_____. *The Pilgrim Chronicles: An Eyewitness History of the Pilgrims and the Founding of Plymouth Colony*. Washington, D.C.: Regnery History, 2014.

Graham, Billy. *Just as I Am: The Autobiography of Billy Graham*. New York: HarperColllins, 1997.

Granberg-Michaelson, Wes. "Think Christianity is Dying? No, Christianity is Shifting Dramatically." *Washington Post,* 20 May 2015.

Grant, Robert. "The Textual Tradition of Theophilus of Antioch." *Vigiilae Christianae*. Vol. 6. No. 3. (July 1952).

Graves, Dan. "John Frith Burned for Beliefs." www.christianity.com/church/church-history/timeline/1501-1600/john-frith-burned-for-beliefs-11629954.html.

Green, John Richard. *History of the English People*. London: Macmillan, 1885.

Gregory, D.S. *Why Four Gospels?* New York: Sheldon Publishing, 1876.

Greider, John C. *The English Bible: Translations and History*. Bloomington: Xlibris, 2013.

Gurkhow, Lazer. "Purim: When Hebrews Became Jews." Israel National News. 11 June 2017.

Gutjahr, Paul C. *An American Bible: A History of the Good Book in the United States, 1777-1880*. Stanford: Stanford University Press, 1999.

Guy, John. *Mary Queen of Scots: The True Life of Mary Stuart*. Boston: Houghton-Mifflin, 2005.

Hall, Edwin. *The Puritans and Their Principles*. New York: Baker and Scribner's, 1846.

Hall, Timothy L. *American Religious Leaders*. New York: Facts on File, 2003.

Hamilton-Hoare, Henry. *The Evolution of the English Bible*. London: John Murray, 1902.

Hamlin, Hannibal. *The Bible in Shakespeare*. Oxford: Oxford University Press, 2013.

Hammond, Joseph. "Christian Disunity." *The Church of England Pulpit and Ecclesiastical Review*. Vol. 48. No. 1225. (July-December 1899).

"Hampton Court Conference." Manuscripts Collection. Mss Eu F89/102. Box 5A. British Library.

Hanbury, Benjamin. *Historical Memorials Relating to the Independents or Congregationalists*. London: Fisher and Son, 1839.

Haraszti, Zoltan. *The Bay Psalm Book: The First Book Printed in British North American, 1640*. Mineola: Dover: 2016.

Harley, Lewis R. *The Life of Charles Thomas, Secretary of the Continental Congress and Translator of the Bible from the Greek*. Philadelphia: George Jacobs, 1900.

Harnack, Adolph. *History of Dogma*. Neil Buchanan, editor. Boston: Little and Brown, 1905.

Harper, Jennifer. "Museum of the Bible to Open Near U.S. Capitol. *Washington Times*. 10 July 2017.

Harris, Tim. *Rebellion: England's First Stuart Kings.* Oxford: Oxford University Press, 2014.

Hart, Darrel. *Calvinism: A History.* New Haven: Yale University Press, 2013.

Haskell, Caleb. *Caleb Haskell's Diary, May 5, 1775-May 30, 1776.* Lothrop Withington, editor. Newburyport: 1881.

Haskell, David. "Liberal Churches Are Dying. But Conservative Churches are Thriving." *Washington Post.* 4 January 2017.

Hausser, Ludwig. *The Period of the Reformation, 1517-1648.* Wilhelm Oncken, editor. New York: American Tact Society: 1873.s

Haynes, Alan. *The Gunpowder Plot: Faith in Rebellion.* Dover: Alan Sutton, 1994.

Hayward, C.T.R. *Saint Jerome's Hebrew Questions on Genesis,* Oxford: Oxford University Press, 1995.

Haywood, John. *Northmen: The Viking Saga, AD 793-1241.* New York: St. Martin's Press, 2015.

Heather, Peter. *The Fall of the Roman Empire: A New History of Rome and the Barbarians,* Oxford: Oxford University Press, 2006.

Hebrew Bible Old Testament: The History of Its Interpretation. Magna Saebo, editor. Göttingen: Vandenhoeck & Ruprecht, 2008.

Hefele, Charles J. *A History of the Christian Councils to the Close of the Council of Nicaea in A.D. 325.* William R. Clark, translator. Edinburgh: T&T Clark, 1871.

Hendrix, Scott A. *Martin Luther: Visionary Reformer.* New Haven: Yale University Press, 2015.

Henry, Matthew. *Revelation.* Alister McGrath and J.I. Packer, editors. Wheaton: Crossway Books, 1999.

Herbraeolus. "To Mr. A.P. on His Proposal and Translation of the 68 Psalm." *The Gentleman's Magazine and Historical Chronicle.* Vol. 6. (1736).

Herl, Joseph. *Worship Wars in Early Lutheranism: Choir, Congregation and Three Centuries of Conflict.* Oxford: Oxford University Press, 2004.

Hibbert, Christopher. *Tower of London.* New York: Newsweek Books, 1971.

Hill, C. E. "The Debate Over the Muratorian Fragment and the Development of the Canon." *Westminster Theological Journal.* Vol. 57. No.2. (Fall 1995).

Hill, Christopher. *The English Bible and the Seventeenth Century Revolution.* London: Allen Lane, 1993.

Hilliam, Paul. *Elizabeth I: Queen of England's Golden Age.* New York: Rosen Publishing, 2005.

Hinson, E. Glenn. *The Church Triumphant: A History of Christianity Up to 1300.* Mercer: Mercer University Press, 1995.

History of Books and Printing. Paul A. Winkler, editor. Engelwood: Information Handling Services, 1978.

A History of the Book in America: The Colonial Book in the Atlantic World. Hugh Amory and David D. Hall, editors. Chapel Hill: University of North Carolina Press, 2010.

Historical Dictionary of the British Empire. James S. Olson and Robert Shadle, editors. Westport: Greenwood Press, 1996.

"The History of Wycliffe." Wycliffe Bible Translators. www.wycliffe.org/about.

Hoak, D.E. *The King's Council in the Reign of Edward VI.* Cambridge: Cambridge University Press, 1976.

Hodge, Archibald A. and Benjamin B. Warfield. "Inspiration." *The British and Foreign Evangelical Review.* Vol. 117. (July 1881).

Hoffman, Joel. *In the Beginning: A Short History of the Hebrew Language,* New York: New York University Press: 2004

Holmes, Urban T. and Alexander H. Schultz. *A History of the French Language.* New York: Biblio and Tannen, 1928.

The Holy Bible: Containing the Old and New Testaments, Translated Out of the Original Tongues and With the Former Translations Diligently Compared and Revised by His Majesty's Special Command, AD 1611, London: British and Foreign Bible Society, 1967.

The Holy Bible, King James Authorized Version. New York: American Bible Society: 1865.

Hooper, Finley and Matthew Schwartz. *Roman Letters: History from a Personal Point of View.* Detroit: Wayne State University Press, 1991.

Hull, Robert F. *The Story of the New Testament Text: Movers, Materials, Motives, and Models.* Atlanta: Society of Biblical Literature, 2010.

Hunt, Gaillard. *The Seal of the United States: How It Was Developed and Adopted.* Washington, D.C.: U.S. Department of State, 1892.

Inge, Janet. *Johann Gutenberg and His Bible: A Study.* New York: Typophiles, 1988.

The Illustrated Bible Dictionary, J.D. Douglas, ed. Leicester, UK: Inter-Varsity Press, 1980.

The International Standard Bible Encyclopedia. James Orr, editor. Chicago: Howard-Severance, 1915

Ironsides, H.A. *I and II Timothy, Titus and Philemon.* Grand Rapids: Kreger Publications, 2007.

Isaacs, Ronald H. *Why Hebrew Goes from Right to Left.* Jersey City: KTAV Publishing, 1992.

Jackson, Jeremy. *No Other Foundation.* Westchester: Cornerstone Books, 1980.

Jackson, Joseph. *Market Street, Philadelphia: The Most Historic Street in America.* Philadelphia: Joseph Jackson, 1918.

James I and VI: Ideas, Authority and Government. Ralph Anthony Houlbrook, editor. Hampshire: Ashgate, 2006.

Jefferson, Thomas. *The Writings of Thomas Jefferson.* Paul Leicester Ford, editor. New York: G.P. Putnam's Sons, 1904.

Jenkins, Everett Jr. *The Creation: Secular, Jewish, Catholic, Protestant and Muslim Perspectives Analyzed.* Jefferson: McFarland Publishing, 2003.

The Jewish Encyclopedia: The History, Religion, Literature and Customs of the Jewish People. Isadore Singer, editor. New York: Funk and Wagnalls, 1902.

Jewish Renaissance and Revival in America. Eitan P. Fishbane and Jonathan D. Sarna, editor. Lebanon: University Press of New England, 2011.

Johnson, Alan F. and Robert E. Webber. *What Christians Believe: A Biblical and Historical Summary.* Grand Rapids: Zondervan Publishing, 1993.

Johnston, Andrew. *The Protestant Reformation in Europe.* London: Routledge Publishing, 1991.

Jones, Gwyn. *A History of the Vikings.* Oxford: Oxford University Press, 1968.

Josephus, Flavius. *Jewish Antiquities.* William Whiston, editor. London: Wordsworth Editions, 2006.

_____. *The Jewish War.* Martin Hammond, translator. Oxford: Oxford University Press, 2017.

Josephus, Flavius and William Whiston. *The Genuine Works of Flavius Josephus, the Jewish Historian.* New York: William Borradaile, 1823.

Journals of the Continental Congress, 1774-1789. Worthington C. Ford, editor. Washington, D.C.: U.S. Government Printing Office, 1906.

Joyner, Charles. *Down by the Riverside: A South Carolina Slave Community.* Urbana: University of Illinois Press, 1984.

Kahn, Lily. *The Routledge Introductory Course in Biblical Hebrew.* London: Routledge Publishing, 2014.

Kamen, Henry. *Philip of Spain.* New Haven: Yale University Press, 1997.

Katsh, Abraham Isaac. *The Biblical Heritage of American Democracy,* New York: KATV, 1977.

Katz, Hava. "The Dead Sea Scrolls Exhibition." Israel Antiquities Authority. www.antiquities.org.il/scroll_eng_new.aspx (accessed 8 June 2017).

Keller, Timothy. Kingdom Centered Prayer. www.gospelinlife.com.

Kelly, Balmer H. *The Laymen's Bible Commentary*. Louisville, John Knox: 1959.

Kelly, John D. *Jerome: His Life, Writings and Controversies*. New York: Harper & Row, 1975.

"Ken Taylor, Translator of The Living Bible, Dies at 88." *Christianity Today*. 10 June 2005. www.christianitytoday.com/ct/2005/juneweb-only.

Kendall, Joshua. *The Forgotten Founding Father: Noah Webster's Obsession and the Creation of an American Culture*. New York: G.P. Putnam's Sons, 2011.

Kennedy, Hugh. *The Great Arab Conquests: How the Spread of Islam Changed the World We Live In*. Philadelphia: Da Capo Press, 2007.

Kennedy, J.F. Illustrated Sketches of the Countries and Places Mentioned in Bible History. Philadelphia: American Sunday School Union, 1847.

Kenyon, Frederic George. *The Bible and Archaeology*. New York: Harper Brothers, 1940.

_____. *Our Bible and the Ancient Manuscripts*. Eugene: Wipf and Stock, 2011.

_____. *The Reading of the Bible: As History, as Literature and as Religion*. London: J. Murray Publisher, 1944.

Kholodiuk, Anatoly. "Exhibition: 'Tischendorf, In Search of the Oldest Bible in the World,' Opens in Leipzig Library." *Orthodox Christianity*. 18 February 2011.

Kincaid, Paula R. "Three Presbyterian Denominations Experience Growth in the Number of Churches in 2014." *Presbyterian News and Analysis*. 5 June 2015.

King, David W. *The Bible in History: How the Texts Have Shaped the Times*. Oxford: Oxford University Press, 2004.

The King James Bible, 1611-2011: Prehistory and Afterlife. Tibor Fabiny and Sara Toth, editors. Budapest: L'Harmattan, 2016.

The King James Bible After 400 Years: Literary, Linguistic and Cultural Influences. Hannibal Hamlin and Norman W. Jones, editors. Cambridge: Cambridge University Press, 2010.

Kitchen, Kenneth A. *On the Reliability of the Old Testament*. Grand Rapids: William B. Eerdmans Publishing: 2003.

Knecht, R.J. *Catherine D'Medici*. London: Routledge Publishing, 1998.

Kooi, Christine. *Calvinists and Catholics During Holland's Golden Age: Heretics and Idolaters*. Cambridge: Cambridge University Press, 2002.

Koop, C. Everett and Francis Schaeffer. *Whatever Happened to the Human Race?* Wheaton: Crossway, 1978.

Krukel, James. "On the Bible and Literary Criticism." *The Journal of Biblical Literature*. Vol. 105. No. 3. (September 1986).

Krummell, D.W. *The Bay Psalm Book Tencentenary, 1698-1998*. London: Bibliographical Society, 1975.

Kutluk, Thomas. "Breakthrough at Eskimo Point: God Used an Icy Plunge to Redirect this Eskimo's Life." *Testimony: The Alliance Witness*. Vol. 120. (January 2, 1985).

Lacombe, Michael A. *Political Gastronomy: Food and Authority in the English Atlantic World*. Philadelphia: University of Pennsylvania Press, 2002.

Lacy, Barbara E. *From Sacred to Secular: Visual Images in Early American Publications*. Newark: University of Delaware Press, 2007.

Lanchester, H.C.O. *The Book of Genesis*. Cambridge: Cambridge University Press, 1924.

Larue, Gerald A. "Ancient Jewish History: Who Were the Hebrews?" Jewish Virtual Library. jewishvirtuallibrary.org.

Latimer, Hugh. *Selected Sermons of Hugh Latimer*. Allan Chester, editor. Charlottesville: University of Virginia Press, 1968.

Laugrand, Frederic and Jarich G. Oosten. *Inuit Shamanism and Christianity*. Montreal: McGill-Queens University Press: 2010.

_____. "Reconnecting People and Healing the Land: Inuit Pentecostal and Evangelical Movements in the Canadian Eastern Arctic." *Numen*. Vol. 54. (2007).

Lauret, Rene. *France and Germany: The Legacy of Charlemagne*. Chicago: Henry Regnery Company, 1964.

Law, Ernest P. *Hampton Court: A Short History of the Royal Manor and Palace*. London: George Bell and Sons, 1900.

Law, Timothy M. *Origenes Orientalis: The Preservation of Origin's Hexapla in the Syrohexapla*. Gottingen: Vandenhoeck and Ruprecht, 2011.

Leary, Lewis Gaston. *The Book-Peddling Parson: An Account of the Life and Times of Mason Locke Weems*. Chapel Hill: Algonquin Books, 1984.

Lechler, Gotthard V. *John Wycliffe and His English Precursors*. London: Religious Tract Society, 1904.

Lee, Morgan. "Many Practicing Christians Agree with Marxism." *Christianity Today*. 10 May 2017.www. christianitytoday.com/news/2017/may/many-practicing-christians-agree-marxism-worldviews-barna.html.

Lee, Sidney. *Queen Victoria: A Biography*. New York: Macmillan, 1908.

Leibovitz, Liel. "Should Hebrew Be Israel's Official Language?" *Tablet*. 12 September 2014.

Letters of Delegates to Congress, 1774-1789. Paul H. Smith, editor. Washington, D.C.: Library of Congress, 1931.

Letters to King James VI. Anne MacDonald, editor. Edinburgh: Maitland Club, 1835.

Lewis, Jack P. *The Day after Doomsday: The Making of the Bishops' Bible*. Eugene: Wipf and Stock, 2016.

_____. *The English Bible: From the KJV to the NIV: An Evaluation*. Grand Rapids: Baker Book House, 1991.

_____. "What Do We Mean by Javneh?" *Journal of the Bible and Religion*. Vol. 32. No. 2. (April, 1964).

The Library of American Biography. Jared Sparks, editor. Boston: Hilliard and Gray, 1836.

Life of William Whittingham. Mary Anne Greene, editor. Westminster: J.B. Nichols: 1870.

Lightfoot, J.B. *On a Fresh Translation of the English New Testament*. London: Macmillan, 1871.

Lightfoot, Neil R. *How We Got the Bible*. Grand Rapids: Baker Book House, 1963.

Lim, T.K. *Edible Medicinal and Non-Medicinal Plants,* New York: Springer Science and Business Media, 2016.

Lindsey, Thomas. *A History of the Reformation*. New York: Charles Scribner's Sons, 1906.

Living Traditions of the Bible: Scripture in Jewish, Christian and Muslim Practice. James E. Bowley, editor. St. Louis: Chalice Publishing, 1999.

Loades, David. *Mary Tudor*. London: Amberly Publishing, 2012.

Lockard, Craig A. *Societies, Networks and Transitions: A Global History*. Stamford: Cengage Learning, 2015.

Lockyer, Herbert. *All the Apostles of the Bible*. Grand Rapids: Zondervan Publishing, 1972.

Loewin, Henry. *Ink Against the Devil: Luther's and His Opponents*. Waterloo: Wilfrid Laurier University Press, 2015.

Lohse, Berhard. *Martin Luther: An Introduction to His Life and Work*. Philadelphia: Fortress Press, 1986.

Louth, Andrew. *Greek East and Latin West: The Church AD 681-1071,* Crestwood: St. Vladimer's Seminary Press, 2007.

Love, William D. *The Fast and Thanksgiving Days of New England*. Boston: Houghton Mifflin, 1895.

Lowenstein, David. *Treacherous Faith: The Spectre of Heresy in Early Modern English Literature and Culture*. Oxford: Oxford University Press, 2013.

Lowndes, J.J. *Memorials of Miles Coverdale*. London: Samuel Bagster, 1838.

Lufton, Lewis F. *A History of the Geneva Bible: Welcome Joy*. Providence: Fauconberg Press, 1966.

Lunberg, Marilyn J. "The Discovery of the Dead Sea Scrolls." West Semitic Research Project. www.wsrp. usc.edu/educational_site/dead_sea_scrolls/discovery.shtml.

Lupton, Lewis F. *Welcome Joy: A History of the Geneva Bible*. Riverside: Olive Tree, 1975.

Luther, Martin. *Martin Luther's 95 Theses: With the Pertinent Documents from the History of the Reformation*. St. Louis: Concordia Publishing House, 2004.

_____. "A Mighty Fortress is Our God." Thomas Carlyle, translator. *The Lutheran Hymnal*. St. Louis: Concordia Publishing House, 1958.

Lyle, Anthony. *Ancient History: A Revised Chronology*. Bloomington: Authorhouse, 2012.

Macalister, R.A. Stewart. *Bible Side-Lights from the Mound of Gezer: A Record of Excavation and Discovery in Palestine*. London: Hodder and Stoughton, 1907.

MacCulloch, Dairmaid. *The Boy King: Edward VI and the Protestant Reformation*. Berkeley: University of California Press, 2002.

MacFarlane, Charles. *The Cabinet History of England*. London: Charles Knight, 1845.

Mackay, Christopher A. *Ancient Rome: A Military and Political History*. Cambridge: Cambridge University Press, 2004.

Mackintosh, James. *The History of England*. London: Longman, Orme, Brown and Green Publishers, 1838.

MaGrath, Alistar E. *In the Beginning: The Story of the King James Bible and How It Changed a Nation, a Language and a Culture*. New York: Anchor Books, 2012.

McGrath, Charles. "Why the King James Bible Endures." *New York Times*. 23 April 2011.

Man, John. *Gutenberg: How One Man Remade the World with Words*. New York: John Wiley and Sons, 2002.

Manual of Councils of the Holy Catholic Church. Edward H. Landon, editors. London: Francis and John Rivington, 1846.

"Manuscripts in the British Library: Lindisfarne Gospels."www.bl.uk/collection-items/lindisfarne-gospels.

Marsden, Richard. *The Text of the Old Testament in Anglo-Saxon England*. Cambridge: Cambridge University Press, 1995.

Marsh, George P. *The Origin and History of the English Language*. New York: Charles Scribner's Sons, 1892
_____. *The Excavation of Gezer, 1902-05 and 1907-09*. London: John Murray, 1912.

Marshall, Paul A, Lela Gilbert and Nina Shea. *Persecuted: The Global Assault on Christians*. Nashville; Thomas Nelson, 2013.

Marston, Jerilynn Green. *King and Congress: The Transfer of Political Legitimacy, 1774-1776*. Princeton: Princeton University Press, 1987.

Martin, Colin and Geoffrey Parker. *The Spanish Armada*. New York: Penguin Books, 1989.

Martin, Gary D. *Multiple Originals: New Approaches to Hebrew Bible Textual Criticism*. Atlanta: Society of Biblical Literature, 2010.

Martin Luther, the Bible and the Jewish People: A Reader. Brooks Schramm and Kirsi I. Stjerna, editors. Minneapolis: Fortress Press, 2012.

Mary Tudor: Old and New Perspectives. Susan Doran and Thomas S. Freeman, editors. Basingstoke: Palgrave Macmillan, 2011.

Mason Locke Weems: His Works and Ways. Emily E. Ford Skeel, editors. New York: Plimpton Press, 1929.

Mather, Cotton. *Magnalia Christi Ameicana: The Ecclesiastical History of New England*. Hartford: Silas Andrus, 1855.

Matusiak, John. *James I: Scotland's King of England.* Strand: The History Press, 2015.

Maynard, Theodore. *The Crown and the Cross: A Biography of Thomas Cromwell.* New York: McGraw-Hill, 1950.

McDonald, Lee Martin. *The Formation of the Biblical Canon: The Old Testament.* London: Bloomsbury, 2017.

McMahon, Matthew. *The Life and Times of John Wycliffe: Morning Star of the Reformation,* London: Religious Tract Society, 1884.

Merritt, Jonathan. "Mega-Church Pastor's Scandalous Take on Scripture." Religious News Service. 1 May 2014.

The Message: The Bible in Contemporary Language. Colorado Springs: NavPress, 2002.

Metzger, Bruce C. *The Bible in Translation: Ancient and English Versions.,* Grand Rapids: Baker Academic, 2006.

_____. *The Canon of the New Testament: Its Origin, Development and Significance.* Oxford: Oxford University Press, 1987.

_____. "The Geneva Bible of 1560." *Theology Today.* Vol. 17. No. 3. (1 October 1960).

_____. *Manuscripts of the Greek Bible: An Introduction to Palaeography.* New York: Oxford University Press, 1981.

Middlekauff, Robert. *The Glorious Cause: The American Revolution, 1763-1789.* New York: Oxford University Press, 1982.

Miller, George L. *The Shekinah Glory.* Maitland: Xolon Press, 2007.

Miller, Perry. *An Errand into the Wilderness.* Cambridge: Harvard University Press, 1956.

_____. *The New England Mind: From Colony to Province.* Cambridge: Belknap Press, 1953.

Miller, Stephen M. and Robert V. Huber. *The Bible: A History.* Oxford: Lion Books, 2015.

Milligan, George. *The New Testament Documents: Their Origin and History.* London: Macmillan, 1913.

Milman, Henry Hart. *Annals of St. Paul's Cathedral.* London: John Murray, 1868.

"Ministry." Crossway Books. www.crossway.org/ministry.

Monter, William. *Judging the French Reformation: Heresy Trials by Sixteenth Century Parliaments.* Cambridge: Harvard University Press, 1999.

More Than A Memory: The Discourse of Martyrdom and the Construction of Christian Identity in the History of Christianity. John Leeman, editor. Leuven: Uitgeverij Peeters, 2005.

Morini, Massomiliano. *Tudor Translation in Theory and Practice.* London: Routledge, 2017.

Morley, Henry. *A Miscellany Containing Richard of Bury's Prohibition, the Basilikon Doron of James I.* London: George Routledge, 1888.

Monro, Alexander. *The Paper Trail: The History of an Unexpected Revolution.* New York: Alfred A. Knopf: 2016.

Morris, Henry M. *The Genesis Record: A Scientific and Devotional Commentary on the Book of Beginnings.* Grand Rapids: Baker Book House, 1982.

Morton, H.V. *Travels in Rome.* New York: Da Capo Press, 1957.

Mottram, Stewart. *Empire and Nation in Early English Renaissance Literature.* Cambridge: D.S. Brewer, 2008.

Moynahan, Brian. *God's Bestseller: William Tyndale, Thomas More and the Writing of the English Bible – A Story of Martyrdom and Betrayal.* New York: St. Martin's Press: 2002.

Mozley, J.F. *Coverdale and His Bibles.* Cambridge: James Clarke, 2004.

Muchnik, Malka Marina Miznik, and Tania Gluzman. *Elective Language Learning and Policy in Israel.* London: Palgrave Macmillan UK, 2016.

Munson, W. Donald, Jr., Bible Lecture. Montreat-Anderson College, 17 April 1978.

Murphy, Anne. *Thomas More*. Chicago: Triumph Books, 1997.

Murray, Hugh. *The Travels of Marco Polo*. New York: Harper Brothers, 1851.

Museum of the Bible.www.museumofthebible.org/museum.

Mykytiuk, Lawrence. "Archaeology Confirms 50 Real People in the Bible." *Biblical Archaeology Review*. Vol. 40. No.2. (March-April 2014).

Naaman, Nadav. "A New Appraisal of the Silver Amulets from Ketef Hinnom." *Israel Exploration Journal*. Tisip Kuper-Blau, editor. Vol. 61, no. 2 (2001).

Neal, Daniel. *The History of the Puritans or Protestant Non-Conformists*. Boston: Charles Ewer, 1817.

Neale, J.E. *Queen Elizabeth I*. Chicago: Academy Chicago Publishers, 1992.

The Nelson Study Bible: New King James Version. Earl D. Radmacher, editor. Nashville: Thomas Nelson, 1997.

Neusner, Jacob. *A Life of Rabban Yohanan ben Zakkai*. Leiden: E.J. Brill, 1977.

The New Bible Dictionary. J.D. Douglas, editor. Wheaton, Illinois: Tyndale House Publishers, 1982.

The New Cambridge History of the Bible: From 1750 to the Present. John Riches, editor. New York: Cambridge University Press, 2015.

New Dictionary of the English Language. New York: Thomas Nelson and Sons, 1922.

The New Encyclopaedia Britannica. Chicago: *Encyclopaedia Britannica*, 1974.

The New International Dictionary of Biblical Archaeology. E.M. Blaiklock and R.K. Harrison, editors. Grand Rapids: Zondervan Corporation, 1983.

"New Life Version." Bible Gateway. www.biblegateway.com/versions/New-Life-Version--NLV-Bible/#vinfo.

The New Westminster Dictionary of Church History: The Early, Medieval and Reformation Eras. Robert Benedetto, editor. London: Westminster John Knox Press, 2008.

Ngo, Robin. "The 'High Place' at Tel Gezer." *Bible History Daily*. 13 August 2016.

Nichols, Charles Lemuel. *Isaiah Thomas: Printer, Writer and Collector*. Boston: Club of Old Volumes, 1912.

Nicklesburg, George W. *Jewish Literature Between the Bible and the Mishnah: A Historical and Literary Introduction*. Minneapolis: Fortress Press, 2005.

Nicolas, Nicholas H. *The Literary Remains of Lady Jane Grey*. London: Harding and Triphook, 1825.

Nicholls, Mark. *Investigating the Gunpowder Plot*. Manchester: University of Manchester Press, 1991.

Nicholson, Adam. *God's Secretaries: The Making of the King James Bible*. New York: HarperCollins, 2003.

Nida, Eugene A. and Charles R. Taber. *The Theory and Practice of Translation*. Lieden: Brill, 2003.

"The NIV's Commitment to Accuracy." Biblica: The International Bible Society. www.biblica.com/niv-bible/niv-bible-translation-accuracy.

Nolan, Edward N. *A History of India and the British Empire of the East,* London: Viscount and Clark, 1878.

North, David. *A Short History of the King James Bible: From Tyndale to Today*. Cambridge: Cambridge University Press, 2011.

Norton, David. *A Textual History of the King James Bible*. Cambridge: Cambridge University Press, 2005.

Novak, Ralph Martin. *Christianity and the Roman Empire: The Texts*. Harrisburg: Trinity, 2001.

"Obituary: Sir Frederic George Kenyon." *Scripture: The Quarterly of the Catholic Biblical Association*. Vol. 5, no. 5. (January-March 1953).

Ogilve, Sarah. *Words of the World: A Global History of the Oxford English Dictionary*. Cambridge: Cambridge University Press, 2013.

The Old English Gloss to the Lindisfarne Gospels: Language, Author and Context. Julia Fernandez Cuesta and Sara M. Pon-Sans, editors. Berlin: Walter de Gruyter, 2016.

Old, Hughes Oliphant. *The Reading and the Preaching of the Scriptures in the Worship of the Christian Church.* Grand Rapids: William B. Eerdmans, 2004.

Olasky, Susan. "Femme Fatale." *World Magazine.* 29 March 1997. https://world.wng.org/1997/03/femme_fatale.

Olsen, Ted. "Correcting the 'Mistakes' of the TNIV and Inclusive NIV, Translators will Revise NIV in 2011." *Christianity Today,* 1 September 2009. www.christianitytoday.com/news/2009/september/correcting-mistakes-of-tniv-and-inclusive-niv-translators.html.

Olson, Roger E. *The Story of Christian Theology: Twenty Centuries of Tradition and Reform.* Downers Grove: Intervarsity, 1999.

O'Malley, John W. *A History of the Popes: From Peter to the Present.* New York: Rowan & Littlefield, 2010.

"Open Doors World Watch List, 2017." Open Doors USA. www.opendoorsusa.org/christian-persecution/world-watch-list.

The Origin of the Bible. Philip Wesley Comfort. Carol Stream, Illinois: Tyndale House Publishers, 1992.

"Our History." Biblica – The International Bible Society. www.biblica.com/about/history.

The Oxford Companion to Christian Thought: Intellectual, Spiritual and Moral Horizons. Adrian Hastings, Alistar Mason and Hugh Pyper, editors. Oxford: Oxford University Press: 2000.

The Oxford Dictionary of the Christian Church. F.L. Cross, editor. Oxford: Oxford University Press, 1997.

The Oxford Dictionary of the Jewish Religion. Adele Berlin, editor. New York: Oxford University Press, 2001.

The Oxford Encyclopedia of the Books of the Bible. Michael D. Coogan, editor. Oxford: Oxford University Press, 2011.

The Oxford Guide to Ideas and Issues of the Bible. Bruce M. Metzger and Michael D. Coogan, editors. Oxford: Oxford University Press, 2001.

The Oxford Handbook to the Bible in Early Modern England, 1530-1700. Kevin Killeen, editor. Helen Smith and Rachel Willie, Oxford: Oxford University Press, 2015.

The Oxford Handbook to Cuneiform Culture. Karen Radner and Eleanor Robson, editor. New York: Oxford University Press, 2011.

The Oxford History of Anglicanism. Jeremy Morris, editor. Oxford: Oxford University Press, 2017.

The Oxford History of Byzantium. Cyril Mango, editor. Oxford: Oxford University Press: 2002.

The Oxford Illustrated History of the Reformation. Peter Marshall, editor. Oxford: Oxford University Press, 2015.

Pache, Rene. *The Inspiration and Authority of Scripture.* Chicago: Moody Press, 1969.

Packer, J.I. *God Has Spoken: Revelation and the Bible.* Grand Rapids: Baker Book House, 2000.

_____."*Sola Fide:* The Reformed Doctrine of Justification." www.ligonier.org/learn/articles/sola-fide-the-reformed-doctrine-of-justification.

Papers of the Continental Congress, 1774-1789. Washington, D.C.: National Archives and Records Administration.

Parker, C.C. *Codex Bezae.* Cambridge: Cambridge University Press, 1996.

Parker, David C. *Codex Sinaiticus: The Story of the World's Oldest Bible.* London; British Library, 2010.

The Parliamentary History of England: From the Earliest Period to the Year 1803. London: T.C. Hansard, 1806.

Patterson, W.B., *James VI and I and the Reunion of Christendom.* Cambridge: Cambridge University Press, 1997.

Paul, William E. *English Language Bible Translators*. Jefferson: McFarland, 2003.

Peacham, Henry. *Peacham's Compleat Gentleman, 1634*. Oxford: Clarendon Press, 1904.

Pears, Thomas C. "The Story of the Aitken Bible," *Journal of the Presbyterian Historical Society*. Vol. 18. No.6. (June 1939).

Penrose, J.D. *An Outline of Christianity: The Story of Our Civilization*. New York: Bethlehem Publishers, 1926.

Penry, John. *The Notebook of John Penry, 1593*. London: Royal Historical Society, 1944.

Percy, George. "A Trewe Relacyon: Virginia From 1608-1612." *Tyler's Historical and Genealogical Magazine*. Leon G. Tyler, editor. 1922.

Perkins, Pheme. *Gnosticism and the New Testament*. Minneapolis: Ausburg Fortress, 1993.

Perry, Marvin. *Western Civilization: Ideas, Politics and Society*. Boston: Cengage Learning: 2009.

Persaud, Raj and Peter Bruggan. "British Opinion Polls Reveal a Dramatic Decline in the Impact of the Bible on the UK." Huffington Post UK. www.huffingtonpost.co.uk/dr-raj-persaud/british-opinion-polls-rev_b_5870786.html.

Personalities of the Early Church. Everett Ferguson, David Scholer and Paul C. Finey, editors. London: Routledge Publishing, 1993.

Peters, Edward. *Inquisition,* Berkeley: University of California Press, 1989.

Peters, F.E. *Muhammad and the Origins of Islam*. Albany: State University of New York Press, 1994.

Peterson, Roy. "The Forbidden Bible." Fox News. 29 January 2015. www.foxnews.com/opinion/2015/01/27/forbidden-bible.html.

Philbrick, Nathaniel. *Mayflower: A Story of Courage, Community, and War*. New York: Viking Penguin, 2006.

Pilch, John J. *Choosing a Bible Translation*. Collegeville: Liturgical Press, 2000.

"Point Your Heart to True North." Holman Bibles. www.bhpublishinggroup.com/category/bibles.

Polo, Marco. *The Book of Marco Polo the Venetian*. Henry Yule, editor. New York: Charles Scribner's, 1903.

Poole, J.B. and R. Reed. "The Preparation of Leather and Parchment by the Dead Sea Scrolls Community." Technology and Culture. (1963).Vol. 3. No.1.

Pope, Robert Martin. *An Introduction to Early Church History: A Survey of the Relations Between Christianity and Paganism in the Early Roman Empire*. London: Macmillan Publishing, 1918.

Porter, Stanley E. *Constantine Tischendorf: The Life and Work of a 19th Century Bible Hunter*. London: Bloomsbury Publishing, 2015.

_____. "Hero or Thief: Constantine Tischendorf Turns Two Hundred." *Biblical Archaeology Review*. Vol. 41. No. 5. (September-October 2015).

Potter, David. *Constantine the Emperor*. Oxford: Oxford University Press, 2013.

The Prayer Book of Queen Elizabeth, 1559. Edinburgh: Grant Publishing, 1911.

"Preface to the English Standard Version." Crossway Books. www.esv.org/resources/esv-global-study-bible/preface-to-the-english-standard-version.

Price, David and Charles C. Ryrie. *Let It Go Among Our People: An Illustrated History of the English Bible from John Wyclif to the King James Version*. Cambridge: Lutterworth, 2004.

Price, Ira M. *The Ancestry of Our English Bible: An Account of Manuscripts, Texts and Versions of the Bible*. New York: Harper & Brothers Publishers, 1956.

Price, James. "Memorable Places Within the Bounds of the United Presbyterian Presbytery." *Journal of Presbyterian History*. Vol. 6. (1911-1912).

Price, Maurice. "The Hebrew Text of the Old Testament." *The Biblical World*. Vol. 37. No.4 (April 1911).

The Puritans: A Sourcebook of Their Writings. Perry Miller and Thomas H. Johnson, editors. New York: Harper & Row, 1963.

Puritans and Puritanism in Europe and America: A Comprehensive Encyclopedia. Francis J. Bremer and Tom Webster, editors. Santa Barbara: Clio, 2006.

Radosh, Daniel. "The Good Book Business." *The New Yorker.* 18 December 2006. www.newyorker. com/magazine/2006/12/18/the-good-book-business.

Rainolds, John. *John Rainolds' Oxford Lectures on Aristotle's* Rhetoric. Lawrence Green, editor. Newark: University of Delaware Press, 1986.

Reader's Guide to Judaism. Ralph Terry, editor. London: Routledge, 2000.

Records of the English Bible, 1525-1611. Alfred W. Pollard, editor. London: Oxford University Press, 1911.

Reeves, Eileen. *Evening News: Optics, Astronomy and Journalism in Early Modern Europe.* Philadelphia: University of Pennsylvania Press, 2014.

"The Reformation Study Bible (ESV)." http://www.ligonier.org/store/the-reformation-study-bible-esv-hardcover.

Reif, Stepan. "Impact on Jewish Studies of a Century of Genizah Research." *Jewish Studies at the Turn of the 20th Century: Biblical, Rabbinical, and Medieval Studies.* Judit T. Borras and Angel Saenz-Badillos, editors. Leiden: Brill Publishing: 1999.

"Religious Landscape Study." Pew Research Center on Religion and Public Life. www.pewforum.org/religious-landscape-study.

Religious Policy in the Soviet Union. Salerna Petra Ramet, editors. Cambridge University Press, 1993.

Reports of Cases in the Star Chamber and the Court of High Commission. Samuel R. Gardiner, editor. Westminster: Nichols and Sons, 1886.

Reu, M. "Luther's Journey to Rome." *Lutheran Church Review.* Vol. 36. No. 2. (February 1917).

Revelation and the Bible, Carl F. Henry, editor. Grand Rapids: Baker Book House, 1958.

Riddle, Matthew B. *The Story of the Revised New Testament, American Standard Version:* Philadelphia: Sunday School Times, 1908.

Roberts, Bleddyn J. *The Old Testament Text and Versions: The Hebrew Text in Transmissions and the History of the Ancient Versions.* Cardiff: University of Wales Press, 1951.

Robertson, A.T. *Studies on the Texts of the New Testament.* New York: Doran Books, 1926.

Robinson, Ellis. *A Commentary on Catullus.* Oxford: Clarendon Press, 1889.

Robinson, John A.T. *Redating the New Testament.* Eugene: Wipf and Stock, 1976.

Roitman, Adolfo. "The History, Architecture, and Symbolism of the Shrine of the Book." *Israel Museum Journal.* Vol. 15. (1997).

Romantic Biography of the Age of Elizabeth. William Cooke Taylor, editor. London: Richard Bentley, 1842.

Rosefielde, Steven. *Red Holocaust.* London: Routledge, 2010.

Rosseau, John J. and Rami Arav. *Jesus and His World: An Archaeological and Cultural Dictionary.* Minneapolis: Fortress Press, 1995.

Ruciman, Steven. *The Fall of Constantinople, 1453.* Cambridge: Cambridge University Press, 1965.

Ryken, Leland. *Understanding English Bible Translations: The Case for an Essentially Literal Approach.* Wheaton: Crossway, 2009.

_____. *Wordly Saints: The Puritans as They Really Were.* Grand Rapids: Zondervan, 1991.

Ryrie, Charles C. "The Inspiration of the Bible." Supplement to the Ryrie Study Bible. Chicago: Moody Press, 1994.

The Ryrie Study Bible: New American Standard Translation. Charles C. Ryrie, commentary. Chicago: Moody Press, 1978.

Saad, Lydia. "Three in Four in U.S. Still See the Bible as the Word of God." Gallup. 4 June 2014. www.gallup.com/poll/170834/three-four-bible-word-god.aspx.

Sáenz-Badillos, Angel. *A History of the Hebrew Language.* Cambridge: Cambridge University Press, 1993.

Salom, A.P. "The New English Bible: A Preliminary Critique." *The Ministry,* Vol. 6. No. 10. (October 1961).

Sanders, James A. *The Dead Sea Psalms Scrolls.* Ithaca: Cornell University Press, 1967.

Sandys, John Edwin. *A History of Classical Scholarship: From the Revival of Learning to the Eighteenth Century.* Cambridge: Cambridge University Press, 1908.

Salisbury, Neal. "Red Puritans: 'The Praying Indians' of Massachusetts Bay and John Eliot." *The William and Mary Quarterly.* Vol. 31. No.1. (January 1974).

Schaeffer, Francis. *He Is There and He Is Not Silent.* Carol Stream: Tyndale House Publishers, 1972.

_____. *How Should We Then Live: The Rise and Fall of Western Thought and Culture.* Wheaton: Crossway Books, 1976.

Schaff, Philip. *History of the Christian Church.* New York: Charles Scribner's Sons, 1910.

_____. *The Revision of the English Version of the Holy Scriptures.* New York: Harper and Brothers, 1875.

Scharf, John T. and Thomas Westcott. *History of Philadelphia, 1609-1884.* Philadelphia: L.H. Wescott, 1884.

Schofield, John. *Philip Melanchthon and the English Reformation.* Burlington: Ashgate Publishing, 2006.

Schreiner, Thomas R. *Interpreting the Pauline Epistles.* Grand Rapids: Baker Academic, 1990.

Scripture and the Scrolls: The Bible and the Dead Sea Scrolls. James H. Charlesworth, editor. Waco: Baylor University Press, 2006.

"Scrolls from the Dead Sea: The Ancient Library of Qumran and Modern Scholarship," U.S. Library of Congress, www.loc.gov/exhibits/sc rolls.

Seiss, Joseph A. *The Apocalypse: Lectures on the Book of Revelation.* New York: Cosimo Classics, 2007.

A Select Library of Nicene and Post-Nicene Fathers of the Christian Church. Henry Wace and Philip Schaff, editors. Oxford: Parker Publishing, 1890.

Sergeant, Lewis. *John Wyclif: Last of the Schoolmen and First of the English Reformers.* Harrington: Delmarva Publications, 2013.

Shamir, Avner. *English Bibles on Trial: Bible Burning and the Desecration of Bibles, 1640-1800.* London: Routledge, 2017.

Shillington, V. George. *Reading the Sacred Text: An Introduction to Biblical Studies.* London: T & T Clark: 2002.

Shirer, William L. *The Rise and Fall of the Third Reich: A History of Nazi Germany.* New York: Simon & Schuster, 1960.

Showalter, Brandon. "China on Track to Have World's Largest Christian Population by 2030." *Christian Post.* July 21, 2016.

Silver, Sandra Sweeney. *Footprints in Parchment: Rome Verses Christianity, 30-313 A.D.* Bloomington: Authorhouse, 2013.

Skeat, Theodore Cressy. *The Collected Biblical Writings of T.C. Skeat.* J.K. Elliott, editor. Leiden: Brill Publishing, 2004.

Skelton, Debra and Pamela Dell. *Empire of Alexander the Great.* New York: Chelsea House, 2009.

Smith, Andrew. *A Study of the Gospels in the Codex Alexandrinus.* Leiden: Brill Publishing, 2014.

_____. *A Study of the Gospels in the Codex Vaticanus.* Leiden: Brill Publishing, 2014.

Smith, John. *Travels and Works of Captain John Smith, President of Virginia and Admiral of New England, 1580-1631.* Edward Arber, editor. Edinburgh: John Grant, 1910.

Smyth, John Patterson. *How We Got Our Bible*. New York: James Pott, 1909.

Snyder, Timothy. "Hitler v. Stalin: Who Killed the Most?" *New York Review of Books*. 30 March 2011. www.nybooks.com/daily/2011/01/27/hitler-vs-stalin-who-was-worse.

Somerset, Anne. *Elizabeth I*. London: Wiedenfeld and Nicholson, 1993.

Souter, Alexander. *The Text and Canon of the New Testament*. New York: Scribner's Sons, 1913.

Spar, Ira. *Cuneiform Texts in the Metropolitan Museum of Art*. New York: Metropolitan Museum of Art, 1988.

Sparks, Jared. *The Life of George Washington*. London: Henry Colburn, 1839.

Sproul, R.C. *Soli Deo Gloria: Essays in Reformed Theology*. Phillipsburg: Presbyterian and Reformed Publishing, 1976.

Spurgeon, Charles. "Scala Santa." *Sword and Trowel*. Vol. 4. (January 1874).

St. Sepulchre's History. www.stsepulchres.org/our-community/history.

Stavans, Ilan. *Resurrecting Hebrew*. New York: Random House, 2008.

"State of the Bible, 2017." 4 April 2017. American Bible Society, http://news.americanbible.org/blog/entry/corporate-blog/2017-State-of-the-Bible-Report-Offers-New-Insights-into-Bible-Engagement.

"State of the Bible 2017: Top Findings." www.barna.com/research/state-bible-2017-top-findings.

Stayer, James M. *The German Peasants' War and Anabaptist Community of Goods*. Montreal: McGill-Queens University Press, 1991.

Stetzer, Ed. "A Closer Look: The Historical Reliability of the Old Testament." *Christianity Today*. www.christianitytoday.com/edstetzer/2012/february/closer-look-historical-reliability-of-old-testament.html.

_____. "If It Doesn't Stem Its Decline, Mainline Protestantism Has Just 23 Easters Left." *Washington Post*. 28 April 2017.

Stewart, Alan. *The Cradle King: The Life of King James VI and I – the First King of a United Britain*. New York: St. Martin's, 2003.

Stine, Philip C. *Bible Translations and the Spread of the Church*. Leiden: E.J. Brill, 1990.

Stock, Eugene. *The Story of the Bible*. New York: E.P. Dutton, 1906.

Stokes, George. *The Lives of the English Reformers*. Philadelphia: Presbyterian Board of Publication, 1870.

Stone, Larry. *The Story of the Bible: The Fascinating History of Its Writing, Translation and Effect on Civilization*. Nashville: Thomas Nelson, 2010.

Strand, Kenneth A. *Early Low-German Bibles*. Grand Rapids: William B. Eerdmans Publishing, 1967.

Streeter, Tom. *The Church and Western Culture: An Introduction to Church History*. Bloomington: Authorhouse, 2008.

Strong, James. *Strong's Exhaustive Concordance of the Bible*. Peabody: Hendrickson Publishing, 2007.

Strype, John. *The Life and Acts of Matthew Parker*, Oxford: Clarendon Press, 1830.

_____. *Memorials of Thomas Cranmer: Wherein the History of the Church and the Reformation of It*. Oxford: Oxford University Press, 1840.

Stuart, James. *James VI and I: Political Writings*. Johann P. Somerville, editor. Cambridge: Cambridge University Press, 1994.

Studies on the Texts of the New Testament and Early Christianity: Essays. Daniel Gurtner, Juan Hernandez Jr. and Paul Foster, editors. New York: Doran Books, 1926.

Sullivan, Edward. *The Book of Kells*. London: The Studio, 1920.

Sussman, Lance J. *Isaac Leesman and the Making of American Judiasm*. Detroit: Wayne State University, 1995.

Swartzwald, Jack L. *The Collapse and Recovery of Europe, A.D. 476-1648*. Jefferson: McFarland, 2016.

Szasz, Margaret Connell. *Indian Education in the American Colonies, 1607-1783*. Lincoln: Bison Books, 2007.

Tacitus, Publius Cornelius. *Annals of Imperial Rome.* New York: Penguin Books, 1956.

_____. *The Histories of Tacitus.* London: Macmillan Publishing, 1907.

Tagart, Edward. *Sketches of the Lives of the Leading Reformers of the Sixteenth Century.* London: John Green, 1843.

Tawil, Hayim and Bernard Schneider. *Crown of Aleppo: The Mystery of the Oldest Hebrew Bible Codex.* Philadelphia: Jewish Publication Society, 2010.

Taylor, James D. *Documents of Lady Jane Grey: Nine Day Queen of England, 1553.* New York: Algora Publishing, 2004.

Taylor, Jerome. "Fragment From World's Oldest Bible Found Hidden at Egyptian Monastery." *Independent.* 1 September 2009.

Taylor, John J. *A Retrospect of the Religious Life of England: The Church, Puritanism and Free Inquiry.* London: Trubner, 1876.

Tedder, Dale Jr. "United Methodist Authority and the Question of Inerrancy." Florida Confessing Association. http://ucmpage.org/fa_cm/cmfa_3.htm#N_1.

Teems, David. *Tyndale: The Man Who Gave God an English Voice.* Nashville: Thomas Nelson, 2012.

The Temple Dictionary of the Bible. William Ewing and John Ebenezer Thomson, editors. London: J.M. Dent, 1910.

Terry, Milton Spencer. *Biblical Hermeneutics: A Treatise on the Interpretation of the Old and New Testaments.* New York: Phillips & Hunt, 1983.

Tertullian, Quentus Septimius. *Apology De Spectaculis.* T.R. Glover, translator. Cambridge: Harvard University Press, 1931.

Textus Receptus Bibles. www.textusreceptusbibles.com/Interlinear/42015007.

Thiessen, Henry C. *Introduction to the New Testament.* Grand Rapids: Eerdmans Publishing, 1954.

Thomas, Isaac. *The History of Printing in America.* Albany: Joel Munsell, 1874.

Thomas, Jane Resh. *Behind the Mask: The Life of Elizabeth I.* New York: Clarion Books, 1998.

Thompson, Robert E. *A History of the Presbyterian Churches in the United States.* New York: Charles Scribner's, 1895.

Tierny, Brian. *Origins of Papal Infallibility, 1150-1350.* Leiden: E.J. Brill, 1972.

Tolerance and Intolerance in the European Reformation. Peter Grell and Bob Scribner. Cambridge: Cambridge University Press, 1986.

Tracts on Liberty of Conscience and Persecution, 1614-1661. Edward B. Underhill, editor. London: J. Haddon, 1846.

Trevelyan, George Otto. *The American Revolution,* New York: Longman and Green, 1922.

Trout, Dennis. *Damasus of Rome: The Epigraphic Poetry,* Oxford: Oxford University Press, 2015.

Tulloch, John. *Leaders of the Reformation: Luther, Calvin, Latimer and Knox.* London: William Blackwood: 1859.

Tulse, Henrico. *History of the Church of Great Britain: From the Birth of Our Saviour to Until the Year of Our Lord 1667.* London: Philip Chetwin, 1674.

Turnbull, Robert. *Christ in History.* Boston: Phillips and Sampson Publishing, 1854.

Twilley, L.D. *The Origin and Transmission of the New Testament.* Grand Rapids: Eerdmans Publishing, 1957.

Tyler, Moses Coit. *The Literary History of the American Revolution 1763-1783.* New York: G.P. Putnam's Sons, 1897.

Tyndale, William. *Doctrinal Treatises and Introductions to Different Portions of the Holy Scriptures.* Henry Walter, editor. Cambridge: Cambridge University Press, 1848.

_____. *The Obedience of a Christian Man.* Introduction by David Daniell. London: Penguin Books, 2000.

Tyndale's New Testament. William Tyndale, translator. Introduction by David Daniell. New Haven: Yale University Press, 1989.

Underhill, Henry Bean. *The Struggles and Triumphs of Religious Liberty.* New York: Lewis Colby Publishers, 1851.

Usher, Roland G. *The Pilgrims and Their History.* New York: Macmillan, 1918.

Vacchio, Stephen J. *Job in the Ancient World.* Eugene: Wipf and Stock: 2006.

Van Der Toon, Karel. *Scribal Culture and the Making of the Hebrew Bible.* Cambridge: Harvard University Press, 2007.

Ver Steeg, Clarence L. *The Formative Years, 1607-1763.* New York: Hill and Wang, 1965.

Vermes, Geza. *An Introduction to the Complete Dead Sea Scrolls.* Minneapolis: Fortress Press, 1999.

Von Harnack, Adolf. *Monasticism: Its Ideals and Its History.* Charles R. Gillet, translator. New York: Christian Literature Company, 1895.

Von Tischendorf, Constantine. *The Revised Versions of the New Testament: With a History of the Revision.* St. Louis: Scammel Publishers, 1881.

_____. *Travels in the East.* London: Longman, Brown and Green Publishers, 1851.

The Vulgate Bible: Douay-Rheims Translation. Swift Edgar, editor. Cambridge: Harvard University Press, 2011.

Waddington, John. *John Penry: The Pilgrim Martyr, 1553-1593.* London: W.F.G. Cash, 1854.

Wallace-Hadrill, D.S. *Christian Antioch: A Study of Early Christian Thought in the East.* Cambridge: Cambridge University Press, 1982.

Warfield, Benjamin B. *The Inspiration and Authority of the Bible.* Phillipsburg: Presbyterian and Reformed Publishing Company, 1948.

_____. *The Printing of the Westminster Confession of Faith.* Philadelphia: MacCalla, 1901.

Watson, Alexander. *History of the New York Bible Society.* New York: Anson Randolph, 1858.

Watt, William Montgomery. *Muhammad: Prophet and Statesman.* Oxford: Oxford University Press, 1961.

Watts, Steven. *The Republic Reborn: War and the Making of Liberal America.* Baltimore: John Hopkins Press, 1987.

Wayland, John W. *The Apostles: Who They Were and What They Did.* Elgin: Brethren Publishing, 1907.

Webster, Noah. *History of the United States.* New Haven: Durrie and Peck Publishing, 1832.

Weeter, Mark. *John Wesley's View and Use of Scripture.* Eugene: Wipf and Stock, 2007.

Wegner, G.S. *6,000 Years of the Bible.* New York: Harper and Brothers Publishers, 1963.

Weir, Alison. *Henry VIII: The King and His Court.* New York: Ballantine Books, 2009.

Weldon, Anthony. *The Court and Character of King James.* London: John Wright, 1650.

Wenhan, John W. *Christ and the Bible.* Downers Grove: InterVarsity Press, 1973.

Werrell, Ralph S. *The Roots of William Tyndale's Theology.* Cambridge: James Clark Publishers, 2013.

Werthwein, Ernst. *The Text of the Old Testament: An Introduction to Biblia Hebraica.* Erroll F. Rhodes, translator. Grand Rapids: William B. Eerdmans Publishing, 2014.

Wesley, John. *The New Testament with Explanatory Notes.* Halifax: William Morrison, 1869.

West, Gerald O. *The Stolen Bible: From the Tool of Imperialism to African Icon.* Leiden: Brill Publishing, 2016.

Westbrook, Vivienne. *Long Travail and Great Paynes: The Politics of Reformation Revision.* London: Kluwer Academic, 2001.

Wescott, Brooke F. *A General View of the History of the English Bible.* London: Macmillan, 1905.

"What is *The Message?*" NavPress. www.navpress.com/what-is-the-message.

"When Was the Bible Written?" Biblica: The International Bible Society, https://www.biblica.com/resources/bible-faqs/when-was-the-bible-written/.

White, Cynthia. *The Emergence of Christianity: Classical Traditions in Contemporary Perspective.* Minneapolis: Fortress Press, 2011.

Wielander, Gerda. *Christian Values in Communist China.* London: Routledge, 2013.

Wifstrand, Albert. *Epochs and Styles: Selected Writings on the New Testament, Greek Language and Greek Culture in the Post-Classical Era.* Lars Rydbeck and Stanley E. Porter, editor. Denis Searby, translator. Tubingen: Mohrs Siebeck, 2005.

Wilson, Bird. *Memoir of the Life of the Right Reverend William White.* Philadelphia: James Kay, 1839.

Wilson, Derek. *The Peoples' Bible: The Remarkable History of the King James Version.* Oxford: Lion Hudson, 2010.

Williams, Charles Harold. *William Tyndale.* Nashville: Thomas Nelson, 1969.

Winthrop, John. *Life and Letters of John Winthrop.* Robert C. Winthrop, editor. Boston: Little and Brown, 1869.

_____. *Winthrop's Journal, 1630-1649.* James K. Hosmer, editor. New York: Charles Scribner's Sons, 1908.

Winworth, Anders. *The Conversion of Scandinavia: Vikings, Merchants and Missionaries in the Remaking of Europe.* New Haven: Yale University Press, 2012.

Wolfenden, John. *Treasures of the British Museum.* New York: Viking Press, 1972.

Wooly, Leonard. *Ur: The First Phases.* New York: Penguin Books, 1946.

Workman, Herbert B. *Persecution in the Early Church.* Manchester: Epworth Press, 1923.

The Works of the English Reformers: William Tyndale and John Frith. Thomas Russell, editor. London: Ebenezer Palmer, 1831.

The Works of Martin Luther. Adolph Spaeth. Philadelphia: A. J. Holman, 1915.

The World of John Winthrop: Essays on England and New England, 1588-1649. Francis J. Bremer and Lynn A. Bohtelo, editors. Boston: Massachusetts Historical Society, 2005.

A World History of Christianity. Adrian Hastings, editor. Grand Rapids: William B. Eerdmans, 1999.

Worth, Roland H. *Church. Monarch and Bible in Sixteenth Century England.* Jefferson: McFarland, 2000.

Wright, John. *Early Bibles of America: Being a Descriptive Account of Bibles Published in the United States, Mexico and Canada.* New York: Thomas Whitaker, 1894.

Yadin, Yigael. *The Message of the Scrolls.* New York: Grosset and Dunlap, 1961.

Yamauchi, Edwin. *The Stones and the Scriptures: An Introduction to Biblical Archaeology.* Grand Rapids: Baker Book House, 1972.

Zylstra, Sarah E. "The Most Popular and Fastest-Growing Bible Translation Isn't What you Think It Is." *Christianity Today.* 13 March 2014. www.christianitytoday.com/news/2014/march/most-popular-and-fastest-growing-bible-translation-niv-kjv.html.

Index

Mark (biblical writer). *See* John Mark
Martin, Gregory, 154
Marshall, William, 194
Marxism, 239
Mary I of England (queen) (aka Mary Tudor; Mary, Queen of Scots), 113, 132, 146–50, 152, 153, 154, 155, 156, 157, 161
Masoretes, 38–39
Masoretic text(s), 28, 39, 213
Mather, Cotton, 187
Matthew, Thomas, 141
Matthew (apostle), 47 (icon), 48, 49, 64
Matthew Bible, 141, 142, 147, 158
Matthias (apostle), 49
Matusiak, John, 168
Maximus Thrax (emperor), 77
Mayflower Compact, 182, 184–86, 187
McKean, Thomas, 203
Mehmed the Conqueror, 89
Melanchthon, Philipp, 111
membrane (origin of the word), 13
Message, The, 231–32
Millenary Petition, 167–68
Moabite Stone, 31
More, Thomas, 124, 126, 131–32, 133, 134, 135
Mosaic covenant, 32–33, 34
Moses ben Asher, 45
Muhammad, 85–86
Munson, W. Donald, 81
Muratorian fragment, 75
"Murderer's" edition (of the Bible), 178
Museum of the Bible (Washington, DC), 244

Nag Hammadi artifacts, 70–71
Nash Papyrus, 44
National Council of Churches, 222
National Reich Church, 235
Nebuchadnezzar, 22, 31
Nero, 73, 74, 77
Nesuton, Job, 189
Neuman, Salid, 213
New American Standard Bible (NASB), 223, 225–26, 236
New English Bible (NEB), 224
New Geneva Study Bible, 234

New International Version (or, NIV), 228–29, 230, 232, 243, 236
New King James Version (NKJV), 229, 230–31, 236
New Life Version, 220, 221
New Living Translation, 225, 236
New Revised Standard Version, 222, 230
New Testament. *See* chapter 3, "The New Testament" (46–66)
　date of authorship of the books, 54
　languages of the, 61–63, 64
　number of books in the, 63
　oldest New Testament manuscripts discovered, 54–56
　overview of the books of the, 63–66
Newton, Isaac, 8–9
New York Bible Society; New York International Bible Society (later, Biblica), 227, 228
Nicholas of Hereford, 99
Ninety-Five Theses, 105, 106, 108, 109, 116, 124
"Non-conformists," 157, 169, 172
Northern Renaissance, 101–2, 115

Odoacer, 89
Old Testament. *See* chapter 2, "The Old Testament" (25–45)
　canonization of the, 37
　the four sections of the, 36
　major manuscripts, 43–45
　organization of the thirty-nine books in the Protestant, 37
　overview of the collective story, 34–35
　writers of the, 36–37
Open Door World Watch List, 235
Ophites, 69
Origen, 64, 75, 84
"Oxford Standard Edition," 179
Oxford University Press, 224

Packer, J. I., 233, 240–41
paganism, 69
Paine, Thomas, 199–200
pantheism, percent of "practicing Christians" who agree with some aspects of, 239
papacy, 83, 103, 118. *See also individual popes by name*